D1536781

Tips for Trolling the Web

- Bookmark any sites that you plan to revisit.
- Use multiple browser windows.
- When using a search engine, the search results after the first 20 or so tend to be off target.
- Give your browser a decent-sized cache to speed the loading of Web sites.
- Conserve bandwidth by closing your Internet connection when you're not using it.
- Guard personal information. Be wary of anyone who asks for your real name, address, or phone number.
- Click the Reload button when a page stalls while loading. Chances are, the page will reload without stalling.

Message Abbreviations and Emoticons

Abbreviation	What it means
BTW	By the way
IMO	In my opinion
IMHO	In my humble opinion
LOL	Laughing out loud
OIC	Oh, I see
OTOH	On the other hand
ROFL	Rolling on the floor laughing

Emoticon	What it means
:-)	Happy days are here again!
:-(	Oh, too bad.
;-)	Wink, wink!
:-o	Oh, no! I'm shocked!

Micons Used ... Book

...is a model ...r design.

...e site contains lots of graphics.

A browser plug-in is recommended.

$ A fee is required.

Files for down-loading are available.

Sound files are available.

Video clips are a featured element.

File uploads are possible.

Online shopping is offered.

You must sign in.

Message boards are available.

Online chat is offered.

The site is of special interest to non-Americans.

Your Favorite Sites

This book is all about *my* favorite sites; the least I can do is provide this space for you to make notes of your own. While you're writing them here, don't forget to bookmark them in your browser!

Site Name
_____

URL
_____

Site Name
_____

URL
_____

Site Name
_____

URL
_____

Site Name
_____

URL
_____

Site Name
_____

URL
_____

Site Name
_____

URL
_____

Site Name
_____

URL
_____

Site Name
_____

URL
_____

Site Name
_____

URL
_____

Site Name
_____

URL
_____

Site Name
_____

URL
_____

Site Name
_____

URL
_____

Important Search Engines and Directories

If you absolutely can't find the site you're looking for, try these helpful search engines and directories:

AltaVista
www.altavista.digital.com/
Sophisticated Internet searching.

Dogpile
www.dogpile.com
Multiengine searching worth barking about.

Excite
www.excite.com
News, directories, oh, and searching, too.

EZ-Find
www.theriver.com/TheRiver/Explore/ezfind.html
Several search engines on one page.

Galaxy
www.einet.net/galaxy.html
Great directory, excellent advanced searching.

HotBot
www.hotbot.com
Wild design, great results.

Inference Find
www.infind.com
Search results classified for you.

Infoseek
www.infoseek.com
Handy search/directory page.

Internet Sleuth
www.isleuth.com
Utilizes hundreds of topical search engines.

LookSmart
www.looksmart.com
Directory with useful design.

Lycos
www.lycos.com
Search lots of spots on the Internet.

Magellan
www.mckinley.com
Directory with site reviews.

MetaCrawler
www.metacrawler.com
Lets other engines do the work.

ProFusion
profusion.ittc.ukans.edu
Fast multiengine searching.

Starting Point
www.stpt.com
Small, compact Net directory.

WebCrawler
webcrawler.com
Veteran search engine with new directory.

Yahoo!
www.yahoo.com
The granddaddy of Internet directories.

INTERNET
DIRECTORY
FOR
DUMMIES®

2ND EDITION

by Brad Hill

Revised by Rev Mengle

IDG Books Worldwide, Inc.
An International Data Group Company

Foster City, CA ♦ Chicago, IL ♦ Indianapolis, IN ♦ New York, NY

Internet Directory For Dummies® **2nd Edition**

Published by
IDG Books Worldwide, Inc.
An International Data Group Company
919 E. Hillsdale Blvd.
Suite 400
Foster City, CA 94404
www.idgbooks.com (IDG Books Worldwide Web site)
www.dummies.com (Dummies Press Web site)

Library of Congress Catalog Card No.: 98-87432

ISBN: 0-7645-0436-3

Printed in the United States of America

10 9 8 7 6 5 4 3 2

2O/ST/QS/ZZ/IN

Distributed in the United States by IDG Books Worldwide, Inc.

Distributed by Macmillan Canada for Canada; by Transworld Publishers Limited in the United Kingdom; by IDG Norge Books for Norway; by IDG Sweden Books for Sweden; by Woodslane Pty. Ltd. for Australia; by Woodslane (NZ) Ltd. for New Zealand; by Addison Wesley Longman Singapore Pte Ltd. for Singapore, Malaysia, Thailand, and Indonesia; by Norma Comunicaciones S.A. for Colombia; by Intersoft for South Africa; by International Thomson Publishing for Germany, Austria and Switzerland; by Distribuidora Cuspide for Argentina; by Livraria Cultura for Brazil; by Ediciencia S.A. for Ecuador; by Ediciones ZETA S.C.R. Ltda. for Peru; by WS Computer Publishing Corporation, Inc., for the Philippines; by Contemporanea de Ediciones for Venezuela; by Express Computer Distributors for the Caribbean and West Indies; by Micronesia Media Distributor, Inc. for Micronesia; by Grupo Editorial Norma S.A. for Guatemala; by Chips Computadoras S.A. de C.V. for Mexico; by Editorial Norma de Panama S.A. for Panama; by Wouters Import for Belgium; by American Bookshops for Finland. Authorized Sales Agent: Anthony Rudkin Associates for the Middle East and North Africa.

For general information on IDG Books Worldwide's books in the U.S., please call our Consumer Customer Service department at 800-762-2974. For reseller information, including discounts and premium sales, please call our Reseller Customer Service department at 800-434-3422.

For information on where to purchase IDG Books Worldwide's books outside the U.S., please contact our International Sales department at 317-596-5530 or fax 317-596-5692.

For information on foreign language translations, please contact our Foreign & Subsidiary Rights department at 650-655-3021 or fax 650-655-3281.

For sales inquiries and special prices for bulk quantities, please contact our Sales department at 650-655-3200 or write to the address above.

For information on using IDG Books Worldwide's books in the classroom or for ordering examination copies, please contact our Educational Sales department at 800-434-2086 or fax 317-596-5499.

For press review copies, author interviews, or other publicity information, please contact our Public Relations department at 650-655-3000 or fax 650-655-3299.

For authorization to photocopy items for corporate, personal, or educational use, please contact Copyright Clearance Center, 222 Rosewood Drive, Danvers, MA 01923, or fax 978-750-4470.

About the Authors

Brad Hill spends most of his time with computers and considers them living creatures with personalities. For this reason alone, he should be treated with caution. Nevertheless, this affinity with digital life forms has led him to the far corners of cyberspace.

Brad is the author of nine books about the Internet and personal technology. *World Wide Web Searching For Dummies,* 2nd Edition, has been a *Publishers Weekly* bestseller, and the first edition of the *Internet Directory For Dummies* was a Book of the Month Club catalog selection. Get Brad talking about the Internet and you can barely shut him up — as a result, he has appeared widely on television and radio, including CNN, *Good Day L.A.,* Turner Entertainment Network, and over 50 radio programs. His loquaciousness makes him an easy interview for journalists, and Brad is often quoted in magazine and newspaper articles about the Internet experience.

Brad's impassioned advocacy of the Internet led him to the position of National Media Spokesperson for WebTV when that online service was introduced. He is also the author of *WebTV For Dummies*. Brad has been involved in managing portions of the CompuServe and WOW! online services.

Brad is listed in *Who's Who* and is a member of The Author's Guild. He enjoys hearing from people and can be reached electronically at his Internet e-mail address: brad@njcc.com.

* * *

Rev Mengle is old enough to remember disco, complete with a leisure suit high school graduation photo that he's too embarrassed to show his co-workers. He worked for 12 years at a daily newspaper, and when the first Macintosh entered the newsroom, he was put in charge of using the Mac to create newspaper graphics. He even had a whole hour to learn how to use the Mac before being asked if he could draw a map for that day's edition. He then got hands-on Windows experience a couple of years later when the paper went to a paginated layout system. Thankfully, Rev wasn't in charge of that, and the experience added to his growing appreciation for computers.

Rev moved on to IDG Books Worldwide, Inc., where he was a project editor for two years. He edited a wide variety of books — on topics as diverse as Web pages and database programming to cocktail parties and sailing — but enjoyed every one of them and appreciated working with some great authors. And after completing this edition, you can believe that Rev has an even better appreciation for just how great those authors were.

This isn't Rev's first authoring venture for IDG; he also contributed to the award-winning *PCs For Kids & Parents*. Rev now works on a new product team at IDG Books and can be reached at rmengle@idgbooks.com.

ABOUT IDG BOOKS WORLDWIDE

Welcome to the world of IDG Books Worldwide.

IDG Books Worldwide, Inc., is a subsidiary of International Data Group, the world's largest publisher of computer-related information and the leading global provider of information services on information technology. IDG was founded more than 30 years ago by Patrick J. McGovern and now employs more than 9,000 people worldwide. IDG publishes more than 290 computer publications in over 75 countries. More than 90 million people read one or more IDG publications each month.

Launched in 1990, IDG Books Worldwide is today the #1 publisher of best-selling computer books in the United States. We are proud to have received eight awards from the Computer Press Association in recognition of editorial excellence and three from Computer Currents' First Annual Readers' Choice Awards. Our best-selling ...For Dummies® series has more than 50 million copies in print with translations in 31 languages. IDG Books Worldwide, through a joint venture with IDG's Hi-Tech Beijing, became the first U.S. publisher to publish a computer book in the People's Republic of China. In record time, IDG Books Worldwide has become the first choice for millions of readers around the world who want to learn how to better manage their businesses.

Our mission is simple: Every one of our books is designed to bring extra value and skill-building instructions to the reader. Our books are written by experts who understand and care about our readers. The knowledge base of our editorial staff comes from years of experience in publishing, education, and journalism — experience we use to produce books to carry us into the new millennium. In short, we care about books, so we attract the best people. We devote special attention to details such as audience, interior design, use of icons, and illustrations. And because we use an efficient process of authoring, editing, and desktop publishing our books electronically, we can spend more time ensuring superior content and less time on the technicalities of making books.

You can count on our commitment to deliver high-quality books at competitive prices on topics you want to read about. At IDG Books Worldwide, we continue in the IDG tradition of delivering quality for more than 30 years. You'll find no better book on a subject than one from IDG Books Worldwide.

IDG
BOOKS
WORLDWIDE

John Kilcullen
Chairman and CEO
IDG Books Worldwide, Inc.

Steven Berkowitz
President and Publisher
IDG Books Worldwide, Inc.

Eighth Annual
Computer Press
Awards ≥1992

Ninth Annual
Computer Press
Awards ≥1993

Tenth Annual
Computer Press
Awards ≥1994

Eleventh Annual
Computer Press
Awards ≥1995

IDG is the world's leading IT media, research and exposition company. Founded in 1964, IDG had 1997 revenues of $2.05 billion and has more than 9,000 employees worldwide. IDG offers the widest range of media options that reach IT buyers in 75 countries representing 95% of worldwide IT spending. IDG's diverse product and services portfolio spans six key areas including print publishing, online publishing, expositions and conferences, market research, education and training, and global marketing services. More than 90 million people read one or more of IDG's 290 magazines and newspapers, including IDG's leading global brands — Computerworld, PC World, Network World, Macworld and the Channel World family of publications. IDG Books Worldwide is one of the fastest-growing computer book publishers in the world, with more than 700 titles in 36 languages. The "...For Dummies®" series alone has more than 50 million copies in print. IDG offers online users the largest network of technology-specific Web sites around the world through IDG.net (http://www.idg.net), which comprises more than 225 targeted Web sites in 55 countries worldwide. International Data Corporation (IDC) is the world's largest provider of information technology data, analysis and consulting, with research centers in over 41 countries and more than 400 research analysts worldwide. IDG World Expo is a leading producer of more than 168 globally branded conferences and expositions in 35 countries including E3 (Electronic Entertainment Expo), Macworld Expo, ComNet, Windows World Expo, ICE (Internet Commerce Expo), Agenda, DEMO, and Spotlight. IDG's training subsidiary, ExecuTrain, is the world's largest computer training company, with more than 230 locations worldwide and 785 training courses. IDG Marketing Services helps industry-leading IT companies build international brand recognition by developing global integrated marketing programs via IDG's print, online and exposition products worldwide. Further information about the company can be found at www.idg.com.   1/24/99

Authors' Acknowledgments

Brad Hill

Mary Bednarek and Gareth Hancock of IDG Books Worldwide conspired to have me write the first edition of this book, and I'm grateful not only for the opportunity but for their support throughout the project.

Tim Gallan filled the crucial, ever-unsung role of editor, and his calm expertise made things easier every step of the way. Thanks also to Mary Goodwin for her always excellent suggestions, and finally, to Kim Darosett for her fastidious work.

Mary Corder got me into this whole business in the first place, which I'll never forget. (I mean that in the most positive sense!)

Finally, I thank my lucky stars that I have the best Internet service provider anyone could hope for: New Jersey Computer Connection. I've used all the big ones, but nothing beats a reliable local service — especially for someone who lives on the Net as much as I do. Thanks to Brian and the whole crew at NJCC for uninterrupted excellence.

Rev Mengle

I'd like to thank Brad Hill for leaving me such an excellent legacy; Diane Steele, Mary Bednarek, Mike Kelly, and Seta Frantz for conspiring to get me involved in the project (Mary, not that I'm a conspiracy theorist, but are you noticing a trend here?); Rich Graves, Kyle Bowen, and Karen York for their site research; Ted Cains for keeping the whole project rolling along and keeping my old office much neater than I ever did; and Kim Darosett for not losing her mind while editing this book a second time. And I'd also like to thank my wife, Karen, and my two boys, Joshua and Austin, just for being. I promise to reintroduce myself soon. Very soon.

Publisher's Acknowledgments

We're proud of this book; please register your comments through our IDG Books Worldwide Online Registration Form located at http://my2cents.dummies.com.

Some of the people who helped bring this book to market include the following:

Acquisitions, Editorial, and Media Development

Project Editor: Ted Cains

Acquisitions Editor: Joyce Pepple

Copy Editors: Kim Darosett, Darren Meiss

Technical Editor: Dennis Teague

Site Researcher: Kyle Bowen

Product Development Administrator: Richard Graves

Media Development Editors: Marita Ellixson, Joell Smith

Media Development Coordinator: Megan Roney

Associate Permissions Editor: Carmen Krikorian

Editorial Manager: Colleen Rainsberger

Media Development Manager: Heather Heath Dismore

Production

Project Coordinator: Karen York

Layout and Graphics: Lou Boudreau, Angela F. Hunckler, Jane E. Martin, Brent Savage, Rashell Smith, Michael A. Sullivan

Proofreaders: Kelli Botta, Michelle Croninger, Christine Snyder, Janet M. Withers

Indexer: Sharon Hilgenberg

Special Help: Publication Services

General and Administrative

IDG Books Worldwide, Inc.: John Kilcullen, CEO; Steven Berkowitz, President and Publisher

IDG Books Technology Publishing: Brenda McLaughlin, Senior Vice President and Group Publisher

Dummies Technology Press and Dummies Editorial: Diane Graves Steele, Vice President and Associate Publisher; Mary Bednarek, Director of Acquisitions and Product Development; Kristin A. Cocks, Editorial Director

Dummies Trade Press: Kathleen A. Welton, Vice President and Publisher; Kevin Thornton, Acquisitions Manager

IDG Books Production for Dummies Press: Michael R. Britton, Vice President of Production and Creative Services; Cindy L. Phipps, Manager of Project Coordination, Production Proofreading, and Indexing; Kathie S. Schutte, Supervisor of Page Layout; Shelley Lea, Supervisor of Graphics and Design; Debbie J. Gates, Production Systems Specialist; Robert Springer, Supervisor of Proofreading; Debbie Stailey, Special Projects Coordinator; Tony Augsburger, Supervisor of Reprints and Bluelines

Dummies Packaging and Book Design: Patty Page, Manager, Promotions Marketing

◆

The publisher would like to give special thanks to Patrick J. McGovern, without whom this book would not have been possible.

◆

Contents at a Glance

Cartoons at a Glance

By Rich Tennant

"Ronnie made the body from what he learned in Metal Shop, Sissy and Darlene's Home Ec. class helped them in fixing up the inside, and then all that anti-gravity stuff we picked up off the Web."

page 187

page 39

page 325

"IT WAS ACTUALLY ON THE WEB ONE NIGHT THAT CAPT. AHAB CAUGHT UP WITH HIS OBSESSION."

page 285

"NOW, THAT WOULD SHOW HOW IMPORTANT IT IS TO DISTINGUISH 'FERTILIZING PRACTICES' FROM 'FERTILITY PRACTICES' WHEN DOWNLOADING A VIDEO FILE FROM 'THE INTERNET.'"

page 83

"SINCE WE GOT IT, HE HASN'T MOVED FROM THAT SPOT FOR ELEVEN STRAIGHT DAYS. ODDLY ENOUGH THEY CALL THIS 'GETTING UP AND RUNNING' ON THE INTERNET."

page 9

"Awww jeez. I was afraid of this. Some poor kid, bored with the usual chat lines, starts looking for bigger kicks, pretty soon they're surfin' the seedy back alleys of cyberspace, and before you know it they're into a file they can't 'undo'. I guess that's why they call it the Web. Somebody open a Window!"

page 229

page 139

Fax: 978-546-7747 • E-mail: the5wave@tiac.net

Table of Contents

∙∙

Introduction

The World on a Platter

● ●

*W*hen I first began talking with the editors at IDG Books about an Internet Directory, the need for an outline became apparent. In the words of one editor, I was to "reduce the world to three pages" before knowing if the project was feasible. I reduced, boiled down, coalesced, and rearranged. Feasibility ensued. And this, to make a long story short, is the result: the world between two bright yellow covers. But that doesn't sound elegant or glamorous enough, so I'll call it the world on a platter. Tempting in its variety, highly seasoned with humor, and ready for you to dig into.

The World Wide Web is aptly named in two respects: It is worldwide, and it's a tangled web. Surfing is easy, and the snarled threads with which cyberspace is woven add pleasure to wandering. Even searching for specific stuff has become fairly easy with the help of online directories and search engines. (You may want to check out my book *World Wide Web Searching For Dummies* for the full scoop on locating great sites.) But neither browsing nor searching can compare with being served a planet on a platter — a broad array of well-chosen sites, fully reviewed in the kind of immortal prose that makes grown men weep, dancing with helpful and informative micons (I'll get to them in a minute), all served up by an elegant butler dressed in formal evening clothes (that would be me). Of course, you have to take my word about the evening clothes.

This book serves three purposes:

1. Saves you time.

I don't waste your time or mine with sites that don't cut the mustard. (If you've ever tried cutting mustard, you know how difficult and messy it can be.) Every location described in this book is a winner in at least one important aspect and usually in several aspects. Occasionally, to keep you up-to-date, I include a site that every self-respecting netizen must know about, even if I don't personally take a shine to it. But overwhelmingly, the sites reviewed in these pages are the luster of the Web.

2. **Gives you ideas.**

   Most people get on the Web for the first time, flounder around a bit, get their bearings, develop some preferences, find some favorite locations, and before too long, they're in a surfing rut. This book can explode your ruts by opening your eyes and mind to whole categories of Web sites (like continents of the world) that you may never have thought of exploring. And believe me, as much as I love computers, flipping through a book is much easier than spending hours scrolling through an online directory.

3. **Holds your coffee.**

   I'm not recommending high intakes of the black nectar, don't get me wrong. But when you're enjoying a steaming double-light semi-decaf nutmeg-sprinkled mocha triple latte and can find no safe place to rest your mug, this book with its thick cover is a stalwart and helpful companion.

Who Are You?

Well, that's a rude question if I ever heard one. To save you further embarrassment, I'll answer it for you. If you've picked up this book, you either have an Internet access account, may have one soon, or know someone who logs on to the Net and could use the judicious selections herein. I've covered a lot of bases with that sentence, my point being that this book is for everyone interested in the Internet, regardless of experience. Now, don't go trying to tell me that you have more experience than I do because I'm utterly without a life thanks to the Internet, and I'm sure you have some semblance of a life, right? If you're not yet wired into cyberspace (What *are* you waiting for? We miss you in here.), this second edition of *Internet Directory For Dummies* tells you what you're missing and what you have to look forward to. If you're a new cybercitizen (Welcome!), I can point you toward stuff that would take forever to find on your own. And if you're a veteran, I know you'll find new sites in this book. As a fellow veteran, I know how much fun it is to check out other people's discoveries.

Forget the "Dummy" label. You and I both know you're no dummy, regardless of your Net experience or lack thereof. We just got in the habit of calling these books *...For Dummies,* and now we can't stop. However, I assure you that I don't assume anyone reading these reviews has lots of Net-savvy smarts or experience with online multimedia. Appendix A explains the essentials — what you need to know to explore intelligently, including information about modems, Usenet newsgroups, and plug-ins. Appendix B offers some tips to give you a smooth ride while surfing the Net.

How to Read This Book

Hey, reading this thing isn't homework. You're not required to read this book from cover to cover. If you read it straight through, I'd fear for your sanity. No, this book is for browsing. Start with the Table of Contents to see how everything is broken down. Then flip to a section that attracts your interest and rummage among the reviews. You can either manually type in any site's URL or use the included CD, which contains links to every site listed in this book.

The book is divided into *parts,* each representing a broad subject area. Sections and subsections within each part contain the site selections. Here's a brief, inadequate rundown of what's in each part:

Part I: Internet and Computer Help

Part I reviews online Internet directories, search engines, technology news sites, and places for downloading software. Its four sections gather sites to help you keep up-to-date with technology news, find the right software for your computer, and navigate around cyberspace.

Part II: News and Information

You can find general, what's-happening-today sort of news sites in this part, and I also include a section on finding weather forecasts on the Web. News broadcasts, financial news, online magazines, and virtual newspapers get their own sections in Part II, as well. Wondering about *push* services that send customized news directly to your computer? Part II has a section for those services, too.

Part III: Research and Education

All right, down to work. Time to learn things. Part III spells out where to go for sites about science, history, politics, health, religion, and social issues. It's not all a grind, don't worry. In fact, informative Web sites generally have a good dollop of entertainment value, living up to the computer-age term *edutainment.* A homework section points kids and parents to safe and productive sites for young learners. Part III even has a reference section describing online dictionaries, encyclopedias, and atlases.

Part IV: Sports, Entertainment, and Leisure

All kinds of leisure activities, hobbies, sports, and recreation are covered in Part IV. Sports megasites are a big attraction for many people, and they're well represented. Beyond following professional sports, Part IV contains reviews of amateur sporting and recreation sites. Home maintenance, though it may not always seem like much fun, goes in this part. Travel sites comprise a large and important section, and fashion is displayed in fine style.

Part V: Shopping and Services

The Internet isn't all for show — it can actually do things for you. Web services, in fact, are becoming a larger part of the overall mix, and Part V tells you what kinds of services are available, from college search pages to online brokerages to virtual shopping malls. This part is the most commercial portion of the book because many (but by no means all) service sites charge money for their services.

Part VI: Cultural Arts

This part includes recommended sites for following movies, television, theater, books, music, and celebrities. The "Entertainment News and Gossip" section reviews some of the glitziest sites on the Web. Fine aspects of culture are covered in the — what else — "Culture" section.

Part VII: Fun and Free Stuff

The Internet is a give-and-take experience. You keep selecting what you want as you go along. You can meet other people on the Web in many different ways, and the "Meeting Places" section of this part explains where to go for online communities. This part also covers sites for kids and sites with all kinds of jokes, games, contests, and puzzles. Audio and video sites — the ones that *stream* content through your web browser — also are covered in this part.

Part VIII: The Part of Tens

This part is where the book takes "the road less traveled," as Robert Frost said. (He didn't say it directly to me.) Part VIII features sites that select and rate unusual new sites as they're created, sites for senior citizens (a fast-growing Web market segment), and quirky locations highlighting bizarre topics.

The Appendixes

I've already mentioned two appendixes in the back of the book: Appendix A, with Internet basics, and Appendix B, with Net surfing tips. But wait — just like the famous Ginsu knife offer, there's more. Flip to the back and you'll also find Appendix C, which contains fabulous information about the fabulous software on the fabulous CD that comes with this fabulous book — the CD contains all the software you need to get on the Internet. Talk about one-stop shopping.

Micons (Mini Icons) Used in This Book

I want you to get as much information as possible with a quick glance at the reviews in this book. The reviews aren't long, but you may want to browse them to get the gist fast and then read them further if you're interested. In addition to ultra-short banner descriptions for each reviewed site, you can see whether the site has some special characteristics by checking for the following micons:

When a site offers a space for talking in real time with other visitors, this micon is present. Participating in chat rooms (and sometimes message boards) often requires registering at the site, so you may see this icon with the Sign-In micon.

Sites marked with this micon have software for downloading. The software may be a helper program that displays the site differently than your browser does, or the site may specialize in storing software programs for downloading.

$ Some commercial sites charge money to see some pages, or, in rare cases, to see any pages. I use this micon when most of the site's content or the most important content is available only to paying subscribers.

★ ★
★ ★   John Keats once wrote that "A thing of beauty is a joy forever." Well, the
Internet hasn't been around forever, but many Web sites are a joy.
This micon celebrates sites that mix outstanding design with outstanding
content.

Lots of graphics slow down the display of Web pages for most viewers. (If
you have ISDN or a faster connection, either at home or work, graphics may
not make much difference.) I mark graphics-intense sites with this micon.

One of the beauties of the World Wide Web is that anyone anywhere can
access the sites. But many of the sites have a decidedly North American feel
to them. This micon highlights sites with special features that appeal to a
more global audience.

Interactive message boards are a nifty way of communicating with other
people who share an interest. I find message boards more and more often in
Web sites of all sorts, often paired with chat rooms.

Some sites rely on content that can be experienced only with one or more
plug-ins that work with your browser (see Appendix A for details). For a site
to offer *only* plug-in content is very rare, but I've supplied this micon when
the best experience of the site is compromised without certain plug-ins.

When items are for sale through a Web page, this micon appears. Some
online stores replicate a merchandise catalog without offering an online
ordering system, in which case they don't get this Shopping micon. You
must be able to actually order a product through the Web site in order for
the site to gain the Shopping micon.

I'm sorry to report that an increasing number of sites require you to register.
Registration is usually free (I tell you in the review when it isn't) but is
sometimes arduous. At its most harmless, registration just takes your name
and e-mail address. At its most obnoxious, it demands all sorts of information about your demographic niche and tastes and then forwards this
information to marketing departments.

If audio clips are a conspicuous element of a site, you see this micon. In
many cases, you hear the audio parts through a plug-in, but some sites
include tiny audio files — sound effects, not music — that don't need plug-
ins. For that reason, you may see this micon without the Plug-Ins micon.

You can contribute stuff to some sites. Uploads can be as large as an audio
file of your latest musical creation or as small as a paragraph of writing that
you type into the site. This micon signals all kinds of upload possibilities,
even if it's just the opportunity to type a question to an online health site.

As with the Sound micon, the Video micon tells you when video clips are a
featured element of a site.

Hey, Write a Letter!

To me, that is. I like getting mail, especially the digital kind. Knock on my virtual door at this address:

```
brad@njcc.com
```

In the meantime, happy reading, browsing, surfing, searching, chatting, messaging, downloading, listening, and everything else you can do on the Net.

Part I
Internet and Computer Help

The 5th Wave — By Rich Tennant

"SINCE WE GOT IT, HE HASN'T MOVED FROM THAT SPOT FOR ELEVEN STRAIGHT DAYS. ODDLY ENOUGH THEY CALL THIS 'GETTING UP AND RUNNING' ON THE INTERNET."

In this part . . .

*1*nternet and computer help on the World Wide Web is like first aid in a hospital. The fact that the Internet is a common interest among almost everyone *on* the Internet makes sense. Assistance comes in the form of directories that map the Internet terrain, search engines that encourage searching for topics by keyword, download sites for acquiring software through your modem, and high-tech news sites that help explain the Internet and computers.

Directories

galaxy The professional's guide to a world of information.

Home
What's New
Add Your Site
Advanced Search
Info & Help

DO YOU
KNOW WHO I AM?

Web Search

Search here, or use *Galaxy's advanced search* for more
options.

Professional
Directory

The Web's resources, compiled for professionals.
Business And Commerce   Medicine
Community   Reference
Engineering And Technology   Science
                               Social Sciences
                               Leisure And Recreation

Galaxy Directory   **Business and Commerce**
                   Business General Resources · Consumer Products and Services · General Products and Services

Community
Births · Charity and Community Service · Consumer Issues · Crime and Law Enforcement · Culture · Death ·
Education · Environment · Family · Gender Issues · Health · Home · Immigration · Law · Libraries · Net Citizens ·
Networking and Communication · News · Paranormal · Politics · Religion · Safety · US States · Urban Life ·
Veteran Affairs · Weddings · Workplace · World Communities

www.einet.net/galaxy.html

The World Wide Web is many things, but one thing it's not is organized. Nothing is in its right place because, in cyberspace, there are no places. Web sites simply exist in the void of virtual reality, and although you can easily click your way around by following hyperlinks, you may not be able to easily find exactly what you're looking for. Finding specific information is where Web directories come in handy — in fact, these directories are essential. World Wide Web directories are like maps of the cyber-landscape, organized into topics that help you narrow down your browsing.

Most Web directories are basically the same, using a multilevel system of organizing Internet subject matter. The top level of a directory usually offers between eight and twenty main topics, with each topic linking to a second level of subtopics. The largest directories go down eight or ten levels — each level more specific and detailed than the last — with links to Web pages starting with the second or third level.

Web sites differ in how they organize their topics and whether they review the linked sites. Many directories also supply other kinds of information, such as news headlines, personalization features, weather updates, and other newsy items.

By the way, you may wonder what the difference is between directories, reviewed here, and search engines, which

I talk about later. The basic difference is that Web site creators have to register with directories in order to be listed, and you only get these registered sites in their categories when you use the directory. Search engines, on the other hand, take your search request and send out software robots (sometimes nicknamed *bots*) to find matches. In shopping terms, using a directory is the same as limiting yourself to what the store has in stock, which is fine *if* you like the selection. If you don't, then you can special order, which is what a search engine does.

General Web Directories

General Web directories attempt to map out the Web in the broadest possible strokes. The following directories encompass a broad range of general topics, although they vary in the depth of their coverage of those topics. Some directories attempt to list every site on the Web, whereas others strive to spare you the stress of being overwhelmed by handpicking sites to include in the listings.

Excite

www.excite.com

Good selection of sites plus some brief reviews: Excite calls its directory topics *channels,* presumably in deference to the broadcast sensibility sweeping the Internet. Excite presents its directory information as a mix of site links and magazine-style information flow. Every second level of the directory includes headlines related to the topic, and sometimes other miscellaneous features crowding around the subtopic directory list. Clicking a subtopic gets rid of the channel stuff and takes you to the heart of the Excite directory: reviews and links. In each subtopic, Excite reviews selected

12 Directories

sites and provides bare links to many other unreviewed locations. The reviews are Excite's way of saying, "These are the most important sites in this category," and that editorial discrimination is a great help in finding good stuff. Excite has been around for a long time (by Web standards), and it exercises good judgment.

Galaxy

www.einet.net/galaxy.html

Web directory geared toward professionals: If you don't like small type, forget about Galaxy. But if you can stand squinting at tiny letters, this Web directory has some things going for it — some peculiarities, too, but I want to concentrate on the positive. Geared toward professionals but useful for everyone, the directory contains links to many academic and professional organizations, and its subcategories are especially helpful to specialists in the fields represented by the main topics. The directory is very deep and displays the second and third levels simultaneously, which is very convenient and doesn't force you to lurch back and forth between two pages when tracking down a topic. Surprisingly, the directory is weak in the business and investing fields.

Infoseek

www.infoseek.com

Popular Internet directory: Following current trends in Web directories, Infoseek provides more than just a multilevel table of contents for the World Wide Web. Links take you to locations for finding people, e-mail addresses, maps, chat sites, and other Internet attractions. For the global community of netizens who don't live in the United States and for whom English is not their native language, the international directory, found at the bottom of the home page, is a resource *fantastique*. Each country link

provides a complete Web directory in that country's language. The main English directory has a couple of useful top-level subjects, including Getting It Done, listing practical and productive sites. Shopping also gets its own subject heading. Infoseek claims to be the Web's largest directory, which is difficult to evaluate. But it's unquestionably one of the best.

LookSmart

www.looksmart.com

★ ★
★ ★

Internet directory with a uniquely useful design: The innovative LookSmart directory presents such a different and sensible approach to mapping the Web that you can't help wondering why other directories haven't thought of the idea — or at least copied it. What's so special? As you drill deeper into the directory, LookSmart uses an original design to show your *entire* search path on one page. Other multilevel directories replace the first level with a second-level page when you click a topic, and as you go deeper, the directories continue hiding your earlier topic pages. This feature makes it much easier to retrace your steps intelligently, without the tedium of using the Back button. LookSmart isn't as comprehensive as some other directories (if it was, the unique display system wouldn't be possible), but it does contain good choices, and each site comes with a brief review.

Lycos

www.lycos.com

Magazine-style Web directory: Lycos has been around since the earliest days of Web mapping and has undergone several fundamental changes. In its current incarnation, the Lycos directory has the appearance of a Web magazine divided into 22 main subjects. Each topic also lists some subtopics on the home page, so you can click Buy a Car under Auto and go directly to that page, for example. As you explore the directory, you get more than subtopics and links to Web sites. Headlines and reviews jockey for screen space and your attention, and a Top 5 percent feature attempts to segregate the Web's best sites from the vast wasteland of mediocrity. Searches may seem superfluous but are actually good for coming up with new ideas. The directory's new look does a nice job of categorizing a mishmash of features and subject angles on each screen. And links at the bottom of the page provide Lycos directories in a number of languages.

Magellan

www.mckinley.com

Each site in the directory is reviewed: Magellan tosses its hat into the crowded ring of World Wide Web directories with a service that won't make you jump up and down or write home, but may make you shift in your seat and think about your mother. A review directory, Magellan provides one-paragraph, witty reviews of selected Web sites. The site then limits the directory to those reviewed sites, which is unusual. In every category, you know you're seeing a list of sites that have passed some sort of criteria and have at least been checked for basic functionality. The downside, of course, is that the Magellan directory isn't very large compared to competitors that list unreviewed sites. If you prefer reliable, high-quality sites to sheer volume, Magellan is a good place to find them.

Starting Point

www.stpt.com

★ ★
★ ★

Small, compact Net directory: Working with the idea that a picture is worth a thousand — or at least a few hundred — words, Starting Point takes a graphical approach to Web navigation. Does it live up to its slightly awkward slogan, "Everything You Need to Work the Web . . . Every Day"? Although Starting Point doesn't have the complexity of Yahoo!, Lycos, or the other monsters, you may prefer the coziness of the site as well as the wealth of links here. The directory is three levels deep, with the second and third levels combined on the same page to make searching a quick experience. The directory selections contain nothing unusual, and no descriptions or reviews clutter the tastefully laid-out pages. You won't give up your job to roam this site, but it is — as the title suggests — a starting point.

WebCrawler

webcrawler.com

A new directory attached to an old search engine: Born as a student project in 1994, WebCrawler began as one of the very first Web search engines. Although it enjoyed a loyal group of users, WebCrawler nevertheless was threatened by obsolescence until rejuvenating itself with a recent facelift and feature upgrade. The site now looks good and sports a brand new directory alongside its keyword search features. Among its 16 main directory topics are a few unusual attractions, such as People & Chat and Games headings. The Relationships category is also original, leading to a range of sites from poetry to sexuality. The site handpicks and reviews every site in the directory, making WebCrawler one of those directories that sacrifices quantity for quality — usually a favorable trade-off for the average user.

Yahoo!

www.yahoo.com

The granddaddy of Internet directories: Yahoo! Internet directory — probably the best known of all online maps and one of the most visited Web sites of any kind — is characterized by sheer massiveness. The directory is an awesome testimonial to the huge complexity of the World Wide Web. Extending as deep as eight levels in some topics, Yahoo! attempts to link to every site on the Web. The directory probably doesn't quite accomplish that noble goal, but it comes as close as anyone could want. From the top level, shown on the home page, click any of the 14 main topics to start your excursion into hyperlink heaven. At the bottom of the home page, you find small links to World and Metro Yahoo! directories, which are independent maps to Web sites relevant to specific geographical regions. Yahoo! gives a somewhat impersonal feel to the directory. Only small, tasteful graphics compete for your attention with the serious task at hand — finding your way around the Web. Yahoo! doesn't review sites, although the sites' creators enhance a certain percentage of the links with one-sentence descriptions. The main benefit of this pervasive starkness? The directory is fast and almost never stalls. Yahoo! is the directory to use when you don't want to miss a single site.

Other Stuff to Check Out

gv.tinet.ie
netscape.yahoo.com/guide
www.aol.com/netfind
www.cyberspud.com
www.eyeontheweb.com
www.i-explorer.com
www.selectsurf.com

Specialized Internet Directories

Many directories address only a portion of the Internet — the Usenet newsgroups, for example, or a single subject area of the World Wide Web. Some of the smaller directories are either too frivolous or don't work well enough for me to include them. The following sites provide a valuable, specific service.

Achoo

www.achoo.com

Directory of healthcare sites: Can you think of a better name for a directory of online healthcare services? Achoo isn't to be sneezed at. It provides over 8,000 links to healthcare information resources on the Net. Achoo divides its Directory page into three categories: Human Health & Disease, Business of Health, and Organizations & Sources. With those links, you can telescope your way down to almost any aspect of health, illness, treatment, and recovery, and find a place on the Web to read more about that subject. Also, on the top-level directory page, you find a Headline News link, which is devoted to healthcare news items (broken up into convenient categories), and a Site of the Week link. Perhaps the most impressive feature is a searchable database of healthcare companies and topics. You can ferret out articles on any subject. If an apple a day keeps the doctor away, visit this site while you're eating it.

Click

www.click.toplinks.com

Web directory for teens: Unlike Yahooligans!, which provides all ages of kids with a child-safe directory of Web sites, Click is just for teens. The directory's graphics make the site appealing and stylish (although the motifs slow down page loads). The top-level topics favor quirkiness over completeness — Create, Fun, Learning, Life, Looks, Music, Net, On Top (of news and happenings), and Sports are the main subjects. Each main topic has up to 18 subtopics, which lead to handfuls of links. The directory's careful selection is reassuring, and the directory includes a brief review of each site. As you explore the links chosen by the Click directory, the sites may give you a kid-safe impression; however, Click neither guarantees site quality nor describes its screening process.

Deja News

www.dejanews.com

Directory of Usenet newsgroups: Deja News started out and built its formidable reputation as a search engine for the Usenet newsgroups — the bulletin boards

of the Internet community. Very recently, Deja News expanded its site to include a multilevel directory, which it again restricts to the Usenet newsgroups. Anyone who has ever scoured a gigantic master list of the thousands of individual newsgroups trying to find a particular one — like beer making or a fan club for a rock band — can see how valuable a newsgroup directory could be. On the top level, Deja News presents nine basic topics, from which you can click your way deeper into the directory. At the bottom level of any particular topic, a list of relevant newsgroups enables you to read and participate in any newsgroup or perform a keyword search within that newsgroup. You may want to use a dedicated newsgroup program rather than the Deja News interface for reading and posting messages, but the directory can at least find the best groups for you.

Parents, one warning: As I mention in Appendix A, Usenet newsgroups are an adult feature of the Internet. That means Deja News probably isn't something you want to let your youngster browse around unsupervised.

The Huge List

thehugelist.com

Big Net directory with unusual topics: The Huge List lives up to its name. Although it doesn't compare in "hugeness" to the vast Yahoo! directory, it makes up the difference with a unique structure and unusual topic headings. A whopping 34 main topics stretch down the left-hand menu frame, including some rare subjects (for Internet directories, anyway) such as Apple Macintosh, Disabled Persons, Free Webspace, Internet Providers, Motorcycles, Web Tools, and Women's Web. After you click a heading, the main topic list remains visible on the page. Every directory page has a remarkable feature: You can enter your e-mail address so that the site notifies you when that directory

16   Directories

page is changed or updated. Another nifty feature is the THL Remote link, which opens a small browser panel containing all the first-level topic headings. The Remote Link panel operates just like another (small) browser window, and you can keep it open as you wander around the Web with your main browser window. The panel enables you to conduct a Huge List search from anywhere on the Web.

World Wide Web Pavilion

**www.catalog.com/tsw/Pavilion/
    pavilion.htm**

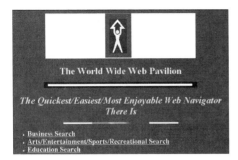

Fast Internet directory: The World Wide Web Pavilion offers one great feature that's sometimes frustratingly lacking in other directories: speed. This site's menu system of Web links is lightning fast. Whether speed makes up for the World Wide Web Pavilion's relatively modest scope of Web sites — not to mention the eye-popping yellow-on-blue color design of some pages — is up to you to determine. Your brain may also be twisted by some odd directory placements, such as Art Galleries under the Business heading. Nevertheless, the World Wide Web Pavilion is a good place to zip in and out of when you want to check out some links without brewing a pot of coffee while complicated pages slowly display on your screen. The site is strongest in the education, government, and science listings.

WWWomen

www.wwwomen.com

A directory of sites for women: Women are a minority in the Internet citizenry. You can show a friend what she's missing by taking her on a cruise through this specialized directory. The top-level menu includes standard topics — such as Arts & Entertainment, Community & Government, and Science & Technology — with a slant toward women's interests. You also find more specifically focused feminist topics, such as Women's Resources, Women & Computers, and Women Throughout History.

Yahooligans!

www.yahooligans.com

Kid-safe Internet directory: In many ways, the Internet is an adult environment, but there's no reason why that should be exclusively the case. Kids tend to be skilled at using computers and are intrigued by cyberspace. Aside from steering kids away from encountering adult content on the Net, a kid-oriented directory is a big help in finding sites that are either generally appropriate or specifically designed for children. Yahooligans! is the first, best, biggest, and most strictly regulated directory on the Web. A division of the famous Yahoo! general Web directory, every site on every Yahooligans! Directory page is cleared by the Yahoo! staff. Kids can use Yahooligans! to find homework-helper sites, read about science, locate safe chat environments where other kids hang out, track school Web projects around the world, and generally have a domain that they can call their own.

Other Stuff to Check Out

www.blackworld.com
www.clearinghouse.net
www.e-map.com
www.everythingblack.com

Downloads

www.buydirect.com

In the past, people used the Internet mainly for downloading. Mostly a university tool, academicians used the young Net to find and acquire research files from colleagues around the world. Today, the World Wide Web brings the Internet into homes and shifts attention to multimedia information and commerce. But downloading is still available on the Internet — more than ever, in fact. With personal computing becoming a mainstream aspect of modern life, the Internet contains more programs and files to download than were ever imagined ten years ago.

Downloading through a web browser is an easy matter, with no special knowledge required. In most cases, you just follow hyperlinked instructions until your browser pops up a window asking you

where you want to store your new program on your hard drive. (The process is just like saving a file during a word-processing session.) Then you just wait for the transfer to take place, which can take less than a minute or more than an hour, depending on the size of the file you're acquiring.

Downloading is usually reserved for sites that specialize in offering programs and files. This section reviews the best of these sites. A few of the sites maintain enormous inventories of available files, like software supermarkets. Other sites fill more specific niches, such as games or screen savers. But all these selections provide a good interface for browsing and initiating downloads.

Betabase.com

www.betabase.com

Test programs before they're released commercially: Beta is a term denoting software still under development but functional enough to be tested. The brave souls willing to subject their hard drives to immature programs are called *beta testers.* Betabase.com acts as a clearinghouse for beta programs, their developers, and the testers. Windows and Macintosh beta software is available for downloading from the Betabase section — it's easy to become a beta tester. The Betabase Bulletin Board is a major site feature, enabling software developers to post requirements for special testers (fluent in certain languages, for example) and allowing testers to compare notes. The Betabase News is a free e-mail newsletter that keeps you up to speed about beta software and testing needs. Finally, the Betabase Reviews offer evaluations of prominent prerelease software, such as evolving versions of Netscape Communicator or Hot Java.

18 Downloads

BuyDirect.com
www.buydirect.com

Buy software online: BuyDirect.com is a download site devoted to commercial software sold through the Internet. Commercial programs differ from shareware in the method of payment. Neither type of software is free, but you pay for a commercial program before acquiring it, and you pay for shareware after using it for a trial period and then deciding to keep it. The programs sold through BuyDirect.com are mostly Internet assistance programs like browsers, chat clients software, server utilities (such as MPEG-encoding programs), Java programming tools, and other development and communications tools. The new arrivals and top sellers links cut to the chase if you visit the site often or want the best of the best. If you're looking for a specific program and you're not sure which category to find it in, the all products a to z link is a handy index. When you select a download, the site requests a billing address and credit card information. Then you start the download, make yourself a snack, and soon you have your new software. Using the BuyDirect.com site is a lot quicker than going to the store, and the selection of Internet-related titles is better.

Dave Central
www.davecentral.com

Handpicked shareware and freeware: Dave Franklin created a terrific download site that has become a staple on bookmark lists everywhere. The site concentrates on only Internet freeware, shareware, and commercial demos. You won't find any word processors, screen savers, or database programs here, but you do find a good selection of handpicked and reviewed e-mail programs, programming

aids, newsgroup readers, conferencing software, and other Internet-related stuff. Graphically, Franklin models the site after a Windows File Manager, with category folders stretching down the left side of the screen. Click any folder to see subcategories within it; by using this method, you eventually reach the programs themselves. The site treats each program in royal fashion on its own download page with a screen shot, description, price, and link to the Web site of the company or individual author of the program. For quality selection and good descriptions, you can hardly do better when browsing for Internet software than Dave Central.

Download.com
www.download.com

Huge selection of shareware: Download.com is a major portion of the CNET Web site and one of the most important download pipelines on the Web. Taking the appearance of an online magazine, Download.com splashes headlines about new software and provides links to special pages for downloading new programs. The huge site is organized into categories of software — Business, Games, Home & Personal, Internet, Utilities, and so on. The Weekly Picks link is for the cream-of-the-crop software, while the At a Glance section helps those who like to keep up with the latest thing find out what's most popular, what's new, and what the site considers its top picks. Each category link leads to a second-level page with subcategories and more headlines. The site really amounts to a multilevel directory of software, listing the actual programs on the third level. Download.com contains both shareware and commercial programs in its archives (whereas a sister CNET site, Shareware.com, is limited to just shareware and freeware). If a program charges for downloading, you'll find a link to a different CNET-affiliated site called BuyDirect.com (also reviewed in this section). You find most of the BuyDirect programs in the Internet category. Each listed program shows the date that the site added it to the database, plus the number of times users have downloaded it — high download numbers can sometimes indicate good quality, or at least popularity. Single paragraphs (usually single sentences) describe the programs and list the size of the software, so you know roughly how long you'll tap your fingers while it's downloading.

Dr. Download

www.drdownload.com/home.htm

Essential downloads for Internet beginners: Dr. Download is the fictional creation of the marketing company responsible for this award-winning site. The site writes all of its text — introductions and reviews — in the doctor's highly personable, informal voice, which makes browsing fun. Dr. Download avoids any kind of graphic organization in favor of running text, which is great for beginners but a little inconvenient for more experienced netizens. More than just a good read (provided you *can* read the black text on the greenish-brown background), Dr. Download cuts through the shareware jungle by selecting and offering only handpicked programs, purporting to save you tons of time downloading worthless

software. The categories are freebies, games, utilities, and audio/video. The site covers PC and Mac programs with admirable equality, and the good doctor sticks to the basics. In the Utilities department, for example, if you're already equipped with standard compression programs (such as WinZip or Stuffit Expander, which you find on the accompanying CD), then don't look here for fancier or more esoteric stuff. Dr. Download is a good starting point for the shareware beginner.

File Mine

www.filemine.com

Game and other shareware downloads: File Mine is a magazine-style download source with a strong emphasis on games. Going the extra mile toward user-agreeableness, File Mine automatically keeps a personal page for you, which lists every file (program) you select. Selecting doesn't necessarily mean downloading; it just means adding to your personal page and viewing a review. Your personal page keeps the list intact even if you leave the site, so you can return hours, days, or weeks later to review your selections and download them. The impressive game library contains arcade simulations, adventure games, strategy brain exercises, sports, and role-playing games, among others. File Mine also stores work stuff — Internet programs, general utilities, commercial demos, business and education software, and others — but go for the games first.

FilePile

filepile.com/nc/start

Enormous selection of computer files for downloading: FilePile is a mile-high pile of stylish files. Claiming to be the largest indexed collection of files in the world — numbering over 1.2 million files — the

20 Downloads

site is impressive indeed. Lest you think FilePile is a megamarket of over a million software programs, you should know that many of the files in this library are images and other multimedia elements, not programs. The added breadth of making multimedia files available for downloading is the site's strongest point. After all, you can get software programs from Jumbo, Download.com, and other better-organized sites than this one. But the selection of pictures, audio, and font (typeface) files is a terrific resource for fun and productivity. The site is a bit difficult to browse effectively, forcing you to rely on the keyword search engine.

Galt Shareware Zone

www.galttech.com

Unusual selection of shareware: Galt Shareware Zone doesn't try to be comprehensive, smartly leaving that arduous goal to the software supermarkets like Jumbo (also reviewed in this section). Instead, the nerdy-looking site concentrates on certain shareware niches and offers an unusual and fun collection of programs. The site highlights screen savers with about 1,400 programs. A Top-20 Games section contains handpicked shareware game programs. Perhaps the most remarkable section is the Desktop Themes area, which offers packages of desktop pictures and window color combinations for Windows 95 users. (You must have Microsoft Plus! on your computer along with Windows 95.) You can galvanize the appearance of your computer desktop with a Hawaiian islands theme or an *Austin Powers* motif (among many others). Shareware Zone is fun browsing if you're not looking for aisles and aisles of programs.

Jumbo

www.jumbo.com

Shareware supermarket: As the name implies, Jumbo goes for sheer size, archiving over 250,000 programs in a wide range of categories for your downloading pleasure, and the site enables you to find out for yourself what's good and what isn't. You can check out some software reviews before committing yourself to the download, but in many cases, you have to rely on brief (often one sentence) descriptions. The site divides each classification — Business, Entertainment, Games, Homework, Internet, and others — by computer platform (Windows 3.*x*, Windows 95, Macintosh, and so on). A keyword form lets you search for specific titles. Downloading is usually just as simple as clicking an icon. Jumbo is a supermarket for software, with no sign of a selection or testing process, so it's best for experienced computer users and software addicts.

Macdownload.com

www.zdnet.com/mac/download.html

Vast software selection for Macs: I don't know this for a fact, but I suspect that somewhere recently a Mac user died and insisted on "Gone to Macdownload.com" being inscribed on his tombstone. He'll have plenty to check out. The site groups its offerings in 17 categories, listed on the left side of the home page. Everything from Fonts/Publishing to Games to software for the Newton is included. The individual pages include not only the software, but a five-mouse rating system and the number of times the software has been downloaded — a good clue as to what's popular. New software is noted (and also grouped on a separate page). The individual software pages add a general description, the file size, purchase information (freeware or shareware, and the cost), and what anti-virus program was used to check the software. One tip: You're better off sticking with the links that you're given than clicking the Site Map link in the upper-left corner. That link creates another window with the map to the entire ZDNet site, not just Macdownload.

PC Magazine Downloads

www.pcmag.com/download/dl-
  home.htm

 ★★
★★

High-quality free downloads from the magazine: PC Magazine Downloads appeals to the same people who read *PC Magazine* — highly computer-literate, software-enchanted users. The site is technical, no doubt about it, offering downloads of past PC Tech sections of the magazine, plus the actual software benchmark tools that the magazine uses to compile its renowned equipment reviews. Nongeeks can find value in the site by going straight for the PC Magazine Free Utilities link, which contains the biweekly selected utility programs featured in the magazine and enables you to download them for free. The programs are freeware, not shareware, and uniformly excellent, making them the best and most famous bargains on the Net (with the exception, perhaps, of Microsoft Internet Explorer, a free world-class web browser). Another good link for the average surfer is Internet Utilities, which features a selection of handy Internet programs.

Screen Savers a2z

www.sirius.com/~ratloaf

Shareware and freeware screen savers: If you think the best thing about your computer is what happens to the screen when you're not using it, visit Screen Savers a2z. Even if you're only moderately entranced by pictures and designs that play across your monitor when your computer is idle, you may want to start or enhance your collection with a few well-selected downloads from this site. You don't have to be a screen-saver zombie to enjoy the large catalog of screen savers here. Many screen savers are small, quick downloads, so within minutes you can be wasting your time gazing helplessly at colorful animations. My only complaint about this site is its alphabetical organization. The site could improve by categorizing the screen savers by type — slide show, animation, abstract design, and so on. Still, Screen Savers a2z is good grazing.

WinFiles.com

www.winfiles.com

Shareware for Windows 95, 98, CE, and NT: Good Web sites strive to stay current, and this site recently changed names (from Windows95.com) to reflect an updated mission: To serve all Windows users, no matter — to quote the site — "which 'flavor' of Windows they're running." WinFiles.com is not a Microsoft site, and you can't download the Windows 95 or 98 operating systems from it, nor from any other site on the Net — you must purchase them in a store or bundled with a new computer. But if you're looking for shareware add-ons, utilities, bug fixes (sorry, Microsoft — I know you don't like the word *bug*), or device drivers for Windows 95, 98, CE, and NT, then WinFiles. com is the place to go. Thorough and well

22 Search Engines

organized, the site uses a Windows 95-type window as its main menu. Searching the site using keywords is a user-friendly experience, allowing you to narrow the search to certain kinds of software or broaden it to cover the whole site. Clicking the Windows Shareware icon on the home page takes you to the Shareware Collection page, where you find the Windows 95/98, NT, and CE icons. (Nice attention to detail, too: The icons use drawings of computers appropriate for each particular operating system, such as a palm computer in the icon for Windows CE.) The shareware selection is very large, including subdivisions like Multimedia and Graphics Tools, Productivity Tools, Information Management, Shell and Desktop, and many others. Winfiles.com is a tremendous downloadable shareware resource exclusively for Windows users.

Other Stuff to Check Out

meccaworld.com
www.download.com/Browsers/
    ?st.dl.fd.tb.br
www.geocities.com/SiliconValley/Park/2061/
    index.html
www.q-d.com/swc.htm
www.shareware95.com
www.ukshareware.com

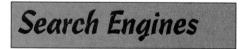

www.altavista.digital.com

In the great quest to find what you want in the midst of ever-increasing Internet sprawl, search engines help by compiling huge indexes of Web sites and letting you search them with keywords. *Keywords* are like hints that you give the search engine to help it find what you need. A keyword search string, as they're called, can be as simple as *movies* or as complex as *old movies humphrey bogart*. Most search services offer a simple interface for doing quick searches and an alternative interface — usually called Power Searching or Advanced Searching — for more complicated search strings.

The real purpose of search engines is to save you hours of browsing — which is not to say that browsing isn't fun. In fact, the World Wide Web was built on the delights of browsing. But when you want to find something fast, use your favorite search engine.

Broad search engine sites maintain indexes of the entire World Wide Web, and sometimes they invite you to search the Usenet newsgroups as well. Some of the following sites are *multiengine* services, which send your keywords to more than one of the popular search engines. The advantage to multiengine sites is that you don't need to scurry around from one search engine to another if you want to try several. The disadvantage is that these sites access only the simplest functions of each search engine — if you want to use the advanced searching functions, you have to do some scurrying.

One other note: By their very nature, search engines show results that include international sites. (After all, that's why they call it the *World* Wide Web.) However, not every search site includes search *pages* that cater to non-Americans. In this section, I've restricted the use of the International micon to those sites that include non-English instruction.

AltaVista

www.altavista.digital.com/

Sophisticated Internet searching: AltaVista grew in fame among search engines during 1995 and 1996, gaining a sort of most-favored-engine status among savvy netizens. More recently some other search services, particularly HotBot, have gained their share of headlines and eclipsed AltaVista's reputation to a certain extent. Nevertheless, AltaVista remains one of the premier search engines, with some unique features for advanced keyword searching, and should be on the bookmark list of anyone serious about finding stuff on the Web. You can also search the Usenet newsgroups by clicking the Search Usenet link. Want to search for documents in a non-English language, like Estonian or Icelandic? No problem. Simply click the appropriate language in the Search the Web for documents drop-down box. If you want to go to the AltaVista search network for another country, simply click Our Search Network and use the site map to find the appropriate region. The site also has a nifty feature that invites you to refine searches by selecting and eliminating certain words and concepts from your current search results, narrowing the field of relevant links. AltaVista is a good search engine for exploring advanced options, all of which are explained by clicking the Help link on any keyword entry page.

Dogpile

www.dogpile.com

Simultaneous multiengine searching: A multiengine search service, Dogpile (where *did* they come up with that name?) automatically scours the indexes of Yahoo!, Excite, Lycos, Infoseek, AltaVista, and several other databases, with your keywords. You can select whether to search the Web, newswires

only, Usenet, or two of the three in a certain order, and you can set a time limit (up to a minute in ten-second increments) by which Dogpile must deliver the results. But you can't choose which other search engines from the extensive list participate in the search; Dogpile — like an irrepressible puppy — goes for all the search engines with equal enthusiasm when you tell it to Fetch. Dogpile sorts the results by search engine, so you get Yahoo! results, then Excite, then Lycos, and so on. Dogpile does a good job, even if it doesn't provide enough ways to narrow down the results.

Excite

www.excite.com

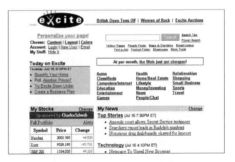

Searching by concept of keyword: Excite has ambitions beyond merely finding good Web sites for you. It is devoted to finding *information,* regardless of what you need. It provides a variety of services that help you find your particular needle in the Internet haystack, including Yellow Pages, maps, a People Finder, and the Email Lookup. (Links for these services appear just under the keyword form on the home page.) In terms of actually searching the Web, Excite is no slouch either. The search engine first gained fame on the Net by introducing a novel idea: searching by concept. Excite enables you to enter keywords and phrases without worrying about the computer taking you too literally or messing around with search operators and the other esoterica of information retrieval. Other search engines have caught up with Excite in this regard, but Excite's engine is still highly regarded. For an easy way to use advanced searching techniques, try the Power Search link.

EZ-Find

www.theriver.com/TheRiver/Explore/ ezfind.html

Several search engines on one page: EZ-Find serves as a consolidator of search engines, giving you access to several services on one page. Head over to the EZ-Find URL and check out the buttons beneath the keyword entry form — each button sends your keyword search request to a different major search engine. Underneath the buttons, some drop-down menus, using basic functions that all the search engines understand, enable you to determine how you want your keywords interpreted. Bear in mind that EZ-Find can't search with all the different engines simultaneously — you can use only one engine at a time. The benefit to using EZ-Find is having a central location for accessing each search engine. Any drawbacks? Well, yes, now that you ask. You don't have access to advanced search features — you must visit the search engines' sites to access special keyword options.

Galaxy

www.einet.net/galaxy.html

Fast searching with a unique design for narrowing results: You wouldn't think that so many ways to search the Internet could exist, but Galaxy adds yet another permutation to the variegated world of Web search engines. The simple search page isn't anything special — enter a keyword or three, wait a few seconds, and you're bowled over by a flood of results. Galaxy really shines when you use the advanced search feature to narrow down the results. Click the advanced search link to see another keyword entry form;

this time it's surrounded by a couple of drop-down menus for refining the search. The lower drop-down menu is a list of directory topics (from the Galaxy directory, which is reviewed in the Directories section), letting you restrict your search to any specific field. This option is a bigger deal than it may seem at first. Try a search on the keyword *Paris* with the drop-down menu selection Every Topic. You get lots of results. Now go back and narrow the results instantly by selecting Business and Commerce or Government. Only those sites that match the topic show up in the result list, and you can repeat the process as often as you need to. It's an instant way of filtering search results, and Galaxy is unique among search engines in using this method.

HotBot

www.hotbot.com

State-of-the-cool Net searching: HotBot takes its name from the software robots that automatically scour the World Wide Web for new sites. All search engines use some kind of software 'bot, sometimes called a *spider* or *worm*. HotBot is a search service developed by HotWired, the online version of *Wired* magazine. If you've ever subjected your optic nerves to the crazy color clashings of the magazine or the Web site, you won't be too startled by the eye-boggling ambiance of the HotBot pages. Wear sunglasses if you must, but do try the fast, accurate, comprehensive search engine hiding beneath the Day-Glo home page. Drop-down menus surround the keyword form and enable you to refine your search right from the start — no need to click over to a Power Search page as many other engines require. If you crave even more control over your searches, click More Search Options. That opens even more options for limiting the range of your search, and you can use any or all the menus at once. Setting a date range, media type, page type, or location can really cut to the chase in serious searches. You may need to experiment to get the hang of all the options, but it's worth enduring a learning curve to find information more quickly. HotBot is state-of-the-art searching.

Inference Find

www.inference.com/ifind

Great organization of search results: This search engine almost didn't make it into this book. Face it: Inference Find is a dumb title. However, I've never seen search results displayed with the organization of this engine, and I want everyone to experience it. Inference Find puts six search engines — WebCrawler, Yahoo!, Lycos, AltaVista, Infoseek, and Excite, at the time of this writing — to work for you, and then tidies up the results. Links that match your keywords don't come back in an incoherent jumble, making it impossible to distinguish one site from another without linking over to them. Inference Find classifies the links by type. For example, a recent search on the word *Paris* grouped together links that were part of the same domain (such as sites from Paris), commercial sites, nonprofit sites, and so on. The engine divided the search results into nine categories, and the search itself didn't take any longer than normal. For that kind of service, I can put up with a capricious exclamation point and a broken graphic. Inference Find also offers services in a limited number of foreign languages.

Infoseek

www.infoseek.com

Internet, Usenet, and e-mail searching: The Infoseek search engine is particularly user-friendly in several important ways. One of the first features you notice on the home page, right under the main keyword

entry form, is a selection of option buttons that determine the domain of your search. The default choice is the Web because most people look for Web sites on a particular subject. But people are beginning to search the Internet's resources from other angles, so Infoseek also lets you define newsgroups, wire service sites, and business sites as channels within which your keywords search. Another convenience: When you enter keywords, using quotation marks around a phrase keeps the keywords intact and in order, and capitalizing the first letter of keywords alerts the search engine that you're looking for a proper name. These conveniences make keyword searching a more intuitive experience, which is always welcome.

The Internet Sleuth

www.isleuth.com

Hundreds of topical search engines in one location: If one site exists that may reset your standards of combing the Net for information, it's The Internet Sleuth. It's a combination directory and keyword search service that uses the familiar multilevel, topical directory structure to provide hundreds of highly specific keyword search databases. The Internet Sleuth is basically a collection of every search engine in every subject area imaginable. Click the News link on the home page and you see a collection of keyword-based search engines for the Associated Press, *The Christian Science Monitor, USA Today,* and several other databases on the Web. This incredible

26 Search Engines

resource lets you zoom in quickly on articles and other research materials by restricting the search to specific Web locations. For serious and highly specific searches, The Internet Sleuth is the real stuff.

Livelink Pinstripe

pinstripe.opentext.com

Standout business searching: The former Open Text search site has evolved into this somewhat specialized search site. Hey, everyone needs to find their niche in life. And Pinstripe serves its niche well with a main Search page that allows you to limit your search to business types. Why is this important? Imagine how many businesses have "American" in their titles. But if you're looking for, say, American Airlines, you can just click the Transportation radio button. If you want a trucking company, just click the Transportation link, and you can further refine your search to Truck Transportation. The home page also includes tabs for other search areas — Finance, News, Company/People, Employment, Travel, and Discussion. Each tab page has not only a keyword search box and additional tabs, but links to related sites as well. All told, Livelink Pinstripe works hard to live up to its motto of being "The Source for Business Knowledge."

Lycos

www.lycos.com

Basic Internet searching: The Lycos search engine is almost as quirky as its directory (which I review in the Directories section). A drop-down menu — which is all the rage in search engines these days — lets you determine what portion of the Internet you want to limit your search to. The Web is one portion, obviously. The other selections enable you to search just for sounds, pictures, personal home pages created by individuals, or recipes. What an esoteric collection of possibilities! Scouring the Web for sound and

picture files is definitely useful, and I'll let you decide the value of the other choices. The Lycos Pro Advanced Search link takes you to a custom search page that gets a little fancier with keyword options using more drop-down menus. (These menus really are very chic.) You won't mistake the advanced options for the sophistication of AltaVista or HotBot (both reviewed in this section), but Lycos gives you a little more control over your search results.

MetaCrawler

www.metacrawler.com

Piggybacks on other search engines: Typically, search engines rely on home-grown indexes of Web sites to deliver quick search results. Search services constantly update their private indexes by using automatic software robots to find and classify new and updated Web pages and then add them to their indexes. When you perform a keyword search, the search engine isn't really scurrying around the Web on your behalf — it's scurrying through the index, which is much faster. MetaCrawler differs from other engines because it completely lacks an index. Instead of building its own database of Web sites, MetaCrawler borrows other indexes by submitting your search request to Infoseek, Excite, AltaVista, and other engines; MetaCrawler then organizes the results in its own format to present them to you. MetaCrawler's searches take a little longer, but they consolidate the advantages of several search engines.

ProFusion

profusion.ittc.ukans.edu

Flexible and fast multiengine searching: ProFusion is a multiengine search service along the lines of Dogpile and MetaCrawler (both reviewed in this section); however, it has a couple of unique features that set it apart. First, you can choose (from a list of eight major services) which search engine you want your keywords sent to. You can even choose more than three engines and then request that ProFusion settle on the *fastest* three for any given search. You can also specify that ProFusion search the Web or Usenet, although it's not a unique feature for a multiengine page. The update feature is singular, letting you perform a search again, either right away or any time in the future if you bookmark your search results page. However, for some reason ProFusion wants you to register (for free) to use that particular feature. Peculiar, but not offensive.

WebCrawler

webcrawler.com

The search engine for Internet "voyeurs": Let's get the formalities over with. WebCrawler is one of the oldest of all search engines, and if the search box on the home page isn't enough, you'll also find links underneath the box that can help you locate information on a number of other topics. There. Now to the good stuff: Click the Games channel, and then click Search Voyeur. *Voilà!* You now see a Java streaming ticker across your screen, displaying the keywords and phrases currently being searched by other WebCrawler users. The site protects privacy by not displaying the identities of the people conducting those searches. (WebCrawler has no way of knowing who is behind any web browser during the 5 million search requests entered every day.) Web-search voyeurism isn't the point; the fun comes when you click a keyword as it streams past — WebCrawler displays the results of the search on your monitor. Seeing mangled misspellings is also hilarious, in a mean sort of way. Whether you swipe some-body else's search phrase or use your own, you get a compact list of result links, unaccompanied by descriptions or reviews. Click the Help button for an

excellent online tutorial on how to use the WebCrawler system.

Yahoo!

www.yahoo.com

Search the best directory on the Web: Yahoo! is better known as a Web directory than a search engine (see the directory review in the Directories section earlier in this part), and it doesn't implement a keyword-based search service. Yahoo! functions in two ways. First, like any other Web search engine, it links you to sites that relate to your keywords. Secondly, unlike other such services, it links you to different parts of its own directory. Such seemingly prideful self-referral is justified because the Yahoo! directory is so vast and complex. You can easily get lost within the many levels and thousands of pages of the directory, so any pointers are welcome. When you enter a keyword on the Yahoo! home page and hit the Search button, the results come in two parts: Yahoo! directory pages that match your keywords and outside sites that do the same. The integration of two types of search results makes for longer pages that take more time to browse through and can be confusing. Some of the search engines reviewed in this section are easier to use, have clearer search results, and review some sites for your convenience. Yahoo! may not be the friendliest search service, but it does help you make sense of the huge Yahoo! directory.

28 Technology News

Other Stuff to Check Out

home.microsoft.com/access/allinone.asp
www.albany.net/allinone
www.itools.com
www.nlsearch.com
www.thrall.org/proteus.html

You won't be surprised that on the Internet, the great technical innovation of the 1990s, you find an abundance of high-tech news — enough information, in fact, to warrant a whole section in this book. The field of technical news covers computers, software, the Internet and online services, and all the commentary, speculation, and general ranting that accompanies news about such a volatile industry. Some of the sites that I list in this section represent the best that the World Wide Web has to offer in terms of page design, content quality, and interactive features — naturally, a site that wants to be your news source for high-tech subjects will try to impress you with its Net-savvy Web design.

Note: Just as the computer age has made it easier to cross international boundaries, so it has made technology reporting a more international affair. Most of these sites run stories based on merit, not the geographic source, so one story from Silicon Valley may be followed by another one from Tokyo. That means that you can consider them all international sites.

Tech Headlines and News

The following sites are the best sources of raw technical news in the typical Internet headline-link format. Headline links lead to story summaries and complete articles or wire service reports. Generally, these types of sites strive to get you up to speed quickly and don't hamper the process with unnecessary graphics — unlike the online editions of some technical magazines that want to be pretty as well as useful.

CNET

www.cnet.com

Massive technology news site with plenty of audio: CNET is a Web legend in its own time. Almost like a small online service in its ambitious scope, CNET boasts more than one million members, which is impressive even when you consider that member registration is free. CNET treats media as a big playground, refusing to restrict itself to the Internet alone. The tremendous wealth of RealAudio content in the site makes CNET resemble nothing short of an online radio station devoted to technology reporting. (CNET also produces a number of TV shows, which enhance and are enhanced by the site.) Links to other CNET sites, which include software reviews, a game center, learning resources of various kinds, and many more features that I can't describe here enliven the trademark yellow-bordered pages of the CNET site. The old saying applies: If you visit just one technology news site, make it CNET.

CNN Science and Technology

www.cnn.com/TECH/index.html

Science and high-tech news: The CNN Science and Technology site belongs on your bookmark list if you like a blend of technology news that goes beyond computers and the Internet. Recent CNN Sci-Tech stories included the Mir space station, the search for a sunken World War II aircraft carrier, and how the standard Hollywood movie solution to a meteor heading toward Earth (blow the meteor up) is probably exactly what space rangers should *not* do. Of course, the site mixes in the usual range of computer, semiconductor, and Web news, all covered with CNN's customary thoroughness and straightforward style. Web site reviews comprise a separate section, and you can also explore recaps and enhancements of CNN's technology television shows.

Computer News Daily

www.computernewsdaily.com

★★
★★

Commentary on high-tech news: You won't have difficulty finding technology news headlines on the Web; hard news sites abound. Computer News Daily (CND) makes a claim on your attention span by presenting a softer side of high-tech news: columns and opinion articles. CND acts as a news agent, collecting the best of technology writing from cyberspace and displaying it in one consistent interface. Happily, you don't click outside of the site when following a headline link, as is the case with many other news sources that don't write their own journalism. You're likely to read an article from the Cox News Service or the New York Times Syndicate, but CND always sets the article against an easy-on-the-eyes background. Keyword searching is available, and discussion message boards provide a forum for rehashing today's news with other users.

Good Morning Silicon Valley

www.sjmercury.com/gmsv

News from the epicenter of high technology: The idea of Silicon Valley (the portion of northern California around Palo Alto where many high-tech firms are headquartered) being its own socio-economic region is reinforced by a major Web news site devoted to it. Good Morning Silicon Valley (can you imagine Robin Williams screaming that into a radio microphone?) is a production of the *San Jose Mercury News,* a print newspaper emphasizing technology. (San Jose is right next to Palo Alto.) This aggressively updated site has four revolving editions. First Light is an early-morning report on the day's agenda of technology news, and the site updates the report at 1 a.m. Pacific time (4 a.m. Eastern time). The later Morning Report is a digest of important high-tech news from a variety of sources. Tech Stocks, updated in the late afternoon (Eastern time), is a daily account of technology from an investor's viewpoint and includes the day's market movements. The evening Tech Ticker is a stream of news tidbits and breaking stories. All sections of the site are archived for the previous month, in a low-graphics interface that crams a lot of information into its quick pages.

IDG.Net

www.idg.net

★★
★★

Impressive array of international technology news: Long before International Data Group founded IDG Books Worldwide, Inc., (which produced the book you're reading), IDG was into technology information in a big way. This site brings together information from the more than 400 worldwide newspapers, magazines, and Web sites that the company is affiliated with. The downside is that to access all the goodies, you have to register. Registration is free, but is a long, painful process roughly equivalent to filling out an insurance form. Shudder. The good news is that IDG.Net uses that information to put together a personal page for you and can even e-mail you updates on everything from Mac news to stock tips. IDG.Net's slick design enables you to get to information in different parts of the world with only a few clicks. A hometown pick? Sure — but a worthy one.

Media Central

www.mediacentral.com

Covers high-tech news and media: Although, strictly speaking, Media Central is a news site about all types of media — including low-tech manifestations like newspapers (remember them?) and magazines (I think I touched one recently) — the site ends up covering a lot of technology news. The technology emphasis is due to the fact that media, in this Infobahn era, inevitably converges with interactivity, networking, and other topics of digital publishing. I would characterize Media Central as a high-tech news site with a publishing angle. The site has a clean, uncluttered look that keeps it moving quickly.

Netly News Network

cgi.pathfinder.com/netly

Commentary on the Internet community: Netly News is a Pathfinder site, which means it falls under the wide umbrella of

Time Warner's Web publication empire. Netly News is mostly a collection of columns, site reviews, and viewer-participation bulletin boards. The Netly News articles range in tone from gossipy to objectively detached, but have valuable links integrated into the text. A recent column, calling the proposed new Internet names plan in the United States an "escape act," linked to the *San Jose Mercury News* story on the plan so that you could read the straight stuff and make up your own mind. I find that the Walter Miller columns ("Trailer Trash on the Infobahn") are good for a laugh or an insight or two. Too bad the site no longer offers new "This Old PC" columns — they offered great advice on low-cost computing.

NewsLinx

www.newslinx.com

International news about the Web: NewsLinx is one of the least attractive sites in this or any category. NewsLinx is also one of the most essential, culling stories from the mainstream press and posting updates throughout the day. The sources are varied, from wire services to other technology news sites, but the focus is the same: the World Wide Web. Headline links are simply posted in batches of five on the home page; during my latest visit, some 76 stories (and one lone straggler at the bottom) were listed. NewsLinx may be the most international resource in this category, putting stories about general technology ("Netizen

Cashes in on Anti-Spam Law," from News.com) next to stories about countries or regions ("In Turkey, Microsoft Thrives Despite Piracy," from Reuters). One big disadvantage is that the headline-only link doesn't give you much information, so you don't know until you click that the "Email Should Be Plain, Not a Pain" story from Yahoo! is actually a commentary from film critic Roger Ebert until you arrive at the story site. Still, the site is searchable, and a three-minute RealAudio summary is available. If you're familiar with Web topics and can skim the headlines for the news you need, NewsLinx is a definite bookmark.

NewsPage

www.newspage.com

$

Excellent directory of technology news: NewsPage enjoys a double reputation for excellence in providing financial news and technology news. The site is therefore a perfect bookmark for anyone interested in money, business, and technology. The stories don't cross over into both fields; for example, you won't see journalism about the business of high-technology companies or the investment opportunities of Wall Street's technology sector. But NewsPage's topic categories are strongest in the two fields, and NewsPage is renowned throughout the Web as a great site for technology news. The site's strongest point is the hyper-organized directory system that lets you bookmark individual pages deep within the directory that are devoted to highly specified subjects. For example, in the Interactive Media section, you can link to the PC-Based Multimedia page that displays headlines related to developments in that hot Web delivery topic. NewsPage offers a few subscription levels, including a free pass that enables you to access all headlines but only some full stories.

TechWeb

www.techweb.com

Roomy site with broad technology coverage: TechWeb, the self-described "Technology Super Site," is a big, well-rounded electronic newspaper about computers, the Internet, shareware, Web technology (like Java), product reviews, and games. The home page is a combination of Top Stories, Headlines, and Quick Hits, with the headlines of all but the latter linked to stories about all aspects of the technology industry. The TechCalendar (found by clicking the Events/Shows link on the home page) is an amazingly comprehensive directory of technology conventions used around the world and is primarily for professionals. The Encyclopedia dishes out over 10,000 definitions of technology terms. And rather than having to read all the interviews, you can listen to some of them with RealPlayer (available for download via the site).

USA Today Tech Report

www.usatoday.com/life/cyber/tech/ ct000.htm

Technology articles from the daily newspaper: Efficiency is the name of the game at this site. Although *USA Today* produces the site, the Tech Report is a Web production separate from the printed newspaper's content. Forget about graphics — they would slow you down. Never mind archiving past stories on a separate page — which would involve time-consuming mouse clicks. Don't look for story summaries underneath the headlines — they would take up valuable screen space and make the home page unwieldy. Instead, you get the day's top technology headlines, updated every few hours or as compelling stories evolve. Beneath the current headlines, you find yesterday's most important headlines, followed by headlines that span back for about one month. Headlines are the

32 Technology News

fastest way to get up to speed on information or backtrack through the news. Special reports spice up the side borders, and you can rummage back through them, too, for the past year's events. This site doesn't mess around; it trims the fat and delivers the goods without any waste.

Washington Technology Online

www.wtonline.com

 ★★ ★★

Technology from a legislative angle: Classy page design and unusual technology stories distinguish the online version of the *Washington Technology* newspaper. A certain local slant is evident in many stories that cover legislative issues on technology. Recent stories included the awarding of a new travel contract at the U.S. Department of Defense. The Washington angle doesn't prevent Washington Technology Online from reporting on Silicon Valley, however. The front page displays the beginnings of the current issue's top stories, but for a more comprehensive overview of the site, I suggest starting with the Table of Contents button. At any point you may bump into a registration request because several portions of the online newspaper are for members only, but you don't have to pay any subscription charges.

Wired News

www.wired.com/news

★★ ★★

High-tech news with an attitude: A division of HotWired, Wired News dishes up a stylish rendition of current technology news laced with the digerati sensibilities of *Wired* magazine, the site's parent organization. The site features about ten headlines at any given moment on the home page, accompanied by story summaries. Click a headline to see the full story. Five main sections divide the site: Business, Culture, Technology, Politics, and General News. Regardless of the category, the editorial viewpoint is that of a computer-savvy, digitally connected, wired-to-the-eyeballs reader. With a recent design change, HotWired abandoned a misguided white-on-black color scheme that previously scorched retinas around the globe. An e-mail update delivers the top stories directly to your mailbox and reminds you to check this site every day. It's a winner.

ZDNNews

www.zdnet.com/zdnn

Respected technology publishing organization: Ziff-Davis (the ZD part of this site) publishes computer magazines. ZDN (Ziff-Davis Network) is a news organization that covers technology subjects. ZDNNews is a top high-tech news source on the Web, unconnected to a specific magazine. Now that the credits are out of the way, I can focus on what this site offers. When you arrive on Page One, you get a rapid-fire burst of news, which is constantly updated throughout the day. The News Bursts headline column links you to stories as they develop and is designed to be a cutting-edge, breaking-news feature. The central portion of the page gives headlines and story summaries, showing off a clever, pun-infested style of news entertainment. If that isn't a fast-enough summary, click Headline Scan. Clicking a ZDTV link gets you access to videos from Ziff-Davis' television arm — it's worth sampling even if you don't generally like taking the time for newscasts. Search engines are *de rigueur* in slick news sites, and ZDNNews provides a keyword form down on the right. This packed site provides a lot of substance to browse through.

Other Stuff to Check Out

free-help.com
www.cio.com
www.dummiesdaily.com
www.tipworld.com

Tech Publications

Web publications covering high-tech subjects are a mix of print magazines gone virtual and *e-zines,* which began on the Internet and serve only a logged-on readership. As in other fields, the online editions of computer magazines may or may not include all the content of the printed edition but almost certainly contain special articles or interactive features specific to the World Wide Web. Subscription costs are rare, possibly because the readers of high-tech magazines are Internet veterans who are accustomed to getting stuff for free, and they don't have patience for the new-fangled commercial sites. When money does come into play, the fees usually apply to only a special portion of the site and not to the whole thing.

Boardwatch Magazine

www.boardwatch.com

Coverage of online services and the Internet: Boardwatch Magazine is well known to veteran online enthusiasts for its balanced coverage. Giving equal weight to the Internet, commercial online services, and local BBS services, the editors of Boardwatch Magazine treat the online realm as a giant, integrated universe of connection possibilities. While other magazines carve out niches based on separating computing dominions — the Web, online services, personal computers, software, Internet culture, and Web site reviews — Boardwatch Magazine holds steady the course of furnishing information for everyone with a modem, no matter what their cyber-space preferences are. The Web site offers an archive of back issues (and one of the most graphically pleasing archive search pages), plus a simple presentation philosophy of the current issue: It's free, no strings attached, and no omissions. One valuable bonus is worth noting: The site includes an online guide to Internet service providers (ISPs).

Byte

www.byte.com

Online magazine about hardware and computer technology: As the Internet revolution has kindled itself into a flame, Byte Magazine has resisted the transient trends and fast-fading fads of computer

34   Technology News

magazine publishing, sticking to its established sober style and hardware-oriented focus. Byte's editorial emphasis is on the broad topic of information management, and it carries articles on server technology, Web site management, intranets, data warehousing, and other high-tech esoterica relating to supervising the flow of data. A glossary helps you come to grips with the advanced treatment of Byte articles, which comes in handy as you're trudging through a dense archive of over 6,000 articles and 3,000 images. Good luck!

Computer Shopper

www.zdnet.com/cshopper

How and where to buy computer stuff: You've seen the bricklike printed magazine in stores. Astonishingly large, you could use it in a weight-training program. When future archaeologists dig up remnants of the late 20th century, they'll look at crumbling issues of *Computer Shopper* and conclude that citizens from the 20th century had greatly magnified cranial capacities. The magazine is like the collected works of Dave Barry stuffed into one volume, except not nearly as funny. In fact, it's a pretty dry read, but the magazine isn't about entertainment; it's about shopping for and buying computers and peripherals. The Web site carries on the tradition but without all the mail-order ads of the printed book. **Tip:** Start with the About us button to help get a grip on all the information. Also, try the e-mail updates.

You can find a related site, called NetBuyer, at this URL: `www.netbuyer.com`. NetBuyer is part of the overall Computer Shopper Web edition and gets you going with the nitty-gritty of comparing brands and networking with other readers. Review columns and weekly special deals from vendors enhance an already excellent resource.

ComputerLife Online

www.zdnet.com/complife

The digital-age lifestyle: We live in the age of computers, a shining time of digitally enhanced fun for the whole family. That philosophy, at least, is the editorial attitude of ComputerLife Online, a Web version of the Ziff-Davis magazine. Articles have a practical bent and a family-oriented angle. Recent features include using a scanner to touch up family photos; how, given the explosion of information technology, you can avoid information overload; and a report on online personality quizzes that you can take ("Are you a Bill Gates kind of guy, or are you more like Elvis?") The site didn't explain what that last story had to do with technology, but go with the flow. The Download section contains basic Internet tools like plug-ins and decompressors — a good download page for Net newcomers. ComputerLife Online is best for relatively new Internet citizens; more experienced residents may crave a little less sugar and a little more edge.

HotWired

www.hotwired.com

Ultra-hip online magazine for the wired generation: Created by the parent organization of *Wired* magazine, HotWired has an independent editorial staff, but it retains the same neon color sensibilities of the print magazine. No matter what your age, you can join the wired generation by visiting HotWired's techno-attitudinal domain, from which you may eventually emerge with your mind altered and your optical synapses twitching. Famous departments include Webmonkey, which offers you assistance in developing your own site; Net Surf, which has site reviews; Dream Jobs, the hippest and most digitally literate listing of high-tech professional positions; and the Beta Lounge, which rocks your computer with RealAudio DJ ruminations. After you finish, recover from the HotWired experience in Talk.com, the Java-enabled chat area.

Macworld/MacWeek

macworld.zdnet.com

Information feast for Mac lovers: Die-hards who vow to give up their Apple Macintosh computers only at gunpoint — and there are a few, my editor included! — may find this site to be an information oasis in a PC desert. A joint product of IDG and Ziff-Davis (two heavyweights in the technology information business), the site includes elements of *Macworld* magazine and *MacWeek,* which leads to a somewhat schizophrenic design. But don't despair, Mac lovers: In this case, two is better than one. Clicking on the Current Issue under Macworld at the top of the home page leads you to virtually the entire magazine online, complete with features, news, reviews, and the like. Back issues even include special inserts. Back on the home page, the MacWeek section includes current headlines; clicking on one takes you to a story page, from which you can click Home to access more stories. Some stories include video: One recent offering was the QuickTime movie that Steve Jobs (he's still the head of Apple at the time of this writing — again) played at Macworld Expo.

Nando Times InfoTech

www.nando.net/nt/info

Online technology journalism: The Nando Times, the Internet's largest Web-only newspaper, serves up high-tech news in a spacious format — almost too spacious, come to think of it. The front page would be more useful if Nando compacted it into a smaller screen space, but that's a quibbling detail. One nice feature of the front page is that it displays the exact posting time of the headlines, so you can see just how up to speed you are on the news. Nando differentiates columns by putting the author's name in capital letters in the headline link. Another nice feature — not uncommon — is that when you call up a story, the right of the window includes headline links to the other stories so that you can jump to the next story without having to return to the home page. And Nando Times InfoTech isn't one of those sites that forces you to ponder life's unanswerable questions while its pages begrudgingly display.

PC Magazine Online

www.zdnet.com/pcmag

Computer reviews and columns from the printed magazine: Many people consider *PC Magazine* a kind of computer bible. The biweekly magazine for hard-core PC users (not Macintosh loyalists) puts out the best hardware tests in the industry, includes a great range of software reviews, and has renowned columnists. *PC Magazine* is the kind of must-have publication that thousands of people subscribe to year after year and read from cover to cover the day it arrives; they even save the issues for future reference. The Web site lets you throw out all those back issues by archiving the PC Labs hardware reviews. The site includes much of the printed material, enhanced by Internet snazz like Java applets and continually updated site recommendations. Wondering about John

Dvorak's column, one of the prime features of the magazine? It's there. Even if you do read *PC Magazine* cover to cover, the online edition is a definite bookmark.

Popular Mechanics

popularmechanics.com

Low-tech, science, and engineering: If your impression of the venerable *Popular Mechanics* magazine has a musty aura to it — bolstered by the publication's decades-old emphasis on predigital tinkering with the nuts and bolts of hobby endeavors like building your own radio — then you must visit the so-called Popular Mechanics PMZone, a dynamic, interesting, rejuvenated Webzine. Wearing its many Web site awards like medals of honor on its title page, PMZone tells you up front that you need fast equipment to get the most out of the site. If you have the hardware, enter via the Shockwave route. What you find is not exactly your father's *Popular Mechanics.* Inside, however, PMZone still covers standard electronics and mechanical engineering issues. Automotive and Home Improvement sections preside. For more modern coverage, click the Science or Technology buttons. You can chat or browse the message boards in the User's Forums area, but if you care to participate, you need to register (for free). The message boards are among the best discussion forums I've seen on the Web — intelligent, detailed, and informative.

WorldVillage

www.worldvillage.com

Award-winning, informative community: A uniquely designed e-zine, WorldVillage serves up software reviews, directories of downloadables, game reviews and tips, and interactive community features. It's a magazine; it's a news source; it's an online community. The site's home page mixes content links with ads, but the Village Online page clearly breaks out the key sections, including Games, Kidz, Chat, and Download. Clicking Village Online and any location opens a new browser window, so you can explore new areas without losing the home page. WorldVillage is fun but never loses sight of its mission to be informative and useful. Its awards are deserved.

Yahoo! Internet Life

www.zdnet.com/yil/

Internet navigation, lifestyle, and Web culture: In a strange reversal of the typical magazine's migration from print to virtuality, Yahoo! Internet Life began as an e-zine and developed into a print magazine, eventually settling into both realms comfortably. Because Yahoo! is a preeminent Web directory, part of Yahoo! Internet Life's charter is to evaluate, review, and recommend Web sites. But Yahoo! Internet Life stretches the editorial focus way beyond being a mere review sheet in its coverage of Internet culture in a broad sense. A well-rounded e-zine in its maturity, Yahoo! Internet Life sports feature articles on the Net lifestyle, daily horoscopes, opinion columns, daily downloads, and a rich collection of featured site links. Much of the site's content is original (not copied from the print magazine).

ZD Internet Megasite Magazine

www.zdimag.com

Simply enormous: Ziff-Davis publishes a number of well-known and widely read computer magazines, some of which enjoy their own Web editions. ZD Internet Megasite Magazine is a separate Internet-only publication, consolidating the tremendous news-gathering and editorial resources of the Ziff-Davis publishing organization. The site's ambitious scope and depth are impressive; feature articles are interesting and dig deep. The Internet Labs section probes software and delivers test results. The ISPZone contains news and analysis about Internet on-ramps and connection services. Cyberstats charts cyberspace trends, and Devtools reviews electronic publishing programs for everyone. You get the picture — lots of departments in this content-rich site.

Other Stuff to Check Out

netpcreview.com
www.chips.navy.mil/chips
www.cpost.mb.ca
www.hyperzine.com
www.internet-magazine.com/home.htm
www.macaddict.com
www.machome.com
www.tcp.ca
www.zdnet.com/icom/e-business/index.html

38 **Technology News** _____

Part II
News and Information

In this part . . .

We've come a long way. From town criers to the first newspapers, from radio to television, and now the Internet. News reporting has shrunk the world as much as any contemporary cultural force. Television takes viewers directly to the scene of breaking news, but it turns them into completely passive recipients of the news director's choices.

Choice is the Internet's strong point. More immediate than newspapers and more varied than television, the Net offers a perfect alternative for anyone who likes getting certain types of news at certain times — with no waiting. This part explores the many types of news sites: financial news, online newspapers, up-to-the-minute current news, phone books and e-mail directories, and even weather.

Financial News

abcnews.com

Money is a huge topic both on and off the Internet. Financial news appears on the World Wide Web in the form of headlines — just like general news stories — and publications that deal with business and investments. This section deals with financial information as a topic separate from financial services, which deserve (and get) their own section later in this book. Here, I gather the best sites for keeping up to speed with today's breaking news from Wall Street and other financial markets, plus the best locations for enjoying the commentary and articles in the online finance publications. The Financial Services section includes online brokerages, stock quote and portfolio sites, and investment advice assistance.

Because the Web includes so many financial news sites, I'm reluctantly forced to omit some good locations. In particular, I concentrate on including free sites, because many financial news sites charge a subscription rate for access. This omission doesn't reflect any judgment about sites that require a fee; as you discover these sites on your own, you may decide the information is worth paying for. (I subscribe to a couple myself.) Sometimes, a site presents most of its information without charge, but withholds a special section or two for subscribers only.

An exception to this section's free-site rule is *The Wall Street Journal* site, which

is subscription-based. I include it here because of its prominence in the landscape of financial news on the Web.

Financial Headlines and Wire Services

Financial news headlines on the Internet usually get the same treatment as general news. Headline hyperlinks lead to full stories. Financial news consists of stories related to business, corporations and the people who run them, global marketplaces in which goods and services are bought and sold, stock markets, real estate, and investments of all types. Although I cover stock quotes — which I consider a financial service within the scope of this book — in the Financial Services section, many of the news sites offer market quotes as a side attraction. Some financial news sites are spin-offs from larger online news organizations, and others are self-contained, money-only information sources.

ABCNews.com: Business

abcnews.com

★ ★
★ ★

Compact updates of essential business news: You have to access this site by clicking the Business link on the ABCNews.com home page, but make the effort. This site's great layout makes finding information easy. The site divides stories into coherent sectors — such as International, Tech Biz, Industrial, and Services — and manages to clearly present the headlines even if they're drastically compacted. Any downside? Well, when you click a headline, you often get Associated Press (or other wire service) copy. Nothing wrong with that, but the pages display slowly, and you can

42 Financial News

get wire services a lot more quickly on other sites. That's not to say the site has no original material — I particularly enjoyed the recent article on "cool clothes" with built-in ventilation. Still, organizational flair is what puts ABCNews.com: Business on the map.

ABS Live

www.abslive.com/mainabs.html

Highly interactive investment news: ABS is the Atlantic Broadcasting System, and the company has gained recognition for its innovative financial Netcasting. For example, from the ABS Live Web site you can listen to the traders in the Chicago futures pit (sounds like they're battling snakes, but actually they're just trading commodity shares) in real time. For this treat and other ABS programming, you need a web browser equipped with the RealAudio 5.0 plug-in (accessible from the site). During market hours, if you keep your RealAudio player parked at the ABS Live site, you can hear market updates revised every half hour. A standard array of stock quotes and charts supplements the RealAudio programming. You can also download special software that *pushes* (automatically sends you) financial headlines, or you can sign up for market analysis e-mails.

Bloomberg News

www.bloomberg.com/welcome.html

Profound depth of international financial coverage: You'd think getting to the point would be easy for a site that specializes in — and excels at — providing a concise briefing on the day's top business news. Suffice to say that even though the Bloomberg News home page has some nice charts, getting beyond a couple of cursory headlines takes an annoying number of clicks. To get the briefs beyond the headlines, click News; for more, click Top News, Company News, or whatever your particular interest is. I prefer to skip the headlines entirely and go straight to these areas: Equity Previews, Equity Movers, or — best of all — Major Newspaper Headlines. The last feature is a daily digest of top stories from newspapers around the world, sorted by country. If you want — no, *need* — to know major stories in today's Portuguese or Turkish press, scoot your browser to the Bloomberg News site. If you want even more international news, go back to the home page and click the U.K., Australia, Japan, or Latin America options in the International section.

Briefing.com

www.briefing.com/schwab

Professional-quality analysis of investment news: Briefing.com is one of the most respected sources of *daily* stock market news. The Short Stories feature — not as literary as you may think — describes the fortunes of individual companies making news during the course of the business day. For example, if a brokerage company changes its evaluation of a company's stock, the news hits Short Stories almost immediately. Briefing.com provides at least a dozen other potently useful news formats, including technical stock analysis, earnings estimates and calendars, splits calendars, StreetBeat analysis, and much more. Just browsing through the Briefing.com site is an education in itself. Other investing sites license the

Briefing.com news updates, which is an indication of the site's value. Another indication is that you must pay a subscription fee to access all the features of the Briefing.com site — however, the site shows you enough for free to decide whether a trial subscription is for you.

Business Wire

www.businesswire.com

Bulletins from the business world: Not much happens on the Business Wire site during weekends, but on business days, look out. Business Wire is a resource that you can quickly become dependent on for hourly headline updates on corporate culture, stocks, and general finance. The site breaks down headlines by the hour that it posts them, enabling you to track the news through the day. Clicking a headline takes you to the full story, and because Business Wire is — as the name implies — a self-contained wire service, all the content is original. The stories on the Business Wire site are widely relied upon for breaking news of executive movements within corporations, mergers, stock splits, and more general news that impacts companies and their stockholders. The hourly headlines alone make the site darn handy, but the site provides much more. The site also presents news on health, entertainment, trade shows, and other topics, although the information isn't as complete as the front headline page of business news. And don't be surprised if some of the headlines are in non-English languages.

CNN Financial Network

www.cnnfn.com

Enhancement of CNN's financial cable network: If you follow the CNNfn cable TV channel, the corresponding Web site is a useful supplement. It fact, the Web site

almost acts as a replacement because with the appropriate plug-in — Vxtreme, which you can obtain by following a link from the fn on-air page — you can watch the channel through your web browser. Assuming you don't consider the Web a surrogate television, you can use the site to read headlines, stories, and feature articles on hot business topics. One great feature: a Web recap of Digital Jam, the morning segment of CNNfn devoted to technology companies. If your schedule doesn't allow you to see CNNfn live, just catch up on the stories later on the Web. Although more comprehensive sites exist on the Web, CNNfn does a good job of enhancing one of the most important financial TV networks.

Corporate Financials Online

www.cfonews.com

Limited but useful company information: Many sites in this section provide general business and financial news in a variety of formats, styles, and angles. If you hanker for wire reports about particular companies, especially if you're in a browsing mood, try Corporate Financials Online for electronic press releases and SEC (Securities and Exchange Commission) filings on individual publicly held companies. Why should you be in a browsing mood? Because this page doesn't furnish a search engine, and you're limited to a preset list of companies. The list of companies isn't bad — a finer, more upstanding list of companies would be hard to come by — but it's a drop in the bucket compared to the total number of public companies that file press releases and SEC reports. Making up for that deficiency, Corporate Financials Online offers a few links to other information sites.

44 Financial News

Industry.net

www.industry.net/news

★★
★★

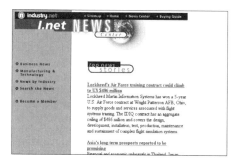

Beautifully organized business news: Designed with simplicity that's easy on the eyes, Industry.net presents linkable headlines to stories and press releases on business topics. The site uses a double-classification scheme that enables you to browse through headlines either by industry segment (Aerospace, Computers, Environmental, Pharmaceutical, and so on, accessed via the News by Industry link) or by geographical region (U.S. regions and states, accessed by the Sitemap link at the top of the page). Furthermore, you can cross-reference your efforts by searching the database of stories using keywords on the Search the News page. You have the option of Simple and Advanced keyword forms, the latter inviting you to define a date range within which the site searches for your keyword(s). Industry.net leans toward manufacturing coverage, so it isn't as complete as the NewsPage site (also reviewed in this section), but it's also not as cluttered with options. The entire site is free, though registration is encouraged.

News Alert

www.newsalert.com

Excellent searchable database of financial news: I tried. I tried to stump the search engine at News Alert. I ran the search engine through my engine-buster test of arcane keywords, and it passed effortlessly. Now, I have to devise a new test, but you don't want to hear about my troubles. While I'm griping, get your browser over to News Alert for an impressive array of news categories ranging from stock quotes to headlines to marketplace digests. Free registration gives you total access to the site, bestowing upon you the title of Free Explorer (oh pul-eeze, couldn't the site have a less hokey name?). The registration also enables you to create a personalized page and receive e-mail alerts on late-breaking events. Overall, News Alert isn't terribly innovative, but it does offer a coherent package of information.

NewsPage

www.newspage.com

Well-organized directory of business news: NewsPage is a can't-do-without site for many people who get their business news on the Net. The Daily Business News is a directory-style database of headlines divided into topics. The topics reflect a strong emphasis on technology companies but also include a good representation of banking, finance, defense, energy, environmental, healthcare, transportation, and insurance news. Clicking a main topic displays a list of subtopics, from which you link to a list of headlines within that subtopic. Stories marked *Basic* are free; you must pay for other stories on a per-view basis, by giving NewsPage some billing information. The shining feature of this Web site is its organizational structure, which enables you to bookmark subtopic pages for quick access to highly specific news in a certain business segment. Because a short paragraph summary of the full story accompanies each headline (free or pay), just a glance gets you up to speed on a lot of news.

Silicon Investor

www.techstocks.com

  $

Network with other investors: Silicon Investor (SI) takes a different approach to providing financial news by empowering individuals to network with one another. The idea is that individual investors are often experts in specialty areas, such as a small niche of a market segment or a single company and its stock. Providing an online place where individual investors can meet to share research and speculation is the mission of Silicon Investor. You find charts and stock quotes on the Web site as well, but the overwhelmingly dominant feature of the site is its system of message boards. The site is like a small online service devoted to stock and option investments.

Several features set Silicon Investor apart. SI is by far the largest networking tool for investors on the Internet — not counting the Usenet newsgroups — with thousands of *threads* (discussion topics) organized in dozens of categories. The site leans toward technical stocks (Internet companies, biotechnology research, computer builders) and small companies (penny stocks and companies listed on the low-cap bulletin board of the NASDAQ system), but any company and any topic are open for discussion. Silicon Investor started out as a free service, but it now charges for membership. By choosing an unusual lifetime plan, your fee is $200 for unlimited access forever. (Whether the plan refers to your lifetime or the lifetime of the site is anyone's guess.)

Yahoo! Finance

quote.yahoo.com

Broad range of financial and investment information: This site was previously known as Yahoo! Quotes — the name was recently changed to reflect the broadening content of this excellent site. Most people who manage investments online use Yahoo! Finance dozens of times every day. The blazing speed (thanks to no graphics whatsoever) that characterizes all Yahoo! pages mixes well with the wealth of features and links. You'll find yourself flipping back and forth between pages, amazed by how quickly you can get up to speed with news about an individual company or the stock market as a whole. Because the site continually updates throughout the day, you're likely to find new headlines every time you hit Reload. On the left side of the page, you find categories leading to all kinds of topical information — from mutual funds to bonds to international business headlines. The famous Motley Fool service — an online investment advice company that began on America Online and now is found on the Web — has a home on Yahoo!.

The site also includes a stock chat area frequented by online investors (it's rarely empty), currency exchange rates, and an earnings report calendar, which market timing specialists make good use of. If you're a real fan of interactivity, try out the Stock/News Ticker, which places a live ticker on your computer screen that displays stock prices, weather, and sports scores. At the center of all these attractions is the stock quote feature that enables you to look up several stock quotations at once, including performance charts. (See the "Financial Services" section of Part V for other financial service sites, including stock quote services.) Yahoo! Finance can be described in one word: Invaluable. Indispensable. (Oops, that's two.)

Other Stuff to Check Out

www12.asiaonline.net/finance/default.asp
www.bizday.com
www.fnsg.com
www.investors.com
www.moneynet.com/home/MONEYNET/
    homepage/homepage.asp
www.newswise.com/menu-bz.htm
www.onfile.nl/newsbrokers

46 Financial News

Financial Newspapers and Magazines

In this part, I assemble the top financial news publications. Most of the sites are online versions of print magazines and newspapers, with only a few originating on the Web. There is always the question of whether an online magazine (or newspaper) edition is merely an advertisement for the printed version, is an exact replication of the printed version, contains some material from the printed version and some new content, or is a wholly original publication with its own editorial staff. In most cases, online financial news publications present a mix of articles from the current print edition along with features that work best in the computer world, such as searchable databases and past issues that are archived for browsing. Plus, of course, the inevitable promotions for subscribing to the printed edition.

Barron's Online
www.barrons.com

 $

Professional analysis and commentary on business and investing news: Barron's is a weekly newspaper containing expert commentary on stocks, bonds, options, and the corporate maneuvers of public companies. It's one of the most respected and widely read financial publications. The online edition has a subscription plan for online readers that bundles The Wall Street Journal Interactive Edition with Barron's Online. Not only does Barron's Online contain much of what you find in the newspaper version (all the feature articles and columns), but it makes good use of the computer's ability to access and cross-reference data, enabling you to use tricks such as searching for all the references to a

certain company in recent issues of *Barron's.* The site also includes an impressive array of stock charts and other company data. Barron's Online is far more than a simple translation of a great newspaper to the online realm — I recommend it to all serious investors who have online access.

Business Week
www.businessweek.com

$

Online edition of famous financial weekly: People in the business world rarely like to give things away for free, so it shouldn't be a surprise that the folks at *Business Week* have started to charge for some areas of their site. Never fear, though: You can still browse quality daily news stories, analyses, special content available only in the online edition (called BW Plus!), and research on the "Company of the Week" for free. Try to go much beyond that, like to one of the stories in the current issue, and you'll be asked to subscribe. No free trial period, either; like I said, they don't give it away for free. The good news is that the subscription price is reasonable, and if you subscribe to the printed version of *Business Week,* you can subscribe to the Web site for free. If you subscribe, mark Thursday nights on your calendar of online events. Thursday is when the virtual edition of *Business Week* is posted to the Web site (you can search an archive for back issues). The site presents the entire weekly edition in a clear table of contents format, including international stories, columns, the Editor's Memo, book and technology sections, economic trends, news analysis, and all the other features that have made *Business Week* staple reading for business executives.

The Economist
www.economist.com

 $ ↘

World business and political news: The days when the sun never set on the British Empire may be over, but the British-based *The Economist* continues bringing quality coverage from the far corners of the earth. Fortunately, netizens can share the excellent coverage. *The Economist*'s Web site, like many others, is a mixture of free and fee. The free stuff includes a smattering of articles from the printed edition. Subscribing (about $48 in the United States, ß62 in Britain) adds 50 additional articles from the printed edition of *The Economist* and numerous other features, including all the color maps and charts of the printed edition and some of the photographs. The coverage is truly global. Headlines during a recent visit ran the gamut from "Cleaning Up Indonesia's Banks" to "Why Is Wyoming Failing?" The site gives you ten free log-ins just by going through a free registration process, so you can weigh whether or not the additional features are worth the cost. You can also subscribe to e-mail political and business updates by registering. And don't forget to download the free screen saver — when your coworkers see it on your computer, it'll leave them wondering just how big a raise you got.

Fortune

www.pathfinder.com/fortune

Online version of a great magazine: *Fortune* is part of the Time Warner family of magazines, existing within the Pathfinder family of Web sites. (Pathfinder is Time Warner's main Internet publication.)

That explains the annoying menu bar at the top of the page that leads to other Pathfinder sites. Below that menu bar, however, you'll find a sampling of stories from the current edition of *Fortune*. If you want the full menu, simply click Contents on the left side. The right side of the home page includes links to daily and special features. One recent offering included the entire *Fortune* Global 500 list — the magazine's renowned examination of the world's largest companies — that you could search using your criteria. The list also included links to company profiles, which include enough numbers to make any accountant leap for joy.

Mutual Funds Magazine Online

www.mfmag.com

Highly useful evaluator of mutual funds: You have a couple of choices with the online version of *Mutual Funds Magazine*. Register free of charge for basic access to the site's contents or subscribe (yes, with real money) for complete access to all the site's features. The smart approach is to try the free registration first and see if you develop a craving for the hidden features. My advice is to subscribe to only the greatest, most valuable sites that fit your needs because so much free information pervades the Internet. Assuming you choose the free registration route, you'll probably be as irritated as I was to have a user name and a password assigned to you, both comprising an unpronounceable glut of letters and numbers — impossible to either memorize or change. Bad move. Invoke the Muse of Web Site Design to whisper a better solution in somebody's ear. In the meantime, your mood should perk up when you see the weighty selection of calculators, performance evaluators, profiles, rankings, and other tools for distinguishing mutual funds. Hmm, not bad — maybe it's worth trying to remember that my user name is 885A3.

48 Financial News

The Red Herring

www.herring.com

Business news with a loyal following: The Red Herring is one of the breed of "secondary" financial publications, not as famous as *Barron's* or *The Wall Street Journal,* but respected in many financial circles and even regarded with fierce loyalty by a band of investors who find its brand of information and advice particularly useful. Maybe the "we try harder" philosophy is at work with this Web site, because it's exceptionally designed and informative. Highly opinionated, as an advice magazine should be, *The Red Herring* doesn't ever deliver news without some spin or analysis. You won't find a registration button anywhere (although you can sign up for a weekly e-mail bulletin). The site offers a keyword search entry form right on the front page for tracking down articles and columns on specific companies. Emphasizing IPOs (Initial Public Offerings) and under-publicized companies, The Red Herring site appeals to investors searching for the undiscovered gems in the stock world. This site provides a great tool for investigating low-profile stocks that may be good values.

SmartMoney

www.dowjones.com/smart

★★
★★

Concise evaluations of investment opportunities: Any serious voting on Most Improved Web Sites has to include SmartMoney in the Financial News category. SmartMoney went from a dark typeface against a black background to a tasteful, elegant site that's easy on the eyes and (if you follow the site's advice) healthy for your pocketbook. The only downside is that the graphics on the home page and the monthly issue's full table of contents page (which you can get to by clicking This Month) take some time to download. Though this site is still more self-promotional than many online editions of printed publications (a "Top 15 Reasons to Subscribe" link greets visitors brazenly), the good news is that the virtual magazine matches the printed version in content. You don't need to register, either.

USA Today Money

www.usatoday.com/money/mfront.htm

Tons of information and bright colors: Information reigns supreme at the Web translation of the financial section of *USA Today,* starting with the familiar, colorful banner at the top of the page and continuing through the data-rich stories, graphs, and tables. The site displays quickly — thanks to minimal graphics — and is an excellent bookmark for getting crucial information fast. Want to see the current performance of about 30 market indexes? How about statistics on certain industry groups? Need to know the equity options enjoying highest volume, gains, and losses? For research-intensive information, USA Today Money is an easy solution. Extras include financial calculators and recommended reading. But the hard data is the meat of the site — or the brown rice for vegetarians.

The Wall Street Journal Interactive Edition

info.wsj.com

★★
★★ $

A variety of free and subscription business news: This Financial News section wouldn't be complete without a reference to the Web site of the famous institution of financial publishing: *The Wall Street Journal* (WSJ). The Web site contains a goodly amount of information — albeit, in English — for investors interested in Europe, Asia, and the Americas. The WSJ was one of the first publishers to attempt a Web site that charges for admission (you pay by the month or annually). The Interactive Edition contains some special content that you won't find in the newspaper, and the subscription cost is reasonable. To be fair, let me advise you that, in my experience, you can locate most of the information offered to subscribers at the WSJ Web site elsewhere free of charge. Some online investors feel the time-honored newspaper is really charging for its name, rather than its content. The choice is yours, and the best strategy may be to try the site for a month or two. The URL that I provide leads you to a front page Directory of Services (and a gorgeous page it is); click the subscribing link to find out more, or check out some of the free features, such as business headlines.

Worth Online

www.worth.com

Special content not found in the magazine: The online version of *Worth* magazine seeks out the community aspects of the Internet — an angle disregarded by many financial publications. In addition to articles about building an investment portfolio, Worth Online offers message boards for readers to chat with one another. The site's content is a mix of new material prepared just for the virtual edition and reprints of articles from the magazine. The site offers daily updates reflecting current stock market news as well as a search engine to find specific info quickly. Peter Lynch, the well-known financial author, is a frequent columnist for *Worth,* and you can browse through the complete collection of his contributions. The *Worth* editors are enlightened by the potential of Internet publication and have gone far beyond merely translating magazine content to a Web site. Worth Online is a unique publication that takes advantage of the Net's peculiar features and is updated often enough to maintain interest while staying abreast of the evolving Web aesthetic. Nice job.

Other Stuff to Check Out

www.businesslife.com
www.thebiz.co.uk/default.htm
www.upside.com
www.xtra.co.nz/independent/index.html

www.almanac.com

50 Magazines

Yes, magazines do appear on the Internet. Convenient, don't you think? Just tuck your computer under your arm and log on to the Web in your doctor's waiting room. Okay, electronic magazines aren't quite as portable as the printed versions, but they do have some unique features — such as interactivity — that make them more useful than their real-world siblings. Electronic magazines often include community features like message boards or chat rooms. Another commonplace feature is an e-mail newsletter or bulletin that notifies you when the site adds something cool. Back-issue searching is also nifty, enabling you to find articles from a year or two (or longer) ago by using search keywords.

This section is for general-interest magazines and newsmagazines. Basically, you find either online editions of printed magazines that you're probably somewhat familiar with and may subscribe to, or electronic-only publications that originated on the World Wide Web. In almost all cases when a printed magazine exists, the site makes some kind of pitch to get you to subscribe to the printed version. However, the magazine must be more than a mere promotion for the printed edition to make it into this section. Having some of the interactive features I just mentioned helps, as well as carrying some (or all) of the articles in the printed magazine along with fresh content unique to the online version. The best sites have all three.

Online Editions of Printed Magazines

The following sites are the best online editions of general and news magazines that you can find on the virtual newsstand — a very comprehensive newsstand in some cases. Most of the sites are free, although you never can tell when an online magazine is going to start charging

for some of its content. When the magazines do charge, they usually charge for access to a section of the site, not the whole thing, and often they provide you with a free trial subscription to that section. Occasionally, an online magazine reserves valuable content for its print-version subscribers, leaving online readers a compelling reason to subscribe to the printed version.

The American Spectator

www.spectator.org

Politics and entertainment coverage: A monthly review of news and commentary, *The American Spectator* saves most of its articles for subscribers to the printed magazine. However, it does create some fresh material for its online audience as well — for example, a schedule of online report updates appears on the home page. Politics is the main order of the day in The American Spectator domain, but movie reviews also get some reportage on Thursdays and Fridays. The editor, R. Emmett Tyrrell, Jr., writes a weekly syndicated column that the site adds on Fridays.

Atlantic Unbound

www.theatlantic.com/coverj.htm

News and commentary with literary sensibilities: Atlantic Unbound is the online venture of *The Atlantic Monthly,* and it was created to have an independent spirit. Although the editorial staffs of the printed and virtual magazines overlap in some areas, and both staffs work in the same office, Atlantic Unbound is meant to be an "accompaniment" to its famous printed counterpart, with fresh content and interactive features that can only be implemented in an online publication. Happily for readers, the publication transposes much of the printed material to the Web site and enhances it with links to primary sources, related articles, special content, and audio files. In addition, you find a *lot* of material unique

_____

to the online edition, certainly enough to encourage subscribers to read both versions. The Post & Riposte section is a reader forum in message-board format. (You must register to post a message.)

LIFE

pathfinder.com/Life

Gallery of photographs and past features: In a curious publishing strategy, the online edition of *LIFE* magazine doesn't include any articles or photographs from the current edition. This strategy comes as something of a surprise when you visit the table of contents (by clicking the LIFE Magazine link on the home page) only to find that none of the article titles are hyperlinked to anything. Don't spend too much time running your mouse cursor futilely over them — take my word for it. Instead, take advantage of the offerings on the home page: the Picture of the Day, usually a dramatic wire-service shot; This Day in LIFE, a nice almanac feature offering a daily quote, famous birthdays, and historical events; and Photo Week, a collection of the best wire-service shots that you can choose to have rotate automatically if you have a Java-enabled browser. Still not satisfied? Try the Features link, where you can pick from a variety of photo features, some exclusively online (like a recent tribute to the late Frank Sinatra). If you're still not satisfied, try the searchable Cover Collection or the Site Index, where you find past features and picture galleries archived for browsing.

Maclean's

www.macleans.ca

News from a Canadian perspective: *Maclean's* is a respected Canadian weekly print magazine that covers international news, sometimes from its unique perspective as a neighbor of the United States. A nicely uncluttered front page presents the current issue's cover (click it to see the cover story) and a Top Stories button, which links to the weekly table of contents. Only about half the content of the printed version is available on the Web. Without the Maclean's Forum, where you can post comments about the cover story, and Web Picks, which selects Web sites related to the current issue, you wouldn't have much of a reason to visit the Web site if you already buy the magazine — unless, of course, your local newsstands don't carry it. Come to think of it, the archive of past stories is very worthwhile, too. Foreign readers now have an easy way to get the Canadian angle on the news.

Media Bypass

www.4bypass.com

$

Alternative (and sometimes flaky) perspectives on the news: When you want to catch up with semi-legitimate, conspiracy-tinged alternatives to the normal news spin, try Media Bypass. Every monthly issue has a main story focus, ranging recently from convicted Oklahoma City bomber Timothy McVeigh's essay on U.S. policy toward Iraq to an article on "The Anthrax Hoax and where it all leads." Media Bypass presents some interesting perspectives without the wild-eyed, hyperbolic writing style that would turn off any serious thinkers. You can get to the main story for free, but you'll need to subscribe to get to the rest of the stories. A subscription costs all of $5 per year. So save up by skipping that burger and fries and give Media Bypass a try when you're bored with the mainstream news.

52 **Magazines**

National Geographic

www.nationalgeographic.com/media/ ngm

Wild animals, primitive tribes, and other explorations: Which would you rather do: Join the National Geographic Society and receive the magazine, or enter an online discussion on how stock car racing got to be so popular in the United States? If you're already a subscriber to the magazine and don't care to rehash the calamities of ancient history, skip both options and tangle your horns with the editor over what cover to choose for the next issue — a fun bit of interactivity on the Web site. The main focus of the National Geographic Web site is the preview section showing some of the stories and world-class photographs slated to appear in upcoming issues. The Resources section can be valuable for teachers and parents, and the The Society area describes the mission and current activities of the National Geographic Society.

Old Farmer's Almanac

www.almanac.com

Essential trivia and folk wisdom: If a certain type of magazine exists that benefits from the unique qualities of Internet publication, including daily updates and computer searching capabilities, it's a magazine with lots of information, reams of minute data, and swarms of tiny factoids. *The Old Farmer's Almanac,* the yellow bible of long-range weather forecasts, obscure historical allusions, folksy advice, and the last word on tidal events, is a perfect candidate for an effective online incarnation. No devotee of country wisdom will be disappointed with the result. The yellow home page and old-style typography puts you right at home, and the forum discussions invite you to marvel with others. Check out Today in Weather History to find out that

18 inches of snow fell on a certain date two centuries ago. Armed with such essential trivia, you can proceed confidently with your day.

Paris Match

www.parismatch.tm.fr

Ooh-la-la: Paris Match is written for the citizens of *la belle France,* but fortunately the Web site offers an English version, too. If you live in Paris, you probably buy the magazine at the newsstand, but Americans can get that sophisticated, continental feeling by checking out the increasingly bilingual online edition. The magazine isn't completely comprehensible to the English-limited reader yet, but it's getting there. At the moment, you can read selected articles (the headlines are still mysteriously in French, but the stories are translated). *Paris Match* fancies itself a newsmagazine, but pictures play a large part in its content, and *Paris Match* is justifiably famous for its photojournalism. One bit of advice: Put on a pair of sunglasses before the site comes up. Bright background colors? *Oui!*

Reader's Digest World

www.readersdigest.com

★★
★★

Brief literature, research journalism, and humor: If you think of *Reader's Digest* as a somewhat stodgy, if venerable, recycler of literature and inspiring all-American stories first published elsewhere, visit the online site for a jolt of disillusionment. Reader's Digest World is one hip, technically advanced, glowing point of cyberspace. The humorous anecdotes that are such a popular part of the printed magazine are prominently featured on the site. In fact, true to *Reader's Digest* tradition, you can submit stories through the Web site to Life in These Cyber States or Laugh Lines. The archive of funny yarns is a nice resource for public speakers. Multimedia games and invitations to forum discussions keep the site highly interactive.

Redbook

homearts.com/rb/toc/00rbhpc1.htm

Pop journalism, mostly for women: *Redbook* has dropped its past literary emphasis and settled into articles about diet, health, marriage, kids, and beauty. Calling itself a "Married Girl's Survival Guide," the Web site is an attractive construction with an unobtrusive Java banner highlighting a feature article. The virtual pages don't present all the content from the print edition (*Redbook* wants you to have some reason to buy the real thing, supposedly), but you can search for back articles and talk in discussion forums on the Web site. The site has a number of sly solicitations, but it's not necessary to register, unless you want to join a discussion forum — and even then you can register as a guest. One other note (or warning): The site has three ads at the top, at least one of which almost always connects you to an online shopping site.

The Saturday Evening Post

www.satevepost.org

Humor, pictures, and not enough articles: Don't let the relatively long download time (considering the number of graphics on the page) drive you away from The Saturday Evening Post site prematurely. Click one of the content links halfway down the page. *The Saturday Evening Post*

keeps much of its political commentary and opinion articles for the printed magazine, but the site serves up a helping of cartoons, humor, and a gallery of artwork by Norman Rockwell and other *The Saturday Evening Post* illustrators.

TIME

pathfinder.com/time

Broad news coverage: This site is no mere subscription billboard. *TIME* has created a substantial, informative, interactive source of news. *TIME* floated around cyberspace in well-publicized moves from America Online to CompuServe, where it enjoyed a short-lived electronic life. Today, the magazine has settled comfortably into a high-rise on the World Wide Web, where a daily edition of the printed newsweekly deserves frequent visits. The site posts stories in a complete version with small pictures that don't gum up your bandwidth. Interestingly, a Search button lurks next to the top stories, inviting you to call up information related to the story's topic. You don't need a special program to participate in the Community section's message boards, which carry serious discussions on every news topic under the sun. Chats for *TIME* and other Time Warner publications are now found on Yahoo! Chat, but you can find a schedule on the TIME site.

U.S. News & World Report Online

www.usnews.com

Great use of the Internet by the staid weekly: If you visit this site, you're likely to be impressed by the presentation of stories embedded with a liberal number of hyperlinks to locations providing background or related news. Interactive features greatly enhance The News You Can Use section, which is transplanted from the magazine. Check out the Site Index link to see just how extensive — but not expensive (U.S. News & World Report Online is free) — the site is. If you sign up for the e-mail reports, you aren't badgered incessantly by site promotions, but you receive occasional newsy updates.

Other Stuff to Check Out

dolphin.gulf.net
www.ecola.com/news
www.esquireb2b.com/main.html
www.newsweek.com
www.swoon.com/mag_rack/gq.html
www.utne.com

News E-Zines

Electronic magazines, or *e-zines,* are a phenomenon of the digital age. They take advantage of the unique formatting, news delivery, archiving, and interactive possibilities of the World Wide Web. The following magazines don't have a printed counterpart, and such electronic publications are a bit less stable than the listings in the previous portion of this magazine section. The reason for the relative instability has to do with commercial realities — online editions of printed magazines can support their expenses by selling subscriptions and advertising in the printed book, whereas electronic magazines must live on just ads, in most cases. (None of the following sites charges subscription fees for access.) The result: E-zines come and go more frequently than online editions of printed mags.

American Newspeak

www.scn.org/news/newspeak

Satirical commentary of news and newsmakers: American Newspeak presents cerebral, humorous commentary on current events. As a satirical e-zine, it shows its intellectual roots by often forgoing graphics in favor of a mostly text interface. You don't find headline humor in American Newspeak — rather it's a thoughtful digestion of news, followed by withering, caustic comments. For example, it labeled a recent decision to limit the number of Kenyan runners in American marathons as "what is believed to be the first time American athletes have received protection from a nation with an average income worth less than two pairs of Nikes." Doublespeak is disparaged at every opportunity. Check the site on Mondays, which is when the e-zine posts weekly updates. The site archives its ruminations to some degree — it saved about 20 of the top stories for 1996 and still has its "Greatest Hits of 1995" available. American Newspeak: Jay Leno it's not, but a sort of mild version of Dennis Miller it is.

Fortean Times

www.forteantimes.com

Bizarre news: The Fortean Times is a weekly e-zine repository for weird news that wouldn't fit into any other magazines. From haunted houses to pasture-prowling large cats to plummeting cows, the Fortean Times honors any and all possibilities. Not as fictitious as a supermarket tabloid, the site does its share of debunking, revealing the truth about urban myths along the way. The e-zine supplies some interactivity by means of a voting booth for registering your favorite area of interest — conspiracy, cults, or parapsychology — or your pick for the next month's cover (my vote: "Beavers on the Moon"). Forget about message boards and chat rooms, unfortunately (they would doubtless contain some great topics), but the site does sell some unusual merchandise.

Weekly Wire

www.weeklywire.com/ww/current/ ww_contents.html

Offbeat news and cultural reviews: Providing news for the fearless, Weekly Wire is a compendium of a little hard news mixed with a lot of commentary, columns, reviews, and offbeat reporting. Culture coverage finds a home here, from music to movies to books. Weekly Wire sports an impressive list of contributing publications, mostly newspapers from around the United States. The very attractive site design is icing on the cake.

Other Stuff to Check Out

www.dominis.com/Zines/

Newspapers

Printed newspapers are still uniquely portable and entertaining. But an astounding number of them — global, national, and local publications — have turned to the Internet to supplement the service that they provide to readers. In some cases, the paper's content is duplicated exactly on the Web; in other cases, the content is enhanced considerably through back-story archiving, the addition of multimedia features like audio and video clips, color pictures in almost all cases, and some interactive jazz, such as automatic clipping services, e-mail delivery, or immediate-response classified ads.

This section has two parts. First, I review the newspapers themselves. Because I don't want you to have to hire a truck to get this book home, I sadly eliminate some wonderful online newspapers and include only the most impressive Web creations. In particular, I leave it up to you to find online papers that are local to your town or region — you may be surprised how many you find. Fortunately, the second part of this section helps you find the local publications; this section contains several directories (virtual newsstands) to newspaper sites all over the Web.

Online Newspapers

This section is a directory to the finest, most extravagant newspaper creations on the Web. All the listings review big-city or national newspapers, although the Net includes hundreds of fine local publications. Most of these online newspaper editions are based in the United States — although I go abroad in a few of my recommendations. They all represent online versions of printed papers, except one — The Nando Times, which is a Web-only paper (that is, if it makes any sense to call an electronic product "paper").

56 Newspapers

Asahi.com

www.asahi.com/english/english.html

A Japanese perspective: Asahi Shimbun is a Japanese news organization that publishes the *Asahi* newspaper and, more recently, the English translation of some news stories for publication on the Internet. Asahi.com is not a full-featured online edition in the same sense as most of the other sites I mention in this section. Starting out less ambitiously, Asahi.com merely translates several dozen top stories from the current issue and presents them as a simple list of links. But fancy layouts and lots of pictures aren't the point here. Browsing the stories is a good way to get an Asian perspective on global news, or to access stories that wouldn't be covered in the press of other countries. The front page contains a handful of links — to see the others, click the English here button.

The Boston Globe Online

www.boston.com/globe/

Plenty of updates: The Boston Globe takes a fairly typical approach to online newspaper design. Feature stories begin on the front page and provide links to their completion on other pages. A menu bar on the left of the page takes you to other sections of the paper, including Latest News, which is one of the most valuable features. The Latest News section, unique to the online edition, breaks down news into typical categories (sports, national, international, Washington, business, technology, arts and entertainment, and as a regional touch, Northeast) and updates stories in those categories every five minutes. This section is a great way to stay up to speed on a developing major story, especially if the story is transpiring in New England. On every page, a keyword entry form invites you to Search the Globe, but the results are restricted to either today or yesterday. This unusual limitation may lead you to look for an archive of back issues and stories — I'll save you the trouble. Try the Archives link on the Table of Contents page. Unfortunately, the Archives page hits you with another restriction: Searches are free, but reading the full text of a retrieved article costs money, so you must set up an account. Never mind — this site is so stuffed with great features that you must explore it yourself to get the whole picture. A photo gallery of the week's best pics, the entire *Boston Globe Magazine* section, classifieds, a crossword puzzle, and comics are some of the attractions of one of the top online newspapers around.

Chicago Tribune

www.chicago.tribune.com

Nice design with a Windy City slant to the news: Some online newspapers try to throw as much information in your face as possible, starting at the front page. Others prefer the uncluttered look, favoring simplicity to overwhelm their audience. The Chicago Tribune Web site values brevity and attempts to save visitors time by condensing its content. The concept works but seemingly at the expense of comprehensiveness. If you take a look at the front page, your first impression is that the online edition doesn't have much to offer compared to some other virtual newspapers. That impression is false, and the best way to cure it is by clicking one of the links along the left edge, and then clicking whichever of the new links interests you. The publication emphasizes Chicago-area news and sports, of course, but it also carries major-league national reporting.

The Christian Science Monitor

www.csmonitor.com

★★
★★

Great international news with a dollop of inspiration: One of the most renowned and respected newspapers in the world, *The Christian Science Monitor* goes beyond its spiritual underpinnings by delivering concise, accessible, comprehensive, and intelligent reporting of international news. The global news organization has always embraced alternative media, producing a radio news network several years ago and an Internet site more recently. In fact, Monitor Radio is incorporated into the site with a RealAudio archive of shows — one of the best features. The front page is a marvel of modest yet promising design; it's easy on the eyes yet indicative of the substance that waits inside. The site provides a navigational shortcut with a drop-down menu leading to different sections. (Try the Weekly News Quiz.) Clicking Today's Paper takes you to the online version of the day's print edition, with a link to a text-only path. You're in molasses territory at this point, and unless you have a chore to do away from the computer, I recommend taking the text route. As if the site didn't provide enough excellence on its own, you can get *The Monitor* (text version) delivered to your e-mail box every day (for a charge of about $5.00 per month).

The Detroit Free Press

www.freep.com

News, multimedia reviews, and an upbeat style: The Freep (I didn't make it up; that's the paper's online nickname) packs

an entire index of the site onto the front page and somehow manages to keep the info coherent. Top-story headlines and summaries stretch down the right side, whereas a site index menu keeps pace on the left; the featured story takes up the middle. The Freep goes for multimedia in a big way, because audio clips accompany music CD reviews (you need RealPlayer). The Browsing section (find it via the Site Index) surveys bumps in the cultural landscape with an emphasis on high-tech pathways like CD-ROMs and Web sites. Movie reviews show their star rating before you link to the full text, in case you just want the very short story. Overall, the tone of The Freep leaves behind the gray sobriety often associated with major newspapers, even their online editions, and provides a site that's both informative and fun.

International Herald Tribune

www.iht.com

Worth digging beneath the mediocre front page: Being The World's Daily Newspaper must be hard, and perhaps the pressure has distorted the judgment of the editors responsible for the online edition of the *International Herald Tribune.* A lukewarm, undistinguished front page is marred by a garish pitch for subscribers to the print newspaper and probably prevents the site from getting as many readers as it deserves. The content is tremendous, just poorly presented. But it's worth digging for. Days of the week links at the top of the page take you to the past six editions. Or zip straight to individual columnists for sports, news, and financial dispatches with a global perspective. Although you have to keep disregarding that darn in-your-face subscription plea, forge ahead with the knowledge that the *International Herald Tribune* has invaluable articles, columns, and global dispatches — and a free Web site.

The Jerusalem Post

www.jpost.co.il

News with an Israeli perspective: The Internet edition of *The Jerusalem Post* is renowned for its professional design and complete coverage of local (Israeli) and global news coverage. Having access to an English translation of a newspaper from another country, with its unique perspectives and attitudes about the global news arena, is unusual. The information is especially valuable when the newspaper is local to a region that is perpetually torn by controversy and political unrest. Any student of Israeli-Arab relations should check this site for non-Western viewpoints. On a lighter note, for anyone planning a visit to the ancient city of Jerusalem, the Tourism section contains updates on travel highlights. On a *much* lighter note, check out the Dry Bones cartoon page. A small clock at the bottom of some pages reminds you of the local Israeli time of day. Readers who really like the newspaper and don't want to miss a single day can sign up for e-mail delivery for about $5 per month.

Los Angeles Times

www.latimes.com

★ ★
★ ★

Tremendous example of what an online newspaper can be: Surfing into the Los Angeles Times site is like going out to buy an economy car and coming home with an 18-wheel truck. This site is massive. However, the front page does a great job of clarifying your options by providing six (count 'em: six) drop-down menus right at the top for choosing sections, plus a keyword search form on the left. Those six drop-down menus take six major classifications — News, Entertainment, Sports, Business, Classifieds, and Southern California — and dissect them into mini-parts like science news and college basketball. Archiving is valued at the *L. A. Times,* and you can pore through back articles, movie reviews, and so on. This newspaper is as sprawling and diverse as the city it represents. Check it out to see a model of what an online newspaper can be when ambition matches user-friendliness. Just don't get too lost in the site, or you may never get out.

The Nando Times

www.nando.net

★ ★
★ ★

A truly virtual newspaper: Most of the newspapers I'm tossing at you in this section are online editions of well-known print publications. The Nando Times, by contrast, is a completely virtual publication created on and for the World Wide Web. Global in scope, Nando covers politics, sports, entertainment, and high-tech news. The site's design offers the main material in the center of the page and links (global, nation, sports, politics, business, and so on) down the left — although the links look a lot like pills from a teenage pharmacist. One failing is that throughout the site, Nando has a tendency to present headlines in long lists rather than grouping them more compactly. Still, the long, unimaginative page does give you the scoop on Nando's extensive contents. And the News that Moves section has interesting and timely animations.

The New York Times

www.nytimes.com

The gray lady dances on the Net: Striking a nice balance between graphics and text, The New York Times Web site displays modified front pages to its various sections, conveying the basic visual impression of the famous Times layout, without the graphic load that would slow down the pages. If you want a more streamlined route, click the Low Graphics link for a simple, text-based table of contents (the Table of Contents link reaches the same destination). From the table of contents, you can link to the front page or any section, including the reputable Op-Ed page. CyberTimes deals with high technology and the Internet. The site partially presents The Sunday Times, where you can access articles at least a day early. Special reports (like the groundbreaking downsizing report of 1996) are archived for a long time. The site's design is adequate, but the main emphasis is its world-class reporting content.

Newsday.com

www.newsday.com

Maybe more style than substance, but rollicking nonetheless: One of several dailies in New York City, *Newsday* reflects the great metropolis in its bustling and cramped home page. Newsday.com has an aura of almost manic fun in the blinking icons and drawings, promising the bright side of the Big Apple. Cutting to the chase, the home page presents a site index, which is down a little from the featured headlines. Drop-down menus enable you to search various sections of the print edition as well as Associated Press reports. Each section carries its own alphabetical index, making exploration a rewarding experience. The site covers entertainment nicely, especially for regional residents who can take advantage of the live events linked to the reviews. You can also access columnists separately from the other content — always an appreciated feature with a gossipy newspaper. Newsday.com has a rollicking side to it, a breath of fresh air amid the grunge of New York.

Philadelphia Online

www.phillynews.com

Two, two, two newspapers in one: Here's a unique idea: Merge two daily newspapers published in a major city into a single Web site, offering intense coverage of that city's news culture. (Actually, this idea turns out to be not so unique; in fact, combined newspaper sites are a new trend.) Philadelphia Online is the virtual newspaper site for both the *Philadelphia Daily News* and *The Philadelphia Inquirer* — both publications presumably laid to rest all competitive impulses for the sake of enlightened Internet cooperation. Very inspiring. But with its Philadelphia-centric news focus, is there any reason for a nonresident to visit this site? Yes, in fact, there are several. Start with the daily comics, which you can view online and even customize for your browser to eliminate the strips that don't inspire a chuckle. Dataplace, an organized archive of special reports and statistical storehouses (say that a few times fast), is a terrific feature that invites you to search for topics such as the financial health of hospitals, listings of shore properties, and FBI crime statistics. The News Vault requires a monthly subscription and provides access to 15 years of articles (the past 15 years, not the next 15). The Video Vault contains automobile, music, and movie reviews in video format — you need the VDO video streaming plug-in to see them. In short, Philadelphia Online has a strong local slant, with enough broader features to be worth checking out.

60 Newspapers

San Jose Mercury News

www.sjmercury.com

A legendary online newspaper emphasizes high-tech news: Not surprisingly, the first newspaper to receive widespread recognition for its online edition was the *San Jose Mercury News* (SJMN), located in the heart of Silicon Valley, California, where many of the high-tech Internet and computer companies are headquartered. The Mercury News set the early standard for efficient online design of a newspaper, and although many other papers have joined its ranks, it continues to provide an excellent Web site. SJMN highlights Silicon Valley and high-tech stories — as is appropriate in a corner of the world where highway billboards advertise software programs. A recent Web edition, for example, included not one, not two, but three hardware reviews — and an enterprise package with everything (if anything) you could possibly want to know about Beanie Babies. The site is searchable, as a good virtual paper should be, and maintains a seven-day archive.

The Times

www.the-times.co.uk

Dignified to the max: The Times of London, that is. The absence of a city designation in the title reflects the venerable newspaper's austere pride — it's just *The Times*. What other city could you possibly mean, old chap? You don't need good breeding to get into this site,

but you do need to register. (The registration form doesn't ask any embarrassing questions, like what duke you descended from, or whether there are any Whigs in your closet. However, a hilarious formality does prevail. On the first pass through the registration form, I forgot to fill in a *Mr.* title, and my registration was rejected.) The site faithfully replicates the contents of the daily and Sunday papers, and a Personal Times link enables you to set up your own virtual edition.

USA Today

www.usatoday.com

Oooh, fast with bright colors: USA Today on the Web is a sprawling, info-rich, picturesque, bustling, oft-updated site that has grown almost to the point of being overwhelming. Fortunately for the overwhelm-challenged, the site divides its info neatly into categories, just like the printed newspaper, beginning with the identical four sections: News, Sports, Money, and Life. An additional separate section for the weather expands forecasting from back-page status in the print edition to a luxurious, searchable real-time database that enables you to view five-day forecasts for any small city in the United States. The Sports section takes athletic statistics and information retrieval to new highs, demonstrating how Internet technology really enhances a factoid-oriented newspaper like *USA Today.* (The scoreboard pages automatically reload with updates every two minutes — just leave your browser parked there while you do other computer work, and then check in for updates whenever.) As with the newspaper, the online version of *USA Today* is bright, colorful, and simple, and it delivers the essentials quickly, without ever drawing outside the lines.

The Washington Post

www.washingtonpost.com

★ ★
★ ★

Great Internet features and renowned reporting: The online edition of *The Washington Post* combines insider reporting from the U.S. Capitol with a great sense of Internet design. The site provides more information than you can shake a stick at (and if you're shaking sticks at your computer something is dreadfully wrong). Here are a few good ways to approach this news resource. You can click the drop-down menu, which directs you to different sections of the paper. Or click the Today's Paper link to view all the contents from the current print edition. Alternatively, peruse the headlines, stories, features, columns, and sports news from the online edition, by scrolling down the page and browsing links. The online edition updates stories frequently and posts the times at which they're added to the site. Links embedded in the stories (in the online edition stories only) provide background information — one of the best features of online newspapers. And the site has a search box on the home page. *The Washington Post* knows how to take advantage of Internet features without compromising its tradition of great journalism.

Other Stuff to Check Out

new-europe.com
www.asiatimes.com
www.european-voice.com
www.speakeasy.org/nasna/
www.telegraph.co.uk

Online Newsstands

The universe of online newspapers is so immense that you need some help to sort it out. Online directories can be considered virtual newsstands, not because they sell anything, but because they make Web newspapers available by providing

links to them. By using these sites, you should be able to track down just about any paper that has an online edition.

Chaplin News

www.geocities.com/Heartland/2308

★ ★
★ ★

Deep directory to small local newspapers online: Chaplin News is a free site and an impressive accomplishment. One of the few newsstands created by an individual and worthy of serious review, Chaplin News is formatted with frames that organize its mountain of links without sacrificing speed. (No extraneous graphics is the key.) On the home page, click the Newspapers link from the left-hand menu, and you're greeted by a continental breakdown of countries. Some smaller, less Internet-involved nations have only one or two newspapers in the directory, but Chaplin really shines in its exhaustive list of local papers throughout the United States. Divided by state, the database shows an amazing array of regional newspapers that have migrated to the Web. You get a nice presentation, too, with little blinking light things. (Sorry about the technical terms.) Chaplin News is one of the few electronic newsstands that carries the local paper of my town — you may be surprised to find that your local paper is on the Web, too.

InfiNet Newsstand

www.infi.net/newsstand.html

★ ★
★ ★

62 Newspapers

Local newspapers from all over the United States: This site takes a bit of explaining. InfiNet is an Internet service provider specializing in getting newspapers on the World Wide Web. By leasing Internet server space and offering design services, InfiNet is responsible for many of the online editions of small and midsize newspapers around the United States. The InfiNet Newsstand is a directory of InfiNet's news partners — that is, the online newspapers using InfiNet's service. The page has directory value to you and me because it's a listing of links to local newspapers from almost every state. You can click a U.S. map or just check the state-by-state list for a paper local to you. Browsing randomly is rewarding, too, because some local virtual papers are wonderfully designed and produced. Another idea is to track down the publication local to a big news story to see how the regional press covers it. However you use it, the InfiNet Newsstand is a quick and easy directory.

Internet Newsroom

www.editors-service.com

Professional service for journalists, available to everyone: Psst! Over here! As long as you're looking for resources that help you find news on the World Wide Web, why not use one built for the pros? Internet Newsroom is a service for journalists that points them in the right direction when researching stories. Not a newsstand strictly speaking, the site nonetheless contains links to some newspapers and other journalistic outlets. Updated every two weeks, the main value of Internet Newsroom is its categorization of news topics. The site breaks down information into topics of relevance to newswriters, such as law, medical, reference, and politics, and then sends reporters off to sites like the Democratic and Republican National Committees, the National Center for Education Statistics, the National Press Club, and *The Washington Post.* If you like getting a deeper, inside perspective on the news, you may as well approach it the way a journalist would.

NewsLink

www.newslink.org

First-class guide to regional online newspapers: Created by the American Journalism Review, NewsLink combines site-review and newsstand functions into one of the most professional news link sites on the Web. NewsLink attempts a kind of encyclopedic directory that would intimidate most organizations. It not only lists links to regional online newspapers state by state, but further classifies them by type of journalism and frequency of publication, and it even includes links to sites not currently active. (I'm not sure what good that last category does, but it's impressive nonetheless.) The site cross-references the entire database so that you can look up papers by location or by category from a central page. International sites don't get quite the same fastidious treatment, but you can find newspaper sites from all continents easily enough. Because this is the newspaper section of the book, I mention only that portion of NewsLink; however, the site works its magic for online magazines and radio and TV stations as well. Without question — bookmark this site.

World Wide News Sources on the Internet

www.discover.co.uk/NET/NEWS/ news.html

Incredible guide to international news sources: You can find several sources of links to international news sources on the Web, but this site remains the best I've found. The site's excellence is largely due to its frame-based design that invites you to click a letter of the alphabet and then peruse all the countries of that letter and their online news editions. When you select a newspaper site to visit, it appears in the larger frame, so you never really leave the World Wide News Sources site.

This setup may seem possessive, but in fact it's convenient; you can explore a newspaper without concern about losing your place because you're always just a click away (in the smaller frame) from resuming your browse of other international sources. Catch up on Belgian news with the Flemish newspaper *Het Volk* (good luck!); gain a new perspective on world news with the *Hong Kong Standard;* experience the global village by sipping coffee over the *Asharq Al-Awsat* from Saudi Arabia. You'll be amazed at how many international virtual newspapers exist, but one country that you won't find here is the United States.

Other Stuff to Check Out

gallery.uunet.be/internetpress/american.htm
newo.com/news/
www.all-links.com/newscentral/
www.mediainfo.com/ephome/npaper/
    nphtm/online.htm
www.worldwidenews.com

Pushed News

www.pointcast.com

Pushing and shoving was once *the* hot Internet topic. Pushing and shoving news, that is. Normally, the Net is a *pull* medium — that is, if you want to see something, you must pull it to your screen by choosing it. By contrast, television is primarily a *push* medium, because shows are pushed to your screen with no opportunity for interactivity except clicking the remote. The Internet's *push* technology is primarily manifested in news delivery. You can generally get

pushed news for free, and with mixed results. In all cases, you select the sources of information that get pushed to your monitor (called *channels* in most cases), and then wait for the fun to begin.

Push technology isn't quite as hot today, but the technology is hardly going the way of the beta videotape machine. (In fact, the channel technology used by the latest Netscape and Microsoft browsers is a form of push technology. You can read more about this in *Netscape Communicator For Dummies* or *Internet Explorer 4 For Dummies,* both from IDG Books Worldwide, Inc.) Not many push companies exist on the Web at present, and this section gathers the main ones.

AirMedia

www.airmedia.com

You need to buy hardware for this to work: AirMedia is a hybrid product, blending wireless technology with the essentially wired connectivity of the Internet. AirMedia takes breaking news, sports, and financial information from Internet news sources and beams it to U.S. subscribers wirelessly, where it appears on computer screens. In order for this product to work, you must buy an AirMedia receiver (around $100) and special software (free with the antenna receiver). After everything is in place, a stream of news information is relayed to your PC whether you're logged on to the Net or not. (Ha! You can't get away from it!) AirMedia claims that their broadcast coverage area includes 90 percent of the U.S. population; the site has a zip code-based search page to see if your area qualifies. Because you must buy hardware to make AirMedia work, it qualifies as one of the most expensive pushed news solutions. Whether it's the wave of the future, I can't say; in the meantime, AirMedia is for those who like to remain on the cutting edge.

64 Pushed News

BackWeb

www.backweb.com

Daily pushing is less frequent than most:
First, the good news: BackWeb is free. You
download the software, decide what
channels you want to receive, and start
getting periodic delivery of news, entertainment, sports, financial, and weather
content. The company also has a presence in Japan and Europe. Now, the not-
so-good news: The channel selection —
while growing — is broad but not deep.
Using the Channels button to see a
directory of choices, you find many
categories but not many selections within
those categories. BackWeb is a good, easy
way to get your feet wet with pushed
news, but it's hardly state of the art. Most
channels don't deliver content more
frequently than daily (some of them are
weekly or monthly), so BackWeb doesn't
hold much advantage over e-mail delivery
services.

Downtown

www.incommon.com

Put your browser on a leash: All pushed
news schemes try for some angle to set
them apart. Downtown is an interesting
blend of news-pusher and automated web
browser. It accomplishes this mixed
mission by providing preset channels and
by enabling you to create your own
channels from just about any Web site.
The preset channels — which include The
New York Times, DBC Financial News,
USA Today, CBS SportsLine, and others —
serve up pushed information in a special
format. In addition, you can add personal
channels by selecting Web sites; Downtown checks these sites for new content
and gets that new content for you. The
personal channel feature makes Downtown a kind of browse-while-you-sleep
automated browser that saves you the
time of visiting your favorite Web sites in
real time.

Marimba

www.marimba.com

Up and coming, with great features: When
considering pushed information over the
Internet, I must talk about the unique
Marimba system. Like other pushed-news
solutions, Marimba enables you to
subscribe to channels of news content.
But Marimba differs by also establishing a
standard within which that content can
be written. Marimba is like a fancy word
processor that can display artwork and
unusual typefaces — the displayed
document must be *written* in the format of
the word processor in order to work.
Marimba can't select from the news
content of any Web site; rather it must
partner with Internet content providers
who desire to write special content for
Marimba. Fortunately, Marimba has
become an Internet force, and its content
selection is very good and getting better
every day. Your only requirement is to
download Castanet — the tuner that sits
on your computer screen and enables you
to select, or *tune,* the content to receive.
(Fortunately, the download is free.)
Castanet downloads the content from the
selected channels, stores it on your hard
drive, and then updates it whenever
updates are available. In this fashion, you
have dynamic, multimedia presentations
of news, entertainment, financial information, and all kinds of other goodies
streaming off your hard drive, which is
much quicker than streaming off the Net.
Marimba is much more entertainment-
oriented than many pushed-news

systems, dedicating some of the channels to games or chatting.

NewsHound

www.hound.com

 $

Not free, but very obedient: Imagine having a brood of virtual dogs continually sniffing out news on the Internet, retrieving it, and carrying it waggingly to your e-mail box — that's the idea behind NewsHound. It lets you train up to five hounds to fetch different kinds of news, which is then either delivered by e-mail or stored on a Web site for you to read at your leisure. The service isn't free, but $7.95 per month covers unlimited access to full stories retrieved by your robot canines. You can change your news profiles at any time, either on the NewsHound Web site or through e-mail commands sent to a special address. NewsHound won't bring your slippers to you, but it will bring the news — without the slobber.

Personal News Alert

**www.msnbc.com/tools/alert/
    alermain.asp**

Unpredictable, but popular and not too intrusive: MSNBC, the hybrid TV-Web channel produced by an alliance between NBC and Microsoft, has created a pushed news service called Personal News Alert, which works with Windows 95 and Windows NT systems. The service is free, but you must download the Personal News Alert program to use it — don't worry, it transfers quickly (less than a minute even for a 14.4Kbps modem). The program installs itself and immediately begins delivering news alerts to your desktop as long as you're logged on to an Internet connection. Fairly sophisticated custom features enable you to personal-

ize what news you receive. On a broad level, you select topics, and more specifically, you can enter keywords, and stories that include those keywords come winging your way. An interesting feature enables you to set alert parameters for certain stocks, so if the price changes up or down or by a certain percentage in either direction, you get an alert. The alerts show up on the Windows 95 taskbar and can be accompanied by a sound; you can also set Personal News Alert to flash the news window right over whatever you're working on. Five minutes is the shortest time increment possible between alerts. Personal News Alert is quick and easy to set up and is customizable enough to be useful.

PointCast

www.pointcast.com

The original mover: This site started the whole push craze. PointCast came up with a good idea — in place of a screen saver, deliver news to personal computers logged on to the Internet — and a whole industry, even a whole new conception of what the Internet could be, was born. If you buy into the usefulness of pushed news, PointCast has the best selection of content providers (channels). (You're not literally *buying* into it, because PointCast is completely free of charge.) PointCast just recently updated its software to version 2.5, and added a slew of new channels as well. Now you can choose from 28 channels, most from specific sources (*The Boston Globe, The Los Angeles Times, The Wall Street Journal,* and other newspapers and magazines), a few topical (Health, Industries, Lifestyle, and Weather). PointCast earned its honorable place as the grandparent of all push ventures, but its latest update keeps the service young.

Other Stuff to Check Out

www.internetbroadcast.com
www.netdelivery.com

Live news on the Net is a small, but growing, area. As technology inches closer to a *broadband* environment — where most people access the Internet with cable or wireless systems through which Web pages load much more quickly than through modems — you will see more television and radio stations incorporating Webcasts into their operations. In this section, I review the pioneers of Webcasting.

Television and radio networks approach the World Wide Web in several different ways. Certain stations attempt live feeds from the station broadcast over the Internet, with mixed results over modems. Webcasts work better for people using ISDN telephone lines or 56 Kbps modems, but video performance is jerky using a 28.8 Kbps modem. Audio Webcasts, however, work fairly well with the new versions (3.0 or later) of the RealAudio plug-in. Another approach is to archive bits of programming for viewing (or listening) in the future. Archiving goes against the "live news" concept, but when the shows are archived quickly, the news

is nearly live. A third approach relies on tried-and-true text news, which the host broadcast station posts continually to the Web site.

ABC News Reports

www.realaudio.com/contentp/abc.html

The ubiquitous Peter Jennings: This RealAudio site streams frequently updated audio news reports, sports stories, and commentary by Peter Jennings, through browsers equipped with the RealAudio plug-in. The programming will sound much better when the site upgrades to RealAudio version 3.0 (or, even better, 4.0), but even using the relatively scratchy version 2.1, you can enjoy the convenience of getting up-to-date news without staring at your monitor. (The site works fine if you're using later versions of RealAudio.) The news link (just click ABC News) contains the most recently updated news, whereas the Peter Jennings commentary audio clips and the Johnny Holliday Sports programs are *daily* features.

ABC Online

www.abc.net.au/

What's happening in Australia: This ABC stands for the Australian Broadcasting Co., the land down under's only national, noncommercial broadcaster. But what's really intriguing is that this site not only serves as a Web recap of and promoter for some of ABC's radio and TV shows, ABC Online seeks to enhance the Web experience of visitors as well. For example, the Explore Your Interests page (click the Explore home page link) links to the pages of ABC's shows on the topics given (Science, Kids, Sports, and so on) *and* provides links to outstanding relevant Web sites as well — Web sites like the Smithsonian Institute in Science and Amnesty International in Politics. The site also has games and other activities. News? Certainly, on the News link. And visitors who click their way to the World News page can get the day's top stories in Indonesian, Chinese, Vietnamese, Khmer, and Tok Pisin. Oddly, the site's audio clips are hard to find, but the depth of content in other areas more than makes up for that small deficiency.

BBC Online

www.bbc.co.uk

Audio news with a British accent: This URL takes you to the home page of the large British Broadcasting Corporation (BBC) site, from which you need to click the World Service link to navigate your way to the live radio page. The BBC's news and current events programming is renowned throughout the world and is sometimes featured on National Public Radio stations in the United States. BBC Netcasts its programming as much as possible; because a Webcast is global in scope, it must refrain from including some sporting events for which it doesn't have global rights. However, the World Service page's world map links to services for various parts of the globe. Clicking the Audio link zips you to a page that can connect you with the BBC's live feed or to services in other languages — including Arabic, Czech, German, Indonesian, Persian, Russian, and Spanish. Pip pip! You need RealAudio 3.0 or higher for the live feed.

CNET Radio

www.news.com/Radio/index.html

Original audio programming for the Internet: CNET makes a token attempt to cover general news, but its true strong point is the digital revolution, including coverage of computer news, Internet developments, and business news that relates to the high-tech sector. The site offers a variety of programming for live listening, but CNET is not a radio station with continuous broadcasting. Important technology news — Microsoft investing in Apple Computer, for example — is updated with audio commentary throughout the day. Several staff reporters and commentators have scheduled time slots for programs that range in duration from about five minutes to a half hour. CNET covers some technology events — trade shows, keynote speeches, and so on.

C-SPAN Online

www.c-span.org/watch

The thrill of live political wrangling: If you've ever sat in front of the TV, eyes glazed over beyond recognition, stunned by the thrill of watching legislators in live debates over budget resolutions or House members wrangling over proposed tax regulations, you've experienced the excitement of C-SPAN. I can't be the only one who likes the channel, because C-SPAN2 was added to the original cable channel, and both channels are available live through RealVideo on the Web. You need version 4.0 of RealPlayer (which combines RealAudio and RealVideo). In addition to the live television feed, C-SPAN archives special events that you can view at any time — the State of the Union Address and other speeches of slightly less importance. Plan your soporific viewing in advance by consulting the daily schedules for both TV channels.

Fox News

www.foxnews.com

Ambitious, glitzy, bandwidth-hungry multimedia site: The Fox News site enlivens typical news sections with streaming news tickers across the top of the home page, a generous supply of audio and video clips, and a live simulcast of the Fox News Channel. This is one hip, cutting-edge, pushing-the-bandwidth news site, if you've got a fast enough modem and the right plug-ins to enjoy it. You can do pretty well with a 28.8Kbps modem as long as your browser is equipped with RealAudio version 4.0 (also called RealPlayer), which handles both the audio and video programming. If you'd rather skip the multimedia shimmer, use the headline links on the left side of the page. This site has it all, whether you're in a hurry or eager to try out some new plug-ins. Fox News is one of the most ambitious news sites on the Web.

MSNBC

www.msnbc.com

The cable channel's online residence: MSNBC, the hybrid news and entertainment organization created by an alliance between Microsoft and NBC, puts out an increasingly jazzy Web tribute to the multimedia possibilities of delivering news programming over the Internet. The Web site is closely linked with the cable station of the same name and carries some of the shows through browser plug-ins (you need RealAudio to make the most of this site). The more staid news portions of MSNBC include standard topical sections, headlines linking to full stories, and other typical elements of a news site, but with the great graphics characteristic of Microsoft Web pages. An especially nice touch is the addition of submenus that pop up when you move your cursor over a link, saving you one step in the clicking process. Customizing a news Web page is very easy using MSNBC's helpful forms, and you can have your own personal Web page of news delivered to your e-mail box. By the way, if you want to surf over to this site and take your eyes off the monitor, try the Audio Headlines link.

Regional News Network

www.rnntv.com

Audio news coverage of the New York metropolitan area: Regional News Network (RNN) covers the densely populated New York City area, including New York state, Connecticut, and New Jersey. Making use of RealPlayer (which handles video streaming as well as audio), RNN provides a real-time simulcast of the RNN television programming. The site adds weather, sports, and movie reviews to the general news coverage, and you can select an area of the site corresponding to a state or county. Drop-down menus help you navigate around the site, and program guides assist you in connecting Web content with television programming.

Other Stuff to Check Out

www.msnbc.com/onair/nbc/today/
  default.asp
www.nightlybusiness.org

Weather

Almost all weather sites provide data about weather conditions in certain locations. The best ones also furnish forecasts for the following day and sometimes for several days in advance. (For whatever these forecasts are worth.) What you're really looking for is a site that enables you to type in a location (the more specific the better) and get a regional forecast as well as current conditions. The following sites do the best job blending conditions, forecasts, and other weather information.

AccuWeather

**www.accuweather.com/web/
welcome.htm**

AccuThis, AccuThat, AccuNice: Want something simple? Get your local five-day forecast just by typing in your zip code on the front page of this Web site. Want to go all out? Download AccuData, an interface program, and subscribe for access to the impressive database. Satellite and radar images, weather maps, conditions and forecasts, and even such wildly diverse items as soap opera summaries, lottery results, and sports scores are available through AccuData. Pushing the commercial envelope, you can even buy AccuWeather mugs and T-shirts. You can sample AccuData for free through the site before subscribing. With all the information this site offers, it

makes you wonder why anyone would want to buy an electronic home weather station — but they sell one in the AccuStore if you're interested. Go figure.

Automated Weather Source

aws.com

Follows the weather a little too closely: The Automated Weather Source makes a big deal about providing "Real Time Weather," which at first looks like an overrated claim. Hit the Live Local Weather button to view constantly updated weather conditions (no forecasts) from several points around the United States, with more reporting locations being added continuously. Some reporting organizations are local television and radio stations, but the display is nothing special, even though the information is quite current. Back on the home page, try clicking to see the Java page. Now you're talking! This Internet weather technology is worth getting excited about. For a select few locations (more being added soon), you can see a Java-animated display of weather conditions as they evolve second by second. For example, a small animated compass serves as a surrogate weather vane, showing the speed and direction of the wind in real time. You can sit and watch as the breeze changes force and direction in the next city. Can you tell I'm easily excited by technology? If it's pouring rain and you're willing to stare at the screen for a while, you can see the rainfall gauge inch up. The Java application takes less than a minute to load with a 28.8Kbps modem, and it's certainly cool in a geekish sort of way.

CNN Weather

cnn.com/WEATHER

Weather journalism: You'd expect CNN to do a comprehensive, newsworthy job of covering the weather, and it does. Four-day forecasts are available for a huge list of towns in the United States and many

70 Weather

cities around the world. You can gaze at weather maps showing temperatures, system fronts, and satellite data. Furthermore, the site is a kind of weather e-zine, modeled after the big CNN news site. All the stories are weather-related, but in a way that suggests a giant, lurking news organization in the background, cross-referencing all the international stories in search of meteorological components and then filing them on the weather site. The resulting stories are much more journalistic than you usually find on a weather site.

National Weather Service

www.nws.noaa.gov

Weather disaster warnings: The mission of the National Weather Service (NWS) is to protect life and property through the short-range forecast of destructive weather. The organization is primarily known for issuing warnings to local areas that are about to blasted with rain, wind, hail, lightning, or other meteorological affronts. You know the type of bulletin: "The National Weather Service has issued a flood warning and mildew alert for Brad Hill's basement." On the NWS site, you must navigate through a maze of mouse clicks to find conditions or forecasts; I suggest sticking with The Weather Channel or USA Today Weather (both are reviewed in this section) — unless you like to check hourly condition readings for the past 24 hours, which, I must confess, is kind of fascinating. The best use of this site is to go for its strong point: the watches and warnings links on the Current Weather page.

Storm Chaser

taiga.geog.niu.edu/chaser.html

Go get that tornado: The Storm Chaser site is *Twister* on the Web: You can catch some vicarious thrills without mussing your hair, by reading accounts of successful tornado chases and viewing the resulting pictures. If you actually like

throwing yourself in front of perilous weather systems, you'll appreciate the late-breaking chaser weather news. This site handles forecasts a tad differently than The Weather Channel, for example, by dealing with surface and upper air conditions, lightning strike maps, and other happy harbingers of imminent disaster. Storm Chaser Talk deals with chaser ethics and other ruminations on the windy lifestyle. Go for it — just watch out for flying cows.

Storm Watch

www.fema.gov/fema/trop.htm

Warnings of emerging storms: This alarming sounding site is a product of the Federal Emergency Management Agency and provides a variety of weather disaster information. Two main sections define the site: Advisories and Helpful Information. The helpful info ranges from how to file flood insurance claims to how to survive the storm. Ten-day precipitation forecast maps and temperature forecast maps track emerging weather systems, and the advisories bulletin sections are updated every two hours. News releases enable you to follow weather stories, such as tropical storms moving along a coast. As a grand finale of disaster news service, the site provides a search engine for locating news releases about rescue efforts. Storm Watch provides useful information and also sheds light on weather-related disaster procedures. Oh, and if you want to know the names for the upcoming hurricane season's Atlantic storms, they're here, too.

USA Today Weather

www.usatoday.com/weather/
   wfront.htm

That famous U.S. weather map: The home page of this Web site features the trademark *USA Today* color-coded national temperature map, surrounded by a lot of information about weather. A downright educational page, you can read about hurricanes, tornadoes, thunderstorms, and other upsetting weather developments. The Topic Index link is a good place to start, but be forewarned: It's massive. Curious about advection fog? (You and me both.) Can't sleep until you know more about latent and dynamic cooling? Intrigued by the concept of microbursts? Need to clarify your understanding of sling psychrometers? The site links these and hundreds of other topics in a virtual encyclopedia of weather arcana. Of course, you can just get forecasts, too. The USA Today five-day outlooks tend to be simpler to follow than those provided by The Weather Channel Web site. Click the spinning Forecasts globe to try them for yourself.

The Weather Channel

www.weather.com

More than just forecasts: If you've ever sat entranced by The Weather Channel on cable TV, you know that it provides more than just forecasts. In what remains one of the most audacious feats of television programming, The Weather Channel treats meteorological events as if they're fascinating plot lines, like a running soap opera of wind, rain, sleet, and sunshine. The Weather Channel Web site is similarly ambitious, providing an "online magazine" about weather. Headlines and top stories fit under the Breaking Weather category, and a summary of current

conditions for major cities scrolls across the screen. You can look at maps and travel conditions; check out how weather affects boating, gardening, and aviation; and get a local forecast — the main point of the site for most people. Just type in the name of your town or nearest city to see a five-day outlook. If the forecast is *all* you're interested in, your best bet is to bookmark that local page and forgo the informative home page, although it is impressive.

The Weather Resource

www.nxdc.com/weather

Resource for weather information on the Web: Here's the tag line for the Weather Resource: "Bringing the World of Internet Weather to You." Ignoring for a moment the fact that the Internet doesn't have any weather, The Weather Resource contains a truckload of statistics, graphics, weather data, and multimedia side dishes that place it in the big leagues of Web weather whistle-stops (go ahead, say that five times). You must bring a forgiving attitude to the site's page design, which features an absolutely unreadable side menu bar, and instead concentrate on the main links stretching down the home page. After you dig into this site a bit, you'll realize a crucial fact: Most of the data, including maps and forecasting, is attained by linking to other sites, notably The Weather Channel and the National Weather Service, both of which I review in this section. The Weather Resource is exactly what its name implies: a resource to weather information located elsewhere. The beauty of the site is the way that it organizes the resource links. More than a simple directory, it automatically steers your browser to the best location to gather information about tomorrow morning's forecast, fog conditions, gardening and boating, snow, surface maps, or whatever your interest is.

The Weather Underground

www.wunderground.com

Fast and convenient weather updates: The Weather Underground is quick, simple, and to the point. A U.S. map on the home page leads you to state-related weather when you click any portion of it. Alternatively, you can type a town name into the keyword entry form above the map to view current conditions and a three-day forecast. The current conditions are fairly complete and include special warnings when appropriate. Most impressively, the system recognizes small cities and towns. You can customize the home page to automatically display selected towns as *Favorites* whenever you enter the site — pretty nifty. No editorial content appears on this site — no weather news, explanatory articles, or tutorials about weather conditions. The Weather Underground is strictly forecasts and conditions, and it performs this simple task very well.

WeatherLab

www.weatherlabs.com

This one wants to be the best, and soon may be: WeatherLab is an ambitious site: "The world's premier online weather service," in its own words. This organization takes weather very seriously and provides forecasts for 200 cities around the world, supplemented by satellite maps, ski conditions, and air travel delays. Good as it is, WeatherLab is about to get better, with a new, interactive home page that — at the time of this writing — was still in the preview stage. The forecasts presented on this site are extremely detailed, divided into Morning, Afternoon, Evening, and Overnight segments for the current 24-hour period. Large, cartoonlike depictions of weather conditions replace the typical small icons of sunshine, clouds, and rain that grace other forecast pages. Extended five-day outlooks are informationally sketchy. You

can't search the site for your city or town on the current site; you must choose from a state-by-state list of cities. After you track your way to your local forecast, I suggest bookmarking that page to avoid trekking to it the hard way in the future.

Other Stuff to Check Out

www.bbc.co.uk/weather
www.cameronlaw.com/weather.html
www.cncentral.com/weather.html
www.webbers.com/weather

Current events — very current — proliferate on the World Wide Web. Presenting daily news is a task well suited to the Internet, where it doesn't cost much to update facts frequently. All the sites in this section update the news at least daily and sometimes even more frequently.

Almost all daily news sites on the Web use a *headline link* format. This format works by presenting headlines as hyperlinks that display full stories (or one-paragraph summaries) when you click them. Apart from this basic format, tremendous variety ensues. Although many news sites don't bother with multimedia tidbits like audio or video clips, or even graphics that slow down the urgent mission of getting hard news on your monitor quickly, others go the opposite route by throwing everything but the multimedia kitchen sink onto their home pages.

ABCNEWS.com

www.abcnews.com

Solid news and fancy Web tricks: You may want to plan an activity to keep you busy while this home page loads — like reupholstering the couch or painting the kitchen. But ABCNEWS.com is worth the wait, if only for the ultra-cool news ticker streaming across the top. Click a headline as it zooms by to see the full story. If your hand-mouse coordination isn't swift enough for such multimedia parlor tricks, you can always get to the stories in the standard hyperlinked fashion. ABCNEWS.com partners with ESPN Sports to cover athletics, and the weather section delivers local forecasts after you tell it where you're located. By registering for immediate local news, you can link up to your local ABC affiliate and set up a remote browser window with headlines that you can keep on your desktop as you roam the Web. ABCNEWS.com is full of little tricks and interactive snacks — radio news through RealAudio, for example. If you're in the mood for fancy Web tricks, you can do no better than ABCNEWS.com; if you need your news fast, I suggest trying a more sleek site.

CNN Interactive

www.cnn.com

An online news juggernaut: The cable TV news giant makes a big splash on the Internet by providing one of the most-visited sites for daily news. The home page is a marvel of clear efficiency, linking to every portion of the gigantic site without appearing overbearing. The site covers world and U.S. news in detail, and other sections are devoted to Sports, Sci-tech, Travel, Style, Entertainment, Health, Politics, and Travel. The U.S. Local page offers a national map; clicking any region takes you to news pages provided by CNN regional affiliates. CNN Interactive makes good use of video clips in some stories (look for little movie camera icons next to headlines), and has a video archive that you can search. Hyperlinks embedded in the text provide background and related items about public figures and events. You can also customize what CNN news is delivered to you or get free desktop headlines (refreshed every five minutes) while you browse elsewhere on the Web. CNN Interactive is incredibly deep and informative.

Crayon

crayon.net

Interactive, customizable newspaper: Crayon stands roughly for Create Your Own Newspaper, which is just what the site helps you do. Crayon walks you through the process of designing a personal Web page with customized links to news sources on the World Wide Web.

74   Wire Services and Daily Updates

You don't need to know what you're doing or be familiar with Web news sources — Crayon keeps a large, updated database of locations and provides forms for you to check off what you want to appear on your page. The result is a Web page that you can save to your hard drive (Crayon helps you with this part, too) and refer to any time you want by loading it into your browser. (Use the Open selection of your browser's File menu.)

Daily Briefing

www.dailybriefing.com

The mission — surviving the day: The weapon: Daily Briefing, a customizable site created by Timecast, the programming department of RealAudio. The site incorporates some of the best RealAudio news programming on the Net, including (at last visit) ABC, CNET, Fox, and Wall Street Journal audio shows. You can even find movie clips. The update schedule varies depending on the source, but it's never less frequent than daily, otherwise the Daily Briefing mission would be compromised and legions of fans would be disappointed.

Drudge Report

www.drudgereport.com

Controversial commentary, plus a directory: Stark, retro black-and-white page design and a no-nonsense, awesome list of links characterize the Drudge Report's aesthetic toward news. Matt Drudge is the brainstormer behind the site as well as its principal writer — its only writer, in fact. The rest of the site links to other news sources to put you in touch with a truckload of syndicated columnists, wire service agencies, and online newspapers and magazines. The Drudge Report is a tremendous roll call of virtual news publications and personalities. The site's real treasure (besides Matt Drudge's

wide-ranging and entertaining report) is the list of columnists, although a quick description of the column's subject or specialty would be welcome. The Drudge Report site can launch a lot of interesting news surf sessions.

The European

www.the-european.com

What else? European news: Here's a quiz: The European delivers news about what continent? Right you are. The classy site is hindered a bit by slow page displays, due partly to overbearing graphics and partly to — for American viewers — the transatlantic link. News, commentary, sports, and business issues struggle for space amid the blinking graphics. The European can deliver pages laid out in the original newspaper format, but you must have Adobe Acrobat Reader on your hard drive to see them (see the accompanying CD for your copy of Acrobat Reader). Try The European for news from a continental viewpoint.

Excite NewsTracker

nt.excite.com

A good news service from a Web directory site: All the big Web directories and search engines are getting into the news biz by providing some blend of headlines, stories, and links to outside news sources. Excite gets into the act at the NewsTracker site with top-story headlines stretching down the center of the page, ongoing stories in a left-hand menu, and section categories across the top of every page — the typical News, Business, Sports, Entertainment, Sci-Tech, Nation, World, and Lifestyle sections. The news comes from Reuters and other wire sources, but the site presents every story within the Excite boundaries, and the pages display quickly. The Newstracker section doesn't refer to a hard-boiled journalist working on a story, rather it refers to a personal page with chosen topics, a standard feature in the news portions of Web directories. Excite's version of the customize feature isn't quite helpful enough in providing topic suggestions.

The Hays Daily News

www.dailynews.net

Business and general news: The home page of The Hays Daily News gives the impression that you've come across a typical Web news site: headlines, a couple of pictures, and links to other stories. In fact, this site is surprisingly rich in facts, figures, and charts, especially in the Markets section. In this section, you can call up all sorts of data about futures and options, daily charts of the current day's market movements, and other financial info of interest to active investors. Surrounding the business news is a solid range of world news. Harris Enterprises, who produces the site, owns local newspapers around North America, and you can use a drop-down list to view the online editions of any one of them. The main Hays Daily News is national in scope.

InfoJunkie

www.infojunkie.com

Up-to-the-second headlines: InfoJunkie caters to newshounds with ravenous appetites for current news. The InfoJunkie site ferociously updates its information and proudly lists the time that it posts headlines to the site. No original writing graces the InfoJunkie pages; instead, the site gleans its content from other sources and links directly to those sources, which range from Yahoo! wire-service pages to Web editions of computer magazines. Five basic sections, like cutlery around a dinner setting, let you feast on a news diet: News, Technology, Business, Entertainment, and Sports. No audio, no video, no multimedia flab — just a fast central location for fresh news.

LiteNews

www.litenews.com/TODAY/index.html

Gentle, not-so-bad news: When the edge of hard news gets too sharp, surf over to LiteNews for what is described as "The Softer Side of Your News Day." LiteNews stories are informal without being gossipy and emphasize entertainment, weather, and personalities. The site presents less grim aspects of mainstream world news with a gentle touch. LiteNews is light graphically, too, so the pages display quickly. The business section carries some informational graphs and charts, but it relies more on feature stories for its main content. No chat rooms or message boards to let you socialize with other news-weary folk, but links to other news and entertainment sites abound.

Lycos Top News

www.lycos.com/news

Better for browsing the news than searching: Lycos, one of the major Web directories that also provides a news service, takes a hybrid approach to issuing news content. Relying heavily on other sources for stories, Lycos writes its own summaries and creates a two-step process to getting the story. First, click a headline link in the In The News section and read the summary that appears. Underneath the summary are links to longer stories on the topic (typically from Reuters).

Underneath that you'll find links for more information and links to other Web resources — often other news sites carrying the story. These sites may be *The Toronto Star, The New York Times,* or any number of other locations. The Lycos news service is seamlessly integrated with its Web directory, with headlines gracing every main directory topic page. In this way, Web sites become entwined with news stories in a fashion that's either intriguing or confusing, depending on your temperament.

The Morrock News Service

morrock.com/index.htm

For those with no time to spare: Formerly known as The Daily News Current, this site's news is both current, in the timely sense, and a swift-moving stream, as in a river current. The Morrock News Service prides itself on quick updates, original writing, and a sleek, simple page design that keeps the site briskly efficient. The first site update of the weekday is 9 a.m. Pacific time (U.S.), which is a bit late for those on the East Coast of the United States, but the pace quickens during the day. The writers and editors glean their source material from the same places that you and I do — newspapers, TV, radio, and the Net, and then they write original rehashes for the site.

Online NewsHour

www.pbs.org/newshour

Jim Lehrer's Internet home: PBS has been one of the most aggressive enthusiasts of the Internet as a medium for its programming. The Online NewsHour is an Internet version of *The NewsHour with Jim Lehrer.* PBS immediately places every edition of the program on the Web site in RealAudio format (I hope PBS soon embraces RealVideo and posts the video portion of the show as well), and an archive of past programs is likewise available. Very conveniently, the site divides each show into its component interview segments so that you can listen to one portion without having to fast-forward through an earlier portion. Besides the RealAudio programming, check out Interactive Forums on the right side of the home page. The forums represent a type of interactivity typical of PBS, whose programs tend to interface the audience with public figures. Viewers of the forums pose questions to the forum's victims — that is, guests who may be freshman senators or corporate leaders. The guests post responses back to the Web page.

The Positive Press

www.positivepress.com

An inspirational attitude toward general news: A few Web sites attempt to balance the grimness of the current-events coverage that saturates disaster-oriented news outlets, but no site does a better job covering inspirational angles than The Positive Press. The excellence extends through the content, organization, and page design of this site. Four main sections define the site's structure: General, Health, Business, and Light. Ironically, The Positive Press scavenges most of its stories from mainstream news publications and links to the original source in its well-organized headlines. The today's quote link is an original bit of editorial content, as is the Historical Perspectives archive. If you like, you can help spread news of kindness, perseverance, and human strength by interacting with other readers on the message boards.

Russia Today

www.russiatoday.com

An American news source about Russia: Produced by the European Internet Network, Russia Today is the primary online news source featuring stories originating within, and focusing on, Russia. It's not a Russian publication, but most of the datelines cite Moscow or another Russian city, and the reporting is objective and authoritative. Headlines, business, news, and a section called Pressing Issues display dozens of stories that you're not likely to find in any other news site. Text transcripts of the day's important Russian television broadcasts provide one of the most interesting site features. Completely up-to-date in the multimedia department, Russia Today gives you a daily video news update through RealVideo.

TIME Daily

pathfinder.com/time/daily

Daily, bite-sized portions of TIME: TIME Daily, a spin-off of the main *TIME* magazine site, provides brisk updates for the newshound. But TIME Daily is not as aggressively current as the wire-service sites, contenting itself with a major daily overhaul rather than hourly or continuous postings. A tastefully sparse home page includes pictures but doesn't strangle your modem, and a text-only version is available by using a link at the top left of the page. The site limits archiving to a single day, although you have access to "yesterday's" TIME Daily. Embedded hyperlinks — a convenient style used very well at this site — provide background for current stories. You can link over to the main magazine site as well as to the TIME community message boards.

United States Information Agency

www.usia.gov/products/washfile/ latest.shtml

Press releases from the U.S. government: The mission of the United States Information Agency (USIA) is to assist the residents, journalists, and government officials of other countries in better understanding the United States and its official representatives and agencies. The USIA publishes a constant stream of press releases describing every twitch of the U.S. government machine: presidential meetings, speeches, agency appointments, senatorial committee meetings, presidential statements, daily White House reports, and State Department reports. Is it dry? Like eating a burnt bagel with sand on it. The site's main asset lies in delivering the complete text of speeches.

U.S. Newswire

www.usnewswire.com/index.htm

U.S. public policy news releases: U.S. Newswire distributes news for the White House, federal agencies, congressional offices, and other governmental agencies. Its charter is to help distribute news releases that define public policy. The Web site's mission is to make current and archived reports available in a blazing-fast interface that favors efficiency over adornment. Click the Top News button and then click current news releases to cut to the chase. What you see is a list of filed stories, and clicking one story displays the entire text of that story. Notice the utter lack of graphics; not even the thought of a picture slows down this site. You can snake through U.S. Newswire in a flash, getting up to speed with the latest policy statements during idle moments.

WorldNetDaily

www.WorldNetDaily.com

Guide to current news at other sites: Run as a nonprofit corporation (and therefore less inclined to fill your monitor with online advertisements), WorldNetDaily serves as a daily electronic news outlet and self-styled government watchdog, citing the U.S. free press as the abiding principle of its existence. However, rather than protect you from media deception with original investigative journalism, WorldNetDaily merely links to other Web news sources for its stories. The Business section is actually the Money section of the USA Today site, and the TV Guide site provides the TV listings. Still, the site is valuable for its good organization and current news. Think of the time you save by having a site that collects the top stories at any given moment at one place. Because reading WorldNetDaily requires your system to constantly link to other sites, expect to confront registrations and possible page stalls as you navigate around the news sources. On the plus side, you can also expect to discover a lot

of great news sources by just following the WorldNetDaily links.

Other Stuff to Check Out

dailynews.yahoo.com/headlines/
flashnews.com
www.clarinet.com
www.fednews.com
www.newsservice.com
www.upi.com

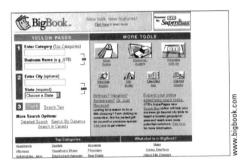

www.bigbook.com

When the CD-ROM revolution hit the marketplace a few years ago, some publishers struck on the idea of putting massive phone books on the discs, figuring that computers were the perfect tools for looking up a phone number. That proposition is debatable, but I (and many other suckers . . . I mean, people) discovered that, indeed, there are advantages to a random-access database over a book. Then the Internet took over, and now you can find phone books of all sorts online.

The traditional phone book models hold true on the Net: White Pages for residential listings and Yellow Pages for business listings. That is, the listings are *called* white and yellow pages; the Web pages themselves may not be colored that way. In addition to white and yellow pages, and perhaps more important than both of them, are the e-mail pages (color unspecified) that enable you to look up a person's e-mail address.

The following are the major people-finding and business-finding Web directories. Separating them into categories is hard because almost all such directories step on each other's toes by dabbling in every kind of lookup service, even if the site's main purpose is yellow pages or e-mail.

One final thought: Just as phone books aren't 100 percent accurate on the day they're published (people do move, you know), online phone books sometimes have old addresses. And I've noticed that not every single geographic area is covered — for example, I've got some good friends in Indiana who don't appear in some of these sites. Still, the listings here are the best the Web has to offer, and the price (nothing) is right.

BigBook

www.bigbook.com

Interactive Yellow Pages: As interactive Yellow Pages directories go, BigBook is currently state of the art. That doesn't mean it's perfect, but it's very useful. More useful than grabbing a real Yellow Pages book and looking something up? Well . . . next, question, please. Logging onto the Internet to find a local hardware store may not be your best use of resources, but using an online Yellow Pages is great for finding a business out of town, as I recently discovered when searching for a dog kennel near an upcoming vacation spot, several states away from my home. In BigBook, you can enter the category of business, or the name of a specific business, plus the city and state. Alternatively, a directory enables you to browse among categories, but the top-level categories are on the broad side. I wouldn't know where to start looking for a kennel by using the directory — it doesn't seem to fit in any of the categories, and the best bet is to

just type **kennel** or **animal boarding.** After you get your search results, all kinds of features come into play, including a personal address book for storing listings that you may want to refer to again and a slick map feature that allows zooming in and out (whee!) and panning back and forth (whoopie!). One nice new feature is that you can run a more detailed search or a Search by Distance. This last feature is particularly handy for overcoming the traditional downside to online directories — that computer directories often take the city literally and don't list businesses in surrounding areas. With BigBook, you can get similar businesses up to 100 miles away from an address. You also can search for Canadian addresses.

Bigfoot

www.bigfoot.com

E-mail lookup service: Big, blue 3-D footprints walk all over the page. That's not the best part of Bigfoot, but it's pretty good. Of course, Bigfoot stakes its claim to the largest e-mail directory in cyberspace (yawn). You also can search for people, Web pages, and Yellow Pages. The e-mail directory fares pretty well on my acid test: myself. The interface is nice and simple, enabling you to search for e-mail addresses and postal addresses (white pages). The white page results come back alphabetized by state (you can't narrow down the state in advance on the home page, unfortunately, so if you're searching for somebody in Wyoming, you've got a lot of scrolling ahead of you) with a residential phone number and info on when the record was updated.

BigYellow

207.51.123.250

Yellow pages plus an e-mail directory: Like any self-respecting Internet directory, BigYellow claims to be the largest of its type, and it may be for all I know. Database size isn't as important with these services as a good interface and ease of use. BigYellow has made some recent

80 Phone Books and E-Mail Directories

changes to deal with the traditional online directory problem — that you can't view listings for an entire region, as you can with a real Yellow Pages book. Clicking the more search options link enables you to include a metropolitan area or specify neighborhoods or suburban areas that you want to search. Sounds a bit snobby, the latter option ("Charles, we're not going to THAT part of town, are we?"), but it's pretty handy for most of us. In real daily life, it's rare that you're unwilling to drive outside a small town to buy paint, for example, or a birthday present for your 5-year-old. Yet BigYellow delivers listings by town or state only, which is too narrow on one hand and too broad on the other. Oh well — complaints, complaints. BigYellow also offers a range of other services like e-mail lookup, Canadian searching, and even contests.

Four11

www.four11.com

Find old friends in cyberspace: No, that's not a typo; it's just one of the most bizarre names on the Web. Especially considering that Four11 has become a famous and much-used location service for long-lost acquaintances. The site has aspirations of being a one-stop search center for e-mail addresses, postal addresses, and business locations, but it's mostly known for locating old friends. It performs this desirable service by maintaining a database of the personal information of its members, and letting

you search through it. It encourages membership, of course, and joining is a good idea because the database is only as valuable as it is complete. Nobody can find *you* if you're not in it. The joining process consists of a bunch of questions and gives you a chance to fill in miscellaneous information about your past that may help someone you knew years ago locate you — for example, the high school or college you attended. Similarly, you can enter where you worked, what your hobbies and association connections have been, and other identifying characteristics of your twisting (not necessarily twisted) life path. On the other side of the fence, as a searcher, you can browse among all the listings that correspond to your college or an old job. It's a pretty great resource, and it gets better all the time as more people join up. And the site speaks a number of different languages.

Internet @ddress Finder

www.iaf.net

Look up e-mail addresses: Internet @ddress Finder (I@F) is the simplest of the people-finders. The search service isn't a white pages directory because it doesn't store postal addresses or telephone numbers. Internet @ddress Finder is also not a yellow pages. It has one mission in life, and one mission only: to locate e-mail addresses. Although I@F boasts of comprising almost 6 million listings in its database, the truth is that it has more trouble finding e-mail addresses than the other services reviewed in this section. I can't explain why, but it scored low on my brutal find-Brad-Hill's-addresses test. However, Internet @ddress Finder does have one unique feature that comes in handy: It searches people *according* to e-mail address. In other words, you type in the e-mail address, and I@F tells you the full name of its owner, plus a bit of other information (nothing juicy).

Switchboard

www.switchboard.com

Find people and then send them a post-card: Switchboard is a people and business finder that claims to be the largest directory of its kind on the Web. (Don't they all?) In fact, Switchboard is easy to use. Searching for someone requires only typing a last name, though the site provides fields for more specific information, like the first name and city. The results include an option to send the found person a card, which you type and Switchboard prints and sends via postal mail (for a price, of course). Switchboard isn't a white pages phone book put online; if you don't register, you don't appear in anyone's search results. Becoming a member is a simple matter of filling in your e-mail address, name, and postal address. The site does include a business search that functions like a yellow pages directory — you browse from a l-o-n-g drop-down menu of business categories and then type in a city location. The resulting listings include an icon for calling up a map.

WhoWhere?

www.whowhere.com

Track people down: That's a pretty evocative title for a Web site. It gets the point across. WhoWhere? tracks down people, with varying degrees of success, either by e-mail or phone and address. It now includes other services like postal addresses (when available); links to send greeting cards; contests; and a 3-D people search page, if your computer has the horsepower. Mine does, but the result — well, let's just say that the page is evolving and isn't as functional right now as the regular search page. Nevertheless, WhoWhere? has established itself as a major people-finding directory, perhaps because of its dead-simple basic interface. Still, simplicity breeds user-friendliness, and there's no way anybody

can get confused or lost on the WhoWhere? home page.

WorldPages

www.worldpages.com

Gigantic, international phone book: WorldPages has a big idea: Combine all the phone books in the world into one gigantic, hyperlinked site. The home page concentrates on the United States and Canada, but click the International Search link for a truly global perspective. Now, the grand ambition has limits. WorldPages doesn't try to provide a common interface for an entire planet of phone and fax numbers. In other words, the site has not created a global database of information (except for the United States and Canada), but it has *found* over 230 directories for more than 100 countries, and it provides links to them. The results can be mixed. Because you're literally clicking around the globe, you may encounter delays, broken sites, and language difficulties. Nevertheless, WorldPages is a tremendous resource. And for you business types, the site also enables you to search by *SIC* codes — numerical assignments designated by the U.S. Government to specify and categorize different types of businesses. In other words, if you can't find that potential client with a normal search, try the SIC code.

82 Phone Books and E-Mail Directories

Zip2 Yellow Pages

www.zip2.com

Yellow pages with memory: I like Zip2 Yellow Pages. Oh, there's nothing unusual about how it starts you off finding a yellow pages listing: You have your choice of typing a business name, typing a business type, or browsing through a directory of common business categories. It's what happens next that I like: Zip2 Yellow Pages asks for your home address, which it remembers, so that you can find stuff near you every time you visit. This feature turns the site into an interactive version of your local Yellow Pages book. If you enter only a state and zip code, you get broader search results than if you enter a city and street address, and I find that the best way to proceed. (Therefore, you must proceed that way, too. Everyone in the world needs to think exactly like me.) Upon selecting a listing, the site links you to a map or written directions — except the directions don't always work. But the map is nice because it can be enlarged or panned in eight directions.

Other Stuff to Check Out

decoder.americom.com
www.555-1212.com/aclookup.html
www.tollfree.att.net/dir800
www.usps.gov/ncsc

Part III
Research and Education

The 5th Wave   By Rich Tennant

"NOW, THAT WOULD SHOW HOW IMPORTANT IT IS TO DISTINGUISH 'FERTILIZING PRACTICES' FROM 'FERTILITY PRACTICES' WHEN DOWNLOADING A VIDEO FILE FROM THE INTERNET."

In this part . . .

From science to politics, health to history, there's a lot to learn in this world. And although you may be able to find a better way to educate than by surfing the World Wide Web, the Internet encompasses an extraordinary range of learning opportunities. You just need to find them. This part is designed to get you started on the right foot (or the left foot, if you prefer) when you're ready to start learning stuff on the Web.

Genealogy

Looking for your ancestral roots on a medium less than a decade old seems rather odd, but genealogy is one of the hottest topics on the World Wide Web. Literally thousands of commercial and reference pages exist to help you in your search for ancestors — and that doesn't even count the thousands of personal sites people have put up with pages titled something like "My family tree."

The following pages are just a sampling of the many Web resources available for genealogists. If you want to dig deeper into your background, an excellent resource is *Genealogy Online For Dummies,* by Matthew L. Helm and April Leigh Helm (IDG Books Worldwide, Inc.).

Family Tree Maker

www.familytreemaker.com

Software and valuable sites: Understand right up front that Family Tree Maker is a software product marketed by Broderbund (one of many genealogy software packages available), and you won't be surprised by how many pages at this site tout the software's advantages. Beyond the commercialism, however, Family Tree Maker has some very valuable free features. Click the Family-Finding Tools link on the front page, and

you're transported to a page with links to the Social Security Death Index, a valuable resource that enables you to track down death records of U.S. residents through their Social Security number; the Genealogy SiteFinder, which has links to some 43,000 Web sites in a directory-style format; and many others. You can, of course, buy the software at the site, but you can also explore a wealth of resources for free just by visiting Family Tree Maker.

GeneaNet: Genealogical Database Network

www.geneanet.org

Search online for surnames: The goal of GeneaNet is simple — to use the Internet's capabilities to build a database indexing all the world's genealogical resources. The resources that GeneaNet focuses on are families studied by genealogists, genealogical publications, manuscripts from libraries and archives, and official sources, such as church registers and government files like deeds. At the time of this writing, GeneaNet had 3.6 million entries and could be accessed in five languages besides English. GeneaNet offers three different ways to search, the easiest being a quick search right from the home page. Simply type in the surname of the individual you seek information on, hit Search, and GeneaNet returns a chart with information about the record (surname, record dates, region, and so on) *and* a link to the record. You can also search a specific country's records by clicking the appropriate flag on the home page, or do an advanced search, which requires free registration.

86 Global Cultures

The National Archives of Canada

www.archives.ca

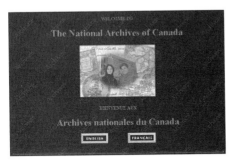

Canadian records and memories: Government records are an important source of information to genealogists, because things like wills and deeds document the kind of who, where, and when information that's so vital to family trees. This site is the online component of The National Archives of Canada, and the site's creators recognize the usefulness of their information to genealogists. Once you get to the title page (by clicking either English or Français on the home page), you find a convenient Genealogy Research listing. Clicking that takes you to an extremely helpful page with a "How to get started" link right at the top. The page also includes tips for using museum resources to do research, and — most importantly — online links to Genealogical Resources in Canada, including Census Records, Wills and Estate Records, Immigration Records, and the like. Other governments also have such information online, but Canada deserves credit for organizing them so conveniently for genealogists.

Other Stuff to Check Out

home.vicnet.net.au/~AGWeb/agweb.htm
www.gendex.com/gendex
www.genhomepage.com
www.iigs.org
www.usigs.org/index.htm

Global Cultures

www.halcon.com/halcon/1ring.html

The Internet is the most international, nation-spanning, global-village-conducive force at the disposal of the common person. Given that fact, you'd think that the Internet would offer a wealth of information about world cultures. In fact, two things mitigate against your seeing a great deal of cultural content on the Web. First, mainstream tastes and priorities prevail on the Net as in other media; most people are interested in entertainment, sports, and news. Second, despite all the global potential, the Net is still primarily an American phenomenon, with U.S. sites comprising most of the content on the World Wide Web.

Nevertheless, you can get a great deal of information about other countries, other lifestyles, and other cultures, sometimes presented with great flair, imagination, and beauty. This section points you toward some of the best sites.

Global Culture Presentations

The following sites represent a broad selection of global culture. My main criteria in selecting these sites are quality of design and information-worthiness, at the expense of methodically documenting every culture on the Web.

African-American Mosaic

lcweb.loc.gov/exhibits/african/
intro.html

African American history and culture: One of a series of Library of Congress (LOC) sites, African-American Mosaic shares the sense of care and comprehensiveness that characterizes the LOC's work on the Internet. The site is a Web version of a recently published resource guide for the study of black history and culture, and in Library of Congress tradition, it doesn't leave anything out. Primarily an illustrated historical text (and a long, multiple-page one), the Mosaic attains true greatness through the hyperlink enhancements that connect its areas with other parts of the Library of Congress Web locations. African-American Mosaic is a real cultural gift on the Web.

The Afro American Web Ring

www.halcon.com/halcon/1ring.html

Linked sites of interest to African Americans: Called a "ring" because the sites in the ring form a chain that eventually links back to the home page, The Afro American Web Ring is an eclectic group of personal and commercial pages. The link for the entire list is hard to find (it's the word "here" in the third paragraph), but the list displays 20 links at a time, with short descriptions. The AAWR also has a navigation menu that you can find about halfway down the home page; use it to go to the previous page or next page in the ring, or to see links for the previous five or next five pages in the ring. (Bad news: The five-link pages offer no descriptions

whatsoever.) However you choose to navigate, you'll find a lot of pages in the link — 988 on my visit, everything from virtual shrines to famous people (such as supermodel Tyra Banks) to personal pages to genealogy pages for African Americans. The site also touts a search engine called — I am not making this up — "Soul Search," but it wasn't working during my last visit.

Note: If you like the ring concept, you can find more rings at www.webring.com.

Asiaweek Online

www.pathfinder.com/
@@9zCX6kA3RAIAQFsz/Asiaweek/

The online edition of Asiaweek *magazine:* Asiaweek Online, the virtual edition of *Asiaweek* magazine (a Time Warner publication), contains every bit of content from the printed magazine. It covers political and cultural news in India, Taiwan, Indonesia, North and South Korea, Cambodia, and other Asian nations. A Newsmap feature enables you to navigate the week's news by country. From movie reviews to Asian stock-market reports, from books to currency issues, Asiaweek Online covers the bases in its coverage of Asian news.

Celtic Net

www.majestictech.com/the-celtic-net/

Gaelic and Scottish culture: Celtic Net charms you right off by playing an Irish jig in MIDI format (if you have the Crescendo plug-in) on its home page. Celtic music, in fact, is a special focus of this site, devoting a page to bagpipes and other pages to highlighting traditional bands. The site provides a history of the Scottish tartan (useful if you have no idea what a tartan is) and a directory of Scottish clans (indispensable if you've misplaced your own directory). A nod to Highland dancing and a Gaelic dictionary round out the site. Some of the explanatory material is original writing, and in some cases, the links take you to other sites.

Cultural Bridge Productions

www.culturalbridge.com

Essays on world cultures: When you're in the mood for a good intercultural read, head over to Cultural Bridge Productions. Formatted as a travelogue and emphasizing Asian cultures, the site consists of several lengthy articles describing ventures into Japan, China, Thailand, Malaysia, and a few other locales. Not a practical travel site in the slightest, the text rhapsodizes (sometimes amusingly) about native culture from the viewpoint of daily life. The essays are liberally illustrated with embedded pictures. The organization could be a little clearer; each country has several associated pages and several feature departments, but the only way to access everything is to scroll through the pages sequentially. That linear design, which ignores the random-access quality of the Internet, makes Cultural Bridge Productions a better site for leisurely browsing than for dedicated searching.

Dolce Vita

www.dolcevita.com

Italian travel, cuisine, and culture: This beautiful site offers a variety of travel tips but is more than just another globe-trotting site. Dolce Vita documents the culture and lifestyle of Italy through pages devoted to cuisine, fashion, design, and art. Most of the information is related to visiting Italian cities and sites, but Dolce Vita is a cultural education even for nontravelers. Check out the Wine & Cuisine page for seasonal recipes and tutorials on Italian wines.

Flags of the Native Peoples of the United States

users.aol.com/Donh523/navapage/
    index.html

Photos and histories of Native American flags: This site is pretty much what its name says that it is: pictures of Native American tribal and national flags. Created by the North American Vexillological Association (*vexillology* is the study of flags), the site is more than just a gallery of flag photos — although such a gallery would be interesting by itself. Each flag is accompanied by a history of the tribe, nation, or confederacy, replete with details on tribal characteristics and geographical locations. The site amounts to a tutorial overview of Native American people and traditions.

The Island

www.paddynet.com/island/index.html

Irish visitor information: Which island? Ireland. The home page of this informative site starts with a Gaelic quote: "Fáilte chuig an Oileán!" Roughly translated, that quote means "Faulty chugs in the oil!" (Think twice before believing my translations.) The Island covers Irish topics as broad as history and mythology, and as specific as local geography and attractions. Some pages are wonderfully illustrated with ink-drawn maps. The Ancient Sites (not referring to encrusted Web sites) page brings attention to Newgrange, which usually takes second place to Stonehenge in popular attention. The Island is a wonderful Web site with a modest demeanor.

Jewish Culture and History

www.igc.apc.org/ddickerson/
　　judaica.html

Global Jewish culture: This page is an excellent resource for finding a wide range of Web sites concerned with Jewish culture. The long, mostly textual home page offers a tremendous wealth of links, with full descriptions, and deserves a bookmark on the list of anyone who is interested in global Jewish tradition. The only other pages present images of synagogues in Poland — beautiful photographs. Audio files provide a surprising multimedia touch by sounding the blast of a shofar and a cry of "Shalom!"

Shtetl: Yiddish Language and Culture

sunsite.unc.edu/yiddish/shtetl.html

Yiddish culture: One of the coolest features of this site is the Yiddish-Hebrew-English-German-Russian dictionary, which defines words in all languages (from an English list) by displaying a picture of the word and placing translations around the graphic. Naturally, given this space-consuming format, the site doesn't include many words. The rest of the site is a collection of links and Jewish cultural information, ranging from synagogue histories to archives of personal letters from pre–World War II Poland.

The Web of Culture

www.worldculture.com/index.html

World cultures: The Web of Culture takes a categorical approach to the world's cultures. The home page lists 28 categories ranging from cuisine to religion, and then offers a hodgepodge of information on each topic. I wouldn't call this site an encyclopedia by any means — you never know what you're going to get in each category. But that's part of the charm. You can check the local currency for most countries; find an embassy or consulate in the U.S.; see schedules of holidays in different countries; and even submit an e-mail question to the site, which is a nice interactive opportunity for kids.

World Culture

www.wsu.edu:8080/~dee

World-culture courses online: World Culture is a modern production of Washington State University in the United States, but it covers peoples and countries around the world. The site was designed primarily as "an Internet classroom and anthology." If you're interested in the former, registration information is available; however, anyone with the desire to broaden their cultural knowledge may appreciate the depth of material World Culture offers. Click the Contents link, and you'll find learning "modules," an anthology of readings, a glossary of world cultures, full-color atlases, and links to other Internet resources. The modules include both general topics ("What Is Culture?") and specific world cultures. Say your interest is China. World Culture has modules devoted to "Ancient China," "The Chinese Empire: From the Ch'in to the Yuan," "Ming China," "Ch'ing China," "Modern China," and "Chinese Philosophical Traditions." The people behind World Culture have even grander designs for the future; given what they've accomplished already, this is a site to watch.

Other Stuff to Check Out

dolphin.upenn.edu/~vision
www.ai.mit.edu/~isbell/HFh/black/
  bhcal-toc.html
www.blacknet.co.uk/index.htm
www.cs.org

Global Culture Resource Directories

The sites in this section focus on directing you to other sites that document global cultures rather than providing that information themselves. These sites are specialized directories to cultural and ethnic resources on the Internet.

Asian American Resources

**www.mit.edu/afs/athena.mit.edu/user/
  i/r/irie/www/aar.html**

Lists of Asian-American Web sites: A strange outer-space page design graces the Asian American Resources site, but that design doesn't detract from the usefulness of the directory. This site directs you through lengthy lists of Web links in a few broad categories, including Organizations, Media, and Personal Home Pages. Each category has a few subdivisions, but the subdivisions don't make

reading the yellow-on-black text any easier. Still, fried retinas are a small price to pay for the best selection of Asian-American sites on the Web.

Index of Native American Resources on the Internet

**hanksville.phast.umass.edu/misc/
  NAresources.html**

Lists of sites on Native American culture: This fine directory of Native American culture Web sites is divided into a few general topics: Culture, Language, History, Health, Education, and Indigenous Knowledge. Within those lists — particularly the Indigenous Knowledge category — lie some of the most fascinating Native American sites in cyberspace. A large Native American Art category contains numerous subcategories dedicated to cultural expression, each containing an exhaustive list of links. Anyone interested in Native American heritage should bookmark this astonishing directory.

LatinoWeb

www.latinoweb.com

Lots of info on Latino culture: LatinoWeb has a tidy appearance that belies its deep resourcefulness. Set up like a directory (primarily because it *is* a directory), LatinoWeb directs viewers to categories like Art, Book Stores, Business, Education, Music, Personal Pages, and other divisions of Latino Web pages on the Net. Further, the site makes a play for community with its own chat room; you have to register and sign in, but it's free. This specialized directory gets extra points for covering basic Internet sites like search engines and software download sites.

Other Stuff to Check Out

resi.tamu.edu/bright.html
heather.cs.ucdavis.edu/pub/README.html
oss.ufl.edu/lacasita
www.indiana.edu/~aaamc/index.html
www.ollusa.edu/alumni/alumni/latino/
    latinoh1.htm

Health

Health is a topic that just about everyone's interested in. The Internet is an information phenomenon that meshes perfectly with the modern trend of taking personal responsibility for your own health and empowering yourself with freely available knowledge. A schism has developed in the health field over the past 20 years, separating mainstream medical treatments from so-called alternative or holistic treatments. Holistic medicine ranges from chiropractic (which has gained some mainstream acceptance) to acupuncture, dietary healing, and even esoteric modalities such as aromatherapy and healing meditation. Accordingly, I divide this section into sites that deal primarily with medical awareness and sites that focus on alternative and self-treatment.

Alternative and Holistic Health

The holistic health movement is based on the principles of self-awareness and noninvasive treatment of conditions. Most practitioners advocate staying healthy through proactive dietary and lifestyle choices. The following sites embrace holistic principles to one degree or another.

Alternative Medicine Digest

www.alternativemedicine.com

Online digest of journals: Alternative Medicine Digest is a printed magazine that scours many journals of alternative treatment and then summarizes the current news for readers. The virtual edition runs the same content as the magazine, plus an assortment of features that are unique to the Internet, such as community boards, chat rooms, and online shopping. Feature articles run the gamut from research pieces to anecdotal healing experiences; medical doctors primarily write the columns. Regular departments include Natural Pharmacy, The Healing Grocery, Alternative Pet Care, The Politics of Medicine, and Prescribing for Yourself.

Ask Dr. Weil

cgi.pathfinder.com/drweil/

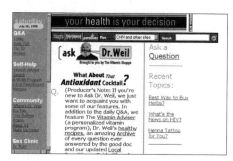

Q & A with Dr. Andrew Weil: Dr. Andrew Weil — he of the gigantically bushy beard, best-selling books, and talent for explaining medicine appealingly — made his first Internet splash on the Hotwired site, where he answered uploaded questions daily. He has since moved to the Pathfinder site, where he performs the same affable and valuable service. Every weekday, a new question (it could be yours!) is posted to the doctor, who answers by blending his medical expertise with a holistic sensibility. His responses often recommend natural remedies and are usually informed by an awareness of vitamins, minerals, and (sometimes) herbs. At the same time, Weil is thoroughly grounded in mainstream medical reality, and this blend of mainstream and alternative medicine is what makes him so appealing to many people. Ask Dr. Weil archives all the question-and-answer sessions, making the site a treasure of wisdom on a multitude of health subjects.

Holistic Internet Resources

www.hir.com

Overview of holistic medicine: Many Web sites are dedicated to various forms of holistic therapy — acupuncture, yoga, vegetarianism, and others — but precious few sites offer a comprehensive overview of holistic medicine. Holistic Internet Resources is a start. The Internet Resources section of the site is actually less important, in my opinion, than the Articles and Book Reviews portion, where you can link quickly to explanations of various holistic healing modalities and read brief reviews of a wide range of publications. The site could use more of both articles and reviews, but again, it's a start. You should also check out the Holistic Internet Community, undergoing some changes at the time of this writing, but available at www.holistic.com.

Planet Health

www.planet-health.com

Alternative/holistic health resources: Planet Health aspires to be the deepest health resource site on the Internet, and although quantitative judgments like that one are hard to verify, this site certainly is a must-bookmark site. The Health News section sports health-related headlines that link to full stories on preventive and crisis medicine and research. Another section, LifeView Health Appraisal, is a health-assessment questionnaire that formulates a customized list of sites that are relevant to your condition. Real Life Resources is a compilation of offline resources for reaching preventive goals such as quitting smoking, losing weight, reducing stress, and eating better. Finally, an online resource guide features a dedicated Health Explorer search engine. Planet Health is well rounded and broadly useful.

WellnessWeb

wellweb.com

A robust site emphasizing preventive medicine: WellnessWeb has been called one of the best 100 sites of all time and, furthermore, one of the five best in the health arena. This site lives up to its soaring reputation by connecting health professionals with regular folks who are interested in learning more about their own health, and then binding the whole thing together with articles, columns, message boards, and a loose organization that encourages bookmarking multiple pages. The site is much larger than it appears when you first glance at the modest home page. Dig deep into the research and reference sections, or spin off into one of the three main site divisions: Alternative/Complementary

Medicine, Conventional Medicine, and Nutrition/Fitness. You can't surf away from WellnessWeb without having learned something — and without wanting to return soon.

Other Stuff to Check Out

cybertowers.com/selfhelp/index.html
www.ivanhoe.com
www.womencare.com
www.worldguide.com/Fitness/hf.html
www2.healthyback.com

Mainstream and Medical Health

When the chips are down, most people rely on the established medical community to diagnose and treat illness. Generally, mainstream medicine is geared toward healing ailing conditions instead of maintaining healthy conditions, but preventive medicine is gaining ground. In addition to institutional sites, this section includes some health-news sites that cover primarily mainstream issues.

American Cancer Society

www.cancer.org/frames.html

Information on the ACS and on cancer: The American Cancer Society (ACS) has a broadly utilitarian site that provides information, hope, and resources for anyone who is touched by cancer. Anyone who is seeking detailed answers to difficult questions about specific cancers would do better elsewhere on the Internet and certainly offline. Much of the space and tone of this site are taken up with self-promotion. The ACS lauds the progress made in cancer research and treatment during this century, and it presents information with a positive spin designed to encourage donations and

membership. Some detailed information *is* available about ACS programs, events, and the research gains of the past year in particular cancers.

CNN Health

cnn.com/HEALTH/index.html

Links to CNN health-news stories: If you seek the broadest possible approach to medical and health news, you can't do better than CNN Health, which delivers objective journalism on every aspect of health and sickness. Following the tried-and-true headline-link method, the main portion of the site is strictly a news source that dishes up stories as they break, regardless of the subject. One new bonus: an In-Depth Information list that enables you to seek information on particular afflictions. Well illustrated with photographs, CNN Health doesn't dabble much with other types of multimedia. Like other portions of the CNN online universe, the site's stories are enhanced by embedded links that lead to background or related information.

Go Ask Alice

www.goaskalice.columbia.edu

Alice rules: Go Ask Alice, the central feature of Columbia University's Healthwise Web site, is a database of questions and answers on all sorts of health conditions. Alice, a fictional computer character, responds at great length — and with surprising wit and style — to selected questions. You can enter your own query at the bottom of the Ask Alice! page and then search the database to see whether the question has already been answered. Searching first and asking later probably is better, actually, because almost any question that you can think of is in the database. Questions in seven areas — sexuality, sexual health, relationships, alcohol and other drugs, fitness and nutrition, emotional well-being, and general health — are accessible by clicking the appropriate home page icon. If you do search, try a single keyword; in many cases, you get multiple results to simple searches. Each response is almost an article of valuable information, making Healthwise (and dear Alice) a veritable encyclopedia of health knowledge.

Mayo Clinic Health O@sis

www.mayohealth.org

Health news and resources: One of the foremost medical clinics in the world has done a fine job of creating a Web site that delivers both general health news and resources on specific conditions. As such, Mayo Clinic Health O@sis is one of the best health sites on the Net. You can search the site by keyword, use the online glossary, and even shop in the virtual store, but the Resources sections (nine of them, each of which essentially comprises a miniature site) are the site's anchor. Each Resource area — O@sis Library; Allergy & Asthma Center, Alzheimer's Center, Cancer Center, Diet & Nutrition, Heart Center, Pregnancy & Children, Medicine Center, and Women's Health — includes such things as reference articles, links to other relevant Web sites, a quiz, and an invitation to ask a question of a Mayo medical staff member. The answers to questions are posted and archived on the site. A free e-mail newsletter, *Housecall,* is available; just provide your name and e-mail address. Mayo Clinic Health O@sis is a channel for Microsoft Explorer Version 4.0.

Men's Health

www.menshealth.com/index.html

Online edition of Men's Health *magazine:* Men's Health is a magazine for men whose idea of health is glistening abs and a strong sex drive. Well, that description may be an oversimplification, but male beauty and persuasive power over the opposite sex certainly play large roles in the publication's editorial content. The cover of the June 1998 issue pictures a buff model taking his shirt off to flash those pecs, which pretty much represents the editorial ideal of male health. But don't get me wrong; as the magazine says in its tag line, the online version features "tons of useful stuff," including a question-and-answer column that invites you to ask a question about a health concern. Daily Tips is another virtual column that centers on fitness and is archived for rewarding browsing of past tips.

Mental Health Net

www.cmhc.com

Directory of online mental-health resources: For professionals and laypeople alike, Mental Health Net is an impressive resource for searching or browsing. The site is a highly categorized directory of Internet sites dealing with various types of mental, psychological, and personality disorders; it offers a smattering of current news headlines on the side. Particularly impressive are the resource links for professionals, which contain an astounding number of links, all of which are reviewed and described. Throughout the site, you're invited to vote on the quality of any link that you find. One thing is for certain: You won't have trouble finding links. The creators of this site scoured every part of the Internet (including newsgroups and mailing lists) for relevant resources.

Women's Health

www.nytimes.com/women

The New York Times site on women's health issues: Women's Health, a Web production of *The New York Times,* has a staid, almost gray, journalistic style. Within the site's hallowed cyberhalls, though, you're treated to a learning experience enhanced by good organization and classy cross-referencing, which generally results in your finding more than you expected to. One of the best features is located at the top right of the home page, where you find a drop-down list of 29 health conditions, such as arthritis, high cholesterol, and depression. Each option leads to a page of information and resources that are presented from a woman's viewpoint but that in fact contain knowledge of interest to everyone. A Bookshelf section (for which you may have to use a link on a secondary page) enables you to browse current health titles, and the Resources link leads to an annotated guide to dozens of other Web sites.

Women's Health Interactive

www.womens-health.com

A friendly, interactive place for women to discuss health: I don't know why Web publishers don't seem to care about the health of men, but the fact is that women's health is much better represented on the Internet, and both of the women's health sites that I review (the

other is called Women's Health, also in this section) are too good to leave out. Women's Health Interactive is more of a community than Women's Health, although less journalistic. This site strives to be highly interactive, as the name implies, with questionnaires designed to assess your gynecological condition (men: don't bother). Online conferences with medical experts are features, as are e-mail discussion groups. A detailed registration process is encouraged but not necessary before you browse the informational parts of the site or participate in the assessments.

Your Health Daily

yourhealthdaily.com

News and message boards: Your Health Daily is primarily a news service, but it makes an attempt to attain community with the inclusion of message boards. The home page lists current health headlines. This site was the first health-news Web site (to my knowledge) to break the story of digital X-rays in August 1997. For a real browsing experience, go straight to the Health Topics link and choose among the 23 health subjects under which past articles are archived. Choosing Sexual Health, for example, delivers recent articles on every aspect of the subject, ranging from HIV to self-treatment of yeast infections in women. Choose Elderly to read news about a regenerating gene clone or an article about geriatric care. The real benefits of Your Health Daily are quick access to these back articles and organization that makes the site rewarding to browse.

Other Stuff to Check Out

www.comed.com/empower/welcome.spml
www.intelihealth.com
www.lycos.com/health
www.medscape.com
www.priory.com
www.psynet.com
www.shapeup.org/sua

I'll be honest with you — history is not the most ragingly popular topic on the Web. (I won't tell you what topic is, but you can probably guess.) Most people, besides history hobbyists, probably don't want to be reminded of their terrible school days, during which history was the most lifeless class in the world. The topic has little commercial potential, which keeps corporations out of the picture. So the historical pages that exist on the Net are produced by history buffs who are expressing their hobby online and by foundations whose job is to lose money putting up Web sites that most people won't look at.

The thing is, however, that some of these sites are absolutely among the best things on the World Wide Web — beautifully produced, educational, and (dare I suggest it?) even fun to browse. I include this section in the book to save you the trouble of scratching around for the best history sites, which you probably never would have done anyway. So get to work — tomorrow I'm giving you a quiz.

American Memory

rs6.loc.gov/amhome.html

U.S. history: A production of the Library of Congress in cooperation with numerous private partners and contributors, American Memory is one of the most worthwhile history and educational sites on the World Wide Web. A virtual, interactive, multimedia museum of American tradition, history, and lore, American Memory is beautiful to look at, easy to use, and filled with impressive surprises. Searching or browsing by exhibit title, topic, library division, or type of multimedia display, any visitor is likely to be stunned by the depth and care with which this collection was assembled. You'd do well to click the Sound Recordings or Motion Pictures link for collections of historical audio and video playback programs. A couple of the more spectacular recent additions include a history of Northern California folk music from the 1930s and the Spanish-American War in motion pictures. Plug-ins are a must for getting the most from this site, but you can find plenty to read, too. No short review can convey the scope and value of this site; even a casual history buff is greatly rewarded by visiting it.

Archiving Early America

earlyamerica.com

Archive of 18th-century American documents: Rarely are historical subjects presented with such flair and humor on the Web as they are on the Archiving Early America site. If you want to start your exploration with a laugh, click Enter the World of Early America and then go to the How to Read a 200-Year-old Document link, which amusingly explains the substitution of *f* for *s* in many old printed documents. A scrolling banner on the home page tells you what happened on the current date in the 18th century, lending an ironically up-to-the-minute quality to this archive of the antique.

Message boards are divided into moderated discussion forums. The site's strongest quality lies in its valuable digital archives of source material — original newspapers, maps, and writings — from the 18th century. You can display newspaper articles written by George Washington on your monitor. I can think of no other site that does a better job of bringing history to life with the help of the Internet.

The '80s Server

www.80s.com

Review of the 1980s: History doesn't have to be old history, does it? Besides, the 1980s seem to be a long time ago as the world approaches the new millennium. The '80s Server is a thorough, detailed romp through the 1980s. The home page asks you to choose between a fast or slow path; my recommendation, if you have a fast modem and computer, is to take the fast route. The straight text menu of the slow page is just so bogus! This comprehensive site covers just about every aspect of 1980s life, from sports to money to movies. Surprisingly, this site charges a subscription membership (for about $5 per month), for which you get free e-mail (remember, you already have e-mail if you're logging onto the Internet from home) and access to the 80s Jukebox — an admittedly cool feature. Nonsubscribers can still access some of the features; click the Inside Skinny text link near the

bottom of the home page for a page that shows you what's free and what isn't. The best place for subscribers to start on this busy site: Megalibrary.

1492: An Ongoing Voyage

sunsite.unc.edu/expo/1492.exhibit/
  Intro.html

Commemoration of the discovery of America: This virtual exhibit is produced by the Library of Congress, reflecting the library's ongoing commitment to put historical displays on the World Wide Web. This particular exhibit is less of a multimedia extravaganza than some other Library of Congress sites are; it basically consists of long stretches of text illustrated, to a moderate degree, by photographs. The narrative, which begins long before Columbus made his voyage, describes the pre-Columbus cultures of North and Middle America, and then swings over to Spain and the Caribbean world, documenting life in the 15th century. Finally, the Christopher Columbus: Man and Myth section takes you through the European claim on North America. A detailed outline of the site's contents provides links to each portion and subchapter.

Grolier's World War II Commemoration

www.grolier.com/wwii/
  wwii_mainpage.html

War history: With content taken from the *Encyclopedia Americana,* the World War II Commemoration site is a complete multimedia history of the great war. The main article is divided into four large sections, including a gallery of photographs and an archive of air combat films. After absorbing the text, you can take a 25-question test — which, fortunately, is not required. A section of World War II Web links rounds out the site. Admittedly a bit on the dry side, this site provides one of the best histories of the seminal event of the 20th century on the Net. Grolier's is not a free site overall, but you can access this entire commemoration without charge, and boy, is it worth it.

The History Channel

www.historychannel.com

History is the greatest show of all at The History Channel: The History Channel Web site tries to put the fun back into history, probably in recognition of the fact that fun was painfully extracted from the history learning process for most people. The Fun & Games section does this directly, recently offering to let viewers uncover the secrets of a pharaoh's tomb. You don't even have to ask your mummy! The Great Speeches section and the This Day in History link transport you back in time through audio and video clips. One recent day featured U.S. President Franklin D. Roosevelt's speech to Congress the day after the Pearl Harbor attack, and a video clip of Nelson Mandela during the South African leader's fight against Apartheid. The history store offers online shopping, primarily for historical videos, and message boards enable you to meet other history buffs. As expected, you can look up the broadcast schedule for The History Channel cable network.

History Net

www.TheHistoryNet.com

★★ ★★

A browser's paradise: Probably the best all-around history site on the Web, History Net displays a front page that immediately makes clear that the site contains too much information to absorb in any one sitting. Some of the main sections are World History; American

History; Personality Profiles; Great Battles; Arms, Armies, and Intrigue; Interviews; Aviation and Technology; and Homes & Heritage. The site is updated weekly, with new features coming online for each update. A site map and search engine are available (thank goodness!). Message boards with predetermined topics provide a forum for meeting other history mavens. Keep in mind that History Net doesn't attempt to provide a sequential or comprehensive version of any nation's history; rather, it displays articles and feature presentations. The site is a hobby page, more suitable for browsing than for serious research.

Library of Congress

marvel.loc.gov

Historical research: Although one spin-off site of the Library of Congress, American Memory, is reviewed in this section and another (Thomas) is reviewed in the Politics section, you shouldn't miss out on the overall LOC site. Even if you check out only the Exhibitions section, which has permanent virtual displays on the African-American Mosaic; Declaring Independence: Drafting the Documents; Scrolls from the Dead Sea; architect and designer Frank Lloyd Wright; and other subjects, the experience is worthwhile. The site is an astonishing resource — the kind of site that justifies the entire Internet. You also can access a raft of research services from (no surprise) the Research Tools section. All the sections and spin-off sites, including American Memory and Thomas, have indexed drop-down lists of their tables of contents on the Library of Congress home page, making this site one of the most intelligently organized Web sites.

Museum of London

www.museum-london.org.uk

museum of
LONDON

Welcome to the Museum of London,
the largest, most comprehensive city
museum
in the world, telling the fascinating
story
of London from prehistoric times to
the
present day.

500,000 YEARS IN THE MAKING

Ancient to modern London history:
Advertised as having been 500,000 years
in the making, the Museum of London
attempts to track the city's history from
prehistoric times to the present. Perhaps
the real museum does exactly that, but
the online galleries have a more modest
scope. Angling into London history
through children, entertainers, traffic,
and other aspects of daily life, the site's
exhibits use text and photography to
document changes in lifestyle and urban
development over the past couple of
centuries. The site is beautifully designed, although the graphics are heavy
enough to cause some delays, especially
for American netizens.

National Archives and Records Administration

www.nara.gov

Government documents: National Archives
and Records Administration (NARA) is
the government agency that stores and
ensures the accessibility of essential
national records. "Where should I put the
Marshall Plan?" "I know — let's create an
agency with a difficult-to-pronounce
name!" That's basically how the site got
started. But the whole thing sounds drier
than it really is, and the NARA site is a
great historical trip — especially if you
spin off to the Online Exhibit Hall. One
recently featured exhibit was *When Nixon
Met Elvis,* which is a far cry from viewing
a dusty copy of the Marshall Plan. A
Research Room is for more serious
endeavors, while The Digital Classroom

offers material and sample lesson plans
for teachers. The online gift shop displays
souvenir merchandise but sells it only
over the phone.

Smithsonian Institution

www.si.edu

*History of the Smithsonian and the United
States:* The Smithsonian Institution site
conveys as much of the institution's own
150-year history as anything else, but that
amounts to a general history of the
United States. The site ladles out self-
promotion with a big spoon, but it also
includes drop-down menu links that bring
the vast Smithsonian-related resources to
your computer. For example, you can
check out Smithsonian's fabulous
AIR&SPACE magazine from the site, or
learn about the Mpala Research Centre in
Kenya. The rich site is a delightful place
to spend a few hours exploring the past.

Other Stuff to Check Out

library.byu.edu/~rdh/eurodocs
lists.village.virginia.edu/sixties
sunsite.utk.edu/civil-war
www.americanheritage.com
www.currenthistory.com
www.english.upenn.edu/~jlynch/18th
www.historyplace.com
www.jcu.edu.au/aff/history
wwwsun.redstone.army.mil/history/
   women.html

Homework Sites

ENCARTA.
online

Aprende algo
nuevo hoy!

Click here for English *(North American)*
Click here for English *(World)*
Klicken Sie hier für Deutsch
Haga clic aquí para español
Cliquez ici pour le français
Clicca qui per l'italiano
日本語
Klik hier voor nederlands

encarta.msn.com/LanguageChoice.asp

100 Homework Sites

The classroom extends onto the Internet in the form of homework sites that help kids with research issues or actually provide answers. Most homework sites focus on math or science, but I unearthed some English, social studies, and literature sites. When you think about it, homework sites are beneficial in two ways: Such sites not only encourage resourcefulness on the part of children, but also teach kids about computers and the Internet.

Question-and-answer sites are the most popular form of Web-based homework helpers. Some of the following sites provide bare facts, however; others are primarily link sites that point to other research stations on the Net.

Ask Dr. Math

**forum.swarthmore.edu/dr.math/
dr-math.html**

Math help for students ages 5 to 18: Dr. Math is a landmark homework-helper site on the Web, furnishing problem-solving assistance for kids between the ages of 5 and 18. (A new section of the site answers questions at the college level and beyond.) Anybody can send a question to Dr. Math, and the answers are added to the archive. Produced by Swarthmore College, the site provides answers that are authoritative and trustworthy, and includes explanations about *how* the answers are reached. Browsing the archive is an education in itself, even if you don't have a specific problem that needs solving. The site is set up as a directory. You first choose a broad age group and then choose among a list of topics — Algebra, Calculus, Addition, and so on. A list of submitted questions is displayed; you click one to see the answer. The service accepts all types of math questions, from specific equation queries to general requests for explanations of math terms. The answers are generally encouraging and clear.

B. J. Pinchbeck's Homework Helper

tristate.pgh.net/~pinch13/

Subject resources: Bruce Pinchbeck (B. J., or Beege) is a 10-year-old who, with his father, scoured the Internet for good homework sites. Compared to the 6th Grade Brain Bank, which invites viewers to pitch in with their favorite links, this site is much more formal, professional, even verging on commercial (it has its own sponsors), and, I might add, much more comprehensive. The link lists that B. J. and his dad organized are awesome. Set up as a directory, the site lists several main topics: Reference, News and Current Events, Math, Science, Social Studies, English, History, Computers and the Internet, Foreign Languages (non-English, that is), and Music and Art. The actual links weigh in at between 50 and 120 per topic. Each link is described in a single sentence — enough to give you the gist of a site's content before you link over to it.

Britannica Online

www.eb.com

$

Online version of the Encyclopedia Britannica: The famous *Encyclopedia Britannica* reproduces all its content in an online format at this site, for an experience that is truly . . . well, encyclopedic. Unfortunately, the site isn't free. Britannica Online is one of the few learning Web sites that charges a monthly subscription rate, but it also offers a free trial period. If your children get hooked during the free trial (or if you do), you may have to fork over the subscription fee to feed the learning habit. A subscription may be worth the cost, especially if you don't have an encyclopedia in book form. Britannica Online doesn't jazz up its articles with multimedia features; because the encyclopedia is the world's best-known text authority on world knowledge, perhaps the editors feel that it doesn't need extra sheen online. But Britannica Online does go all out for its Spotlight Archive features, which can be accessed from the home page. Two recent offerings were a deep examination of the June 1944 D-Day invasion at Normandy, complete with radio broadcasts and newsreels, and a photograph- and information-rich exhibit on the *Titanic*.

Encarta Online

encarta.msn.com

State-of-the-Net virtual schoolhouse: The Encarta Online site is the online version of the famous Encarta interactive encyclopedia from Microsoft. The first thing you tell Encarta is which of the eight languages (including two versions of English) you want the information in; after that, to borrow a well-worn Microsoft advertising slogan, it's "Where do you want to go today?" The site's three main links are Explorer, where students can delve into the topic of the day (oceanography, during my last visit); Schoolhouse, which offers resources for teachers; and Find, which enables you to search for information straight from the Encarta database. The site is graphically rich but manages to display without much delay. You have to look just a little bit more to find the link to the Encarta Online Library, a professional-level research site containing almost a million articles from diverse sources. The Online Library charges a subscription price, but the rest of the site is free. If you know someone who just remembered that they have a term paper due tomorrow, Encarta Online is a good place to start. Right now.

Grasshopper

members.aol.com/eduscience/
    index.html

Science-site resources: Grasshopper helps kids hop over to science sites on and off the Web. Not, strictly speaking, a homework-answer site, Grasshopper nonetheless helps kids find resources for their

science projects. The list of Web sites includes online museums, zoos, and magazines. The offline sites likewise include museums. The site is as simple as sites get, with minimal graphics and basic, high-quality lists.

Homework Central

www.homeworkcentral.com

"The Biggest Study Site on the Internet": My grade school teachers used to tell me that no one likes a braggart, but Homework Central just might live up to its lofty motto. The site offers research for 2,200 subjects in some 21 categories ranging from Arts to History (with separate categories for United States and World) to Science. Homework Central's offerings are so deep, in fact, that it didn't live up to its "Just Three Clicks And You're In" boast when I went looking for cloning sites under the Science category. I needed six clicks from the home page to the story. No big deal: Each click offered me more specific subgroups, so I didn't mind. And the site also offers special categories for elementary school children (grades 1 through 6 in the United States), teachers, parents, and scholarships. Done? Not yet. The site also has links to school sites (elementary, secondary, college, and university) around the world. Whether the links include "all" such links, as Homework Central claims, is anybody's guess, but I quickly surfed to pages for schools in Kenya and California. Sure,

Homework Central brags a little, but when it comes to content, Homework Central delivers.

Homework Help

www.startribune.com/stonline/html/
    special/homework

Message boards for students: Homework Help provides a communal resource for homework-burdened kids in six broad topic areas: English and Literature, Social Studies/Civics, Science, Math, World Languages, and Elementary School Topics. The site is communal because it uses message boards to post questions and answers so that students can help one another. In addition, many teachers volunteer their time to respond to student queries. In an Internet environment in which children really shouldn't visit the adult-oriented Usenet message boards, Homework Help is a terrific substitute. The messages are not threaded — that is, you don't see a map of queries and responses — so the site gets a little disorganized sometimes. But the informal learning atmosphere in which everyone works on everyone else's problems makes the slight confusion worth it. And a search engine is available.

Knowledge Adventure Encyclopedia

www.adventure.com/encyclopedia/

Interactive encyclopedia: This terrific resource for kids (and adults, for that matter) is part of the broader Knowledge Adventure site, which is reviewed in the "Kid's Sites" section, located in Part VII of this book. The Encyclopedia, which stands alone as a wonderful homework site, is powered by a keyword search engine. Just type a subject (**dinosaurs**, for example, or **weather**) to see a link list of subtopic entries. You also can search for information in nine general categories

(such as Aviation, the Human Body, or Undersea Life) or choose the Browse all of the entries link to avoid the keyword searching. The writing in the Knowledge Adventure Encyclopedia is clear and on the simple side. Pages tend to be short, with a preference for multiple short entries instead of a few long ones. Kids up to the age of 14 get the most out of the Encyclopedia, with older children perhaps being frustrated by the lack of depth or adult language. The site offers no multimedia gems, such as audio clips or video footage, so the Knowledge Adventure Encyclopedia doesn't compare with the glitz of a CD-ROM encyclopedia. The site's true value lies in its inter-activity and in the ease with which you can search it.

Mad Scientist Network

www.madsci.org

Real answers from a sane scientist: This site makes science fun. By following the provided instructions, kids can ask the mad scientist questions. The site recommends that kids browse the extensive archives of already answered questions — which, in fact, is an education all by itself. The Mad Scientist Library discusses how to find science resources on the Net and contains links to some of those resources. The site doesn't answer questions about personal health conditions or queries about how to find stuff on the Internet. Aside from volume and quality of information, the site is distinguished by its almost-psychedelic design.

Shakespeare Bookshelf

www.ipl.org/reading/shakespeare/
    shakespeare.html

Links to a glossary of Shakespearean terms: The fact that the Shakespeare Bookshelf contains every word of every Shakespearean play is impressive, but not impressive enough to make it a great homework site. After all, the plays are not hard to acquire in the real world. What makes this site remarkable are the embedded hyperlinks. Every word of every scene that had a different meaning when Shakespeare wrote it is hyperlinked to a glossary that defines it. This glossary clarifies many a passage and educates young readers in the English language of the Elizabethan period.

6th Grade Brain Bank

www.zygomedia.com/61wc

Cooperative site for sixth-grade students: Patrick White, having successfully navigated sixth grade with the help of the Internet, created this Web space to assemble links to useful homework sites. He invites (practically begs, really) other kids to submit links and divides the spoils into the categories Math, Science, English, Social Studies, and Other Homework Links. The lists are not comprehensive, by any means, but Patrick has good taste in homework sites. Even more valuable than just another homework resource is the cooperative nature of the site: Every visiting child can get in the act by seeking out and submitting good homework locations on the Web.

World Factbook

www.odci.gov/cia/publications/ factbook/index.html

Basic information on all countries: This site is for pure, no-frills research on the basic data of any country in the world. World Factbook is produced by the Central Intelligence Agency, so you can be sure that it's pretty accurate. The preceding URL takes you to a master alphabetical listing of countries. Click any country to view a jam-packed information page about that nation, including maps (viewable and downloadable), population figures, geography, government, economy, transportation, communication, and defense characteristics. The World Factbook doesn't waste time with unnecessary graphics or commentary, so it's a quick and complete data resource to use when you're working on reports.

Other Stuff to Check Out

forum.swarthmore.edu
sln.fi.edu/tfi/hotlists/kids.html
trfn.clpgh.org/Education/K12/homework
www.cwa.co.nz/eduweb/edu/worlded.html
www.hiwaay.net/homework

Politics

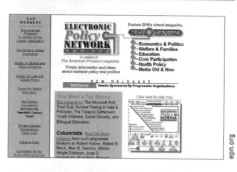

Two basic kinds of political pages are on the Web: sites that explain politics and sites that serve some government function. I cover both kinds in this section. General political sites are close in content to general news sites because much of today's mainstream news is political in nature. Still, the specialized political news sites go deeper into the political stories and are more satisfying for people who follow politics closely.

About Politics

In this section, I include online political publications; public-policy-explanation sites; political commentary; and the Electronic Frontier Foundation, which uniquely covers online political issues. I also include Web sites for the three largest U.S. political parties, because I don't consider them to be fitting for the Government Pages section.

CNN/TIME AllPolitics

allpolitics.com/1998/index.html

Daily political news: For a totally political brain hit, you can do no better than the CNN/TIME AllPolitics site. Formatted like an electronic newspaper, the site provides daily updates of headlines and in-depth stories that should sate anybody's appetite for government and candidacy news. An in-depth link takes the coverage to a more profound level, and an analysis page offers commentary. Occasional contests and a bulletin-board section provide the site's main interactivity and community feeling. Multimedia is disregarded in the pages of AllPolitics, for the most part; the site is just a good read.

The Daily Muse

www.cais.com/aschnedr/muse.htm

Irreverent political commentary: Tired of the straight, sober, grave, righteous approach to political news? Do you crave a little irreverence with your morning news infusion, laced with cynicism and a caustic bite? Get your browser over to The Daily Muse for an opinionated

rundown, tongue planted firmly in cheek, of the day's political events. Nobody gets off the hook at this site, which often lambastes both sides of any issue. Darting in and out of stories with two-line commentaries that both enlighten and denigrate political personalities, The Daily Muse dishes up its blighted reportage in easy-to-take bites of acerbic wit. The site's catchphrase is "Rewriting history in real time." Don't miss the revisionist humor of this site.

The Democratic Party Online

www.democrats.org/online.html

Partisan politics: Democratic: Like an online pep talk, the Democratic Party's Web site pushes for activism and involvement while dishing up partisan articles, press releases, and commentary on current events in Washington. You can join the party right through its site and learn about becoming a precinct campaign leader. A party calendar and list of headquarters sites keeps you in touch with the real world, and a newsletter keeps you informed of the site's changes. (Don't worry — I'm taking a bipartisan approach in this book. The Republican Party Web site is reviewed in this section, too.)

Electronic Frontier Foundation

www.eff.org

Civil-rights organization for the online community: The Electronic Frontier Foundation (EFF) is the most high-profile, influential, grassroots, Netcentric civil-rights organization. By "civil rights," I mean electronic civil rights, as in the rights of netizens. The EFF is concerned with the wired issues of the virtual community and with civil liberties as they apply to cyberspace. The organization publishes a newsletter (which is available at the site), and it informs the Internet community about policy crises, issues that need immediate action, and pending legislation. This Web site is an incredible resource for getting up to speed with online issues. That blue ribbon that you see on so many Web sites comes from the Electronic Frontier Foundation, which encourages any site owner who is concerned about free speech to download and display the ribbon.

Electronic Policy Network

epn.org

Public policy resources: The Electronic Policy Network is a sprawling site that encompasses several other spin-off sites. You may want to bookmark the home page, from which you can launch your way to the many individual sections, or you may want to browse those sections and bookmark individual portions. Idea Central is one major spin-off that is itself divided into a few Web publications: Economics & Politics, Education, Welfare & Families, Civic Participation, Health Policy, and Media Old & New. The Electronic Policy Network is produced by an alliance of mostly not-for-profit policy organizations, including the Center for Law and Social Policy, the Center for Media Education, and the Citizens Fund. With too much content to describe adequately in a short review (a search engine helps make sense of everything), the Electronic Policy Network is a meaty site and definitely worth a visit.

Libertarian Party

www.lp.org/lp/lp.html

Libertarian politics: The Libertarian Party is the third-largest political party in the United States. Nevertheless, many people don't have a clear idea what the party's philosophies, platforms, and public policy positions are. The Libertarian Party site is clear, if nothing else — no fancy graphics, but a coherent explanation of what the party is all about as well as its history and current activities. The Statement of Principles (on the Philosophies and Positions page) lays out the low-government, equal-rights, individual-centric policy of the party. The Info by State link is a good resource on party officials, including e-mail addresses (when available).

Mojo Wire

www.mojones.com

Online edition of Mother Jones *magazine:* Mojo Wire is the online version of *Mother Jones,* the liberal, grassroots bimonthly U.S. publication that has grown more stridently political over the years. Treading the narrow territory between mainstream and alternative reporting, *Mother Jones* attempts visionary thinking and in-depth reports turned in well ahead of the media pack. The same ideals inform Mojo Wire. The site is a little heavy on magazine promotion, but not too distractingly. A recent issue featured a commentary on how the awful John Wayne movie *The Conquerors* actually had some insights on the recent nuclear bomb tests in India and Pakistan; an article on how big business groups are trying to get around U.S. laws banning trade with some foreign countries with poor human rights records; and a report on the implications of the boom in biotechnology (plus, as they say on Madison Avenue, much more). Join the mailing list to receive bulletins from the site.

Public Affairs Web

www.publicaffairsweb.com

Comprehensive political information: Public Affairs Web has high aspirations: It wants to be the only Web site that you need for all questions of public policy, pending legislation, candidacy, and elections. Click the Main Menu link right away to see what the site is all about. From the Main Menu page, you can link to rosters of elected officials; presidential candidates; candidates for other federal offices; upcoming legislation in each state; information on parties and unions, charities and foundations; media and press information; and much more. The site is a treasure house of information, and it apparently will only get better, with its promise to provide more frequent updates in the near future.

Republican Mainstreet

www.rnc.org

Welcome to Republican Mainstreet!

Republican politics: With all objectivity, there is no comparison between the Democratic Party Web site (reviewed earlier in this section) and the official cyberspace location of the Republican Party. The Democrats should steal the design of the Republican pages or at least borrow some of their attitude. Hip design and far more compelling mudslinging distinguish the GOP cyberspot, not to mention the ultra-cool chat rooms and e-mail lists for the House and Senate. (You need to download a plug-in for chatting.) From the classy home-page

graphic map to the acerbic wit of the Clinton Calendar, the Republicans win votes for Net-savvy sensibilities and style. As for content, I'll stay out of that discussion.

Vox Pop

www.voxpop.org

Useful and informative political resource: Vox Pop has earned laudatory enthusiasm from all over the Net as being one of the indispensable political sites in cyberspace. The site is divided into four main areas. The Jefferson Project is a wide-ranging directory of political sites on the Net. Directory topics on the main Jefferson Project page include Publications, Political Humor, The Left, The Right (equal time, you know), The Radical (it doesn't say to which extreme) Issues and Activists, Political News, Parties, and Government Resources. The Weekly Views is a small section that updates a single editorial every week; invited guest writers pen the articles. The Netgrams section helps you contact your elected legislator by some means: e-mail, fax, or telegram. Finally, The Zipper is a handy service that locates your senator or representative when you enter your zip code.

Other Stuff to Check Out

www.adfa.oz.au/~adm/politics/politics.html
www.clark.net/pub/thomjeff/
www.geocities.com/CapitolHill/7970/
    index.htm
www.trincoll.edu/~pols/guide/home.html

U.S. Government Pages

The following sites are either produced by U.S. government agencies or by independent services that help you contact those agencies.

Central Intelligence Agency

www.odci.gov/cia

Information about the CIA: It's perfectly fitting — this Web site is the only one I've ever seen (and I've examined several sites during the past few years) that confesses that it may be monitoring your movements within the site. The warning is emblazoned front and center on the CIA home page. But click past that daunting welcome, and you'll be all smiles as you trip from link to link, engaging in fun activities and games. Well, no — forget about the fun and games. But the CIA Web site *is* informative, linking you to explanatory text about the agency, its public affairs, publications, and (gulp!) employment opportunities. Watch for my next book: *International Intrigue For Dummies.*

Federal Bureau of Investigation

www.fbi.gov

Information about the FBI: You'd expect a dry approach from this governmental site, but actually, the FBI Web location emphasizes the romantic angle of criminal apprehension, presumably appealing to the boyish spirit that has kids checking the post office for Most Wanted posters. Take your inner child to the FBI's Fugitives page and use the Most Wanted link to see photos and descriptions of the heinous criminals whose seizure is most urgently desired. Descriptions of ongoing investigations (including investigations of tobacco company

executives and the TWA Flight 800 crash) mingle with speeches by the agency's director, Louis J. Freeh (great last name, huh?). A History link provides background on this august agency, and you can read present and past press releases issued by it. And for all you fans of *The X-Files,* the FBI has recently begun posting reports on the existence of UFOs — albeit with "classified" information black-markered out. Maybe the truth is now on the FBI Web site!

Federal Web Locator

www.law.vill.edu/Fed-Agency/ fedwebloc.html

List of government Web sites: When you want to track down the home page of a governmental branch — the House of Representatives, perhaps, or the Supreme Court, or even the CIA — the Federal Web Locator is the site to consult. Browse the Table of Contents link or just scroll down the home page if you want to be amazed by just how *many* governmental Web sites exist. In fact, finding something in that megalist is harder than using the search engine, which is conveniently located near the top of the home page. The keyword entry form makes all the difference.

GPO Gate

www.gpo.ucop.edu

Directory of government databases: GPO Gate, created by the University of California, is the Internet presence of the Government Printing Office. The site is a directory of databases — and if that description seems to be opaque, chalk it up to the huge number of bills, laws, committees, agencies, debates, executive orders, purchase orders, regulations, presidential documents, resolutions, documents associated with the U.S. Congress, and other bureaucratic arcana. All the preceding items are archived in databases that you can access through your computer — personally, I can't think of a better way to spend a balmy Saturday afternoon. The site is great for legislative research and high-school (or college) political-science assignments.

Mr. Smith E-Mails Washington

www.mrsmith.com

E-mail addresses of members of Congress: Ever had the urge to blast off a letter to your government representative but were unsure who that august person was or how to find out? This site is your savior in such moments because it documents the e-mail addresses of senators, representatives, the president, and the vice president of the United States. The directory is organized by state, and tracking down your elected official is a breeze. A couple of warnings apply, however: You must know your congressional district, and some representatives don't have e-mail addresses. Recently, the Mr. Smith E-Mails Washington site broadened its scope by including media addresses, listing editorial e-mail addresses for a large selection of publications.

Peace Corps

www.peacecorps.gov

Information about the agency: The Peace Corps site has a smidgen of historical information (the agency was founded in 1961 by John F. Kennedy) but is mostly a vehicle for promoting current global projects and soliciting volunteers. A complete, multiple-page description of the requirements and the volunteer process are among the most valuable aspects of the site. Browsing through the list of countries that receive Peace Corps assistance is also fascinating; the site includes a fair amount of material about the characteristics and needs of those countries. Getting involved in a Peace Corps project without leaving home is possible, and that possibility is likewise detailed. Press releases about the agency round out the site.

Thomas

thomas.loc.gov

Database of legislative action: A service of the Library of Congress, Thomas provides legislative information via the Internet in a format that continually improves. The search engine was recently overhauled, making tracking down the text of bills much easier. So what is Thomas, exactly? It's a database of legislative action during the current session of Congress, with archives stretching back to the 1970s, in some cases. You can search for a piece of legislation (whether it eventually passed into law or not) by topic, title, popular title, bill number, and bill type. A raft of other features assist in legislative research, including *Congressional Record* text and indexes, frequently asked questions, historical documents (including the Declaration of Independence and the Federalist Papers), explanations of the legislative process, and committee reports.

The United States Senate

www.senate.gov

Information on the Senate: This formal, distinguished site is the cyberspace home of the U.S. Senate, delivering a filibuster on the Senate's history, a rundown of its current legislative activities, a roster of senators, a logjam of committees and their work, links to other sites, and a keyword search feature. The style is appropriately drab — hey, you wouldn't expect a chuckle per page on the Senate site, would you?

White House Briefing Room

**www.whitehouse.gov/WH/html/
   briefroom.html**

Press information: The White House Briefing Room is a spin-off of the White House home page, which I normally don't recommend to anybody; the White House home page is a high-profile, often-visited site, but it doesn't deliver much substance. The Briefing Room, however, is a different matter. Visit this site for daily press releases and briefings of the White House press corps by the press secretary. The Saturday Radio Address is archived in RealAudio, which by itself is worth the surf. The White House at Work section is the only self-congratulatory part of the site, detailing the effectiveness of public policies put in place by the current administration. Everything at this site is archived; you can search the site in the Virtual Library section.

Other Stuff to Check Out

www.intellectualcapital.com/index.html
www.library.nwu.edu/govpub/idtf/
    foreign.html
www.lib.umich.edu/libhome/
    Documents.center/polisci.html
www.vote-smart.org

World Government Pages

I had a professor in college who believed some secret international commission was really running the world. I've never bought that. I don't think there's any global government conspiracy. Now, not being able to get a high-speed line for my modem, *that's* a conspiracy.

Anyway, the following Web sites are for recognized international government agencies. I think my college professor has heard of all of them.

European Union

europa.eu.int

Diverse multilingual site: The European Union has been called "the United States of Europe," only the EU conducts its business in several languages. Fortunately, this Web site was designed with that cultural diversity in mind. The home page greets visitors with "Welcome" in English and ten other languages. Click the one that matches your language skills, and you're transported to a page with news and other basic information about the EU. Dig deeper and you'll find the Dialogue page, a handy little feature that matches which EU country people are coming from and which EU country they want to go to, and offers advice on visiting, doing business, and even looking for a job. The EU site may not be dazzling, but it's quite functional and — perhaps most important — even diplomatic.

Interpol

www.interpol-pr.com

International law enforcement agency: Here's one of life's ironies: The Interpol Web site is one of the best art galleries on the Web. During my last visit, I was able to view a stone head from Beijing and a Pieter Balten painting from the Netherlands, among others. Why is that ironic? Because the full name of Interpol is *Inter*national Criminal *Pol*ice Organization, and all the pictured art is on Interpol's "most wanted works of art" list. This multilingual site gives you the details on Interpol's history and operations. Pretty pictures, too.

NATO

www.nato.int

Information about the alliance: The North Atlantic Treaty Organization (NATO) page is a partially multilingual site, as is appropriate for an international organization, but English comes first on every page and shares the home page with French. As a basic introduction to NATO, you can't do any better on the Web than the Welcome to NATO link and The Organisation (notice the British spelling). News and archived documents have their places at this site, and perhaps the most interesting parts are the summaries of NATO meetings throughout the world. You can link to pages that provide the actual documents and resolutions written and passed during those meetings. Reading the documents is not quite like being at the meetings, but it's almost like reading the minutes, which is about as close as most of us will ever come to attending a head-of-state party in Brussels.

United Nations

www.un.org

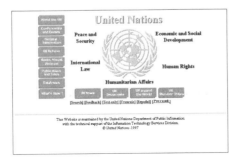

Information about the U.N: The United Nations Web site attempts to set out the overarching mission and current activities of the U.N. in such comprehensive detail as to be the only source necessary for anyone who is researching the multinational organization. The site provides many links, partly because it's highly organized by topics and subtopics, but your perseverance pays off big time in a thorough international current-events lesson. Summaries of ongoing peace missions, for example, include the names of the commanding officers, the size of the forces involved, the participating countries, and detailed background text.

The site covers several broad topics: Peace and Security, International Law, Economic and Social Development, Human Rights, and Humanitarian Affairs. Also useful are the rundowns on how the U.N. works and on the specific job of the secretary-general.

Other Stuff to Check Out

www.agora.stm.it/politic/home.htm
www.gksoft.com/govt/en/oceania.html
www.parliament.uk

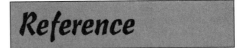

www.cc.columbia.edu/acis/bartleby/bartlett

Quick, which is easier — looking up a word in a dictionary from the bookshelf or logging onto a Web dictionary? (Tick, tock, tick, tock.) The answer: Neither is as fast as guessing. For those of you who believe in the value of accuracy (bah, humbug), going to the bookshelf is probably easier. But online dictionaries and encyclopedias have one great value in that they enable you to search interactively by typing keywords (at least, some of them have this feature). Random access is the big advantage of computers, and it certainly comes into play at reference sites.

Dictionaries

I include all kinds of dictionaries in this section: regular English-word lookups, quotation finders, and even a reverse dictionary that works so badly that it's too funny to miss. The criterion is quality (except for the broken reverse dictionary), and I tried to put together an interesting variety of references.

American Sign Language Dictionary

www.bconnex.net/~randys

Animated dictionary of the language: No dictionary listed in this section makes better use of the Internet's unique qualities than the American Sign Language Dictionary. This site is an *animated* guide to signing words in the language understood by the deaf. A brief history of sign language sets the stage; then an alphabetical directory contains the animations. Choose a letter and then a word beginning with that letter to see how to sign that word. A fast-sequencing series of photographs presents a clear graphic illustration of the hand positions and movements. The movements are crucial because most ASL signs aren't static, but gestured hand positions. (You don't need any plug-ins to view the animations.) This terrific site is the work of an individual, and a great deal of work it is. The dictionary of words is growing, and my hope is that the author will continue this project for a long time to come.

Bartlett's Familiar Quotations

www.cc.columbia.edu/acis/bartleby/ bartlett

Online edition of the dictionary of quotations: As Robert Herrick said in the 17th century, "Nothing's so hard but search will find it out." *Bartlett's Familiar Quotations* has for decades been the preeminent reference book for quotations. Both the book and the online site "may give a useful lesson to the head" (William Cowper). The site gives you a choice of searching by keyword or browsing, for (as James Russell Lowell wrote) "It is the

brave man chooses, while the coward stands aside." Well, that may be overstating the matter. Nevertheless, you can see a list of all quoted authors, either alphabetically or chronologically, cross-referenced to their selected quotes. "Wood best to burn," opined Francis Bacon, adding, "old wine to drink, old friends to trust, and old authors to read" — an apt statement, considering the antique quality of Bartlett's. ("I do perceive that the old proverbs be not always true," said Thomas à Kempis.) You can't find Bill Gates's latest pearl of wisdom in this book; in fact, most of the quotes are a couple of centuries old. But John Milton wrote about the "resistless eloquence" of ancestors, and Samuel Taylor Coleridge referred to the "intelligible forms of ancient poets," so who are we to complain that the old masters hold "undisturbed their ancient reign" (Alfred Domett)?

Elements of Style

www.columbia.edu/acis/bartleby/strunk

Online edition of the book: William Strunk, Jr.'s landmark book of good writing habits is reproduced on the Net at this site, thanks to Columbia University. Entertaining the site is not, but it answers any grammatical question that you can come up with. From spelling to the possessive, from the proper use of clauses to the passive tense, Elements of Style lays down the laws of good English. The home page lists the book's table of contents in hyperlink form, and each section is transposed exactly from the book.

Free On-Line Dictionary of Computing

wombat.doc.ic.ac.uk/foldoc/index.html

Dictionary of computer terms: Non-British users whose browsers are casting their lines across long distances to reach this U.K. site may find it a little slow, but this site is a handy stop in cyberspace. Just don't expect much in the way of visual entertainment — the interface is as bald and text-oriented as it can be. The word entry form is way up at the top of the home page, and you can safely disregard everything else. Just type a computing-related word and, probably before you can pour that tenth cup of coffee (you really should cut back), the site displays an enhanced definition. The enhancement takes the form of hyperlinks that further explain words used in the definition.

Merriam-Webster Online

www.m-w.com

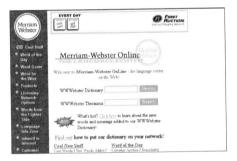

Online version of the dictionary and thesaurus: Merriam-Webster, the famous dictionary company, couldn't resist the impulse to take advantage of the similar-ity of its name to the *Web,* so it put up an interactive version of its dictionary: the World Wide Webster Dictionary. Now the Merriam-Webster Thesaurus (or, to use the proper online vernacular, the WWWebster Thesaurus) has been added to what is now called Merriam-Webster Online. Using the site is a simple affair: You type a word, and a new page tells you what the word means or gives you synonyms. One nice feature is that the definition/synonym pages are cross-linked, so that when you get your defini-tion — for the word *author,* say — you can click the Thesaurus button to see synonyms, such as *genius, talent,* and *precocity.* (Just kidding. But I bet that *obnoxious* is on the list.) By the way, the home page offers a Word of the Day game and other questionably fun word features.

OneLook Dictionaries

www.onelook.com

Definitions searched by keyword: OneLook Dictionaries takes its cue from the multiple-engine search services of the World Wide Web. Those search services enable you to enter a single keyword, which is sent simultaneously to several search engines, such as Excite, AltaVista, and Infoseek. OneLook Dictionaries does essentially the same thing with words that you want defined. Type the word, and the site looks it up in several dozen online dictionaries simultaneously, including specialized technology, medical, business, and computer references, as well as general dictionaries. The results show which dictionaries carry matches to your word and invite you to link both to the definition in each specific dictionary and to the home pages of the dictionaries. Very handy! The site is a one-stop word lookup service that crosses over subject fields and works quickly.

Phrase Finder

www.shu.ac.uk/web-admin/phrases

Find phrases using keywords: Phrase Finder is a unique, questionably useful, but fun reference site that finds phrases related to a word that you type. Type **money**, for example, and receive phrases such as *A penny for your thoughts, A king's ransom, Break the bank, Hard times, Out of pocket,* and *The buck stops here,* plus some head-scratchers such as *Clean bill of health.* The last one (and similar non sequiturs) is the result of the site's literalness, which in this case connects the keyword *money* with the word *bill.* Americans also may be startled by some British phrase connections at this U.K. site. Some of the phrases are enhanced with hyperlinks that lead to historical sources of the phrases and definitions of meaning.

Quotation Search

**www.starlingtech.com/quotes/
search.html**

Funny and modern database of quotes: The Quotation Search site is delightfully contemporary and humorous. The home page presents a quote of the day and quote of the week, but the search engine is at the heart of the site. From a drop-down list, you can choose which of several specialized quote databases to search, including the comedic Deep Thoughts by Jack Handy (of *Saturday Night Live* fame), Steven Wright quotations, Dave Barry quotations, quotes by women, and other categories. (Click the Advanced Search link to search more than one category at a time.) Just type a keyword and see the results. This site is a great way to gather public-speaking quote material and just fun to browse.

Reverse Dictionary

www.c3.lanl.gov:8064/cgi/revdict

Nonsensical definitions: This site is so unintentionally hilarious that I must tell you about it, useless though it may be for serious purposes. The idea is to dash to the Reverse Dictionary site when you have that tip-of-the-tongue inability to come up with a certain word (obviously, not a practical strategy when you're at a dinner party). You type a definition and get back suggestions of suitable words. Now, I'm not a slouch with language and definitions, but I haven't been able to get this thing to make sense even once. Therein lies the fun. First, I pretended that I couldn't remember the word *sarcastic* and typed this definition: *funny, mean, and insincere.* The suggestions? *Grindstone, hovel, purveyor, notwithstanding,* and some four dozen other head-scratchers. Going back to the well, I tried *hide the meaning of,* figuring that the phrase was appropriate under the circumstances. I was looking for *obfuscate* but would have settled for anything remotely in the ballpark. You'll be surprised to know that you can convey the meaning of *obfuscate* with the words *transoceanic* (okay, the meaning of the *Titanic* is hidden under 14,000 feet of ocean), *gunfire* (perhaps the result of obfuscating too much), *graveyard* (the ultimate result?), *toothbrush* (if you can't tell the truth, at least brush your teeth), and *anus* (no comment). As you can see, the Reverse Dictionary has no practical value. But when you want a laugh, you should definitely . . . hmm, what's the word for visiting a site? Oh, yes — you should pantry it.

Rhyming Dictionary

www.cs.cmu.edu/~dougb/rhyme.html

Dictionary of rhyming words: This site, perhaps in an attempt to justify its existence, asks what a user can do with the Rhyming Dictionary and comes up with this answer: "You can use it to help write poetry. . . ." Well, sign me up! I need all the help I can get to produce even awful verses. The process is easy: Just type a single word and get back words that rhyme with it. Use the drop-down list to choose among options that include perfect rhymes, rhymes of the last syllable only, or homophones (words that sound exactly the same but have different meanings, such as *night* and *knight*). Beware — the results page contains a bunch of gibberish at the top (mostly links), and the results lie below. I feel that this site has expanded my artistic potential considerably, and I offer the following verse as evidence:

There once was a man with no spine
Whose name was unfortunate: Schlein.
He tried hard to change it
But couldn't arrange it
And now takes to sloshing cheap wine.

And to think that I'm stuck writing computer books while my art goes unrecognized.

Roget's Thesaurus

www.thesaurus.com

Online version of the thesaurus: The online version of the famous dictionary of synonyms (words that mean roughly the same thing) is a brilliant accomplishment. The only problem is that the home page isn't as simple as it looks. Sure, the little orange box has a Find: word entry box; simply type in the word you need a synonym for and click Now! Try "orange" and you'll end up in the sections related to rotundity ("round as an orange") and probability (as in the phrase "all Lombard Street to a China orange"; no, I've never heard it, either). But what are all those other cryptic symbols right above the Find: box? Links, Watson. Taking advantage of the unique features of the hyperlinked Internet, the site enables you to browse for words alphabetically, or — much more difficult, but strangely enlightening — to search through a directory that classifies all words in one of six orders of being. Taking the latter route may bend your brain out of shape, but why should I be the only one with a twisted mind? Alternatively, save yourself the strain of mind alteration and just use the alphabet links.

Translating Dictionaries

dictionaries.travlang.com

Translations of foreign words: This site is a polyglot's dream come true — a bunch of foreign-language dictionaries all in one place. The languages represented are English, German, Dutch, French, Italian, Spanish, Norwegian, Danish, Finnish, Portuguese, Afrikaans, Hungarian, Czech, Esperanto, and Latin. Not every language is translated to every other language, but some cross-fertilization exists, such as German to French, French to Spanish, and Dutch to German. Each language combination is provided as a link, which, when clicked, displays the appropriate

dictionary with a word entry form. Type a word and get the translation. Some limitations prevail; the word databases are usually constrained to a few thousand words, for example, and the definitions are rather bare, lacking in pronunciations but giving examples.

Web of Online Dictionaries

www.bucknell.edu/~rbeard/diction.html

Directory of dictionaries: Basically a directory of foreign-language dictionaries on the Net, the Web of Online Dictionaries also functions as a quick word definition service in English. The home page, in fact, starts with that feature, presented as a word entry form connected to Merriam-Webster's Collegiate Dictionary. (Hey, even noncollege students can use it.) Scroll down the page to see a list of languages. Clicking any language displays all the Internet dictionaries in that language, listed as hyperlinks. Predicting the quality of the dictionary sites is impossible, but the Web of Online Dictionaries is a terrific resource for translators, students, and anyone else who enjoys words on an international scope.

WordNet

www.cogsci.princeton.edu/~wn

"A Lexical Database for English": WordNet is for serious lexicographers, wordsmiths, and those who enjoy delving deep into the tangled matrix of language, enjoying the complexity of words for their own sake. Created by Princeton University, WordNet can be forbidding, but a little experimenting eases the way. The Use WordNet Online page warning offers a taste of the level at which this site operates: "Please do not request searches that recursively traverse down noun hierarchies from very high up a tree." I wouldn't think of doing such a thing,

much less try to pronounce that sentence. In fact, if I were very high up a tree, the last thing on earth I'd try to do is recursively traverse anywhere. Anyway, get started by choosing either the HTML or Java interface and then typing a word in the entry form. The site crunches its database and returns a definition, along with a drop-down list that offers further choices. You can look up synonyms, hypernyms, and hyponyms, all of which are explained briefly. Fun, huh? Well, as I said, this site is entertaining only for people who love words. For basic definitions, stick to one of the simpler online dictionaries reviewed in this section.

Other Stuff to Check Out

babelfish.altavista.digital.com
wheel.ucdavis.edu/~btcarrol/skeptic/
    dictcont.html
www.plumbdesign.com/thesaurus
www.sti.nasa.gov/nasa-thesaurus.html
www.ucc.ie/info/net/acronyms/index.html

Encyclopedias and Atlases

As I do in the Dictionaries portion of the Reference section, I include all kinds of encyclopedic resources in this section. The emphasis is on quality, and the collection represents a broad range of what you can find on the Net.

American Presidency

**www.grolier.com/presidents/
    preshome.html**

Reference on the U.S. presidency: A spinoff of the Grolier's Online site, American Presidency is free (the larger Grolier's is a subscription site) and excellent. Divided into three main sections (by age groups), Encyclopedia Americana is the best for

adults, featuring lengthy articles on the American presidency and related political subjects, and enhanced by hyperlinked words that lead to other articles and definitions. That would be enough, but American Presidency goes the extra mile with a Commentary section, an Online Exhibit Hall of Presidents (photos and sound clips), historical election results, and presidential Web links. All in all, American Presidency is a complete reference site to the high office and the political institutions surrounding it.

Atlas of the World

cliffie.nosc.mil/~NATLAS/atlas

Maps of cities and countries: You may wonder what an atlas of the world looks like squeezed onto a computer screen. This site is your chance to find out. Most maps displayed on the Web are clickable, but the one displayed on the World page of this site is static; it just sits there. Glumly. You can zoom into more detailed maps the long way around, however, by clicking through the geographical directory links. Start with Europe, for example; choose a country from the next page; then you see a detailed map. The map is still surly and unresponsive, but what can you do with a map that has an attitude? You can follow the preceding process all the way down to the city level. The maps may not be interactive or much fun at parties, but they're some of the nicest that I've encountered on the Net.

116 Reference

Encyclopedia Mythica

www.pantheon.org/mythica

★★
★★

Encyclopedia of world mythologies: This beautifully designed, perfectly operating site is one of the best encyclopedia products on the Web. The site offers both directory browsing and keyword searching; you probably should start with the directory to grasp the extent of the site. Mythologies from Greek, Chinese, Japanese, Egyptian, Persian, Roman, Welsh, Mayan, Native American, and several other cultural traditions are covered. The articles are short to the extent of seeming more like definitions sometimes, but the compensation is the quickness with which the site operates. (The articles have no multimedia elements, although some pictures are gathered into the Image Gallery.) The emphasis is on comprehensiveness — breadth rather than depth. Using the frames version of the site, you see a list of article subjects on the left of the screen; clicking any subject brings the article up on the right side within a second or two. Each cultural tradition has hundreds of entries. The site is a delight to browse.

PC Webopaedia

www.pcwebopaedia.com

Encyclopedia of computer and Internet information: This excellent reference site is an encyclopedia of computer and Internet information, with an interface that looks like a dictionary. PC Webopaedia's database is good, but its cross-referencing of that database is extraordinary, which simply means that you're likely to get much more than you came for — always a happy experience (except at the dentist's office). The home page gives you two basic choices: browsing the directory of terms by category or searching dictionary-style by typing a word. Search if you know what you need; browse if you're just looking.

When you get to a definition of a term, the articles are quite small — more like longish dictionary definitions, really. The articles are enhanced by hyperlinks for certain words that lead to other definitions. Below the definition are links to related Web sites, each of which is briefly reviewed — a feature that goes way beyond the call of duty. Some of the link lists are quite long. All these features add up to an amazingly complete resource for gaining understanding of a computer term or concept.

U.S. Gazetteer

www.census.gov/cgi-bin/gazetteer

Maps of the United States: The folks who run the U.S. census aren't known for their sparkling humor, and this site, which the Census Bureau is behind, is about as dry as sites get, even for a reference product. Not a problem — who wants a map with smiley faces all over it, anyway? The operation of this site is simple: You type a zip code or geographical name (keep it within the United States, of course), and the site spits the formal name of the place and a few basic facts (population and longitude and latitude) back at you. The page also enables you to look up more statistical information in table form, but the map is more fun because you can manipulate the heck out of it. Zoom in or out interactively, add features such as highway markings and various topographical labels, or subtract features. Are you having fun yet?

World Population Figures

home.worldonline.nl/~quark/index.html

Not just population facts: Quick, what's the world's largest airport? Give the answer first in terms of passengers and then cargo. Well, I didn't know either answer, but this site delivers more than just population figures — so much more, in fact, that it should be renamed. The airport data is from the Charts section, which lists the top 25 examples in various categories. More substantial are the country profiles (grouped by region), which work together to dish up just about any kind of fact about a country that you could aspire to know. The site works quickly, and browsing is intuitive.

Other Stuff to Check Out

disserv.stu.umn.edu/AltForm/brl-guide.cgi
www.atlapedia.com
www.cnet.com/Resources/Info/Glossary/
www.hiway.co.uk/~ei/intro.html
www.jcave.com/~bandorm/megaterm/
    megaterm.htm
www.matisse.net/files/glossary.html

Religion and Spirit

www.family.org

Religion is not only a controversial subject, but also one that defies easy description. One person's deep faith is another person's cultish brainwashing. In late-20th-century America, the unorganized, grassroots New Age movement is clearly spiritual but has not coalesced into a religion. As always in this book, I go for variety in this section, trying to paint a broad picture of the types of religion sites that are available.

Christian Sites

My goal in this section is to not promote any particular faith or denomination. I include a Christian portion of the Religion section because this book originates in America, where Christianity is the dominant religion, and also because Christianity is well represented on the Internet. Following are a few sites that accomplish their goals with virtual grace.

Bible Gateway

gospelcom.net/bible?

Bible-search resource: The Bible Gateway is an amazing resource, regardless of your spiritual beliefs. Whether your interest is secular research, worshipful Bible browsing, homework, or any of several other purposes, the Bible Gateway makes scouring the text easy. You can search by passage, keyword, or topic. The home page cuts right to the chase by presenting several word entry forms, inviting you to type a specific passage (by chapter and verse), a keyword, and a word that restricts the search to a certain portion of the Bible. Bible Gateway uses six translations of the Bible and describes the history of each version. A bit farther down the home page is another search form that enables you to call up Bible citations on certain subjects, such as *love* or *miracles.* The results are usefully categorized. Throughout all the search processes, the Bible results are displayed by verse in a format that's both easy to read and to identify by verse number. The site is also accessible in nine non-English languages. All in all, the Bible Gateway does a spectacular job of searching the Bible quickly (it's lightning-fast, really), conveniently, and in a way that emphasizes usefulness and user-friendliness.

Catholic Information Center on the Internet

www.catholic.net

Discussions of Catholicism: The CICI (Catholic Information Center on the Internet) is geared equally toward the practicing Catholic believer and the interested non-Catholic. In fact, judging by the message boards at this site (use the Issues & Fact link on the What's New page), many people who are hostile to Catholicism and papal policy visit the site and participate in its debates. The Issues & Fact section is probably not meant to be the centerpiece of the site, but it attracts huge, controversial conversations about issues such as abortion and papal infallibility, and clearly comprises the most dynamic portion of the CICI. If you're not in the mood to argue, the home page links to a variety of informational pages, offering various teachings and directories.

Catholic Online

www.catholic.org

Information about Catholicism: Catholicism merges with the digital age in Catholic Online, a broad information site that leans heavily on audio- and video-streaming multimedia. Have you ever tuned in to Vatican Radio? Have a listen at this site via RealAudio and try the Eternal World Television Network while you're at it. The video section relies on the VDO Video Player plug-in (which you can easily download from a provided link) and features a few productions from Human Life International. Both the audio and video sections promise increased offerings in the near future. Aside from multimedia, Catholic Online has a beautiful section on angels and saints, as well as a news section.

Focus on the Family

www.family.org

"Dedicated to the Preservation of the Home": Focus on the Family is a U.S.-based Christian organization started by Dr. James Dobson, whose radio program on Christian parenting is now heard daily on more than 4,000 radio facilities in North America and over 70 other countries. You can link to the daily program from this URL, but the Web site goes far beyond just the broadcast. Focus on the Family's many other efforts now include *Teachers in Focus* magazine and *Brio* magazine (the latter for teenage girls), selections of which are available at the site; and lobbying for pro-Christian laws, the current efforts of which are detailed. But the site doesn't forget that it has a Focus on the Family. The Parents' Place community section groups its material according to the child's age, with pages for New Parents, You and Your Toddler, and so on. The pages include links to related past questions that Dr. Dobson has answered, related articles, and "resources" — usually books or tapes that you can buy from the site. "Buy" isn't really an appropriate term — Focus on the Family simply includes a "Suggested Donation" amount, leaving the actual amount to the individual.

Net Ministries

www.netministries.org/nf_index.html

Scripture, sermons, and links: Net Ministries is a Texas-based site that seeks to serve as an online resource for the Christian community. And what a resource it is: Whether you seek a place to worship, guidance in your own devotions, or just want an occasional encouraging word, Net Ministries can help or provides links to sites that do. The site's newest feature, Bible Basics, goes far beyond its title with a wonderful three-frame page setup that includes an index in the left frame and a guide to pronouncing Biblical words in the bottom frame. The main frame is dedicated to the actual text, which begins with a title page that includes the history of the book and an audio clip of how to pronounce the name of the book (handy when you get to Habakkuk). Ready to read? Go ahead — the entire book is online, in not one but six versions, including King James, New International, and Revised Standard. Commentaries and sermon notes are also handy. Too much? A no-frame version of the site is available if needed. Church listings? The site now has links to Web pages of more than 5,600 churches worldwide, from Mexico to Ohio to England to Malaysia to Canada.

Other Stuff to Check Out

tlem.netcentral.net
www.churchnet.org.uk
www.churchsurf.com/index.htm
www.easterbrooks.com/personal/calendar/
index.html
www.goshen.net/directory
www.gospelcom.net/ifc/newsletter.shtml
www.helwys.com/abphome.htm
www.mit.edu/~tb/anglican
www.vog.org

New Age Sites

The New Age is an amalgam of spiritual thought, much of it transposed from ancient teachings. Channeling and angels are two of the hottest topics in the current New Age movement, and I include sites that reflect those trends.

Angels on the Net

www.netangel.com

Information about angels: When you surf to the home page of this site, you're greeted as an Angelic Visitor, and Angels on the Net has had more than 500,000 visitors (angelic or not) during its lifetime. Shopping, chatting, and asking e-mail questions are all part of the proceedings, but the heart of the site is the Stories section. Everyone is invited to contribute stories of encounters with angels — and a skim of the archived accounts clarifies that no objective verification is required. This is a gentle, faithful site for those who have — or want to have — a personal perception of divine protection.

A.R.E.

www.are-cayce.com

Edgar Cayce and reincarnation: Edgar Cayce was perhaps this century's foremost psychic, decades before channeling and trance healing became all the rage, and the Association for Research and Enlightenment (A.R.E.) is the foundation that continues to promote Cayce's work. Performing thousands of trance readings for people all over the world, most of which were transcribed and archived, Cayce assured himself something close to earthly immortality. Much of his work focused on healing and wellness, prophecy of earth changes, ancient civilizations, dream work, meditation, and reincarnation. Although this site doesn't present any transcripts of readings, it does provide a good overview of the foundation's work and the gist of Cayce's message.

ConsciousNet

www.consciousnet.com/index.html

★ ★
★ ★

Links to sites on consciousness-raising:
ConsciousNet is a repository of links to
information, services, and products on
the Web that purportedly raise your
consciousness. Therefore, if your consciousness is afraid of heights, avoid this
site and all other attempts to raise it.
ConsciousNet enjoys the double benefit
of being both a good resource and a
prettily designed one — the latter feature
being extremely rare among New Age Web
sites. The home page lists a couple dozen
subject categories, each of which leads to
a page displaying links around the Web.
The links as a whole have a definite
commercial feeling, lending credibility to
the cynical notion that contemporary
spirituality, under the umbrella of New
Age, is primarily a marketing niche.
Nevertheless, whether you seek information or the latest meditation tape, you'll
probably find something at just the right
altitude in ConsciousNet.

Other Stuff to Check Out

www.aquarianage.org
www.digiserve.com/mystic/
www.earthchannel.com/aquarius/
www.spirituality.org

Other Religious Sites

Religions span the globe and would make
an interesting book in themselves. In this
section, I gather some sites that strike me
as being genuine, caring, and nonpushy. I
also include at least one organization for
sheer interest, even though many people
would characterize it as being pushy to
the extreme.

Al-Muslim

www.al-muslim.org

Information about the Islamic religion: A
sophisticated site with complex frames
and many sections, Al-Muslim serves as a
focal point for practicing Muslims as well
as an information resource for anyone
interested in Islam. Newcomers should go
for the Introducing Islam link first — its
many sections give an overview of the
religion for outsiders. The Women in
Islam section is particularly interesting
because it offers a defense of Islamic
gender traditions that seem strange to
Western cultural sensibilities, such as
polygamy. Al-Muslim also includes a FAQ
(Frequently Asked Questions) link. The
site goes out of its way to provide
information to newcomers.

The Church of Christ, Scientist

www.tfccs.com

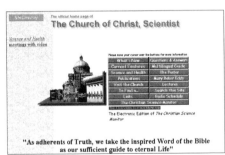

Information on Christian Science: Christian
Science has long embraced multimedia in
a big way, starting with its internationally
renowned newspaper, its radio network,
and (more recently) its excursions on the
Internet. This multilingual home page of
the mother church is a Java-enhanced
marvel of clarity, linking to explanatory
portions of the site that outline exactly
what Christian Science is and pointing
you toward resources for finding out

more offline. The religion's central scripture — *Science and Health with Key to the Scriptures,* by Mary Baker Eddy, the discoverer and founder of Christian Science — is described but not presented in its entirety. You can purchase the book online, however. Audio clips tell you how people have been influenced and healed by Christian Science. A directory of churches and reading rooms, plus a news section, round out the site.

Hare Krishna

www.shamantaka.org

Information on Hare Krishna: You've seen them in airports. You've seen them in local parks. Now, for the first time, see them in hyperlinked glory on the World Wide Web. The exceptionally well-designed and informative Hare Krishna site may surprise you with the depth of its philosophical explanations and art galleries. As an organization that must overcome some public-relations resistance in society at large, the Hare Krishna movement has done a wonderful job of presenting itself on the Web objectively, without defensiveness or undue pressure to join. Every page is interspersed with sacred quotations, and the art galleries really are worth checking out. The Philosophy Section and the Hare Krishna FAQ contain most of the background information that takes your understanding of the movement beyond ecstatic dancing in public places.

Mining Co. Guide to Judaism

judaism.miningco.com

Guide to Jewish Internet resources: This hosted site, like most Mining Co. guide sites, is part destination, part portal. On the destination side, the site offers chat rooms, message boards, stories, jokes,

and features (often multiple-part stories on disparate topics, like dating and Passover, that invite feedback). One unusual feature is that the site also includes RealAudio lessons in the Hebrew language. On the portal side, the guide page has 29 categories of links right on the home page, with more categories just a click away. The links offerings are equally diverse — categories range from Bar/Bat Mitzvah to Clip Art to Israeli Politics to Singles Sites.

Religious Atheisms

www.hypertext.com/atheisms

Resources for research on atheism: Putting the Religious Atheisms site in the Religion section may seem odd to some, but this site is a nonbeliever's encyclopedic guide to atheistic references in literature, both sacred and secular. Brief explanations of atheism are offered, but the site is really about pointing you in the right direction for further research. Scroll down the home page to see a list of Topologies links, which consist primarily of excerpts from writings about atheism by such disparate sources as Martin Buber, various popes, Socrates, and Thomas Huxley. Most of the links stay within the Religious Atheisms site, but the site doesn't hesitate to throw you outside to find, say, an article on whether Hinduism allows atheism. Somewhat scholarly in tone, this site manages to convey a broad overview of the godless perspective.

Religious Quotations and Meditations

bcn.boulder.co.us/community/religious/
   mvumc/mvumcattune.html

Inspirational quotations: This site is just the ticket for a quick hit of inspiration. If your sense of devotion or purpose in life is flagging (whose doesn't flag, at times?), a trip to Religious Quotations and Meditations is like a visit from a pastor. Although generally inclined toward

122 Religion and Spirit

Christian sensibilities (the quotations are taken from the church bulletin of the Mountain View United Methodist Church, which produces the site), the selection process appears to focus more on quality than source. All kinds of authors are represented at this site, including Mother Teresa; C. S. Lewis; Martin Luther King, Jr.; Kahlil Gibran; Rainer Maria Rilke; and Emily Dickinson. Humor is not avoided; Erma Bombeck has a quote on this page. The site organization could hardly be simpler; all the quotes are listed on the long home page. This setup makes random browsing a simple matter of clicking the down-arrow button for a second or two and then reading which-ever quote your browser lands on.

Religious Society of Friends

www.quaker.org

Links to sites about the Quakers: The Society of Friends, otherwise known as the Quakers, founds its lifestyle and worship practices on simplicity and reverent silence. So the fact that the official Quaker Web site is simple to the extreme, even sparse, makes a certain amount of sense. But what this linkfest lacks in fancy formatting, it makes up for in abundant leads to just about every scrap of information on Quakerism on the Web. The Quaker site provides almost no original writing, but you can link to the autobiography of George Fox, the writings of other historical Quakers, modern writings, Quaker history sites, and an incredible number of other Friends-oriented Internet locations.

Scientology Home Page

www.scientology.org

Information on the Scientology religion: Scientology, the personal-improvement movement founded by science-fiction writer L. Ron Hubbard, may not seem like a typical religion. In fact, Scientology can hardly be called typical, but it *is* legally a

religion — and a controversial one, at that. So much publicity has adhered to Scientology in the past couple of years that getting the official perspective from this multilingual page is interesting. In one of the best sections, the president of the Church of Scientology answers more than 100 questions about the organization and its troubled image. Whether Scientology is a cult or a legitimate, valuable religion (or something in between) is a question best answered by each individual. But you shouldn't consider it without getting the story from the source.

Taoism Information Page

www.clas.ufl.edu/users/gthursby/ taoism

Links to translations of the Tao Te Ching: Taoism enjoys the fine distinction of owning one of the most bewildering scriptures ever created, the Tao Te Ching — a poem that both summarizes the mystery of existence and hangs your mind on the nearest clothesline to flutter in the wind. Fortunately, the Taoism Information Page helps by linking you to several translations of the ancient Chinese text, each of which is more opaque than the one before. The Intro-ductions to Taoism or Daoism link is a miniature directory of explanatory texts around the Web, and another section provides links to general information on Chinese philosophy. All joking aside, for those who are attracted to the subtlety and poetry of Taoist texts, the Taoism Information Page is a solid tutorial.

Other Stuff to Check Out

bnaibrith.org
hindunet.org/home.shtml
members.aol.com/gr8tao/index.html
web.bu.edu/STH/Library/contents.html
www.geocities.com/RodeoDrive/1415/
www.math.gatech.edu/~jkatz/Islam/
 L_islamic.html
www.ncf.carleton.ca/dharma
www.zen.org

Science

www.nasm.si.edu

Science makes the transition from the physical world to cyberspace beautifully; in fact, science is a big topic on the Net. Astronomy sites in particular have proliferated like uninhibited rabbits over the past couple of years, and several of the best are listed in this section. Also, broadly scientific sites and organizational Web sites, such as NASA's, keep viewers up-to-date on current projects and missions. Most science sites are free to access. Science sites also tend to be graphically heavy and slow-loading, but the results are often worth the wait.

Science Learning and Resources

I had to make some hard choices in this section because many gorgeous, informative science Web sites are available these days. I could easily have included nothing but space and astronomy sites; instead, I selected a variety of disciplines and design approaches. The following sites represent some of the best science on the World Wide Web, but a little exploring on your own can turn up much more.

American Museum of Natural History

www.amnh.org

Virtual museum: At first glance, the American Museum of Natural History site appears to be nothing more than a brief advertisement for the physical museum in New York City, with little or no informative value of its own. In fact, it just takes a little digging, and before you know it, following one link after another, you're on an interesting knowledge expedition — rather like moving through small exhibit rooms of the museum. No single page gives you too much information at this site, but all the pages add up to a great deal of content. Start on the home page by clicking the Exhibitions link; then follow one of the exhibit trails. (I had great success recently with Fossil Halls.) Pictures, timelines, text with embedded links, and other interactive bread crumbs lead you along on a worthwhile expedition.

Discovery Online

www.discovery.com

Online information from The Discovery Channel: No stranger to multimedia, The Discovery Channel produced groundbreaking CD-ROM products before the World Wide Web was a gleam in a programmer's eye. Now, on the Internet,

124 Science

Discovery Online continues to innovate, educate, intrigue, and sometimes dazzle with an edutainment environment reminiscent of a cross between a CD-ROM program and an electronic magazine. Five main topic areas share the cyberspace: Feature Stories and Expeditions, where the stories are lengthy, richly illustrated, and usually interactive in some way; Mind Games, which challenges the visitor; Animal Cams, where you can switch to live shots of a whale in Oregon or a panda in California; and Conversations, where message boards encourage the growth of community. Discovery Online creates pure Web excellence.

Grand Canyon Explorer

www.kaibab.org/gc_homeh.htm

Information about the Grand Canyon: Wow. Sometimes, you come across a Web site that exploits the possibilities of the Internet so effectively and excitingly — not for commercial purpose, but in the spirit of free access to knowledge or beauty — that you wonder why more sites aren't like it. The reason, of course, is that excellence is rare in any medium. The next time you're in the mood for excellence, nudge your browser to the preceding URL. First, maximize your browser window because you need all the monitor real estate that you can get to view the incredible — one might say canyonlike — depth of features and information. In an exceptional display of consideration for different computer systems, bandwidth choices are offered for each of three site designs: no frames, frames, and Java. (The default is high bandwidth without frames, which works fine with a 28.8 Kbps modem.) A photo gallery, a kids' section, online maps, guided tours, lodging information, back-country information, and history, geology, and weather information are just the beginning of this astounding resource. I'll

stop here, lest this entire section be devoted to one site. Check it out for yourself — you'll be glad that you did.

Hubble Space Telescope Public Pictures

oposite.stsci.edu/pubinfo/Pictures.html

Deep-space photographs: This site looks good on any monitor, but if you have a 17-inch computer screen or are using a WebTV system, you'll really have your socks knocked off by the fabulous space shots in this repository of images from the Hubble Space Telescope. You also may appreciate the depth of the archive and the fine organization, which enables you to track down pictures of planets, comets, nebulae, or whatever your pleasure in heavenly phenomena may be. A general copyright applies to the images, but viewers are welcome to download the pictures to their personal hard drives; so building an electronic collection of the most astounding space photography in the world is a snap.

Human Anatomy Online

www.innerbody.com/indexbody.html

Virtual anatomy: This site is worthwhile only if viewed in a fully Java-enabled browser, such as a recent version of Navigator or Explorer. So armed (pun semi-intended), surf on over to a slick online anatomy lesson. Start by choosing a body section or system from a group of small images. Clicking one image expands it to a large image, interactively loaded with hot spots that change to labels when you move the mouse pointer over them. The site provides no explanatory text for what you're seeing, but you'll sure learn Latin names for muscles 'n' things. (You can tell what an advanced biologist I am.)

The site works beautifully, with almost no loading time for the Java applets that provide the interactivity.

HyperTech

www.thetech.org/hyper

Virtual science museum: HyperTech is an online museum fashioned after the hands-on science museums that kids love to run through, loudly. Although this site is appropriate for younger visitors, it doesn't pander to them and is also informative for adults. Recent exhibits included Lasers, Eye on the Universe, Get a Grip on Robotics, Earthquakes, and DNA. Clicking a topic takes you to the first of several instructional, highly illustrated pages. The discourses are basic but intelligent, neither going too deep nor leaving you frustratingly underinformed.

Invention Dimension

web.mit.edu/invent

Profiles of inventions and inventors: A production of the Massachusetts Institute of Technology, Invention Dimension chronicles the annals of American invention by profiling a different inventor or invention every week. The idea is not necessarily to remain on the cutting edge of new inventions, but to fill in the gaps of the past by describing the significance of past inventors' work. A recent spotlighted Inventor of the Week, for example, was Howard S. Jones, Jr., who made antennas practical for spacecrafts by building them into the casings of missiles. Profiles trace the history, acquisition, and commercialization of inventions, and the inventor archives provide an alphabetical list of biographies.

Museum of Unnatural Mystery

unmuseum.mus.pa.us/unmuseum.htm

Unanswerable questions answered: Mixing a bit of pseudoscience into your educational diet is easy with this online museum, which takes a lighthearted approach to mysteries of the natural world, without denying that the paranormal may just be real. UFOs get a great deal of attention, as does the lingering question of what killed the dinosaurs — one of the pervasive mysteries of science. (It has always seemed obvious to me that the great lizards died from eating too many Twinkies, but most archaeological academies don't consult me on the matter.) Even if the subject matter of the Museum of Unnatural Mystery brings a laugh to your lips, you have to admire the seriousness and objectivity that it brings to its articles. A Children's Reading Room introduces kids to the possibility of esoteric reality.

NASA

www.nasa.gov

Information about the space agency: The NASA site, far from being a bureaucratic placard (like some government agencies' Internet sites), is a vibrant, informative, wide-ranging Web science location that is download heaven if you're interested in multimedia science files.

Today@NASA.gov — a section of the site and a worthy site by itself — provides breaking news about NASA missions and new images from the Hubble Space Telescope. The Photo/Movie Gallery is an almost unbelievable repository of pictures, audio clips, and movies available for viewing online (with the correct browser plug-ins) or downloading.

National Air and Space Museum

www.nasm.si.edu

Information about the museum: Part of the Smithsonian Institution, the National Air and Space Museum Internet site serves largely as an electronic brochure for the museum, supplying schedules, maps, and exhibit information. Those features alone wouldn't get the site into this book, however. Dig a little deeper, in the Online Resources section, and further riches reveal themselves, in the form of picture archives of Apollo missions, museum compendia, online versions of special museum events (such as "Star Wars: The Magic of Myth"), space-shuttle photographs, and much more.

Nature Perspective

**www.perspective.com/nature/
index.html**

A directory of all species: How would you like the job of classifying and describing all life on earth, without being boring? Whoever put together the Nature Perspective site (his name is Ari Kornfeld) did just fine. The site groups all earthly life into four categories — Plantae, Fungi, Animae, Protoctista — and then throws in the biosphere as an added attraction. Maintaining a scientific approach in labeling the subdivisions of life, the site describes them with an informal, accessible style that enlivens the proceedings. The liberal use of photographs to illustrate things really helps.

Nobel Prize Internet Archive

www.nobelprizes.com/nobel/top.html

Information about the prizewinners: The most complete and informative archive of Nobel Prize information, the Nobel Prize Internet Archive elegantly solves the main problem that all such pages face: the relative anonymity of many Nobel Prize winners. The Nobel Prize Internet Archive contains a brief amount of background and biographical information on its gallery of winners, but its main strength is pointing viewers in the right direction to learn more on their own. Links to Web sites that belong to — or discuss — the prizewinners, as well as information on books about the prizewinning topic, are useful research features. Often, the entries link to the sponsoring university's pages that are related to the winning research and to the original papers announcing the scientific results that won the prize. The Nobel Prize Internet Archive is divided into broad disciplines: Physics, Chemistry, Peace, and so on. You don't have to be a Nobel laureate yourself to navigate the site.

SETI Institute

www.seti.org/Welcome-page.html

Information about the search for extraterrestrial life: The 1997 movie *Contact* brought popular awareness to SETI (Search for Extraterrestrial Intelligence), the not-for-profit scientific institute that searches for extraterrestrial intelligence. The agency is not fictional; for years, it has worked through the stigma of scientific incredulity, persevering in the quest for coherent signals from space. The site is no feast for the eyes and doesn't splash any space photos across its pages — after all, the institute searches for ET life but has yet to find anything worth photographing. Instead, the site is full of information about the institute's work and its current projects.

Views of the Solar System

bang.lanl.gov/solarsys/

Travel guide to the solar system: You won't
find a more phenomenal resource for
facts, figures, and views of the solar
system. Views of the Solar System is an
exhaustive compendium of data about
planets, comets, asteroids, and the sun,
yet it manages to avoid stuffiness or
tedium. Pick a planet to see available
images of it, plus all the information that
you could ever want about its characteristics and the exploratory missions
launched toward it. Links to other planet-
specific Web sites are included in the
data. Animations are among the best
features of this site, showing planetary
movement relative to the solar system.
The well-written general descriptions of
each planet are enough for some people,
even without diving into the statistics
and other resources. However you
approach this site, you won't come away
disappointed.

Other Stuff to Check Out

darwin.cshl.org
sdf.laafb.af.mil
sln.fi.edu/planets/planets.html
www.jpl.nasa.gov
www.msichicago.org
www.windows.umich.edu

Science Publications

Most of the following magazines are
online editions of printed periodicals that
either transfer their articles to Web
pages, display new content that's not
included in the printed editions, or both.
One magazine, *Omni,* became so enam-
ored with the Web that it discontinued its
print edition in favor of Internet-only
publication.

Discover

www.discover.com

Online edition of the magazine: Discover
magazine covers the entire world of
science. (That must be why *The World of
Science* is the magazine's tag line.) The
Web site covers the parts of the magazine, including the full text of selected
current and past articles. A high-quality, if
low-volume, list of science links around
the Web is presented in directory style,
making finding other locations in a
certain discipline easy. The site's omissions are a bit frustrating, but no doubt
the editors want you to buy the printed
magazine. If nothing else, the Web
site serves as a sort of partial trial
subscription.

Exploring Online

**www.exploratorium.edu/exploring/
index.html**

Features stories focusing on science:
Exploring Online is a monthly Internet
magazine of science and perception that's
the online companion to *Exploring*
magazine, put out by San Francisco's
Exploratoreum museum. The online
magazine is not a full-featured magazine
like one that you'd find on the newsstands; it consists entirely of one story
per issue, without columns, letters, or
other supplementary material. But the
story does include audio and video clips
(one recent story about memory included
some nice RealVideo reminiscences with
a 101-year-old woman), and each issue
promises an online activity. Back issues of
Exploring Online and its predecessor,
What's New in the World, are available.

128 Science

Popular Science

www.popsci.com

Online edition of the magazine: Popular Science deals with scientific subjects that relate to daily living and the products that everyone uses. A recent online issue covered the proposed new international space station, a new base for further adventures in space. But what if the Russians — who seem to be behind — can't deliver the critical piece on time? And how much do space scientists really know about the long-term effects of being in the gravity-less conditions of space? Exactly that type of issue is explored in the virtual pages of this magazine, which is aimed at the consumer who's interested in how things work and why they're invented. Discussion forums enliven the site, and you don't have to register to join in. Discussions are sometimes marred, however, by messages from people who are trying to sell used equipment.

Science News Online

www.sciencenews.org

A weekly online science publication: Science News magazine built its reputation on weekly delivery of concise, timely bulletins from all facets of the science world, written for the intelligent layperson or semiprofessional reader. Anyone who has a casual interest and soft background in science can stay reasonably up-to-date with *Science News* articles, and now they can do so on the

Web. In addition to posting some of the current week's articles, the site provides back issues, indexes for the current and preceding year, and recommended sources of relevant information outside the site. Like many online magazines, the site is more comprehensive in its archives than in its current issue, thereby motivating you to go buy the magazine.

ScienceDaily

www.sciencedaily.com/index.htm

Current science news: ScienceDaily is an online headline publication covering breaking news in all the sciences. Today's current headlines greet you from the home page. Scroll down to see the Science Channels — 15 categories of science (including Fossils & Ruins, Order & Chaos, Cells & Microbes, Mind & Brain, Circuits & Chips, Health & Medicine, and Matter & Energy) within which recent stories are filed. Reading a current story and then getting background information from the related category provides a highly specific research experience on a science topic. Browsing is fun and informative. The site moves as fast as a hungry cheetah, and summaries are provided if you don't have time for extensive reading.

ScienceNOW

sciencenow.sciencemag.org

$

Great science articles — for a price: Not later, but *NOW.* If you have an urgent need for science news, head over to ScienceNOW for the up-to-the-minute scoop. A production of *Science* magazine, ScienceNOW contains original articles and is updated daily. The depth and breadth of content is impressive, featuring reports on the issues of science industries as well as hard science news. A guide to medical tumors may be placed next to an article about the Department of Energy's shutdown of a lab. Headlines go back one week and then are archived in a searchable database. All this excellent content comes at a price, however. You can look over the home page without any obligation. If you want to see a complete table of contents and article abstracts, though, you need to undergo an almost unbelievably complex and troublesome registration process, apparently designed for those who have scientific degrees. The thorny and exhausting registration process would be a finalist in any contest for the worst such travail on the Web. However, the content — ah, the content — is worth it. If you want to see the full text of all articles, you need to join the American Association for the Advancement of Science, which gives you a paid subscription.

Scientific American

www.sciam.com

Online edition of the magazine: Scientific American magazine has long held a place of honor on the reading shelves of science-educated laypeople. The magazine's articles are learned and assume that you have a scientific background, yet they weigh in a couple of notches below the professional level. The online edition presents most of the magazine's content, and the articles are considerably enhanced by embedded links that lead to background and explanatory information. The ever-popular "50, 100, and 150 Years Ago" column is reproduced in its entirety. Back issues are archived about a year and a

half in arrears. Make no mistake — this site is challenging reading and not designed for entry-level students of any scientific discipline. But *Scientific American* is perfect if you like to keep up-to-date with current research in the multidisciplinary field of broad science.

Sky Online

www.skypub.com

Online astronomy magazine: Sky Publishing Corporation, the creator of Sky Online, produces four popular astronomy magazines, including *Sky & Telescope* and *SkyWatch '98*. The site walks a fine line between sharing content from the magazines and forcing you to get the hard copies. In selecting articles and special features for the site (culled from the magazines), Sky Online provides a pretty dynamic array of attractions. From backyard tips to views of the Mir space station, from an eclipse guide to reviews of telescopes and viewing accessories, Sky Online is a fifth magazine unto itself. By the way, for a related site, check out *Sky & Telescope*'s Weekly News Bulletin at the following URL: `www.skypub.com/news/news.html`.

Smithsonian Magazine

www.smithsonianmag.si.edu

Online edition of the magazine: Text and images from *Smithsonian Magazine* are presented in Web format at this site, along with an extensive photo gallery organized by individual photographers who contribute often to the publication. A directory of topics for browsing past articles and a keyword search engine enhance the site's usefulness. (**Hint:** When typing a keyword phrase, place hyphens between the words to keep them together as a phrase.) *Smithsonian Magazine* takes a scientific approach to community concerns, wildlife habitats, and extreme weather conditions, giving the magazine a blend of science and sociology. A recent issue covered the battle to save endangered elms, how house trailers "have come a long way, baby," and how the blimp population is burgeoning.

Other Stuff to Check Out

BioMedNet.com
nyjm.albany.edu:8000
www.cell.com
www.hq.nasa.gov/office/pao/History/alsj
www.jbc.org
www.math.ruu.nl/hm
www.pnas.org

Social Issues

earthtimes.org

Social issues include all the non-entertainment aspects of a society's daily culture. The topics in this section include environmental concerns, gender issues, not-for-profit organizations, and minorities. These groups' agendas are palpable in most of these sites, which use the Web to gain grassroots support and membership, although the sites never charge for a visit.

Environment

Earth-friendly and animal-savior organizations and publications comprise this section. The sites tend to be modestly designed and quick to navigate.

The Earth Times

earthtimes.org

Online edition of the magazine: The Earth Times *is a printed magazine covering environmental issues and offering an online edition. Global in scope,* The Earth Times *reports on sustainable development in Africa, Asia, the Americas, and Europe. The virtual edition has more news sections than nonbiodegradable peanuts in a UPS package, including Arts & Culture, Business & Investing, Children, Gender Issues, Human Rights, and Population. Each section contains an archive of relevant stories, and the writing is neither as alarmist nor as cynical as you might expect. The Earth Times is upbeat (when possible) and helpful in its suggestions and admonitions. Speaking of helpful, a low-graphics version of the site is available (although the regular pages don't stall your modem), as well as a keyword search feature.*

EnviroLink

www.envirolink.org

Online environmental community: EnviroLink is another one of those "I started it as a freshman in college" success stories. Founded as a simple newsletter in 1991 by a first-year student at Carnegie Mellon University, EnviroLink has grown into one of the most impressive environmental information clearinghouses on the Web. The front page meets three criteria that seem to befuddle others: It's classy looking, informative and useful, and easy to understand. Headlines in the middle link to key news stories and commentaries, many of the former coming from the Environmental News Service. Links on the front page send you to pages where you can Express

Yourself (through chat and message board forums, for which you have to register for free); learn more about organic living and buying "green"; and learn more about animal rights. My favorite is the EnviroArts: Orion Online link, a new collaboration between EnviroLink and The Orion Society that offers some of the best environmental artwork — both literary and visual — on the Web.

Greenpeace International

www.greenpeace.org

Information about the organization: Greenpeace is an environmental action group with claws — but creative claws. The organization specializes in innovative, nonviolent confrontation to expose environmental problems and force solutions. Greenpeace's ideals include the protection of biodiversity, the prevention of pollution, the elimination of nuclear threat, and the promotion of peace. The site's six main sections — Toxics, Nuclear, Atmosphere, Forests, Oceans, and Genetic Engineering — spin off to news pages that display links to press releases about Greenpeace campaigns around the world. The site archives past news and includes a search engine, while the National Offices page includes links to Greenpeace affiliates in several countries with information on how you can get involved.

Sierra Club

www.sierraclub.org

Information about the organization: Maybe you've seen calendars and greeting cards featuring the Sierra Club's renowned nature photography. Those phenomenal photos don't grace the Web site, sad to say, but for environmental news, you'd do well to add the Sierra Club URL to your bookmark list. The news articles at this site are replicated from two publications: *Sierra* (the Sierra Club magazine) and *The Planet* (an activist resource). The writing sometimes veers toward political admonitions but is more likely to be self-empowering by suggesting what the average person can do to help solve environmental crises. The first thing that the Sierra Club wants you to do, of course, is join the organization, and full information on doing just so is provided.

Other Stuff to Check Out

www.cfn.cs.dal.ca/Environment/EAC/
    EAC-Home.html
www.ecology.com
www.igc.org/igc/issues/habitats/
www.nceet.snre.umich.edu/EndSpp/
    Endangered.html
www.nrdc.org/nrdc/field/acti.html

Gender and Sexuality Issues

Always controversial, sexuality issues include gay and lesbian concerns, right to choose versus right to life, and feminism. (The section also includes a men's site — would that be "masculism"?)

Abortion Rights Activist

www.cais.com/agm/main/index.html

Information on abortion rights: The Abortion Rights Activist site delivers news and resources for people who are

132 Social Issues

interested in a woman's right to choose to terminate a pregnancy. The site emphasizes what is called clinic violence — terrorist attacks on abortion clinics. In cooperation with the National Abortion Federation, the Tools for Activists page offers a Community Action Guide to help people get more proactively involved with the issue. A useful state-by-state guide to abortion law is one of the best links, along with an antichoice calendar (a list of upcoming right-to-life demonstrations). The Abortion Rights Activist is balanced on the Net by the National Right to Life site, which is also reviewed in this section.

GLAAD

www.glaad.org/glaad/latest.html

Gay and lesbian activism: The Gay and Lesbian Alliance Against Defamation has created a bold Web site filled with news for the gay and lesbian activist community. GLAADLines offers news headlines about the lesbian, gay, bisexual, and transgender communities. GLAADAlerts is a weekly update of issues and public situations that call for grassroots action, complete with contact addresses for writing protest and opinion letters. A search engine makes finding things easier. The site is designed like an online newspaper, and the wealth of graphics may slow it some. Looks great, though.

Human Rights Campaign

www.hrcusa.org

Information about the organization: The Human Rights Campaign (HRC) sounds like a broader-based civil-rights organization than it really is; HRC works specifically toward equal rights for gay and lesbian people in the workforce and the community at large, but it doesn't deal

with other human rights issues. The Web site describes the work of HRC's Washington lobbyists and citizen advocates. The Human Rights Campaign button on the home page brings you up to speed on the central concerns of the group as it struggles with public issues such as HIV/AIDS, workplace discrimination, marriage legislation, and health. Events listings, an online store, and Web links fill out the site.

Men's Issues Page

www.vix.com/pub/men

Information of interest to men: Men don't seem to have as many issues as women do (given the number of Web sites), but whatever concerns exist are covered on the Men's Issues Page, which is one of the few such sites on the Web. At first glance, the Men's Issues Page looks like an Internet directory to related sites, which would be a fine contribution to Net culture. But the agenda of this site goes way beyond merely pointing to other sites; the approach is more explanatory and even encyclopedic. The links of the directory lead to descriptive pages, some of article length, on domestic violence, single-parenting, economics, legislation, political correctness, and much more. One thing that the site is *not* is terribly current. A little more aggressive updating would help, but the information is worthwhile despite the dusty datelines.

National Right to Life

www.nrlc.org

Antiabortion information: The antiabortion agenda of the National Right to Life organization needs no explanation. The site uses plain design sensibilities and clearly organized content to deliver its message. A multimedia section archives some of the Child Protection Fund advertisements for viewing on your computer. Press releases and news, action alerts, the voting records of legislators, contraceptive-drug information, and abortion information are presented, all from a right-to-life viewpoint. The National Right to Life site is balanced on the Net by the Abortion Rights Activist site, which is also reviewed in this section.

National Organization for Women (NOW)

www.now.org

Information on the organization: The National Organization for Women (NOW) fulfills the basic requirements of activist Web sites by providing an archive of news releases, explanations of the organization's policies, and membership information in a collection of well-designed Web pages. The table of contents, located below the main graphic on the home page, spells out the site's features fairly clearly. A good place to start is the Key Issues section, where you can call up descriptions and activist information related to the key agenda items of feminism: abortion, reproductive rights, economic equality, legislation, lesbian rights, and violence. The site links to other Web resources and provides a complete list of local chapters.

WomensNet

www.igc.org/igc/womensnet/

An online magazine and guide to women's groups: This beautiful site is a combination newsmagazine on feminist issues and a resource guide that supports women's organizations internationally. The home page features action alerts on issues that require immediate grassroots support, as well as headlines. A few feature articles usually are presented as well. At the top of the page is one of the best features of WomensNet: a drop-down Issues Directory menu of topics such as Politics, Media, Violence Against Women, and Economics. Choose any topic and click the button, and the entire home page redisplays with content geared toward your selection. This site has a high-quality design and outstanding content.

Other Stuff to Check Out

www.ibd.nrc.ca/~mansfield/feminism/
www.igc.apc.org/gfw/

Minorities

Various U.S. minorities are represented in the following sites. You may also want to look in the "Global Cultures" section earlier in this part, for sites that deal with indigenous cultures.

Channel A

www.channela.com

Information for Asian Americans: Channel A is a premier Web site for information that is relevant to Asian Americans. Taking a cue from the site's name, the content is largely driven by entertainment but also contains sections on food and culture. The site is exceptionally well designed — a feast for the eyes, not even counting the sumptuous recipes in the Food section. Running throughout the site are links to message boards. Channel A is for the energetic, aware, contemporary Asian American.

Grand Times

www.grandtimes.com

Online magazine for senior citizens: Grand Times is an online magazine for senior citizens who like activity, traveling, and keeping abreast of current trends, cultures, and fashions. The site can't be described as being sumptuous — many of the icon links are bare-line sketches — but the sparseness of the decor somehow fits with the almost breathless, go-out-and-do-it attitude. Interactivity is supported through a call for manuscript submissions; see the About Grand Times link for information. A recent issue featured articles on secrets your cat wants you to know, the wonders of solitude, and "Swiss travel you can bank on." (For more senior-citizen sites, see Part VIII.)

Hispanic Online

www.hisp.com

Online editions of two Hispanic magazines: The online home of *Hispanic* and *Moderna* magazines, Hispanic Online carries stories from both publications. Reviews of Latino-oriented Web sites are also featured. The site has a strongly personal bent, often showcasing people in the Latino community and giving Teacher of the Year and Business Person Showcase awards. The home page fairly heavily promotes the mirror site on America Online and the printed magazines, but the promotion doesn't detract from good design and solid content.

NAACP Online

www.naacp.org/index.html

Information about the organization: The National Association for the Advancement of Colored People (NAACP) is the oldest civil-rights organization in the United States, founded in 1909 by a group of black and white citizens in New York City. The Web site, which was created a bit more recently, presents some history, a sample of NAACP programs, and an Issue Alert section that isn't always as up-to-date as some of the news stories on the home page. You can join the NAACP through the site, and the In Your Community button displays a map that enables you to track down local chapters and officials.

Native American Rights Fund

www.narf.org

Information about the organization: The Native American Rights Fund (NARF) provides legal representation to individuals, tribes, and villages to help deal with the complex laws that affect the lives of Native Americans. The Web site documents NARF's work and offers an on-screen membership brochure, press releases, legal reviews, and profiles of officers. A Resources section offers a library of treaties and laws related to American Indians. In addition, this frequently updated site usually includes a couple of job listings.

NativeWeb

www.nativeweb.org

Information of interest to indigenous peoples: NativeWeb seeks to represent all the indigenous peoples of the planet. The scope of this site is broader than that of an American Indian Web location, in that it displays content that's relevant to South and Central America as well as to North America. To that end, the site uses pages of news, events calendars, and lists of Web resources. A message board invites interactive participation. The Native American Story Telling section is interesting, presenting dozens of tales written in the style of aural tradition. NativeWeb is eclectic, with a more intimate, communal feel than some other, larger minority Web sites.

Other Stuff to Check Out

conbio.rice.edu/nae/index.html
www.inform.umd.edu:8080/EdRes/Topic/
   Diversity
www.ubp.com

Not-for-Profit Organizations

I gathered major not-for-profit organizations for this section, regardless of, and without consideration to, their agendas. So this section is a mixed bag, representing social concerns ranging from senior-citizen rights to international civil rights.

AARP

www.aarp.org

Information about the organization: The American Association of Retired People (AARP) is a huge advocacy force in the lives of millions of older folks, as well as a powerful lobbying presence in Washington. The organization is dedicated to expanding the state of Florida — oh, wait, I got my notes confused. Here we go: The AARP's guiding principle is the independence, dignity, and purpose of senior citizens. The Web site is a basic promotion, with some community features. You can read position papers and advocacy statements and, of course, get membership information. AARP doesn't spur its members to grassroots action on compelling contemporary issues, although it works on their behalf in the legislative bodies. As a result, the Web site is low-key — informative without being admonishing. (For more senior-citizen sites, see Part VIII.)

Amnesty International

www.amnesty.org

Information about the organization: Founded in 1961 in response to the arrest of a group of European citizens for toasting freedom in a bar, Amnesty International provides this dryly informative account of its mission and current campaigns. The site needs some organizational tightening to eliminate the many mouse clicks now required to get anywhere, but that's a small complaint compared to what's available. You can search for news releases by date and receive e-mailed reports with a free subscription. Amnesty International operates primarily by researching and drawing attention to human-rights violations rather than by staging proactive confrontations like those practiced by Greenpeace, the environmental-activism group (whose site is reviewed earlier in this part). The Amnesty International Web site is an important vehicle for staying informed.

ASPCA

www.aspca.org

Information about the organization: The American Society for the Prevention of Cruelty to Animals (ASPCA) has its work cut out for it, as animal abandonment, neglect, and sometimes outright torture seem only to increase with the size of the animal population. Far from taking a grim tone, however (unlike the first sentence of this review), the ASPCA site offers pet-care tips for dogs, cats, gerbils, hamsters, rabbits, and guinea pigs; seasonal pet-tips; and other light features that cater to responsible pet owners. For more serious fare, click the Issues & Advocacy button to learn about the society's activities on the governmental and legal fronts. The Event Calendar lists the many activities and training programs offered by the ASPCA, which is located in New York City.

Children's Defense Fund

www.childrensdefense.org

★ ★
★ ★

Information about the organization: Beautifully designed, newsy, and upbeat, the Children's Defense Fund (CDF) site is a cut above the typical slapped-together, not-for-profit Internet placard. The CDF is a proactive voice for American children — particularly poor, disabled, and minority kids. Primarily an educational institution, CDF encourages preventive solutions to child illness, education dropout, family breakdown, and delinquency. The site presents articles, issues, news reports, action alerts, and links to other sites.

International Committee of the Red Cross (ICRC)

**www.icrc.org/unicc/icrcnews.nsf/
    DocIndex/home_eng?OpenDocument**

Information about the organization: You can easily think of the American Red Cross as being a gigantic, globe-spanning relief organization swooping into war and natural-disaster situations with apolitical medical assistance. In fact, much of the Red Cross's work is accomplished at the individual level, with local volunteers, and involves services as diverse and specific as swimming lessons and blood donations. You can get the gist of international activities by going to the Operations by country page, and connect to national Red Cross or Red Crescent (the name used in predominantly Muslim countries) affiliates by clicking Other Red Cross/Red Crescent servers. The affiliates use their Web pages to varying degrees. At the U.S. Red Cross site (www.crossnet.org, in case you want to go there directly), you can get information, begin the joining process, and even donate money right through the Web site. All in all, you can find lots of ways to help make a difference visiting with the Red Cross on the Web.

National Urban League

www.nul.org

Information about the organization: The National Urban League (NUL), founded in 1910, immediately built a Web site. Well, no, I suppose that act would have been premature, despite the rudimentary design of the National Urban League pages. Style isn't the point, however — social-service and civil-rights information and empowerment are what's relevant. The site provides a complete rundown of

NUL activities, policies, officers, affiliates, resources, and programs. The "To Be Equal" weekly column, written by the president of the National Urban League, is presented and archived at the site. The Job Bank is an interactive form; you fill in information fields and view related job possibilities. The job database is active and blazingly current, and you can request up to 75 listings per search.

National Wildlife Federation

www.nwf.org/nwf

Information about the organization: Education about the environment and action toward saving it are emphasized at the National Wildlife Federation (NWF) Web site. As the largest member-supported conservation group, the NWF reaches out to businesses, individuals, and the government to protect nature. The idea is to inspire people to uphold habits of conservation in both small and big ways. The site is a treasure of infor-mation — much more than I can describe in this section. Updates and action alerts (a proposal to put a road through Alaskan wetlands and challenges to U.S. laws protecting endangered sea turtles, among others) tell you what issues need urgent attention. On a milder note, the site offers articles about collaborative conservation and outdoor activities, schedules of TV broadcasts of environmental shows, and even a kids' section. The NWF would love to have you as a member, but the site doesn't make a big deal about it.

Other Stuff to Check Out

action.org
www.habitat.org/default.html
www.mecca.org/~crights

138 Social Issues

Part IV
Sports, Entertainment, and Leisure

In this part . . .

Having fun is what the Internet is all about these days. The sites listed in this part are guaranteed to make your surfing experience a pleasure. Whether you're interested in entertaining your kids, training your dog, catching the latest fashion news, downhill skiing, or checking on sites in different parts of the globe, these sites have what you need.

Family Sites

The number of family sites that saturate the World Wide Web is really surprising, considering that parents — especially young parents — generally don't have a great deal of time to cruise the Internet. But facts are facts, and family issues — parenting, child health, marriage, sibling relations, and so on — are well represented on the Web.

Note: For more on these kinds of sites, check out *The World Wide Web For Kids & Parents,* by Viraf Mohta (IDG Books Worldwide, Inc.).

Family Activities

Family-activity sites place more emphasis on fun than do the sites in the "Family Resources" portion of this section. The following sites often include some interactivity, allowing families to have fun together online.

Big Families

www.bigfamilies.com

Information and activities for large families: Big Families is somewhat more attractive to parents than to kids, but the site proves to be a good group location nonetheless, especially for the photos. The site is a celebration of large families, which are defined as having at least three children. All such families are invited to upload pictures (instructions are included), and the photo gallery includes numerous shots from large families — including a family of 21. A chat area is available (to Java browsers) but not always in use, and message boards enable you to reach other families by writing notes. (You're required to register, which is free, before you use the message boards, and the site solicits some personal information about your interests and family size in order to create a personal profile. You also can set up a special signature to appear at the bottom of your messages.) You and your family also can upload articles about parenting, covering such topics as breast-feeding and the influence of birth order on children. Big Families is a highly interactive, participatory site.

Family Explorer

www.webcom.com/safezone/FE/ frame4.htm

Simple activities for kids and parents: If you quiver with uncertainty when helping your child with science homework and projects, *Family Explorer* has you in mind. The monthly printed magazine contains about six simple activities, plus a word puzzle, a star chart, and miscellaneous other features. The Web edition provides only samples of the printed version, but the site archives everything. This backlog of activities is what makes this site valuable, even though you get more by subscribing to the offline magazine. The Web edition can be a sort of trial subscription to the printed magazine, enabling you to see how you like it. The clearly written, illustrated descriptions are aimed at adults but can be understood by motivated kids.

142 Family Sites

Family Friendly Sites

www.virtuocity.com/family.html

A directory of approved sites for families:
Family Friendly Sites (FFS) is a self-
appointed approval agency that evaluates
the content on other Web sites. If a site
meets FFS guidelines, it can display a logo
(sort of like the Good Housekeeping Seal
of Approval) on its Web pages. A seven-
step document spells out the guidelines
on FFS's home page, and viewers are
welcome to submit URLs to sites that
they think conform to the standards of
family viewing. More useful than a mere
standard-setting organization, Family
Friendly Sites displays a directory of sites
that bear its emblem, broken into standard directory topic headings. The site is
a good starting point for family surf
sessions.

Family Internet

www.familyinternet.com

Links to family resources: Family Internet
is a lush, gloriously designed site with
surprisingly little original content.
Clicking one of its multitudinous links is
likely to open a new browser window and
send you scuttling over the TotalTV
listing guide or to a site about pets or
family computing. Family Internet is an
astonishingly high-gloss production even
though it's essentially a list of links, and
the slow page displays give you ample
time to mend your clothes. But this site
has a solid benefit: All the links have been
checked out and approved for family
viewing.

Family.com

family.disney.com

A family site from Disney: A production of
the Walt Disney Company, Family.com is
like a daily electronic magazine featuring
articles about travel, kids' issues,
parenting subjects, activities, educational
info, recipes, message boards, and chat
rooms (which were under construction
recently). Bright, colorful, packed with
information, and rich with graphics, this
site leaves you a great deal of time for
quality family interacting while you wait
for the pages to display (a characteristic
of all the Disney Web sites). The
parenting section tackles issues such as
how to face the battle at bedtime, how to
avoid spoiling children, and how children
develop speech over the first five years of
their lives. Kids gravitate to the Activities
area for games and video reviews.

Other Stuff to Check Out

www.contestclub.com
www.famday.com
www.rom.on.ca

Family Resources

Family-resource sites differ from parental-
resource sites in that they include a
child's needs and tastes in their designs.
The following sites differ from purely
kids' sites (which I review in the "Kids'
Sites" section of Part VII) in that they're
appropriate for parents and kids to visit
together.

Dr. Toy

www.drtoy.com

Guide to children's products: Dr. Toy's guide to children's products cross-references every which way. Look up a toy or browse the index of listings, which are organized by the category of toy or the age of the child. Browse sections that list toys, games, educational products, socially responsible items, creative toys, active products, high-tech devices, and audio and video tapes. Although the site evaluates and approves every toy, it doesn't provide descriptive reviews. Instead, it links to the toy's Web site, or at the very least, lists the manufacturer's mailing address and phone number.

Education Place

www.eduplace.com

Ideas and products for kids and parents: Because Education Place is produced by Houghton Mifflin, the activities and products that the site promotes are mostly associated with that publisher's printed materials. Beyond the self-promotion, though, Education Place is a solid value for kids and parents, separately or together. Information on famous authors (which you can find under Author Spotlight in the Reading Room section of The Reading Dimension) links to other sites that are dedicated to those authors. Brain Teasers in the Kids Clubhouse are grouped by grade levels, and the site sometimes features contests. The Link Library alone is worth a visit.

Families Under Construction

www.famucon.com

Advice and resources for building families: Families Under Construction takes the attitude that rearing a family is like building a house — if you use high-quality tools and resources, you get better

results. The site usually offers feature articles, some written by doctors and other authorities, covering issues such as fatherhood roles and getting your family to exercise. A Columns section displays the site owner's acerbic responses to a newspaper's parenting column. The site design, featuring a brick background, emphasizes the construction motif, but rest assured — the site itself is fully functional.

Family PC

www1.zdnet.com/familypc

The family's computer magazine: Family PC magazine has long been the monthly resource of choice for families who are looking for hardware and software evaluations from a parent's viewpoint. In fact, the magazine calls itself "The Home of Family Testing." Don't worry — what gets tested is not your family but the computer products that your family buys. Articles cover games, child safety on the Net, software-content blockers, reviews of digital cameras, and much more. The site is a bible for computer-owning families. The Web edition is comprehensive, with a mix of original content and articles imported from the print magazine.

Family Time

www.homearts.com/depts/family/ 00dpftc1.htm

144 Family Sites

Family issues and advice: Family Time's tag line is "The Practical Art of Nurturing." The site makes good on its promise by producing a comprehensive Web site that addresses the entire family — and the parenting experience — with topics ranging from pregnancy to child psychology to pets. Dr. Joyce Brothers has her own page, as do Peggy Post and Jane Bryant Quinn. Book reviews guide parents to the titles that are best for kids. Chat rooms are available, but they require you to register (for free) and download a program. Message boards are another community feature; they don't use any special software, but you still have to register to use them. Dads, don't leave the site without trying the Dad's Corner section.

Kids' Camps

www.kidscamps.com

Directory of camps: Blending a search engine with a browsing directory, Kids' Camps attempts to help you track down any type of camp anywhere in the United States or Canada. The home page features nine topics, including Residential Camps, Day Camps, Tours & Adventures, Sports Camps, Arts Camps, Academic Camps, and Family Camps. Choose any topic to display a series of drop-down lists for selecting locations down to the state level. **Warning:** The search results sometimes veer toward the unexplainable. Recently, I failed to locate the Interlochen Arts Camp when I searched in Michigan, but I found it in a list of *all* music camps, placed correctly in Michigan. Occasional glitches aside, Kids' Camps offers a good way to get leads on different kinds of summer (and year-round) activities. The site even has a section on adult camps.

Other Stuff to Check Out

griffin.vcu.edu/~dimlist
www.agnr.umd.edu/users/nnfr
www.family.com/Categories/Education
www.family-software.com

Parenting

Unsure parents — and what parent doesn't have moments of uncertainty? — have many virtual resources to rely on. Some of these sites are essentially support groups; others provide more practical content in the way of child activities, games to teach your kids, and parental techniques. Some sites tackle the hard, almost unspeakable issues of parenting; others are softer and more comforting. Generally, parenting sites don't assume a great deal of awareness, expertise, or even interest in multimedia on your part, and they present their content in a straightforward manner.

All About Kids Online

www.aak.com

★★
★★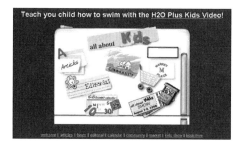

Teach you child how to swim with the H2O Plus Kids Video!

Communal site about kids: Much of the material on this elegantly designed site is taken from *All About Kids* magazine. The online version of the magazine is especially helpful because the printed magazine is sold only in the Cincinnati area. Taking advantage of Internet interactivity features, the site provides a sense of community through the Forum, a series of parenting discussions in message-board format. An excellent list of links to other Web sites is available in the Virtual Community section. Each monthly issue carries a surprisingly large number of useful articles, making All About Kids Online a seemingly bottomless resource.

CreativeKids

www.creativekids.com

Q & A and reviews: If you stop by CreativeKids and dismiss it as just a site that sells software, you're selling the site — and yourself — short. CreativeKids offers some quality family material, not the least of which is ParentsPage. Two doctors contribute to the interactivity of ParentsPage: Dr. Gary Groch, a psychologist, and Dr. Beth Anderson, a Ph.D. with a specialty in education. On the Ask a Question page, both experts are available to answer questions about issues regarding child rearing, and the answers are then posted at the site. Fine as the Q & A feature is, the central attraction of CreativeKids is the software section, which provides a search engine for finding good learning programs for your kids. If you know the title of a program that you want to check out, enter it in the search engine; if you don't, specify an age and subject, and then peruse reviews from a list of approved titles. The reviews are fantastic, providing a paragraph or two of descriptions and a thorough rating system for evaluating features of the software. The site even offers a number of games (some demos) for downloading. ParentsPage doesn't require you to register, but you're invited to sign a guest book.

The CyberMom Dot Com

www.thecybermom.com

Fun and useful parenting site: This fun and resourceful site uses the motif of a rambling old house that has several virtual rooms of activities, software reviews, recipes, garden tips, and an interactive poll. CyberMom Dot Com is stuffed full of reviews, using an oven mitt as a rating-system unit: Five mitts is a scorcher, and one mitt is "definitely undercooked." Motherhood is a lifestyle at this site, extending way beyond bringing up kids. Accordingly, the site provides book reviews; information on money management, relationship and marriage issues; travel ideas; and recipes. The Family Room is the most family-oriented section of the site, providing information about videos, TV shows, home design, and vacations. You can't see everything in one visit to CyberMom Dot Com — a good indication that it deserves bookmarking.

Helping Your Child Learn Science

www.ed.gov/pubs/parents/Science/
  index.html

Spartan but useful site of science activities: This site is dry as a desert. Don't look for any fun graphics or colorful characters to ease your child's journey through the educational maze. In fact, don't look for any graphics whatsoever on this purely textual site — you'll have to add the fun yourself. But this site does start you on the right road to helping your child with science by explaining basic principles of observation and the scientific method, and then proposing fun activities (dryly). Because of the wordy nature of the site and the fact that many activities involve going outdoors, you may want to print individual pages of the activities.

KidsHealth.org

kidshealth.org/index2.html

Information on children's health: KidsHealth.org is, of course, dedicated to the subject of child health. Produced by The Nemours Foundation, the site contains loads of information about child growth, illnesses, infections, immunizations, nutrition, medical tests, conditions and surgical considerations, and modern treatments. The site is divided into sections for parents, kids, and professionals (pediatricians and other health care providers); the serious stuff is reserved for the grown-ups, and the children can play on-screen games related to health. The Health Tip of the Day ensures frequent updates; during a recent visit, the tip was to stick with asthma medicine recommended by your child's pediatrician, and not secretly substitute herbs or other home remedies recommended by friends. The site is searchable by keyword.

KidSource Online

www.kidsource.com

Education and health-care information for parents: KidSource Online is a resource for parents, covering primarily education and health care through articles, reviews, and reports on the state of education. A recent visit turned up articles on teaching children with disabilities, examining the link between childhood obesity and adult health, and keeping kids' teeth safe by enforcing pool rules. The Forums section is a collection of message boards, the stated purpose of which is to connect parents with educators. But the boards also serve as a place for parents to meet one another and discuss issues. Current discussion topics include education, computers, child nutrition, step-parenting, child care, stay-at-home parenting, and learning disabilities.

Learning Train

members.macconnect.com/users/j/ jrpotter/ltrain.spml

Educational activities: The Learning Train has a heck of a lot of cars. Written with care and detail, and without association with any publisher or organization, the Learning Train provides kids' learning activities geared to parents. Many of the activities center on reading, including simple book-making and phonics games. Printing the instructions for future use is a good strategy. A newsletter, *Learning Train News,* carries articles about child care, additional activities, and other parenting issues. Although the site hasn't been updated in a while, it still contains useful links to resources, articles, and reference materials about raising kids.

Librarian's Guide to Cyberspace

www.ala.org/parentspage/greatsites

Internet guide and list of family-oriented sites: The American Library Association feels that the Internet is the most innovative and exciting learning tool of the century, but believes that parents must be aware of the Internet's dangers as well as its advantages. To that end, the Librarian's Guide to Cyberspace helps parents by defining Internet terms, offering a section of safety tips, defining the qualities of a good family (or child) Web site, and listing a directory of more than 700 great sites for kids and parents. The site is quick, simple to use, and a good introduction to cyberspace for nervous parents.

Parent & Child Online

www.parentandchild.com/pcoindex.htm

Essential parenting information: Parent & Child Online (formerly known as Daily Parent) features timely articles about parenting (obviously), health, education, development, safety, food, home, and money. A very simple home page presents these (and many other) topics — each of which contains only one or two articles — in a drop-down list. Most of the sites deal with specific issues, like autism, bed-wetting, stuttering, and so on. You won't be overwhelmed by massive content on this site, but its slim, essentials-only approach is welcome to busy parents who can't spend much time sifting through info-packed megasites. The quality of Daily Parent is good, the pages display quickly, and message boards are available for those who want to linger. Registration is encouraged but not required.

Parent Soup

www.parentsoup.com

Many parents' favorite Web site: Parent Soup is a major Web spot for parents. The site is a cross between an electronic magazine and a community center, featuring deep informational resources and a busy schedule of interactive attractions. Viewer participation is encouraged at every turn, starting on the home page with a daily Parent Poll. Most impressive is the daily rundown of chat topics. On any given weekday, the Parent Soup staff moderates at least a dozen chat sessions, with slightly fewer offered on weekends. The site (part of the iVillage system of chat sites) enables you to choose among chat interfaces, depending on your computer system. Message boards also provide a slower means of discussion, and you must register (for free) to participate. Besides all the interactivity, Parent Soup dishes up software picks and articles that are of interest to parents, both married and single.

ParenthoodWeb

www.parenthoodweb.com

Difficult parenting topics covered frankly: No subject is too controversial or delicate in this frank information resource for parents. ParenthoodWeb tackles questions about pregnancy, breast-feeding, and infant health with a direct, no-nonsense approach that's rare on the Web. Recently, the site discussed bed-wetting, couples who are trying to conceive, children having trouble learning to read, whether or not to let an 8-year-old cry herself to sleep, discipline problems in children of divorcing parents, shopping cart safety for children, and the risks of low-lying placenta during pregnancy — and all that information was just the front page. The chat rooms are equally diverse; one even covers technology subjects. Other sections include an interactive question-and-answer feature, surveys, book reviews, a search engine for browsing by keyword, and a virtual bookstore where you can buy parenting books with a credit card.

ParentsPlace.com

www.parentsplace.com/index.html

Parenting message boards and chat: Operating on the principle that parents are the best resources for other parents, the main function of ParentsPlace.com is to provide a place for parents to meet one another and talk. To that end, the site offers an abundance of message boards and chat rooms, with an active schedule of discussion topics. An incredibly wide range of topics is set up in the message boards, including support groups for different types of child loss. You must register (for free) to participate in both chatting and messaging. ParentsPlace.com has some news and product information, but really, it's a place to connect with other parents.

148 Family Sites

ParentTime

www.parenttime.com

Age-specific information on children:
"Parenting is the most important job in
the world," the site's tag line proclaims,
and few people would argue. (Reviewing
Internet sites ranks a close second.)
ParentTime is a Pathfinder (Time Warner)
site, but it suffers much less from
overpromotion of Time Warner products
than other Pathfinder presentations do.
This site gets down to business, and the
first thing that you can do is take advantage of the personalization feature on the
home page. Click the age of your child
and see a new home page geared to your
particular parenting concerns. If you have
more than one child (not twins), you can
go through the selection process more
than once. The process may seem to be
awkward, but actually, getting age-specific
information without having to search for
it is helpful. Chat rooms and message
boards don't require you to register.

Raisin

www.raisinnet.com

Cutesy site that's frequently updated: All
right, the tag line is cute enough ("Currents for Parents Raisin' Children") and
may be a bit too cute. Raisin is updated
multiple times during the day, bringing
scalding news headlines to your browser.
Are parenting headlines ever that hot,
really? Well, you can count on reading
some fairly esoteric stories about the
maker of the Slinky toy being sold, a
Boston medical center that's taking part
in an Outward Bound program, and a dog
in a classroom. (Those stories are
examples gleaned from actual visits to the
site.) The site has a few departments but
none of the activities, message boards,
tips for parents, or interactive features
that are often available at family-oriented
parenting sites. This site is pure news.

Single Parents Association

www.singleparents.org

Support for go-it-alone parents: For parents
going it alone, the Single Parents Association is a must-bookmark Web resource, if
only for the sympathetic and comforting
tone of its text. The main site links to an
explanation of the organization, membership information, frequently asked
questions, more membership information
organization-chapter locations, and still
more urgings to join. All that stuff is fine,
but make sure you check out the
Parenting Tips link (for informative
essays with useful advice) and the Book
Reviews.

Working Mother

www.womweb.com

Information geared to professional moms:
The online edition of *Working Mother*
magazine is about as down-to-earth as a
site can get. The preceding URL takes you
to the Women's Web site, at which you
must click the Working Mother link. Visit
this site if you're looking for information,
unburdened by graphic glitter. Working
Mother covers topics such as child care
and the best companies for working
mothers; departments cover business,
food, health, kids, politics, and fathers.
Profiles of moms in the workplace are
sometimes featured.

Other Stuff to Check Out

> www.babycenter.com
> www.bguide.com/webguide/parenting/
>   fabfinds.html
> www.earlychildhood.com
> www.familyweb.com
> www.MJBovo.com/Spock.htm
> www.naturalchild.com
> www.npn.org
> www.positiveparenting.com
> www.thekitchentable.com
> www.warmlines.org

Fashion

www.nicolemiller.com

Fashion appears on the Internet with, appropriately, high style. Fashion pages tend to be overdesigned, choking modems all over the world with ravishing graphics. Informational fashion sites tend to be more straightforward, with fashion publications and designer sites pushing the design envelope. The sites in this section aren't focused on selling their fashions online, although they may contain some online merchandise. If you're looking for sites where you can purchase clothes and beauty products online, head over to the Shopping section of Part V.

Designers

Fashion designers, like their uptown stores in New York City, have the most cryptic sites on the Web. Refined and aloof, these pages radiate style and high culture while conveying little information that you can latch onto. Although these sites are showcases, as eye candy goes, the Web has hardly anything better.

Gianni Versace

www.moda.iol.it/stilisti/versace/e/ DEFAULT.HTM

Tribute to Versace's life and work: This English-speaking Italian site is a bare informational tribute to the famous designer, created before Versace was

killed. The site isn't set up as a posthumous tribute but as a living career-in-progress site, which somehow seems to be more impressive when you visit it. The site's two dozen links lead to pages that list Versace's accomplishments as though the site were a résumé. The information is unaccompanied by photographs or other illustrations and consists mostly of simple lists — a list of operas and ballets for which Versace designed the costumes, for example, and a list of celebrities who have worn Versace garments, presumably in prominent situations. The offhand, unpretentious tone of this site underlines the drama and loss of a master's life.

GildaMarx

www.gildamarx.com

Fine and accessible designer site: The motto in the lower right of the home page pretty much sums up what this site is about — "We admire strong women." As if you couldn't tell that from the photos, which during my visit featured women cycling and playing volleyball. Because strong women seemingly don't have a lot of spare time, this site is clear and forthright, presenting only basic information about some of the products in the GildaMarx exercise apparel line. Fortunately, the site does provide clues as to what stores offer the products, or toll-free numbers that U.S. residents can call for more information.

Mr. Blackwell's Wit & Wisdom

www.mrblackwell.com

Pointing out fashion victims: This is a tongue-in-cheek selection for this section, because Mr. Blackwell isn't famous for *designing* clothing but for what he *says* about clothing. Every year since 1960, Mr. Blackwell has unveiled his famous "Worst Dressed List," in which he declares his disapproval of the wardrobes of famous Hollywood women from Lucille Ball to

150 Fashion

Madonna. (The latter drew this 1997 remark: "Let's be blunt: Yesterday's 'Evita' is today's Velveeta.") The list started out as a magazine assignment but is now just shameless self-promotion, which, of course, makes it perfect Web material. You can find all the past lists here, as well as a few lists actually offering fashion accolades. Although the site has no photos of the celebrities named — I'm sure that legal issues are a big reason why — you can buy an autographed picture of Mr. Blackwell. You can bet his picture has been used on a few dartboards around Hollywood.

Nicole Miller

www.nicolemiller.com

★ ★
★ ★

Elegant clothes, elegant site: The Nicole Miller site has one of the most delightful index pages in all of cyberspace — something that looks like a darkened boutique, with tracings of apparel items and word hyperlinks that jump out as you pass your mouse over them. Very chic. So are the offerings, although you can buy only boxers, scarves, ties, and golf shirts on the site. But those items are special — after all, that $60 silk bow tie is a copyrighted print pattern with the year of production right on the label. Limited edition, of course.

Seventh on Sixth

www.7thonsixth.com

★ ★
★ ★

Fashion from many designers: Seventh on Sixth is a Web celebration of the runway scene and designers. The site is simple and elegant. Along the bottom of the home page is a list of designers: Calvin Klein, Hugo Boss, John Bartlett, Perry Ellis, Ralph Lauren, Tommy Hilfiger, and many others. Click a name to see a half-dozen runway photos from recent shows. Simple, clean, and elegant, the site lets the clothes do all of the talking. Seventh on Sixth is a good place to get an overview of current fashions and get up to speed on the designers.

Other Stuff to Check Out

ews.simplenet.com/designer
www.armaniexchange.com
www.donnakaran.com
www.mishatzar.com
www.pathfinder.com/altculture/aentries/o/oldhamxt.html

Fashion Magazines

The fashion magazines in this part are online editions of famous printed publications. These sites are far more newsy than the designer sites and usually are easier for your modem to digest. That's not to say that the magazine sites don't have nice designs — they do, but the designs are mixed with usable information. All these mags are geared primarily to women.

Cosmopolitan Online

cosmomag.com

★ ★
★ ★

Fashion, beauty, and glamour tips: Cosmo packs a great deal of content into its online edition; this site is far more than just a billboard advertising the magazine. For one thing, the Tips are updated weekly and include sections on Fashion,

Beauty, Health, Sex, and Relationships. Frank advice is the hallmark of the *Cosmopolitan* editorial style, and the online edition doesn't shrink from that tradition. Beauty and love are the twin main points in the Cosmo agenda, and the magazine hammers away with circuit-training tips followed by man-woman language translations. Cosmopolitan Online looks fabulous, but the shimmering graphics keep the site moving slowly.

Cover Girl

www.covergirl.com

Makeup and other appearance issues: Cover Girl mixes practical beauty tips with coverage of the modeling scene. The site's content is a relatively static presentation of clothing and makeup advice, with little interactivity and no community. A recent visit told me more than I wanted to know about makeup — but then, makeup is not a subject that I (like most men who aren't Dennis Rodman) have a daily interest in. The site is a detailed tutorial, probably worthy of a college course, in applying synthetic substances to your eyes, lips, face, and nails. Cover Girl provides little coverage of women's concerns aside from appearance; it's purely an online fashion mag.

Elle

www.ellemag.com

French fashion with plenty of photos: Elle is a French magazine with an English printed edition and an English Internet version. The printed content isn't slavishly reproduced in the Web edition, which is a generous way of saying that Elle withholds some articles so that you'll want to buy the magazine. But plenty of stuff is available online, including tons of photographs and Paris-centric coverage of fashion trends. Not to be virtually selfish, Elle provides links to other fashion sites, but the Fashion section is the site's centerpiece — unless you're an aspiring model or a leering gentleman, in which case the model gallery may attract most of your interest. Cindy Crawford, Elle MacPherson, Naomi Campbell, Claudia Schiffer, and many other top models are featured in their own minisections.

Glamour

**www.swoon.com/mag_rack/
  glamour.html**

Interactive fashion and lifestyle: The online edition of *Glamour* magazine manages to look slick without crushing your modem under the weight of heavy graphics — quite a feat in the fashion-mag business. The site is highly interactive, offering surveys ("Are fertility doctors going too far?"), message boards, personal ads, and chat rooms. In a word, this site is *accessible,* which is a breath of fresh air compared with the dark, somber, cryptic, mysterious aura cultivated by many online fashion publications. *Glamour* is really a lifestyle magazine as much as a fashion billboard, featuring articles on navigating the rocky shoals of intergender communications (dates, in other words), work, and health issues. A male-authored column offers a man's view. Registration isn't required, but you can create an alias for personal-ad responses.

Lumiere

www.lumiere.com

Slow pages look dazzling: Almost mystical in appearance as well as name, Lumiere presents a few feature articles covering aspects of fashion and personalities in the industry. The site covered Gianni Versace's murder in front-page style (to the degree that Lumiere can be said to have pages); recent articles included "high-tech solutions to low-lustre complexions" and new techniques in self-tanning. High-resolution photographs give the site an extravagant appearance but slow performance through standard modems. Lumiere archives past features going back a couple of years, making for convenient browsing.

Other Stuff to Check Out

itre.ncsu.edu/gz/fashion.htm
www.apparelnews.net
www.dircon.co.uk/lcf/ntouch.html
www.glamour-illustrated.com
www.hairnet.com
www.lorel.com/~ideas/style/style.html
www.worldstyle.com

General Fashion Sites

Newsy, gossipy, stylish sites covering the fashion industry fall into this section. Typically, these sites display news headlines that link to fashion stories, chic page designs, plenty of photos, and (sometimes) message boards and chat rooms.

CNN Style

www.cnn.com/STYLE

Fashion journalism: Thoroughness, simplicity, and an international scope are the hallmarks of CNN's fashion coverage on the Web. The CNN Style home page is a little more cluttered than other CNN sites but still is very inviting. During a recent visit, one of the main headlines had to do with World Cup–inspired fashions. The headlines on the main page link to full stories with plenty of illustrations and, often, video clips. CNN Style covers anything that's fashion-related, and during nonshow seasons, the site provides more industry news, such as model unionization. CNN Style is a great place to get up-to-date quickly on the entire global fashion scene for the upcoming season.

The Elizabethan Costuming Page

www.dnaco.net/~aleed/corsets/ general.html

For something really different: I'll admit that when I first found this page, my initial reaction was "Who cares about English ladies clothing from the 1500s?" After all, even the tag line of the Overview of an Elizabethan Outfit page admits, "She must be stifling in that thing." But the beauty of the Web is diversity, and few fashion pages cover a topic — even an obscure one — with such obvious affection. The overview page does a nice job blending history with progressive drawings; if you need a visual of the finished product, check out the Elizabethan Costume Gallery pages. Other pages tell you how to sew (yes, sew) virtually an entire outfit, down to the anatomy of a stocking, and the site includes fabric guides. If you need to communicate, the message board section invites you to "Speak Thy Minde." Judging from the volume of postings when I visited, lots of people are interested in Elizabethan costuming. I just hope they're not too stifled.

Fashion Live

www.worldmedia.fr/fashion

The Parisian fashion scene: A glitzy, chic, up-to-date multilingual site, Fashion Live concentrates on the Parisian fashion world. A recent cover story was how French designers were back on the offensive after their country's recent World Cup soccer win. Permanent departments — such as Catwalk Coverage, Trendwatch, Mode Squad, and Paris People — cover the Euro-fashion scene from runway to art studio to model dressing room. The site latches on to broad fashion trends and illustrates, discusses, and fawns over them in great detail. Fashion Live is a sleek site in its well-illustrated presentation, and now links to the online version of Fashion TV, "the world's only 24-hour fashion TV channel." You can watch on the Web with the StreamWorks Player (available for download).

Fashion.net

www.fashion.net

Guide to Internet fashion sites: Fashion.net is a guide to fashion resources and publications on the Web, with a strong community section featuring message boards and chat rooms. The site provides no content about fashion itself, in the way

of articles or original information; Fashion.net is not a magazine. As a community center and link hub, however, the site functions well. The message boards are jammed with friendly chatter about makeup, clothes, modeling, fitness, and with people who are looking for virtual pen pals. The Selected Sites button leads to a directory of fashion logos, each of which is a link to a corresponding Web site.

FirstView

www.firstview.com

$

Online displays of the latest fashions: A photo-intensive site that highlights thousands of current fashions from dozens of designers, FirstView is the place to go for the ultimate in virtual window shopping. (Window shopping without the prices, that is; FirstView doesn't sell or promote any fashion lines.) If you can't wait until the new fashions hit the stores, you can pay for a subscription to the site and see the latest wraps within days of their runway debuts, viewing photographs from the shows themselves. Are you ready for the subscription cost? You'd better sit down — it's about $1,000 per year. Okay, it's only $999. Still, that's *serious* Internet indulgence. Most people no doubt prefer to just register for free and receive e-mail alerts when the photos move from the subscriber area to the free area (about six months after their first showing).

Hypermode

www.hypermode.com/cover/index.html

Dark, almost surreal presentation of underground fashions: With a cynically dark motif and impossibly light green text on a black background, the Hypermode home page sets the bar for unreadable stylishness. Text is not the point, though, as Hypermode takes you on a visual journey through the synapses of the fashion *übermind.* When the site has something important to say, it reverts to boring legibility just long enough to get its point across. Visit Hypermode when you're sated with opulent homages to mainstream European glamour designers and crave underground stylings from the rest of the world. Rich in photographs and awash in its own indecipherable style, Hypermode is an optical odyssey.

NY Style

www.nystyle.com

Fashion magazine and store: NY Style is divided into two broad portions: a magazine and a shopping area. The magazine stretches outward from mere clothing fashion to interior and industrial design and even body fashion, as represented by cosmetic surgery. The site follows the usual e-zine format of features, columns, and departments, with a front page of headlines leading to inner pages of full stories. The shopping section of NY Style features about 40 online shops that sell cosmetics, clothes, books, and jewelry. The interface is a good one, using a common shopping basket for all the stores, which enables you to add items from here and there in just one transaction.

Other Stuff to Check Out

www.bazaar411.com
www.bugleboy.com
www.designercity.com
www.fashionangel.com
www.lookonline.com
www.made-in-italy.com/fashion/fm.htm
www.showbizexpo.com
www.supermodel.com/newswire/index.html

The World Wide Web started out as a hobby. It was invented as a research project, and first adopted by college students for recreational purposes. Although the Web quickly became a commercial venue, it makes sense that you can find plenty of stuff about hobbies online, too. Of course, many of the best hobby pages are put up by commercial companies — an irony that I'll note without further comment. The sites gathered into this section cover collecting, photography, home brewing, and other avocations. My criteria for selecting sites is the inherent interest of the hobby, combined with good site operation.

Apogee Photo Magazine

www.apogeephoto.com

Articles on all aspects of photography: Apogee Photo Magazine is an online photography magazine that cuts netizens a good deal with excellent, free features. The online photo contest (a themed series of contests, actually; watch for the photographic topic and deadline of the next one) is one such feature. A message board and chat room enable you to ask questions and meet other shutterbugs, and a link to an online bookstore is now available. The magazine's articles and regular departments deal with all aspects of photography, ranging from framing to exposure and processing to printing. Recent articles covered dealing with rainy weather when photographing waterfalls. The Apogee Photo Magazine Web site is appropriate for everyone from near-beginners to advanced hobbyists.

Brewery

hbd.org/brewery/index.html

Information on home brewing: The Brewery is a fantastic resource for home-brewing hobbyists and for people whose interest is just beginning to ferment. This site pours out a huge vat of information, articles, links, recipes, archived issues of *Homebrew Digest,* a discussion board, supplier lists, beer-related clip art for use in newsletters, and software for all major platforms related to calculating brewing parameters. There's even an interactive beer recipe calculator. Whew! The site has an intoxicating wealth of resources — it's definitely not a light beer site. Neither is the site fancy in its design, consisting of a single graphic table of contents and then straight text. But because Brewery is basically a dedicated library, the design is appropriate, and you can be glad to be free of slow, unnecessary graphics.

Collector Online

www.collectoronline.com

Online flea market: Collector Online has a handle on a unique concept: an online flea market. Calling itself an antique mall, Collector Online presents many independent antiques dealers (many of them, no doubt, the sort of roving business operators who set up shop in weekend flea markets, as well as stores) in a series of online booths. You can visit a booth, see a list of available antiques (from furniture to knickknacks), link to pictures in some cases, and then call individual dealers for more information. Orders are not transacted over the Web site. However, you can place a Wanted to Buy posting on the site and search the site by keyword.

Collector's Super Mall

www.csmonline.com/stores

Directory of collectibles retailers: Collector's Super Mall isn't really a mall; that fact should be clarified from the start. Unlike other online malls, this site doesn't allow you to transact online purchases, although you can browse a heck of a lot of retail Web sites. That's really the Super Mall's strong point: It's a fine directory of online and offline retailers of collectible merchandise. Some of the sites that Collector's Super Mall links to may offer online buying, but no common shopping cart ties the stores together — a feature that usually defines an online mall. You have two options from the home page: Browse a massive alphabetical directory of all the linked stores or go at it topic by topic. Oh, you can use one other method: Search the site by keyword.

Numismatists Online

www.numismatists.com

Coin sales and collecting information: Numismatists Online is for experienced collectors. At the very least, you should know what *numismatist* means (coin collector). You won't find much beginner's information — well, none. Numismatists Online is basically an online auction for collector coins. The so-called Mock Auction enables you to get your feet wet without putting any real money into play. After you've got the hang of how the auction works, you can bid on a large range of U.S. and international coins and coin sets, offered by several coin dealers and auction houses. The site also has fixed-price sales for the less adventurous (or more sensible). The same auctioncentric approach is taken

156 Home, Garden, and Kitchen

with stamps at Philatelists Online
(www.philatelists.com), which was
created by the same organization. Finally,
the same energetic, auction-loving folks
offer yet another similar site, called
SportsTrade (www.sportstrade.com)
and recently added AuctionVine
(www.auctionvine.com), a site for
wine lovers.

R/C Web Directory

www.towerhobbies.com/rcweb.html

*Information on radio-powered model
vehicles:* A more complete resource and
news guide for fans of radio-controlled
model vehicles is hard to imagine. The
R/C Web Directory does everything
except fly your model plane for you. News
headlines link to stories related to the
surprisingly large hobby industry,
including new developments in all the
accessories that you could want. At the
site's heart is the Web guide directory of
hobby sites, categorized by type of
model: aircraft, cars & trucks, and boats.
If you know about a link that you can't
find in the R/C Web Directory, send it in;
however, this site appears to have all the
bases covered.

Threads Online

www.taunton.com/th

A cyberstitch in time: Threads Online is
the Web version of *Threads* magazine, so
you'll find lots of subscription offers to
the printed magazine and headlines —
but unfortunately not the stories — from
the current edition online. Not to worry.
Threads Online has plenty of other
resources for sewing enthusiasts. The
Design, Techniques, and Fit & Fabric
sections, for example, have lots of articles
from back issues of *Threads.* The site
provides links to other sewing sites, and
an online bookstore is available. And if
you still can't figure out how to make that
zipper invisible, try posting a message. In
the old days, you could get an answer in
your local sewing circle; today, with the
World Wide Web, Threads Online makes
your circle a little more global.

Other Stuff to Check Out

www.auntannie.com
www.beckett.com
www.btha.co.uk
www.ioa.com/home/ggayland
www.justpatterns.com
www.webcreations.com

Home, Garden, and Kitchen

The house, home, garden, and kitchen are
surprisingly well represented on the
Internet. You may think, considering the
fact that fewer women are online compared to men, that home and kitchen

topics would be light. Not so. As this section demonstrates, some spectacular sites on those subjects exist.

Cooking

Cooking has always been a big online topic. When you think about it, computers are a great, if untraditional, way of storing recipes. This section contains some of the best sites about preparing food. Kitchens are covered in the "House and Home" section.

Epicurious Food

food.epicurious.com

Information for gourmets: "For People Who Eat," it says. That doesn't leave out too many folks. And this site deserves a wide audience, replete as it is with information about the love of food, not to mention two magazines — *Bon Appétit* and *Gourmet* — that spin off from the home page. Besides the magazines, three main sections inhabit Epicurious Food: Eating, Drinking, and Playing. That last title is intriguing, but if you're looking for a tutorial on eating spaghetti with your fingers, you'll be disappointed. The section is about etiquette, food implements, festivals, gourmet specialties, and other culinary topics that aren't directly related to recipes and beverages. All the site's sections are woven into a vast, food publication of gastronomic delight, and the Text-Only Index helps sort everything out. When you visit, don't forget to check out the message boards in the Forums link or browse the searchable Recipe database.

Food Channel

www.foodchannel.com

Food-industry news: Food Channel doesn't have the down-home ambience of the more kitchen-oriented sites. The magazinelike site is newsy, savvy about the entire food industry, and ferocious in its intent to keep you informed (and coming back) every day. Health, safety, and awareness of food contaminants are emphasized. All the same, the site's tone is hardly sober or grim. Be sure to visit the Maps & Charts area, which contains some wonderful (if fairly large and slow-loading) pictures representing the social and demographic aspects of food consumption, including a series of alternative food-group pyramids. Food Channel is alert and well designed, with a finger on the pulse of the food industry.

Internet Chef

www.ichef.com

★ ★
★ ★ ■

Worshipful articles on food: Internet Chef calls itself "an electronic archive dedicated to the worship of food." That description is pretty appealing. The site expresses its reverence through monthly articles, columns, a spotlighted recipe every week, and an astounding archive of recipes that should bowl you over in their depth and variety. Three dozen categories of dishes lead to hundreds of recipes in each category. If you can't find a tempting recipe in this treasure trove, then you just aren't hungry. The recipes themselves are geared to the experienced cook, providing instructions like "season lightly" without necessarily telling you what seasonings to use. A handy feature at the bottom of each recipe enables you to e-mail the recipe to yourself (or anyone else, for that matter). This site is wonderfully designed, with snazzy looks where they matter and a more sparse appearance in the recipe section, where you don't want to be delayed by graphics.

Internet Culinary CyberCity

www.culinary.net

Recipes, recipes, and more recipes: This vibrant community is bonkers for recipes (I mean that in the best possible sense). No matter where you are in this packed, tightly organized site, any mention of food or a dish is hyperlinked to a recipe. Then, following whatever story you just finished, you're bound to find several more recipe links. A Recipe Swap section is like a feeding frenzy of culinary concoctions. Registering is encouraged, although necessary only for the interactive features (such as chat rooms), and I suggest joining this joyful and productive cooking community. A good deal of nonrecipe information is available in the Nutrition & Health, Travel & Food, and Photo Gallery sections, among others. This site is a busy one, and getting familiar with it is worth spending the time.

Veggies Unite!

www.vegweb.com

Vegetarian recipes and information: No tofu-loving, meat-declining vegetarian could want a more complete page than Veggies Unite! This site promotes meatless eating with more than 2,700 recipes, a glossary and FAQ (list of Frequently Asked Questions), the Weekly Meal Planner, book reviews, Web links, a newsletter, a few articles, and even a composting guide for putting your table scraps to use in the garden. The recipes are clearly at the center of the site's effort. Divided into food-group categories (bread, beans, breakfasts, sweets, and so on), the recipes range from the ultra-simple (Easy Oatmeal) to the fairly complex (Butternut Squash Sweet Potato Soup). Registration is encouraged but is required only if you want to participate in the chat room or place a personal ad.

Other Stuff to Check Out

newfrontier.com/bravo
www.armchair.com/store/gourmet/
  gourmet.html
www.chefscorner.com
www.cuisine.com
www.gourmetclub.com
www.gourmetworld.co.uk
www.mayo.com
www.outlawcook.com
www.vrg.org

Gardening

Gardening on the Web — you could hardly create a more jarring juxtaposition between high and low tech. Gardening is dirt and water; the Internet is silicon and ether. Still, some Web designers have done a great job of offering growing advice, and the following sites are a few of the best.

The Growing EDGE

www.growingedge.com

Gardening techniques: A bimonthly magazine of gardening techniques, *The Growing EDGE* provides superb coverage of indoor gardening, which is its main claim to fame. In addition to providing articles on greenhouses, growing under lights, and other indoor issues, *The Growing EDGE* reports on hydroponic growing, irrigation techniques, reducing chemical treatment of soils, growing herbs, and other topics of interest to the hobbyist. The editorial viewpoint leans toward organic gardening techniques, grass-roots activism, and a self-sufficient food-growing lifestyle. The Web site reproduces only some of the magazine's content but contains extra information on hydroponics, a Web-site link list, and a store for back issues and books.

Herbal Essentials

**homearts.com/pm/sweatequ/
04herbf1.htm**

Information on growing and harvesting herbs: Guess which magazine produces the Herbal Essentials Web site? Nope — the answer is *Popular Mechanics.* This fact may seem odd, but the site is part of PM's HomeOwners Clinic, which covers many aspects of home ownership. Nothing is strange about the site, though — it's an illustrated, text-based, sequential tutorial on planting, cultivating, and harvesting an herb garden. By *sequential,* I mean that the site doesn't follow the typical menu system of linking randomly to various pages. Instead, you simply read along page by page, clicking a bottom arrow to see the next page, rather like a — what's the name for those things? — oh, yes, a book. Taking you from soil preparation to planting and then running down the essential qualities of basic herbs, the entire site takes no more than 30 minutes to read, even allowing you some time to gaze at the pretty illustrations.

National Gardening Association

www2.garden.org/nga

Former "Gardens for All" online: Founded in 1972, the National Gardening Association (NGA) claims to be the largest member-based, nonprofit organization of home gardeners in the U.S. The NGA has a number of education-oriented programs, so it shouldn't be a surprise that the group is cultivating a following on the Web. The deepest resource on the site is the online version of *National Gardening* magazine, which offers a sampling of the magazine's news and features. Even a sampling suffices, especially with the alliterative headlines ("Fuchsia Flair" was one recent offering). My only complaint during a recent visit is that the stories displayed in long, hard to read, vertical columns, almost begging for a photo to pop in — but none did. You also can find information on NGA's other materials and garden kits, as well as a question and answer section.

Other Stuff to Check Out

armchairgardener.com
gardennet.com
www.ag.uiuc.edu/~robsond/solutions/
    hort.html
www.bhglive.com/gardening/index.html
www.btw.com/garden_archive/toc.html
www.cahe.nmsu.edu/cahe/ces/yard
www.greenhouse-bbs.com/classy.htm
www.herbs-spices-flowers.com
www.hgtv.com
www.mindspring.com:80/~plants
www.netusa1.net/~lindley
www.pathfinder.com/cgi-bin/VG/vg
www.prairienet.org/ag/garden/
    homepage.htm
www.teleport.com/~earth

House and Home

This section covers the home as a hobby and an investment, with an emphasis on maintenance and do-it-yourself home improvements. Many sites help you shop for home appliances such as wood stoves; others are concerned more with instructional advice.

Hearthnet

www.hearth.com

Alternative heating products: Hearthnet is the ultimate Web resource for wood stoves, fireplaces, wood-burning central heating, specialty logs, and other hearth-related appliances. The site is a consortium of retailers and manufacturers in the hearth business and, as such, has a product-oriented quality. You can do preliminary shopping for products and services on these pages, comparing features and price ranges. That's not to say that the site doesn't have plenty of noncommercial information — it does. Hearthnet is an education in state-of-the-art alternative heating methods, discussing the pros and cons of different heating methods, such as pellet stoves. If you're interested in an alternative, ecologically friendly heating source in your home, Hearthnet can bring you up to speed on the possibilities.

Home Central

www.homecentral.com

Home-improvement information: An astonishingly useful site, Home Central single-handedly justifies Internet technology, especially for self-defined house klutzes like me. I'm about as handy as a foot (or is that footy as a hand?), but after browsing this site, I think that even I could handle basic plumbing tasks. Plumbing isn't the only topic covered in Home Central, but it's a major one, along with decks and essentials, like basic carpentry (which for me means hammering a nail without mangling more than one digit). If you haven't yet downloaded the Shockwave plug-in for your browser (you'll find the plug-in conveniently on the CD that came with this book), you have no better excuse to do so than to view the Home Central instructional animations, which make some processes clearer than words ever could.

HomeOwners Clinic

homearts.com/pm/toc/00pmhpc1.htm

Information on home maintenance and repair: Produced by *Popular Mechanics,* the HomeOwners Clinic is a hands-on help site for maintaining your house. The site is especially helpful in the departments of carpentry, appliances, plumbing, and other "hard" topics, as opposed to softer issues such as interior design and gardening. You can search the site by keyword or start with the Solving Problems section — where, if you're like me, you're instantly awed by the main feature presented. The problem-solving table of contents (click the saw at the bottom of the Solving Problems page) is awesome, listing 18 topics, each of which contains up to a dozen subtopics. Pick any of those subtopics (say, Painting New Drywall), and you get a statement of the basic challenge, a quick summary of the solution, and tips on helpful techniques and products. The HomeOwners Clinic doesn't waste your time; it's laid out with the utmost quality and is a homeowner's four-star bookmark.

Hometime

www.hometime.com

Home-improvement plans: Hometime's nuts-and-bolts attitude is evident in its icon design, which features links on a mock blueprint. From the home page, you link to any of several broad categories: Log Cabin, Decks & Patios, Landscape & Garden, Basement Projects, Flooring, Paint & Decorating, and Home Technology, among others. On each topic page, an impressive table of contents links to deeper pages of resources. You soon see that this site has many shopping options, offering books, videos, products by various manufacturers, and even floor plans for sale (which you now can buy online). The site also has an extensive how-to section for each project, and the site describes *many* projects. Because it merges instructions with resources, Hometime is one of the best one-stop, home-maintenance sites on the Web.

Kitchen.net

www.kitchen-bath.com

Information on kitchen improvement: Kitchen.net starts beautifully, in terms of page design, with an attractive home page. The site slips a bit when you get inside, but the pages still deliver good information, even if they're not beautifully presented. The Sweat Equity section offers a mishmash of glossaries, project primers, and fairly deep instructions on a variety of kitchen- and bath-improvement tasks. Dr. in the House is an advice section run by three experts in kitchen and bath remodeling and Karla, the "Misunderstood Elk." These experts talk engagingly about making the most of a small kitchen sink, choosing convection systems, choosing the correct refrigerator depth, improving a basement toilet, and many other down-and-dirty issues. Karla keeps mostly to herself. A buyer's guide and some link lists (including "Dishwasherpalooza!") fill out the site.

LivingHome

206.145.13.222/index.shtml

 ★ ★
★ ★

Informative community for home-owners: What a great site. LivingHome is a newsy community dedicated to all aspects of home ownership, maintenance, decoration, and gardening. Frequently updated, the Daily Dirt section offers a column of tips and contemporary information on all kinds of subjects, ranging from Tupperware to cleaning the fridge. LivingHome is folksy, informal, reliable, and bright. The site is a sort of combination of *Better Homes and Gardens* and "Hints from Heloise." The Forums section includes message boards dedicated to gardening, interior design, remodeling, kitchens and baths, and a growing list of other topics. The Tool Chest is probably the most practical section of the site, providing ideas, plans, and resources for home-improvement projects. The snappy page design doesn't let up throughout the site — LivingHome is attractive, useful, and friendly.

This Old House

pathfinder.com/@@LT2bhgcAYaqw@4i7/ TOH

Home-restoration information from the PBS series and magazine: The well-known TV show and magazine, featuring methodically explained restorations of beautiful old houses, makes a medium splash on the Web. Not everything from the magazine is carried over to the site, and the editors have been sluggish recently about carrying *anything* over. Nevertheless, other features are attractive — two, in particular. The misnamed Encyclopedia is an archive of past projects, presented as illustrated narratives — fascinating chronicles. The Bulletin Boards section hosts an active community of hobbyists and professionals, discussing everything from termites to installing windows. This Old House has an informal, communal feel that makes up for its nonchalance.

Wall & Ceilings Online

www.wconline.com

Directory of manufacturers and service companies: Walls & Ceilings Online advertises itself as being "The Gateway to the Walls and Ceilings Industry" and is primarily a resource directory for manufacturers and service specialists. The Info Base is a collection of resources. You can search the site's article database of past issues of *Walls & Ceilings*, the printed version magazine. Generally, you have to click your mouse too many times to get anywhere in the site, but the information is worth the trouble.

Other Stuff to Check Out

begin.com/fixit
weyrkeep.com/direct
www.nettips.com:80/homepage.html
www.pacificharbor.com:80/whpier/pdd

Judging by the number of fine hiking, hunting, fishing, and extreme sports sites, you'd think that people were taking laptops and wireless modems on their hiking and snowboarding trips. Outdoor sites, generally speaking, tend to contain less state-of-the-art design quality than, for example, entertainment sites created by movie studios. Outdoor-recreation sites are practical and convey information without many fancy (and time-consuming) multimedia gadgets.

The decision was difficult, but for space reasons, I had to eliminate several excellent sites from this section. I concentrate on general, all-purpose outdoor sites as opposed to productions dedicated to skiing or fishing. Hiking, however, being one of the most popular and accessible outdoor activities, is a prominent topic among the following sites.

All Outdoors

alloutdoors.com/Default.html

Hunting and fishing information: With a strong emphasis on hunting and fishing, All Outdoors is a worthy Web site to take along into the blind (except for the fact that the beeps of your laptop may alert game to your presence). Forging a blend of news, equipment reviews, magazine articles (from a variety of sources), an online bookstore, reviews of outdoor-travel spots, and daily features, and a compact and well-designed site, All Outdoors has earned its many awards. The Newsstand link saves you a trip to the real newsstand by collecting current articles from such publications as *In-Fisherman, Sports Afield, Handloader, Texas Fish & Game,* and *Rifle.* The Women Outdoors section may be a welcome addition to female visitors. Message boards help create a communal feeling at the site; each week, a new topic is raised for discussion.

Backcountry

www.flash.net/~bhphiker/BHP

Hiking information: Founded in early 1994, Backcountry is primarily a hiking site, featuring links to Internet hiking resources, photographs, information on hiking clubs, trip ideas, and visitor-uploaded reviews of trails, among other things. The trip reports are informal, full of firsthand information, and incredibly numerous. If you're interested in hiking anywhere from Baja to Berlin, chances are that you can find a review at this site. The Gallery, my favorite section, contains photos contributed by site visitors, as well as links to other graphic collections on the Net.

thebackpacker.com

www.thebackpacker.com

Down-'n'-dirty hiking site: Here's the hype: "Finally, a true, down and dirty, gritty, unsanitary, blood-pouring, sweat falling, peak bagging Internet page." Wow — that's a lot to ask from a Web site, especially the part about pouring blood, which is enough to keep me away from backpacking for life. But you get the gist. This site cuts straight to the chase with gear and trail reviews (the latter searchable by state), a Beginner's Corner, destinations, outstanding photographs, lists of hiking-equipment manufacturers, a Web-site directory, and message boards for networking with other hikers. All this information is packaged in a really nicely designed site. I don't know whether the site is as unsanitary as it thinks it is, but you can always wear a surgical mask while viewing these pages.

Field & Stream Online

www.fieldandstream.com

Hunting and fishing magazine: The virtual edition of the popular, enduring hunting and fishing magazine, Field & Stream Online embraces Internet culture with an electronic publication that uses database searching and multimedia streaming to great advantage. You get the regular features and articles that you'd expect in an online magazine. In the Fishing and Hunting sections, the Fish Finder and Game Finder provide drop-down lists for choosing an animal type and then display all kinds of information, including a guide

to the states where that particular game can be found. Field & Stream Radio is a series of short RealAudio instructional and historical productions; recent topics included Cold Weather Bass Fishing, Women in Hunting, Deer Nutrition, and Buying a Dog. Field & Stream Online has also added a message board site, called Backlash. I guess that's better than Recoil.

Get Lost Adventure Magazine

www.itsnet.com/home/getlost/ mag.html

Humorous outdoor recreation magazine: Now, don't get insulted; this outdoors magazine is telling you to "take a hike" in the most innocent and positive sense. Get Lost has a few unique features, among them a Net Cam that shows you views from around the world — some live camera shots, some photos just a few hours old. You get facts, biographies, and tips on famous explorers, mountains, and expeditions. A Get Psyched page attempts to pump you up psychologically with inspirational quotes ("Do not let what you cannot do interfere with what you can do."). Get Lost adds a healthy dollop of humor in its informational reporting and equipment reviews.

Great Outdoor Recreation Pages

www.gorp.com

164 Outdoor Recreation

Useful and efficient pages: Great Outdoor Recreation Pages (or GORP, as the site amusingly refers to itself) is a feature-packed, sprawling site covering hiking, national parks, canoeing, birding, tours, biking, and just about any outdoor recreation (except walking to your local coffee shop for a cappuccino). GORP is distinguished by its concise and multifaceted information, presented in a series of not-too-long articles organized by location, attraction, and activity. Travel information is highlighted. Community message areas are divided into activity boards: Biking, Paddling, Hiking, Gear, and so on. On the Web, the field of outdoor recreation is crowded, with several excellent pages, and GORP earns a solid place for the quality and quantity of its information.

GreatOutdoors.com

www.gowest.com

Camping and hiking with plenty of multimedia: GreatOutdoors.com is a fantastic Web publication — covering a wide range of outdoor sports — that gleefully makes the most of the Internet's multimedia possibilities. You'll find pages on Climbing, Cycling, Diving, Fly Fishing, Hiking/Camping, Mountain Biking, Paddling, Sailing, Skiing, Snowboarding, Surfing, and Windsurfing. Each category includes such things as destinations, gear, weather conditions, and tips. If you enjoy pictures, sounds, and video, just poke around. RealAudio clips are integrated throughout the site. For example, a recent tribute on the Surfing site showed surfing legend Mark Foo catching a big wave. Unfortunately, the tribute was a posthumous one, because Foo is now riding the big wave in the sky, so to speak, but the tribute was handled honestly and tastefully, conveying his powerful love of surfing while sharing his acknowledgment of the risk

involved. The videos are about half fun and half instructional; the snowboarding videos are particularly helpful for gaining new techniques. Putting multimedia aside for the moment, the rest of Go West is practical and informative. The site encourages community by providing message boards plus a Question of the Week.

Mountain Zone

www.mountainzone.com/toc.html

All aspects of mountaineering: How can one love mountains? Let us count the ways: snowboarding, skiing, hiking, mountain biking, climbing, gawking in fear. Outdoor adventurers may want to disregard the latter one. Mountain Zone is packed with content, from climbing-gear reviews to snow reports throughout North America. Photography, a gentler pursuit than snowboarding down a sheer cliff, has its own section in Mountain Zone. A recent visit displayed incredible reports on an expedition's fight to climb Denali — the Native American word for Alaska's Mt. McKinley. Competition results get lots of coverage, as do travelogues for hikers. Photographic galleries rub elbows with a National Parks directory, and chat rooms feature special guests. Mountain Zone really is, in a word, quite excellent. (I always had trouble counting words.)

Outdoor Resources Online

www.azstarnet.com/~goclimb

Directory of outdoor resources: Fittingly, this directory to outdoor resources is mainly concerned with Web sites. Organized as a typical Web directory, the home page presents basic outdoorsy topics: Sailing, Backcountry, Biking,

Scuba, Skiing, Climbing and Mountaineering, Surfing, and a few others. (Archery and Tennis are promised soon.) Each category links to geographical subcategories, and from those categories, you link to the resources. Most of the resources are physical places, such as a scuba-diving-equipment dealership in Key Largo and a ski resort in Colorado. These outposts have Web sites to which you link to get more information. Some of the directory links lead to other directories or to informational sites that aren't connected to outdoor facilities.

SnoWeb

www.snoweb.com

Reviews of U.S. and Canadian ski resorts: SnoWeb is mainly a review site for ski resorts around the United States and Canada. Featuring in-depth seasonal reviews of Diamond Peak, Kirkwood, Sierra at Tahoe, Alpine Meadows, and other premier ski destinations, SnoWeb also surveys lesser-known spots in the eastern United States, the Rockies, and Canada. Each review covers terrain, snow conditions, seasonal dates, and vertical length information for the resort, and provides descriptive text. SnoWeb is updated more often during the ski season, unsurprisingly, but continues to display its most recent information during the summer.

Other Stuff to Check Out

outside.starwave.com
xenon.stanford.edu/~rsf/mtn-bike.html
www.afn.org/skydive
www.alpworld.com
www.scubacentral.com
www.skinet.com
www.spav.com/default.html
www.spectra.net/~cowboy
www.surfline.com
www.xcski.org
www.xpcsports.com

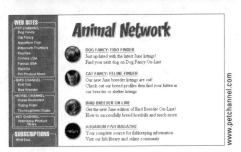

Pets

Pets are a recreational passion for a lot of people, including me. I'm glad to see a fair number of excellent pest, er, pet sites on the Web, which I present in this section. At these sites, you may find grooming hints, answers to pet-care questions, training techniques, and interactive community features for talking with other pet lovers.

Animal Network

www.petchannel.com

Links to Web pet sites: Animal Network is the hub of a vast array of pet sites on the Web. From the Animal Network home page, you can spin off to Dog Fancy On-Line, Cat Fancy On-Line, Aquarium Fish On-Line — you get the picture. From birds to horses, reptiles to ferrets, the Animal Network seems to love them all. Each link goes to an online magazine, trotting out information about breeds, pet care, and pet products. You may want to bookmark Animal Network itself or use it as a hub to find the pages that really interest you and then bookmark them.

Canines of America

www.canines.com

Dog-training information: This dog site has a strong emphasis on training. Although the site provides a certain amount of general pet information, dog-breed links, and community features such as chatting, most of its features deal with dog-training tips, problem solving in obedience training, equipment and manuals for making your dog better behaved, listings of online training seminars (does your dog need to know how to type?), and promotions for the real-world training centers run by Canines of America. This site has real value for dog lovers and training hobbyists.

Cat Fanciers Web Site

www.fanciers.com

How to care for cats: If the Cat Fanciers Web Site were a cat, it would be a plain breed, well-groomed, without glamour or a fancy lineage. This text-based site doesn't gum up your modem with unnecessary graphics but delivers tons of information about felines and their care. From getting a cat to caring for it, cat-breed descriptions to instructions for building a scratching post (for the sake of your furniture), Cat Fanciers covers all the basics straightforwardly and descriptively. Many of the articles are written by veterinarians and animal medical centers, such as the Cornell Feline Health Center. You also can access a few helpful directories, including listings of cat shows, clubs, registries, and shelters.

Pet Channel

www.thepetchannel.com

Pet health and even horoscopes: The Pet Channel is a fantastic resource for pet owners or those who will soon invite pets into their homes. This frequently updated site emphasizes pet health, drawing on the expertise of veterinarians who participate in interactive question-and-answer Web pages. (The site even features a column by a pet therapist.) Pet Channel has a great sense of fun — just check out the Pet Horoscopes section or the Pet Gallery. Find a Pet contains a bulletin board for posting news of lost or

found animals, and the Pet Training area features techniques for getting a dog, cat, or horse under control.

Other Stuff to Check Out

www.cyberpet.com
www.dogworldmag.com
www.petclub.net

Sports

Sports are huge on the Net. The Web is particularly suited to following sports, mainly because it can provide scores with up-to-the-minute currency. You can get up-to-the-second scores from many of the following sites, especially if you have a modern, Java-equipped browser. Furthermore, sports statistics translate well to any computer medium. Live sports still are hard to find on the Net and suffer from limited bandwidth, just like all other types of Webcasting. But the combination of current news and statistical access makes sporting sites some of the most popular World Wide Web destinations.

Baseball

The following are baseball-specific sites that come to life between spring and fall.

The Baseball Server

www.nando.net/SportServer/baseball

International baseball information: Whether you want to check the latest home run statistics in the United States or the professional leagues overseas, this site knows the score. The Baseball Server covers all the international bases by providing news and team standings from Japan and South Korea, in addition to the good ol' U.S. Set up by the Nando Times, a Web-only newspaper (if that's not a contradiction in terms), the site strongly emphasizes the scoreboard. Forget about articles, photo spreads, and caustic commentary from know-it-all columnists, never mind about multimedia, but count on automatically updated scoreboard pages for both the majors and minors. When you need to know whether Hiroshima is gaining ground on Yokohama, you know where to turn.

Baseball Weekly

www.usatoday.com/bbwfront.htm

U.S. baseball information: Several years ago, *USA Today* addressed the need for a dedicated, information-rich publication about baseball by issuing the first edition of *Baseball Weekly,* a year-round compendium of columnists, statistics, individual team coverage, more statistics, minor league coverage, and even more statistics. The online version carries most of the same incredibly comprehensive content, including the valuable Team Reports pages. The writing is informal, even gossipy, and features prominent local sports journalism from around the country. This site has great integrity, presenting its content with nary a whispered plea for subscriptions.

Fastball

www.fastball.com/index.html

From baseball statistics to history: Fastball strives to cover every aspect of baseball, from the hard statistics to soft reminiscences, and it comes close to being a perfectly well-rounded baseball site. You can get scores and current news, of course, and drop-down lists make zipping from the home page to information on your favorite team easy. A forum area called Dugout Chat invites you to interact with other fans and occasional celebrity guests. A minor league section keeps track of schedules, statistics, and standings. The site even has an online store. Fastball is organized nicely but is perhaps overwhelmingly large; click The Site to display a coherent site map.

majorleaguebaseball.com

www.majorleaguebaseball.com

Official Major League Baseball site: This site is the official Web presence of Major League Baseball (MLB). Because MLB, as a corporate entity, is not exactly in the publishing business, you may not expect the Web site to compare favorably with similar sites produced by *USA Today, Baseball Weekly,* or *Sports Illustrated.* In fact, MLB is an attractive magazine-style site, complete with news, standings, scores — the whole shebang. The editorial viewpoint has a promotional tinge — not unexpectedly, considering that Major League Baseball *is* in the promotion business. The site gives a great deal of emphasis to award-winning players of the week, and other high-profile news that glorifies the game. On the multimedia front, the site has a free video archive of great plays — connected to an online video store, naturally — and offers links to Broadcast.com's live audiocasts of ongoing games. You need RealPlayer, but download links are provided.

Minor League Baseball

www.minorleaguebaseball.com

Farm league information: Early in the century, most people in the United States related to baseball through one or more local minor league teams. When radio entered the picture and television began broadcasting Major League Baseball games, the importance of the minors diminished. During the past ten years, though, the sporting community has seen a resurgence of interest in the minor leagues because the majors have become more impersonal and less stable. Minor League Baseball is the Web's premier site dedicated to farm teams and nonmajor pro baseball leagues. Although the Baseball Weekly and The Sporting News sites (both reviewed in this section) cover the minors, that coverage is secondary to their Major League Baseball coverage. Minor League Baseball reports on the entire minor league industry with gratifying thoroughness, from changes in front-office personnel to player stats. Like the minors, this site isn't as glitzy as the major-league sports sites, but that's just fine with me. Even without streaming video clips and Java scoreboards, this site covers all the bases.

Total Baseball Online

totalbaseball.com

Online edition of baseball encyclopedia: Serious baseball fans have a problem when they move from one residence to another: They must find a way to transport *Total Baseball,* the official encyclopedia of Major League Baseball, a legendary book that weighs two-and-a-half tons (approximately). Okay, slight exaggeration there, but the massive tome is like several bricks welded together and contains more information than you ever thought could exist about a game. Putting the encyclopedia on the Web is a natural match. The site is not a complete book-to-Net translation, however, and Total Baseball Online takes a more newsy approach than the book does. It's a bit of

a shame because plenty of baseball and general sports news sites already exist. Nevertheless, Total Baseball is rich in statistical and historical information. Shopping and a chat room are available.

Other Stuff to Check Out

members.aol.com/tomho13/top30.html
rampages.onramp.net/~wordwork/
    index.html
www.sportingnews.com/baseball
www.sportsline.com/u/baseball/mlb

Basketball

Basketball is fairly well represented online, and the following are a few of the best sites.

Basketball Hall of Fame

www.hoophall.com

Virtual museum: The bright-orange home page is an eye-grabber. The Basketball Hall of Fame site should be fouled for garishness: two free throws. The actual hoops Hall of Fame (in Springfield, Massachusetts) is a highly interactive museum in ways that the Web site can't compare with, but if nothing else, the site is an attractive promotion. But that wouldn't be enough by itself to get the site into this section, and the truth is that you can learn a great deal about basketball history, lore, and even current events by touring these pages. The site provides video clips of great moments in basketball history, and you also can shop the virtual gift shop.

The Basketball Server

www.nando.net/SportServer/basketball

Just basketball scores: Part of the series of Sports Servers Web sites, The Basketball Server exists to deliver National Basketball Association (NBA) scores, not general-purpose hoops information. Using an automatically reloading page to keep things current, the scoreboard page is great during the NBA season and useless during the rest of the year. The site has some historical content to fill in the gaps, but it really comes to life when play begins.

College Hoops Insider

www.collegeinsider.com

For college hoops fans: No other sport generates more excitement and interest at a college level than basketball does. College football also is a high-profile sport, but basketball's National Collegiate Athletic Association (NCAA) tournament raises speculation and wagering to a feverish pitch, thanks to its long, relentless elimination process. College Hoops Insider is the Web spot for following the collegiate season. As a relatively new virtual publication, the site adds new features and page constructions frequently, giving it a somewhat fluid appearance, but the already valuable site should only get better. Regional breakdowns of college programs provide a separate page for each team. Game previews and recaps provide informational support for an array of live game broadcasts via RealAudio. And you can discuss the entire college hoop scene with other fans on the message boards.

NBA.com

www.nba.com

The official league site: The National Basketball Association scores a three-pointer with its fast-driving, fancy-dribbling Web site. Covering basic news and inside reports on the NBA draft, NBA.com puts special emphasis on fan interactivity by persuading a revolving cast of players and other NBA pros to answer questions via e-mail. During a recent visit, you could post your queries to newly named Seattle coach Paul Westphal or ask Marty Blake, the NBA's director of scouting, about the then-upcoming draft. Chat-room appearances also are arranged from time to time. Basically, the NBA does a great job of involving the Internet community with the league and pulling the league onto the Net.

On Hoops

www.onhoops.com

Basketball commentary: Most sports magazines, both printed and online, mix news and commentary. On Hoops is a virtual basketball publication that apparently has decided that a niche for just commentary exists. Hip and cynical, the site's attitude ranges from acerbic to caustic and is always lively. The tone is set right from the start — the home page declares, "We have the utmost admiration for the Game and the League and hope not to conflict with any of the League's Internet plans, no matter how boring they may be." The Golden Chuck link takes you to awards, which are now offered in 33 categories. Each monthly installment of On Hoops contains a couple dozen articles offering bemused commentary on current basketball news. The site continues year-round but really heats up during the summer.

Other Stuff to Check Out

www.alleyoop.com
www.tspnetwork.com/courtside

Football (American)

American football — you know, the high-impact, well-padded game for sadistic athletes — isn't as well represented on the Net as some other sports are, but that situation may change as the National Football League (NFL) begins its new promotional phase. In the meantime, the following sites can tide you over.

The Football Server

www.nando.net/SportServer/football

Pro and college football scores: The Football Server rises to the challenge of providing updated scores in the breathless football schedule of one game per week. Well, maybe the schedule isn't so breathless, but football players need plenty of time between games to eat protein and nurture their hostilities. During the entire off-season, The Football Server would have nothing whatsoever to do if it weren't for its NFL and NCAA Football sections. If you're a full-time, all-year football fan, stay up to speed with all the summertime trade, draft, and recruiting activities on both the college and pro levels in those two finely updated sections.

NFL.COM

www.nfl.com

Official NFL site: The official site of the National Football League serves equal measures of league promotion, news, and ladyfinger recipes. (I expect the recipes to have been deleted by the time you read this book.) NFL.COM does a good job of getting fans involved in the site and — more important to most fans — getting sports professionals involved. A chat area holds special live events occasionally, and transcripts of past events are available. You can sign up for an e-mail update on current events and site changes. The site handles preseason news and scheduling with enthusiasm during the late summer, as you may expect from an organization that's trying to gear up its fans for the real thing. You also can view video clips from the season and NFL Films' great library.

Pro Football Hall of Fame

www.canton-ohio.com/hof

★ ★
★ ★

Virtual museum: An eyeball-skewering home-page design grabs your attention with a vengeance, but when you link off the home page, the Pro Football Hall of Fame site gets down to business — the business of promoting a visit to Canton, Ohio, that is. The site contains information on every player immortalized in the hallowed halls, and that gallery alone justifies the site. The most fun and changeable portion of the site is the Weekly Top 20, which updates all-time records in passing, receiving, rushing, and scoring every week during the season. You can glean a nice historical lesson from the Football Decade by Decade section, which is — well, it's obvious what the section is. The Team Histories section also provides decade-spanning perspectives on the coming weekend's tailgate-party opportunities.

Other Stuff to Check Out

www.abcmnf.com
www.shrednet.com/frenzy
www.sportingnews.com/nfl

General Sports News

The following sites include network sports publications and online magazines that cover sports. In many cases, you can subscribe, free of charge, to Java applets that deliver sports scores to your desktop whenever you're logged on, even when you're not visiting the site. In many cases, you also can buy paid subscriptions for special content. Sports sites tend to be slick in the multimedia department, and well-equipped browsers, bristling with the latest plug-ins, make the most of that audio and video stuff.

CBS SportsLine

www.sportsline.com

CBS sports information: Many good sports sites are available, and CBS SportsLine is one of the best. Making great use of Web technology, the site is a multimedia playground in the delivery of sports news, opinion columns, radio programs, and scores. Contests play a big part of CBS SportsLine, and you often find yourself entered in them just by visiting a page. (The contests offer good prizes, too.) One of the best features is City Pages, which presents what are, in effect, separate sites for each of a long list of U.S. cities — the idea being that if you're a New York City sports fan but have relocated to Iowa, for example, you can still follow all the news on your teams. This site has Java scores that can be delivered through a small applet that stays on your desktop, updating itself in real time as you do other work on the computer. In addition to the fancy stuff, the site provides a basic rundown of news on the major sports. Much of the site is free, but some features are saved for paying subscribers (under a monthly or yearly plan).

CNN/SI

www.cnnsi.com

Sports news: That cryptic cluster of consonants stands for the CNN network and *Sports Illustrated,* which are collaborators in this Web venture. The standard sports-news-site formats are followed unimaginatively — not to say that any one site is obligated to break the mold. You'd expect that any *Sports Illustrated* site would be rich with photographs, and online photo galleries are available by clicking the Special Features link on the home page. About ten separate photo essays are presented on subjects ranging (during a recent visit) from Swimsuit '97 to, well, Swimsuit '98 — and lots of other sports in between and since. A desktop scoreboard ticker is available (tickers are all the rage on these sports sites), and some fantasy sports games are offered. The *Sports Illustrated* content — the photo galleries and past material from back issues — is what sets this site apart from others that have slicker multimedia features.

ESPN SportsZone

espn.sportszone.com

Sports news from the cable network: SportsZone is one of the great Web sports sites and probably the most famous. The complete sports service includes terrific photos, updated scores (some scoreboard pages update and reload automatically every minute), feature articles, contests, viewer participation, columns, and live audio. Following the tradition of sports megasites, SportsZone charges for some special content, leaving the rest free of charge. You can get basic scores and news without subscribing, but only members get the more in-depth information about their teams and certain columns. You can see what you're missing at a glance by paying attention to the yellow-and-red tickets next to subscriber-only story headlines. If the site moves too slowly for you, by the way, click the Mostly Text link in the left menu.

Fox Sports Online

www.foxsports.com

Fox sports news: Fox was a late entry into the professional sports field, but the company is making up ground quickly. Fox's U.S. cable network is growing; the company just spent some $300 million to buy baseball's Los Angeles Dodgers; and its Web site is now arguably on the same playing field as those of ESPN and CNN/SI. Fox has tickers, pages on different sports, and interactive features like chat and message boards. Fox also has games and an e-mail newsletter service of the day's top stories. Best of all, the Fox site, unlike CNN/SI or SportsZone, is completely free; now *that's* throwing down the gauntlet.

Interactive Internet Sports

www.iis-sports.com

Sports trivia, predictions, and message boards: This streamlined and entertaining site encourages interactivity among its visitors by staging trivia and prediction

contests. You can try your hand at a selection of daily updated trivia questions covering general sports, football, or baseball. In the Sports Picks section, you can predict game winners and then compare your results with those of other site visitors. (Interactive Internet Sports is *not* a betting site.) Message boards and chat rooms also spark interactivity and get the community feeling going. For pure sports news, you'll have to go elsewhere — Interactive Internet Sports lets newspapers and other sites give you that information. But if you want to go beyond the sports headlines, Interactive Internet Sports is a great site to bookmark.

The Sporting News

www.sportingnews.com

Legendary sports newspaper online: The Sporting News is a venerable newspaper that began as a mostly baseball sheet and then expanded over the decades to include all major sports, with an emphasis on statistics and hard information. Accordingly, the Web site is absolutely crammed with news and features. Knowing where to start is so hard, in fact, that the Customize link saves the day by enabling you to specify what appears on the home page when your browser enters the site. Headlines and articles are supplemented by a vast selection of columnists. You'll also find the statistics that are so important to the printed newspaper in the Vault, a feature deep enough to keep hard-core fans away from family gatherings.

The Sports Network

www.sportsnetwork.com

Sparse design and good sports information: The Sports Network has Web-design problems, but I'm not sure that it cares. I'm not sure that I care, either. The site is surprisingly reliant on text and lacking in the bright graphics, prominent photographs, and loud buttons that adorn most sports sites. Odd typographical errors crop up on some pages. But the site's idiosyncrasies add up to a kind of refreshing charm in contrast to the garish competitiveness of the other Web sports emporiums. The Sports Network saves its biggest feature for those who really want to spend some bucks on their sports coverage: a score pager service.

SportsWeb

www.sportsweb.com

Global perspective on the games: SportsWeb touts itself as "Where the World Comes to Play." Maybe not, but SportsWeb *is* a pretty good place to find out about what's being played around the world. This multilingual Reuters service offers a newspaper-style format, with the main stories headlined down the front page. SportsWeb also offers links to particular sports on the left of the pages — but that's where the truly international flavor of the site begins to appear. Competing for equal time with the links to North America's NBA, NFL, and NHL are links to rugby and cricket. Not international enough? Try the Regional Sections drop-down lists on the right, which enable you to request sports news from countries all around the world. I made my visit during the World Cup soccer (football) tournament, and found the Cameroon page full of stories about questionable refereeing in the World Cup. The multimedia on SportsWeb is nonexistent, but the stories are fresh, and the site's wide variety of coverage makes it a definite bookmark for the discriminating sports fan.

USA Today Sports

www.usatoday.com/sports/sfront.htm

Sports information from the daily newspaper: Data, data, data. If you've ever read the sports section of *USA Today,* the national daily newspaper, you know about its statistics-heavy emphasis on game data. The paper has articles, too, of course, but they tend to be on the short side, following the paper's tendency to deliver news in bite-size chunks. Take the scoreboard page, for example. This page is an auto-refresh affair that updates itself every two minutes, and during a recent early-summer visit, it carried scores for every Major League Baseball game and minor league baseball game in the country. Each major sport has its own home page, linking to news departments and scores. The Digest link is a good place to start when you want a quick update from around the world of sports; this feature is a series of one-paragraph top stories. If you follow primarily one sport, the best plan is to find the relevant front page and bookmark it. The site doesn't have a great deal of multimedia — just timely reporting.

Other Stuff to Check Out

adams.patriot.net/~rbarthle/cal/index.html
chili.collegesportsnews.com
www.afp.com/go/english/sports
www.justwomen.com
www.livestats.com

Other Sports

The sports section in your local paper just can't cover all the sporting events in the world, making the Web the perfect place to check up on those "other" sports that sometimes get overlooked. These sites will help you keep up.

FIFA On-Line

www.fifa.com

World's most popular sport: FIFA stands for Fédération Internationale de Football Association, the world governing organization for football. For you Americans, that's not football played with a pointy pigskin; it's the game that you call soccer. FIFA's ultimate competition is the World Cup, an international soccer — er, football — tournament played every four years. The 1998 World Cup in France has just ended as I write this, so you might think the FIFA Web site will soon go dormant. Wrong you'd be. Click your way to the FIFA Competitions link on any subpage, and you'll discover that FIFA has lots going on all the time. In 1999, for example, the Women's World Cup will be held in the United States, and international youth tournaments take place all the time. This site contains news, updates, regulations, statistics, and helpful links to national soccer — er, football — federations. Stop by FIFA On-Line. I know I'll hate myself for saying so, but it's a kick.

NASCAR Online

www.nascar.com

Stock car racing's online home: NASCAR is the National Association For Stock Car Auto Racing, the governing body of what most people in America simply call "stock car racing." For non-Americans, the sport involves full-sized cars that, except for the bright paint jobs and numbers, look pretty close to what you see on a dealer's lot — but drive a whole lot different. And the folks that run NASCAR have taken great pains to make this Web site one of the best sports sites in cyberspace. Simply put, this site's slicker than Jeff Gordon's Chevy down the back stretch at Daytona. The easy-to-spot links at the top invite you to explore. Information abounds; so does multimedia. Want to see the finish of the latest NASCAR race? Just click the Multimedia link for the AVI file. You also can hear RealAudio files of several of NASCAR's syndicated radio programs. Did I mention that you can shop here, too? Yup, the good ol' boys of NASCAR don't miss a trick.

NHL.com

www.nhl.com

Hockey's hometown on the Web: Of all the North American sports leagues, the National Hockey League (NHL) has arguably the most international appeal. True, the NHL doesn't have Michael Jordan, but it has stars from more countries than the NBA, the NFL, or Major League Baseball. Canada, Sweden, Russia, the Czech Republic, the United States — they're all among the countries represented on NHL rosters. The NHL's Web site does a great job keeping you up-to-date with everything going on in the league. It also has one of the best kids' sections of any professional sports league Web site.

PGA.com

www.pga.com

From tee to shining tee: PGA.com is the official site of the PGA of America, the main U.S. men's professional golfers association. Sure, most of the news stories are about PGA activities, but the information here benefits golfers of all nationalities. The Lesson Tee, for example, gives you tips from teaching pros (such as the recent entreaty to "Eliminate excessive arm movement"). The site's Fitness Center includes an analysis that helps you determine your general fitness level — which, of course, affects your game. Have questions about rules? PGA.com has explanations galore, and if you can't find your particular question addressed, the site has instructions on sending the question to the PGA for a personal e-mail reply.

SkiCentral

skicentral.com

The ski enthusiast's resource: SkiCentral is unlike the other Web sites in this section, because it's actually a search engine dedicated to skiing — except that you really don't need to do much searching to find something useful or interesting. The front-page topics range from news to equipment to conditions. You also can link to pages to download skiing wallpaper for your computer, in case that vacation is a few months away. No matter when your time off comes, the Ski Resort section includes links to more than 600 ski resorts worldwide, which means you can follow the fresh powder around the globe. Good thing SkiCentral's free, because those lift tickets won't be.

TEAMtalk

www.teamtalk.com

British football news: A product of the International Media Services Group, TEAMtalk is a frenetic site that's sometimes brash, sometimes vocal. But that's okay — that's the way Brits are about their football loyalties. (Remember, Americans — that's the game you call soccer.) If you don't want just the General news link on the home page, TEAMtalk divides its coverage of all football things British mainly by team levels, with pages for Premiership, Nationwide (including First Division, Second Division, and Third Division), Scottish Premier, and National Teams. Getting the latest scoop on the team you follow couldn't be easier — you simply click on the team's jersey for a devoted team page with the latest news headlines posted right in front of you. If you don't want to bother to read the stories, no problem. Simply click the Audio link in the lower right, and you have the stories read to you via RealPlayer. Team pages also include links for Results, a chance to get in Your Say, and, of course, Merchandise. One warning: The shopping pages include some of the most intense advertising graphics I've encountered, so your eyes could be in for as big a workout as your wallet.

Other Stuff to Check Out

www.atlasf1.com
www.fia.com
www.lpga.com
www.tennis.com
www.wimbledon.com
www.worldonline.nl/channels/sport/
   formula1

Travel

cityguide.lycos.com

Traveling the world seems to be the most diametrically opposed activity to surfing the Web. Perhaps in some ironic way, that's why so many travel sites exist. Whatever the reason, this section gives you a tour of the best informational travel sites. Allow me to emphasize the word *informational,* because I save *service-oriented* sites for the Travel Services section in Part V of this book. In a way, these sites perform a service by providing information about destinations. But the nuts-'n'-bolts service of making travel reservations and booking tickets is a specialty of another type of site, and I group online travel agents in Part V.

Whether you're armchair-traveling or actually planning a vacation — happy trails! And if you want more information, may I suggest *Travel Planning Online For Dummies,* by Noah Vadnai (IDG Books Worldwide, Inc.).

Destination Guides

Every destination guide on the World Wide Web must strive for some balance between pictures and text, scenery and information. Some sites are well-illustrated travelogues; others are pictorial brochures with a smattering of explanation. The best sites are distinguished by some especially useful informational angle, such as search engines for foreign hotels, currency converters, or interactive global weather guides. The following sites attain a good balance between postcard views and useful information without putting undue strain on your modem.

Arthur Frommer's Outspoken Encyclopedia of Travel

www.frommers.com

Feature-packed travel guide with frank and witty advice: The Frommer's travel site is written in a somewhat bold style and occasionally is as controversial as you may think, judging by the title. Frommer certainly doesn't hold back his criticism in his travel reviews at times, but the main event of this site's soapbox is the daily online travel magazine: Vacations for Real People (which you can reach by clicking the Budget Travel Articles link on the home page). Four or five articles are presented every day on such diverse travel opportunities as lowered airfares from France to Italy and new resorts in the Dominican Republic. Flight, car, and hotel wizards help with travel planning. The site emphasizes discount travel but not at the expense of interest. A personal touch enables you to ask questions of the eminent Mr. Frommer and view his answers. The site proves to be hefty when you dig into it — more than 6,000 pages of tips, trip ideas, and caustic travel journalism.

City Guide

cityguide.lycos.com

Information on world cities: More than it claims to be, City Guide goes way beyond targeting cities as destinations, providing a moderate amount of information on regions of countries as defined by political boundaries, geographical configurations (valleys, mountain ranges, and the like), and ethnogeographic divisions. You can, for example, zero in on the upper Normandy area of France (using the ol' clickable-map trick) and read about not only Rouen, the capital of the region, but also the history and land features of the entire area. City Guide is created by Lycos, one of the major World Wide Web directories, so you may expect the site to be heavy on links to relevant sites. You won't be disappointed. On every page of the Guide, stretching down the right side, is a long list of links, many of them leading to Web sites created by organizations in the city or area that you're investigating. Returning to the Rouen example, you can link to the Web sites of radio and TV stations in the city. The mix of Web searching and original information makes City Guide uniquely valuable.

CNN: Travel Guide

www.cnn.com/TRAVEL

Travel journalism and multimedia: The magazine-style page design is one of the most agreeable features of Web sites, and CNN: Travel Guide uses it well in presenting feature stories and pictures about travel topics and destinations. The magazine metaphor is stretched into the realm of digital interactivity in the Destinations section (click the Destinations link) where you can choose among a long menu of global locations and then click the enticing Take Me There! button. The destinations are all the more imaginative and inviting in their nongeographical names, such as Fall Colors and Music Fests. The result is a travel guide that's such fun to browse that you may lose all track of time. The frames-heavy pages are put to good use in organizing your viewing possibilities, and if you have a fast modem, try using the video and

sound buttons. Otherwise, enjoy the good writing, wealth of pictures, and the atmosphere of wanderlust.

Ecotravel

ecotravel.com

Links to Web travel sites: Ecotravel manages to be gigantic and elegant at the same time. A huge and valuable resource of links to travel sites around the World Wide Web, the site is designed with a simple attractiveness that belies its depth. Serving primarily as a focal point for hundreds of related Web sites, Ecotravel doesn't offer much original information. Still, the site has an editorial point of view, as its name implies, and you can browse links to environmental and conservation sites and travel topics. The fattest section of the site is Destinations, which is a country-by-country breakdown of travel links. Check out Hotel Search, which uses another site's search engine to help you locate a hotel in any reasonably large international city.

Exploration.Net

exploration.net

Virtual exploration of global destinations: Some ambitious Web sites combine deep information with annoying features that make exploring more difficult. Exploration.Net takes both qualities to an extreme with a slick site that presents a stunning wealth of well-organized information. At the same time, its high-graphics, Java-intensive approach just gets in the way. Skip this site if you have a slow modem. But if your connection is fast, you may appreciate the interactive design of a site that looks very much like a CD-ROM presentation. The Live Window is an especially cool feature, displaying a (presumably) live image of Paris, Rome, or any other major destination that you choose. When you get to a location that you want to explore (I'll stick with Paris; I'm in the mood for a croissant), you get a rich menu of links to travel guides, research information, maps, regional resources, local news and weather, transportation, language guides, and much more. Exploration.Net is an impressive one-stop launching pad for virtual explorations around the world — as long as your modem is up to the challenge.

Fodor's Travel Online

www.fodors.com

Trip planning and destination reviews: You can often tell right away when a Web site is going to make your life easier by its clarity of presentation. Fodor's Travel Online isn't such a site, and you may spend a few seconds staring at the home page, wondering what to do next. Here's a tip: Forget the surrounding links and click the center globe. The center globe takes you to the Personal Trip Planner, where you can select a destination from a fairly extensive list. Your choice is the beginning of an interactive survey in which you choose what you want to find out through a series of pages. The process is fun, and it *will* make your life easier. The result is a miniguide from one of the most famous travel directories in the world. You can repeat the process as often as your travel imagination demands, gathering detailed and useful information about cities all over the world. This site is highly recommended.

Microsoft Expedia

expedia.msn.com

Extraordinary travel resource: Expedia, one of the largest and most important travel destinations on the Web, is a combination of magazine, community, travel agent, and resource guide from Microsoft. Offering the feel of a travel encyclopedia, Expedia is lushly designed and gorgeously illustrated. The site is a pleasure to look at (typical of Microsoft sites), and it's hard to leave without discovering something or at least having your wanderlust stimulated. Expedia Magazine usually features a central topic (recently, New England) with relevant stories clustered around it. Research resources are impressive. The World Guide, a virtual encyclopedia to global destinations, is 14,000 pages by itself and represents a masterpiece of Web content unrivaled elsewhere. The site also offers a hotel directory, a currency converter, and a weather section. The map area is detailed and well-implemented. A short review almost insults the depth and care that have been poured into Expedia, so you must simply believe my earnest recommendation: Install Microsoft Expedia permanently on your bookmark list of travel sites.

Pathfinder Travel

pathfinder.com/Travel

Disorganized but useful travel site: Subtitled "Getting Around the Planet," the Pathfinder Travel site suffers a bit from a lack of a defined mission. Even after poking around for a while, you may ask exactly what the site is for. That's not to say that you won't find some darn useful stuff, though, starting with Travel Time, a resource of family travel tips. The mapping section is an interesting collection of regional maps. (Unlike more sophisticated multimedia mapping products, the feature won't create a map with directions for your trip.) A few links to other travel sites round out Pathfinder Travel. Overall, this Web site isn't one that will leave you quivering in your boots, but it's certainly worth visiting.

The Rough Guide

www.hotwired.com/rough

 ★★ ★★

Street-wise budget travel advice: "Savvy. Sensible. Sophisticated." That's the tag line for a hip destination guide produced by HotWired, one of the Web's most *avant* sites. The site's attempt to stimulate discussion on message boards has met with dismal success so far, despite some intriguing topic headers provided by the site, so you should either forget that part or take the initiative to post lots of messages and bring some life to that section. The rest of the site delves into the United States, Europe, Canada, Australia, Mexico, Hong Kong, and India. Clear, simple, colorful maps divide countries into clickable regions, each of which delivers reams of information on history, practical realities of present-day visiting, city transportation, tours, and more. Prices are referenced for everything, fortunately giving you a fairly clear sense of how much it costs to travel around a region. The site assumes that

you have a rough-and-ready attitude about traveling, and the site's unembellished design, although easy on the eyes and speedy through the modem, is a bit confusing to the brain.

Total Travel Network

www.totaltravel.net

Travelogues and trip planning: The best thing about the Total Travel Network is the Travel Tools drop-down box. Scroll down the choices in the box and click one. Depending on your choice, you can perform interactive currency conversions, view a radar image of weather anywhere in the world, determine the local time for any zone, or find the land and air miles between any two major cities. After you have fun playing with the Toy Box, you're left with adventuresome travelogues; trip-planning columns; and lists of links to airlines, auto rental companies, and travel magazines. All this content is good, but the Travel Tools drop-down box puts Total Travel Network on the map.

The Travel Channel

www.travelchannel.com

Travel Channel features: You have to be patient when dealing with The Travel Channel site. For starters, the home page takes a while to load all its images, animations, and Java enhancements (yawn). Second, a big part of the home page is devoted to promoting The Travel Channel networks and their programs and schedules. Skip the hype and go for the Online Stories box (the orange one on the left) and click a story link. The forthcoming pages don't display any faster, but the content is more interesting. Unfortunately, the home page displays only a few stories; to read more, you have to click Online Stories and then wade your way through the Discovery Channel's site (Discovery is the parent of the Travel

180 Travel

Channel). The Faraway Travels link is the key. This site is in dire need of intelligent, user-friendly redesign, but you may like the worthwhile text and images — or you may be better off just watching The Travel Channel on TV.

Travel Source

www.travelsource.com

Links to theme travel packages: This incredible resource puts you in contact with organizations that sponsor travel packages, with an emphasis on theme travel. The home page is Wow! material, displaying an impressive array of theme topics. Serving as the top level of a directory, each theme topic leads to a list of links to Web sites of travel companies that organize tours within that theme. Choose Cycling, for example, to see a page of links to information on cycling expeditions to Europe, pedaling excursions through U.S mountain ranges, and so on. Other themes include Trekking & Walking, Cruises, Ecotours, Bed & Breakfast, Honeymoon Specials, Caribbean, Sports Tours, Sea Kayaking, and Senior Leisure.

Traveler.Net

www.traveler.net/two

Well-organized directory of Web travel sites: This site's parent, *Travel Weekly,* is a printed trade magazine for the travel industry, and the fact that the Web site has an entirely different purpose is somewhat surprising. Meant for consumers and particularly for netizens, Traveler.Net is primarily a gigantic directory of Web travel sites. Now, a travel directory isn't exactly a new invention, and the value of this one lies in how it's organized. Using the big buttons on the left side of the home page, you can view links and short descriptions to U.S. sites; world sites; and Web locations dealing with air travel, cars, trains,

cruises, hotels, tours, and theme travel. The content may sound dry, but you have to get into the links to discover the luster. In the air travel section, in addition to many airline sites, you find a link called Above It All, which deals with Hawaiian sight-seeing planes. Traveler.Net is a valuable, handy resource that exceeds expectations.

TRAVEL.ORG

www.travel.org

Directory of Web travel sites: Although this site may not have the most imaginative name or the most efficient Web design (why do some sites insist on making the home page nothing more than a Click here to enter placard?), TRAVEL.ORG's Directory of Travel provides netizens with a fat directory of Web sites in various categories. A nice list of Bed & Breakfast links is available in the Lodging section. Many of the other categories are broad destinations: Europe, Asia, Islands, and so on. The graphics slow down the site — although a mere text-based design is sufficient for simple directories — but where else are you likely to find a link to a guide on vegetarian restaurants in Norway?

Traveler's Journal

www.travelersjournal.com

Archive of the public-radio broadcasts:
"The Traveler's Journal" is a two-minute
program that you may have heard on
public-radio stations. The Web site is an
archive of the programs, which you can
listen to through RealAudio-enabled
browsers. Click The Program Archives,
and a page appears with links to several
months' worth of programs. Pick a month
and a calendar appears, with each
program briefly described on its day of
broadcast. Each one has a small text link
at the bottom, if you'd rather read than
listen or if you don't have the RealAudio
plug-in. Actually, I find that the best
practice is to initiate the RealAudio
playback and then link up the text to read
along. Too bad that the site doesn't have
any pictures, but it's understandable that
a radio production wouldn't be interested
in visual images. A resource list points
you to a good selection of Web sites.

Weekend Guide

www.weekendguide.com

Tips for weekend trips: The Weekend
Guide's graphics are rudimentary. The
site content looks as though it were
thrown together by a beginning student
of Web design. Obviously, this site is no
Microsoft Web site. Gratifyingly, however,
the information in Weekend Guide is
concise and surprisingly useful. Start by
choosing a country from the menu of
flags. If you choose the United States,
next choose a state from the United
States map. (Stop chuckling over the
dorky map and get on with it.) Finally,
click a button to find out about lodging,
travel, business services, real estate,
shopping, and other travel concerns
within that state. In many cases, a list of
links to local hotels' Web sites appears. If
you're a New Yorker considering a
weekend in Santa Fe or a summer Florid-
ian wanting to chill out in the Carolinas
for a week, Weekend Guide is a great way
to zero in on the right info quickly. You'll
hear no complaints from me about the
way that this site looks (snicker).

World Travel Guide

www.wtgonline.com/navigate/
    default.asp

Online edition of travel reference book:
World Travel Guide is recognized as a
worthy reference book to international
destinations. The online version was
created in collaboration with AT&T. The
Country Factfinder is the central feature
of the site. After you click your way to the
country that you're interested in, all the
information that you could ask for is
tossed in your face — everything from
visa and passport requirements to
accommodation information, social life to
weather, resorts to business concerns to
national history. The site is like a primer
on almost every country in the world. A
special Country of the Month review is of
some interest, but the Country Factfinder
is the main draw at this Web site.

Other Stuff to Check Out

visit-usa.com
www.biztravel.com
www.lonelyplanet.com
www.thetravelguide.com

Travel Publications

Travel publications share some of the
attributes of destination guides but focus
more on feature articles. Because travel
writing is an established literary genre,
some of these sites rely on great
wordsmithery, rather than photographic
displays, to convey a sense of locale.
Other sites attract readers through useful
columns about various aspects of
traveling or searchable databases of back-
issue articles.

182 Travel

bizTraveler

www.biztravel.com/bizTraveler

Travel information for the briefcase set:
The editorial aim of bizTraveler is clear
from its name, and the weekly travelzine
uses computer technology to explore the
political, cultural, social, and economic
aspects of doing business in the country
of your choice. What this basically means
is that you can choose a country from a
long list and see a hyperlinked list of
relevant articles from past issues. This
idea is a good one, even if the pages
display a little slowly, but the feature is
hampered by the lack of original information content that would enhance the site's
value. Because you're limited to a
database of past articles, some country
selections yield much more data than
others. Another big problem: The home
page design doesn't enable you to access
more than a few of these so-called City
Reviews at a time. You have to click off
the home page and use the new links
menu on the left to access the archives.
Still, the magazine is an established fund
of welcome information for business
travelers.

The Connected Traveler

www.travelmedia.com/connected

Exotic jaunts and plenty of humor: A fine
eclectic travel site, without being overtly
weird in its selection of destinations and
topics, The Connected Traveler describes
jaunts such as a visit with Arthur C.
Clarke in his Sri Lanka home and having
drinks at the North Pole with Georgia
Hesse. The online magazine carries an
environmental slant but not to a distracting extent. One of the best features is the
Levity link, which displays hilarious signs
from around the world, such as "Here
speaching American" in Majorca and

"Ladies are requested not to have
children in the bar" in a Norwegian
cocktail lounge. You never know quite
what you're going to get at The Connected Traveler, but everything is
entertaining.

Epicurious Travel

**travel.epicurious.com/travel/g_cnt/
home.html**

Travel and food, a classic combination:
Epicurious Travel is one of the best-
known travel stops on the Web, yet its
raison d'être is a little hard to pin down.
Don't misunderstand me — the site is
wealthy with intriguing travel ideas,
recommendations, and love of food. The
focus is just a little scattered but no
matter. Browsing aimlessly may be the
best way to approach this site. To start,
you may want to scroll down to the
bottom of the home page, where a tiny
drop-down list offers current Deals of the
Week. Alternatively, browse among the
big Places, Planning, and Play buttons.
The Go to Epicurious Food link reveals a
fundamental feature of the site: the
fascination with eating and drinking
around the world. You can find recipes,
menus, and a food dictionary.

Mungo Park

www.mungopark.msn.com

★★
★★

Great travel writing: A Microsoft Network site that's open to the public, Mungo Park is a spectacularly stylish, richly produced magazine on global subjects. Not meant to deliver practical destination information, for the most part, Mungo Park hits its travel topics obliquely — as with Mariel Hemingway's recent article about Ernest Hemingway that serves as a quasi travelogue of Cuba. The writing is top-class, often executed by famous authors or personalities. Mungo Park's self-description — "interactive adventure magazine" — sums the site up perfectly. You may want to sign up for the monthly e-mail alerts on new issues and special chat sessions, if only to remind yourself not to forget about this site; it's a gem.

Travel & Leisure Magazine Online

pathfinder.com/Travel/TL

A smart and efficient online travel magazine: One of the most well-rounded travel magazines online, Travel & Leisure Magazine Online contains about six feature stories per issue. The articles are invariably imaginative, stylishly written, and efficiently presented on pages that don't waste your day displaying. If a half-dozen articles doesn't sate your appetite, visit the More Articles link. A search engine invites you to enter keywords, but the results of any search are limited to the article archive, not to any broader database of travel facts, so you may find it to be as useless as I did. (After striking out with a couple of esoteric search phrases, I gave the search engine an easy one: *New Orleans music.* Nothing.) The site-links page is still under construction but may prove to be useful by the time you read this. For now, treat this site as being the online edition of a good travel magazine, and enjoy the articles.

TravelASSIST Magazine

travelassist.com

An online magazine with a bed & breakfast directory: TravelASSIST is an online magazine with the normal range of destination articles and helpful columns, plus a couple of distinguishing features that make it stand out above the crowd. First, the home page makes it exceptionally easy to browse past articles by linking to them directly, in a long list divided by destination or travel topic. Rather than calling up a list of back issues or forcing you to search through a database by keyword, a juicy list of past articles beckons right from the front page. The Bed & Breakfast directory is a nice affair classified by geographic location and featuring pictures (in most cases) of the inn that you're looking up. This magazine is a good one, providing useful services.

21st Century Adventures

www.10e-design.com/centadv/

Online travel magazine featuring unusual destinations: If you're looking for a simple package tour to someplace like, say, Disney World, this isn't the site for you. 21st Century Adventures is devoted to offbeat, enterprising destination ideas and travelogues. During a recent visit, I found articles on rock climbing in Scotland, white-water rafting in Australia, and hiking the Anza-Borrego State Park in California. Browsing the archived articles is fascinating. And even better is clicking the Virtual Adventure link. What you get is a list of virtual slide shows, complete with soundtracks. You'll need the latest RealAudio plug-in to take advantage, but you can download it from the home page.

USA Today: Travel

www.usatoday.com/life/travel/
ltfront.htm

Travel news from the information-rich daily newspaper: USA Today takes a newsy approach to its online travel publication. General travel news stories ("Vegas visitors hitting the malls more than casinos") dominate the front page, with a featured destination just below and a Travel Tips section in the lower-right corner. Specific tips sections are provided for business and leisure travel, befitting the different audiences. The Business travel today page includes a few quick tips; the meat is provided by the links on the left. Click on your destination (United States, Canada, Europe, and so on) and you'll find more specific "road-warrior" tips for frequent business travelers to that region. The Leisure travel index is a little more relaxed, with a list of recent features on various destinations. The whole USA Today site is searchable, so if you don't find exactly what you want, you can look it up. And links to travel reservation services are provided.

Wanderlust

www.salonmagazine.com/wanderlust

★ ★
★ ★

Weekly online magazine with style and wit: Wanderlust is a virtual spin-off of a larger Web magazine called Salon. The idea behind Wanderlust's editorial choices is to kindle the romance of travel, and as such, the magazine doesn't concentrate so much on destinations as on attitudes

and quests. Recent features included a humorous journalistic account of a Club Med vacation and a search for strange foods around the world. The design is beautiful and simple, with the site showcasing five or six articles at a time. Wanderlust is a weekly publication, and each fresh issue is posted to the Web site on Monday evenings.

Other Stuff to Check Out

www2.journeywoman.com/journeywoman
www.finetravel.com/finetrav
www.globaldialog.com/~tpatmaho
www.onroute.com/destinations/index.html
www.planeta.com
www.travelcorner.com
www.travelmag.co.uk/travelmag
www.ulysse.ca/english

Travel Directories

The Internet is its own domain, completely separated from geography. Well, not completely. The Net does have a physical basis, after all, consisting of real computers existing in real (not cyber) space. Accordingly, some Web directories exist specifically to bridge the gap between cyberspace and physical space by listing Web sites created in certain locations or whose content is dedicated to those locations.

Regional directories can focus on a single country, a selection of countries or cities, or any combination of geographical characteristics. Why would you want to use such directories? They're useful if you're traveling to a region or you're just interested in it. Some listings point to Web sites of practical value when you're in the city or country, like shopping, recreational, or dining opportunities; others are more informational, dealing with history or culture.

Access New Zealand

accessnz.co.nz

Sites about New Zealand: New Zealand may not be the most common destination in the world, but if you ever plan to visit, this site is about as complete a directory to relevant Web sites as you're likely to find. Actually, a combination directory and keyword search engine, Access New Zealand assembles Web sites that you can access by region, domain, or through 21 categories ranging from Agriculture to Weather, Government to Real Estate. The directory is beautifully implemented, showing you how many sites are listed in each group and providing brief descriptions of the linked sites. The directory is admittedly the centerpiece of Access New Zealand, but the maps are helpful, too.

Australian Internet Directories

www.sofcom.com/Directories

Directory of Australian Web sites: I'm not sure why "Directories" is plural in this site's name, because the site is a single guide to Australian Web sites. "The full directory" of such sites, according to the home page, implies that every single Web site originating from down under is listed there. Such a feat would be impossible in the ever-shifting American Web scene, so either this directory is incredibly pretentious, or the Australian Internet landscape is much more stable than elsewhere. No matter. The directory is a good one, covering Travel and Tourism, Personal Home Pages, Government,

Community, Shopping, and other categories. And if you have friends down under, you can look up their e-mail addresses — that way you can warn them you're coming, so they can throw a shrimp on the barbie.

Infoseek Worldwide

www.infoseek.com/
    doc?pg=international.html

International, multilingual Web directories: Brush up your linguistic skills and surf over to Infoseek Worldwide for a reminder that the Internet is a truly global network. That fact is easy for Americans to forget, but Infoseek makes it very clear with a selection of international directories supplementing its main English guide to the Web. Americans won't have any trouble deciphering the United Kingdom directory, but they may need to revive their high school language lessons for nine others: Brazil, Denmark, Germany, Spain, France, Italy, Japan, the Netherlands, and Sweden. In each case, the entire directory is written in the country's native language, including the site descriptions.

Italy on the Net

www.doit.it/feroldi/italynet

An English directory to Italian Web sites: Don't worry: It's in English. Italy on the Net is a guide to useful sites related to Italy and does a good job of mixing together sites from all over the world that have Italy as their main topic. Travelers should appreciate the guide to Italian hotels under the Tourism category. The design of this site is on the clunky side: Is that a circuit board in the background? But the content is worth it, and you can cruise among eight main categories. A word of warning: Although the directory, including site descriptions, is completely in English, it links to pure Italian sites that, in some cases, are written in Italian.

Signpost

signpost.execpc.com

Guide to Web sites about the midwestern United States: Although it doesn't acknowledge the fact up front, Signpost is, to a large degree, a directory for Web sites related to the midwestern United States. Using a great design wherein directory topics are represented by wooden signposts, the five top-level categories aren't that unusual — Business, Community, Government, Recreation, and Entertainment. (A sixth category is a directory of Web sites created by the members of the local Internet service provider that produces Signpost.) Inside the three-level directory pages, you find listings to sites for local churches, entertainment spots, as well as more global listings. Signpost is obviously created for the benefit of its local Internet access customers, but it's valuable for travelers or anyone else in the Midwest.

Yahoo! Regional Directories

**www.yahoo.com/
Computers_and_Internet/Internet/
World_Wide_Web/
Searching_the_Web/Web_Directories/
Yahoo__Regional/**

Growing collection of regional Web directories: The Yahoo! directory and search engine was the first to develop regional directories, and it has widened its advantage by increasing its roster of regional pages. Beginning with San Francisco and Japan, Yahoo! now guides surfers through cyberspace matching the locales of Atlanta, Canada, France, Asia, Miami, and many other cities and countries. The Yahoo! directories link to Web sites useful to both travelers and residents. The directories differ somewhat, but they usually include business, computers, news and media, and community and cultural info. Classifieds, dining guides, and yellow pages are often included as well.

Other Stuff to Check Out

info.fuw.edu.pl/pl/PolandResourceMap.html
peacock.tnjc.edu.tw/ROC_sites.html
serpiente.dgsca.unam.mx/temas_mex.html
thorplus.lib.purdue.edu/inet_resources/
   indiana.html
www.city.net
www.dirglobal.net

Part V
Shopping and Services

The 5th Wave   By Rich Tennant

©RICHTENNANT

"Ronnie made the body from what he learned in Metal Shop, Sissy and Darlene's Home Ec. class helped them in fixing up the inside, and then all that anti-gravity stuff we picked up off the Web."

In this part . . .

Ask not what you can do for the Internet; ask what the Internet can do for you. It can help you find a job, shop, trade stocks, and, after you've made your fortune, book a vacation. This part covers the sites that enable you to do all of these cool things.

Automotive Services

Ready to kick the tires of a shiny new vehicle? That's about the only thing you can't do online anymore. Not only can you get the basics (what equipment comes on a car, and what it will, or should, cost you), you can take virtual tours of the insides of cars. You can't actually buy a new car online yet — what most sites do is take down information about the car you want, and then have an affiliated dealer call you — but don't be surprised to see online car buying available soon.

Note: Automobiles are just one means of transportation that you can find out about online. Want more information? Try *Buying Online For Dummies,* by Joseph Lowery (IDG Books Worldwide, Inc.).

Auto-By-Tel

www.autobytel.com

★ ★
★ ★

State-of-the-art auto site: Auto-By-Tel's home page is dominated by the black FasTrak area on the left for people "who know what they want" and are ready to buy. And if you're one of those people, few sites are simpler than Auto-By-Tel. Simply select the manufacturer that you're interested in, enter your zip code

(or postal code, for visitors to the Canadian page), click Let's Go!, and you're off. As with other sites, your car-buying information is really being forwarded to affiliated dealers who will get in touch with you. Want to research first? No problem — Auto-By-Tel has lots of numbers and lots of advice, and what it doesn't have, it provides links to. The used car purchasing section is especially cool, because not only does it display pictures of the cars, it automatically tells you how far away from your zip code the vehicle is. Perhaps the most innovative feature is that you can fill out financing, lease, and insurance forms online, making the trip to your dealer a short one — once you get to the dealer, of course.

AutoWeb.com

www.autoweb.com

Relaxed but complete: AutoWeb.com isn't as dramatic as Auto-By-Tel, but it's just as thorough. You can arrange to buy new or used, sell your car, arrange financing and leasing, and do research all by clicking the convenient tabs on the front page and following directions. The list of research resources is impressive; equally nice is the easy-to-find list of affiliated U.S. and Canadian dealers, which gives you an idea of how well established AutoWeb.com is in your area. All told, AutoWeb.com does a good job living up to its motto of offering "everything for autos on the Web."

Edmund's

www.edmunds.com

Online version of new and used car price guide: Edmund's produces a book that's sort of a Bible of numbers to U.S. car buyers ready to battle car dealers over the bottom line. Using the guide, you can

190 Automotive Services

look up what the dealer paid for a particular car (or at least, what the experts at Edmund's estimate is the real amount the dealer paid) and negotiate a better deal. The Web site offers the same kind of information, evident from the somewhat plain but very serviceable directory. New car information includes not only the equipment lists and price information, but reviews, pros and cons, insurance costs, and competing models. Edmund's does a nice job keeping up-to-date rebate and recall information, and also provides a link to a service that finds a low-cost dealer in your area. (My advice: Have the Edmund's price sheet handy when the dealer calls, so you can really evaluate how much of a deal you're getting.) Edmund's also offers online truck and used car information, lots of stories with buying tips, a message room, and an online Loan Calculator (which, by the way, doesn't accept commas). As Web sites go, Edmund's isn't a sports car, but it's a good, reliable family sedan.

Microsoft CarPoint

carpoint.msn.com

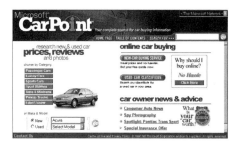

Let Bill Gates help sell you a car, too: Microsoft never does anything in a small way and rarely misses an opportunity to make a computer-related dollar, so it shouldn't be much of a surprise that the software colossus is in the online car business, too. Give CarPoint credit: It has one of the flashiest online car showrooms

around, with top-notch design and features. You can scout out information on new or used cars, submit specs to get a quote from an affiliated U.S. or Canadian dealer, browse the used car classifieds, and generally do just about anything you'd hope to at an online auto site. The cross-referencing is superb, and the news and advice features are more plentiful than other sites, too. The *coup de grâce:* Surround Video clips of the interiors of some cars. Bet you can't guess whose software the clips use.

Trader Online

www.traderonline.com

From sedans to earthmovers: The printed versions of Trader publications are basically classified ads, and Trader Online simply builds on that concept. And does it ever. At the home page, you can select ads for cars, pickups, motorcycles, RVs, big trucks, and heavy equipment. (You can also link to ads for other merchandise; just click Merch.) Trader Online has a classic vehicle page as well. The site basically takes your phone area code or region (Canada and the Caribbean included) and what you want, searches the Trader ad database, and gives you all the appropriate matches. Unlike other sites, Trader Online doesn't act as an intermediary, so you have to make the contact. Fortunately, the site provides contact information. If you're the type who believes in turning over every rock to find a bargain or if you just like to browse without being pressured, Trader Online is for you.

Other Stuff to Check Out

www.cars-on-line.com
www.gmev.com
www.kbb.com
www.theautochannel.com

Classifieds and Job Search Services

www.careerpath.com

Classified ads on the Internet are getting seriously useful. In the past, the idea may have been good, but the implementation verged on awful. Consider that most classified sections of newspapers depend on a local readership for their practicality. The World Wide Web is, to borrow an expression, worldwide. Recently, classified sites have gotten wise to that essential fact and have created international databases divided into local categories, accessible with the help of drop-down menus and other navigational aids. At least, that's how the best sites work. Check out the sites assembled here for a glimpse of how good online classifieds can be.

Note: If you want to do a little more in-depth research on job searching online, try *Job Searching Online For Dummies,* by Pam Dixon (IDG Books Worldwide, Inc.). The book is a great resource for everything involved in using online information to get the job you want, not just finding sites.

America's Job Bank

www.ajb.dni.us

Job listings by category and state: Using a sophisticated and sometimes complex keyword search and sort system,

America's Job Bank helps you navigate a massive database of job listings. You have a choice of searching by menu or by keyword, but either way you have choices to make. If your search results in too many listings, the site won't show them to you (hmph!), so you need to narrow them down right from the start. By selecting a job category and state, you can usually get the listings down to a manageable size. Then you can arrange the display of job listings by salary, location, or job title. All these choices get a bit complicated, but the important point is that America's Job Bank has a ton of listings. And it's free.

Best Jobs in the USA

www.bestjobsusa.com

Job listings with detailed descriptions: One of the strong points of Best Jobs in the USA is its description of jobs, which goes way beyond a mere listing. Some jobs have several paragraphs of descriptive text outlining requirements, company atmosphere, and benefits. Start at the home page and click the Jobs Database link. A page with drop-down menus appears, asking you to choose a state (or all states if you're willing to move anywhere) and enter a job category, a job title or company name, and a keyword, if you'd like to narrow the search. The job categories are broader than at some other sites. The initial result of your search is a simple, raw list of links — click any one of them to see the job description.

CareerPath.com

www.careerpath.com

Classifieds from newspapers around the United States: This incredible service takes a unique approach to listing job openings: It doesn't. That is to say, it doesn't create its own classifieds section. Instead, it borrows the classified databases of newspapers (about 40 of them) from around the United States, which you can search in a few different ways. First, you select a paper based on where you want to work. (You can choose multiple papers.) Then you select a job category from an extensive list on a selectable menu. Then you can type keywords to narrow the search further. This whole procedure is laid out so intuitively that you can't possibly go wrong, and if you do, it's easy to start over.

Infoseek Classifieds

www.classifieds2000.com

Broad array of classifieds: Divided into broad categories that include vehicles, personals, computers, apartment rentals, general merchandise, and event tickets, Infoseek Classifieds covers some unusual bases for a general classifieds site. Most online classifieds are strong in cars and computers and weak in everything else. Infoseek suffers from the same tendency to an extent, but its high name recognition attracts classified posters. You can find some job listings here, but you'd do better with one of the dedicated employment classified sites.

NetJobs

www.netjobs.com

Employment guide for Canada and America: NetJobs focuses primarily (although not exclusively) on Canadian and American technology positions, so if the phrases "code," "interface," and "Does your restaurant deliver?" are familiar, this site is a good place to check. Like many job sites, NetJobs has separate directories for companies seeking employees and employees seeking companies. Click the Job Seekers link to access a page where you can Search Jobs, Post Your Resume (warning — NetJobs charges you for this service), and find Useful Links, among other things. The job search page enables you to search by category, company, and location. You also can search for recent postings — although you have to go to the job description to find out the job's location.

Overseas Jobs Express

www.overseasjobs.com

International job openings and links: The British company behind this site also publishes a print edition, so — surprise! — you'll find lots of invitations on the Web site to subscribe to the biweekly paper. Before you go and spend your money (about $120 a year in the United States, cheaper in Europe) to pick up a subscription, however, try the Web version. You can get a sampling of the advice articles in the paper by clicking the Overseas Jobs Express News link. A recent article highlighted how New Zealand is actually advertising to attract professional immigrants. The International Job Openings page has some of the paper's job openings in some 44 categories ranging from Construction Engineering and Electronics to Arts & Design and Retail. Perhaps the handiest page is the Job Search Resources page, which includes links to job openings around the world. You also can post your resume at the site.

Other Stuff to Check Out

careers.boston.com
classifieds.astranet.com/HCI/bin/nclassy.x/
    hciBHM06
home1.gte.net/shaneh/abc/index.htm
www.infosel.com.mx/bolsaDeTrabajo
www.jobnet.com.au
www.latimes.com/HOME/CLASS/EMPLOY
www.washingtonpost.com/wp-adv/
    classifieds/careerpost/front.htm

Education Services

www.petersons.com

Education is such a wide-ranging field that you *need* a computer just to keep track of all the possibilities, whether you're looking for information on admissions, financial aid, teaching, tests, or careers.

If I expanded the proportions of this section as far as they could go, you would need to hire a bodybuilder to carry the book home for you. Instead, I present a collection of sites representing the multifaceted topic of education, from high school college-prep tests to financial aid, from teaching resources to scholarly Web links.

College Board Online

www.collegeboard.org

Help in taking tests: For those facing crucial tests along the educational path, this site is a nonintimidating way to see how the College Board operates and to find out about its test dates. The site covers SAT testing as well. You can't, unfortunately, take the tests online, but you can prepare for some writing and advanced-placement (college credit) exams by writing practice essays and getting personalized feedback online. Some of the material at the site is geared to guidance counselors, faculty, and admissions staffs, but the SAT Question of the Day is definitely for students. Thank

goodness I'm not one anymore. Every time I give the sample question the old "college try," I end up falling asleep and dreaming about the intellectual rigors of kindergarten.

CollegeNET

www.collegenet.com

Search for colleges using various criteria: The CollegeNET home page was recently redesigned, and the result — well, I thought the use of an outer space motif was appropriate, because I felt like I was trying to read some of the links from across the universe. But no matter. After you get past the front page, the design normalizes, and a terrific search engine opens for your use. You can search for colleges first by type, and then by location (states in the U.S.), enrollment numbers, tuition amounts, and majors offered. You also can search by name, of course. The results link to college Web pages, where available. Scholarship resources also are offered.

ETS Net

www.ets.org

Online site of Educational Testing Service: Educational Testing Service (ETS) — the very name strikes trepidation in the hearts of students everywhere. Well known as an evil lair of kid-torture specialists, ETS devises increasingly efficient brain-picking devices, in the form of multiple-choice questions requiring a number-two pencil, gleefully making young lives miserable. The Web site, sober but friendly, points to a wealth of services for students, parents, and educators. It's amazing how many pies ETS has its fingers in, from testing to careers to financial aid. As a result, the ETS site is a rich resource for information and help. You can view and puzzle through sample test questions (use a number-two mouse, please), and the Colleges & Universities link has great info on admissions tests and getting college credit by testing out of classes.

FinAid

www.finaid.org

How to borrow money for education: The Financial Aid Information Page offers a clearinghouse of information for college students who need tuition help. Maintained by the author of a book on the subject, FinAid contains an astounding wealth of information, including glossaries; FAQs (Frequently Asked Questions); special topics for international and disabled students; links to financial aid Web pages, books, videotapes, and consultants; and much more. All this information makes this site a one-stop resource page. You can access the whole thing easily from a directory-style menu on the home page. This one's a keeper.

Global Schoolhouse

www.gsh.org

Educational technology for teachers: The Global Schoolhouse is a cooperative venture of the Global SchoolNet Foundation and Microsoft. The site is designed for teachers and classrooms, and is of interest to anyone concerned with the use of technology in education. Obviously, the site's viewpoint is that technology is a good thing, and it supports computer networking in the classroom by connecting schools with each other through its directory. School classes can use the Global Schoolhouse to seek out other classes on the Net, by viewing their home pages and by using Microsoft

resources (including free server space) to get themselves on the Web. For administrators, Global Schoolhouse reveals the state of the Internet in education. For teachers, Global Schoolhouse offers practical solutions to getting a classroom online. Free membership offers additional resources, but this site has plenty to offer without joining.

Kaplan Educational Center

www.kaplan.com

Helps students face and take scholastic tests: Kaplan is one of the finest educational service sites on the Net. Seemingly telepathic, the site anticipates all the questions that nervous students ask as they face the important testing milestones along their educational careers. The site answers their questions with deep resources, lots of reassurance, and helpful information that just doesn't quit. When it comes to the SAT, PSAT, GRE, GMAT, and other examinations, Kaplan archives past tests, analyzes strategies, and discusses the relative importance of high or low scores in certain departments. The site is wonderful at giving the admissions process a larger perspective, no matter what your educational level is. The site enables you to test yourself with sample questions, and it dishes up complete sections covering financial aid, careers, medical school, and law school. All kinds of tips spill out of every page, and all the text is full of embedded hyperlinks that lead to nuggets of information. The thoroughness and innovation of the site are hard to convey in a short review — your best bet is to see for yourself.

NASA Online Educational Resources

quest.arc.nasa.gov/OER

Science education resources: If your interest is science education, you've hit the jackpot with this page. In addition to NASA's own educational resources, the site offers a directory of lists to universities and colleges, online museums and expositions, online libraries, collaborative projects, and science education search pages, among others. Any one of these categories could be bookmarked in its own right. I'm impressed by the page design, too: Even though the site is mostly text-based, clicking any category displays a new page with all the main categories still showing and the chosen category broken down into its subcategories. The design makes it easy to shift categories without using the Back button. For sure, if you or your kids enjoy scientific content online, put this NASA resource page on your hot list.

National Education Loan Center

www.schoolfunds.com

How to get government education loans: The National Education Loan Center site has the real scoop on U.S. government education loans. The site lays out all the facts concerning requirements, applications, disbursements, and — unfortunately — paybacks. It tells you when to apply, what the award letter looks like, and even gets you pre-approved online if you care to fill in a reasonably short form. The site could hardly be clearer or more encouraging about financing higher education.

Petersons.com

www.petersons.com

Online college and career guides: Peterson's, the famous college guide company, enables you to access its database of information related to all kinds of education: from kindergarten, to graduate schools, to distance learning. Families who need information on colleges — the database area that put the Peterson's books on the map many years ago — should add this site to their bookmark list. You can browse alphabetically, geographically, by college type, and by religious affiliation; and you can even read campus news from many schools. A search engine accepts keywords, and linked instruction pages help you make sense of all the information offered. Is using this site better than just buying a Peterson's book? It depends. You have more flexible search options with a computer, and the online version is certainly cheaper. You also can get your hands on information about high schools, summer programs, careers and jobs, language study, distance learning, continuing education, educational vacations, vocational schools, and testing — all in one place.

ScholarStuff

www.scholarstuff.com

Directory of education sites: No need for intimidation — ScholarStuff isn't just for scholars, though it *is* scholastic. The site is a directory to educational sites on the Net, with the surprising addition of a chat room. Besides socializing, you can browse through the directory in search of information about colleges and universities, educational software, financial aid sites, and test-help pages. The site even has a directory topic called Greek Life, a resource for fraternities and sororities. The Free Stuff link presents a collection of free offers on the Net — it's a gratuitous link, as almost none of the offers have anything to do with education, but that doesn't diminish its coolness one whit. (Coolness is generally measured in whits.)

196 Financial Services

Teaching and Learning on the WWW

www.mcli.dist.maricopa.edu/tl

Database of educational sites: Using a specialized database of sites related to online courses of various kinds, this site offers a combination of keywords and drop-down menus to narrow your search. The category menu reads like a college catalog: mathematics, law, history, chemistry, religion, literature, and much more. Selecting a category takes you to a page with links and very generous descriptions. Many of the lists contain hundreds of entries, making this site the stellar Web location for finding courses on the Web.

Other Stuff to Check Out

> la.saic.com/edu.html
> www.csu.edu.au/education/library.html
> www.ed.gov/prog_info/SFA/StudentGuide
> www.edurock.com
> www.nelliemae.org
> www.nfsn.com
> www.signet.com/collegemoney
> www.usagroup.com/home.htm
> www.usbank.com

Every site in this section provides a tangible service online, not just a placard for an offline company that provides a service. Fortunately, the fields of investment, business, and personal finance are among the quickest-growing on the World Wide Web. With more sites being added

every week, winnowing the truly valuable from the wanna-bes takes a discriminating sense, and that's the purpose of this section. Here is a directory of the finest financial services that the Internet has to offer. While I've avoided most pay-for-access sites, you can find tremendous value in the sites that follow. (Some sites may charge for certain features.)

Remember to continue exploring on your own because the field is changing very rapidly. Many people feel the age of empowerment for individual investors is at hand, and the changes are being played out on the World Wide Web.

Financial Advice and Information

Beyond brokering trades, providing stock quotes, and portfolio management, one basic financial service remains to be covered on the Web: delivering investor advice. This topic is one of the thorniest landscapes on the Internet, because anyone with an opinion can relatively easily set up a "financial expert" site and even charge subscription rates to access it. There are gems nestled among the piles of mediocrity, though, and this portion of the "Financial Services" section uncovers them. This handful of sites is just a starting point. Anyone interested in online finance can quickly hear about and visit other advice and information sites. Using appropriate caution, you can find your own favorites that meet your particular financial needs.

Note: Investing online is a far deeper subject than anyone can cover just with site reviews. Fortunately, Kathleen Sindell has written an excellent resource called — you guessed it — *Investing Online For Dummies* (IDG Books Worldwide, Inc.). If you're going to spend some serious money investing online, *Investing Online For Dummies* is a very valuable buy.

Merrill Lynch OnLine

www.merrill-lynch.ml.com

★★
★★

Comprehensive financial information: Merrill Lynch, the rock-solid, time-honored Wall Street investment firm, is embracing the Internet big time. And the company is doing a great job of it, I don't mind telling you. Go to the Web site and start with the Merrill Lynch OnLine Today link. It takes you to a multimedia online magazine that by itself is worth a visit to the site, particularly for the RealAudio reports. The Investor Learning Center is another great feature — a virtual online seminar. Likewise the Personal Finance Center and the Business Planning Center. Still more centers: The Family Saving Center and the News & Research Center. Getting the idea that this may be one of the finest financial information locations on the Net? You're right.

The Motley Fool

www.fool.com

★★
★★

Informal presentation of serious investment advice: Strange name for a financial Web site, isn't it? The Motley Fool started with two men offering an investment philosophy on America Online; they're popularity skyrocketed. These men and their organization are now respected throughout the online world, and The Motley Fool is set up as a Web site advice center. You can get stock quotes at the site, but its real purpose is to educate beginning investors in a certain approach (called The 13 Steps) to selecting stock purchases. The "Fool" motif running through every page keeps things fun, but the advice is serious and worthwhile. The site is updated with morning, lunchtime, and

evening news, as well as frequent posting of headlines and articles. Message boards add a community touch, and the whole shebang is as free as air. Becoming a Fool's follower is highly recommended.

Quicken Financial Services

www.qfn.com

Budget and tax planning: Quicken is best known as a software program that helps individuals manage their money. The same company (Intuit) that produces Quicken also makes a tax-preparation program called TurboTax, which is extremely popular. These two prongs of the personal finance fork — budget planning and tax planning — formed the genesis of the Quicken Financial Services site. But that's old history now, because the Quicken site has grown into a vast resource for financial advice. The front page sets the standard, with highlights and news stories in the middle, links to pages on everything from Banking & Borrowing to Saving & Spending. Inside pages typically have more stories and links to features. Finally, online banking is represented by Quicken's BankNOW feature — which is appropriate because the Quicken software program was one of the first forays into the new world of banking by personal computer. The entire Web site is free, although you incur fees when you open an online banking account. The Quicken site, whose purpose partly is to promote the Intuit software, stands on its own as a marvelous financial resource. Beautifully designed, with quick page displays and excellent features, it's worthy of being on many a bookmark list.

Other Stuff to Check Out

www.brill.com
www.elderweb.com/finance.htm
www.tfc.com

Online Brokerages

Online brokerages — sites that replace traditional human brokers by enabling you to buy and sell securities through your web browser — are one of the hot topics on the Web. This directory points you toward the main online brokerages, but more sites are being planned, waiting in the wings even as I write this book. Anyone shopping for an online brokerage should be aware of the basic trade-off when managing a stock, bond, or option portfolio online: You save money on lower commissions but gain some aggravation due to technical glitches. Every site listed here has experienced some degree of technical problems that have, at one time or another, kept its customers from accessing their accounts temporarily. Ironically, online brokerages are very popular among people who trade stocks frequently and need to access their accounts most often — the appeal for them lies in the commission savings. The point is that no Web brokerage is immune to system failure, and it's a young field that's still getting the bugs out. Proceed with caution.

When you set up an account with an online brokerage, the process is similar to opening a checking account at your local bank. The main difference is that you usually must set it up through the mail. Each online brokerage gives contact information for acquiring the necessary forms (in many cases you can request the forms online), which you then fill out and send in with a check to establish your beginning balance. All brokerages have a minimum balance requirement that may range from $500 to $5,000. In most cases, you can transfer securities from an already existing brokerage account, even an offline one. (Unfortunately, it must be *your* account.)

Accutrade

www.accutrade.com

Deep-discount stock and option trading: A quick-displaying Web site and reasonably attractive commission rates (especially for low-premium options) distinguishes the Accutrade online brokerage. Accutrade offers seven methods to conduct transactions, ranging from phone calls to fax machines to using PCs and Macs — even handheld computers with Windows CE work. Accutrade also provides some basic research tools like market news, earnings reports, and stock charts, but the site doesn't even mention mutual funds. You can open an account with as little as $5,000 (sorry — no IOUs are accepted). Trading commissions are based on a flat rate plus a small charge per share bought or sold. Accutrade is in the middle price range of online discount brokerages, with a more expensive commission schedule than E-Trade or Datek, but significantly less costly than Schwab and others.

Ameritrade

www.ameritrade.com

Cheap rates for basic trades: Ameritrade is an amalgamation of the former Aufhauser, Ceres, and eBroker sites and touts one of the lowest equity (read: stock) market trade prices around: $8 over the Internet for an unlimited number of shares. The price goes up if you want to trade over the phone or talk to a broker, of course, but $8 a pop is an eye-grabbing — but not wallet-grabbing — price. Guess the folks at Ameritrade mean it when they say "We never forget it's your money" on the home page. Ameritrade's Web site is fast and reliable, using many of the same screens (like the stock ordering screen) that Accutrade uses. The minimum to open an account is $2,000. Full-time, busy traders should look into Ameritrade if saving money on commissions is a priority.

Datek

www.datek.com

Lowest commissions for online stock trading: Datek takes deep discounting of trading commissions to the max, trading off services in the process. Naturally, the strategy of all deep discount brokerages is to forgo expensive services (like personal interaction with a human broker) to some extent, which appeals to experienced investors who just want to save money on buying and selling stocks that they research themselves. Datek saves such investors a heck of a lot of money, coming in with a flat commission rate (at the time of this writing) of $9.99 per trade — up to 5,000 shares. The commission on the next 5,000 shares costs you another $9.99. While that price is higher than Ameritrade, Datek doesn't charge anything additional for market limit orders or marketable orders that take more than one minute to execute — although if you read the fine print, you find out Datek has a few caveats on the latter. On the positive side, Datek offers *free* real-time stock quotes to its customers, which is very unusual and a great benefit. (***Note:*** The rolling stock quotes at the bottom-left of the front page aren't the real thing. If you look carefully, you'll find Datek is in cahoots with the *Dilbert* zone.) Datek appeals to NASDAQ traders who like moving stocks around quickly, saving money on real-time information.

Discover Brokerage

www.discoverbrokerage.com

Online brokerage for stocks and mutual funds: Discover Brokerage is the face-lifted version of Lombard Institutional Brokerage, created after Lombard and Discover merged, and subsequently absorbed by something called Morgan Stanley Dean Witter & Co. Sheesh. Sounds like something a math teacher would have a student write 50 times on the blackboard as punishment for talking in class. Discover continues Lombard's fine tradition of low commission costs, a great range of services, and a trouble-free reputation. At the time of this writing, Discover's basic market order trade commission was $14.95, and the minimum account size was $2,000. One problem: You can't open the account online. You can send for the forms online, but you have to mail the completed forms to the company's San Francisco office (and Heaven help you if you don't sign the form in black ink). Other than that strangely old-fashioned requirement, Discover Brokerage is a top-notch entry in the online financial field.

DLJdirect

www.dljdirect.com

★ ★
★ ★

Online brokerage with middle-of-the-road prices: A busy and informative home page greets you when you surf over to DLJdirect (formerly PC Financial Network), where you can execute reasonably priced stock trades (a $20 flat fee plus a per-share charge over $1,000 shares), buy mutual funds, and pay rather exorbitant commissions to trade options. DLJdirect offers middle-of-the-road financial services within a Web site that performs extremely well. With quick page displays and well-designed screens, this site demonstrates how an online brokerage should look.

Dreyfus Brokerage Services

www.tradepbs.com

Spartan, efficient online brokerage:
Dreyfus Brokerage Services keeps it
simple and delivers it fast. This Web site
streaks like lightning. No extraneous and
distracting graphics, unnecessary
sidebars, or browser frames (although a
frames version is available). The commission fee schedule is simple too: $15 per
trade, with options executed for $1.75 per
contract ($15 minimum). Don't expect
much beyond simple order execution and
an efficient Web site, though. The order
screens are clear and well designed, but
don't search for in-depth research tools.
This is down-'n'-dirty, stripped-to-the-
bones online brokerage.

e.Schwab

www.eschwab.com

*Online trading from the famous brokerage
house:* Schwab has been a familiar name
in discount brokering for a long time, and
the upstanding firm moved into the
online landscape early in the Web's
development. Before the Internet, Schwab
was synonymous with low trading
commissions. Now, floating in a crowded
sea of online brokerages, e.Schwab is
considered rather on the expensive side
by Net standards, charging about $30 per
trade, with an additional per-share charge
above 1,000 shares. According to the rate
schedule as of this writing, a purchase of
2,000 shares through e.Schwab costs
three times as much as through E-Trade
or Datek. Compensating for higher
commissions, the e.Schwab Web site is
widely known to be rock-solid, rarely
suffering technical difficulties, and the
site offers a special program for those
who prefer a different interface. (The
alternate interface, which can be downloaded from the site, boasts a fresh
design, but the same basic services.)
Schwab also claims to get its customers
better prices on stocks, though some
customers are unsure of this benefit, and
many other brokerages make the same
claim. If you want the security of dealing
with a long-established company famous
for great customer service, then the
higher commissions of e.Schwab may be
for you.

E-Trade

www.etrade.com

Pioneer of online brokerages: One of the
first, and certainly the most famous
online brokerage, E-Trade provides a wide
range of brokering services for trading
financial stocks and options. A true
discount broker, E-Trade charges a flat fee
(currently $14.95 for a PC trade of NYSE-
listed stocks) for the purchase or sale of
an unlimited number of a company's
shares, and option commissions are
competitive. A few things make E-Trade a
leader in the online brokerage race. First
is a true awareness of Internet features
and possibilities — E-Trade isn't a
crossover of an already-existing financial
house but was created specifically to
provide interactive computer brokerage
services. In addition to its Web site,
CompuServe and America Online members appreciate the presence E-Trade
maintains on both those networks — it
provides a margin of safety against
instances when the Web site is out of
service, which happens from time to time.
(But not any more often than other Web-
based brokerages.) E-Trade's strategy
goes beyond merely brokering buys and
sells of securities. An extensive array of
news, research, and charting services are
offered. The amount needed to start a
cash account ($1,000) is among the
lowest on the Internet. And you can try
the E-Trade Game from the front page to
get a taste before you actually part with
any money. E-Trade doesn't provide
everything, but the overall mix of service,
price, and Web performance keeps a lot of
investors happy.

FarSight

www.farsight.com

★ ★
★ ★

Attempting to be a complete financial center: FarSight financial services is a Web location developed by D. E. Shaw & Co., an innovative financial company that has migrated to the Internet with relish. (Which doesn't necessarily mean the company is hot-dogging it.) FarSight's ambitious goal is to surpass current models of online brokerages, online service centers, and online banks. How? By integrating all the features of each of those online businesses into a single online center for personal finance. The FarSight Web site has three main components: a Brokerage section, which lets customers trade securities online; a Banking section that supports checking accounts and a bill-paying feature that automatically writes and sends checks for your regularly recurring expenses; and an Accounts section that enables you to view summaries, histories, and reports of your deposits.

At this writing, FarSight is in a "Pilot" phase but is completely functional. You can open an account, trade stocks, pay bills automatically, and directly deposit paychecks. No minimum deposit was required for a FarSight cash account, and the commission schedule was $20 for up to 1,000 shares. The site is stable and beautifully designed, and downtime for maintenance is scheduled at off-hours. If the FarSight vision is successfully implemented, it could contribute significantly to the online revolution of financial services. This site is worth watching.

Fidelity

personal.fidelity.com/trade/index.html

↘

Relatively expensive online brokerage: Fidelity, home of a famous and diverse family of mutual funds, runs something called On-line Xpress (why should financial geniuses know how to spell?) for its customers. On-line Xpress is just a jazzy name for some optional software that Fidelity offers to help you manage your portfolio. Of course, you have to be a customer to use On-line Xpress. Not a customer? Well, you can become one through the Web page if you like what it offers. Putting an emphasis on Internet security, Fidelity requires you to use a browser that supports 128-bit encryption, which is to say, any recent version of Navigator or Explorer, American version. (Non-American versions don't support such strong encryption and don't work on Web Xpress.) Notwithstanding an emphasis on mutual funds, Fidelity customers can trade regular stocks on the ol' Xpressway (with or without On-line Xpress), as well as buy various insurance products and financial planning services. Fidelity differs from a standard, new-fangled online brokerage in that it provides a Web interface for services that have been established for years. The result is less flexible and more costly than you can find elsewhere, but Fidelity is a great company with which to shop for mutual funds.

J.B. Oxford & Company

www.jboxford.com

Relatively new online brokerage: Recently making its splash into the online trading pond, J. B. Oxford is staking its claim to fame on low commission rates (at this writing, $15 per trade, with unlimited shares, plus a fee if you want the actual stock certificates mailed to you) and a selection of services. You can buy mutual funds through the Web site in addition to regular stocks, and — more unusually — you can shop for and buy insurance products. Basic quotes and charts are provided. A remarkable aspect of the price schedule involves working with a live broker if that's your preference; the cost of trading goes up to only $20 per trade, which is very much on the inexpensive side. The Web page has some confusing points, but the mix of features is interesting.

Quick & Reilly

www.quick-reilly.com

Online brokerage struggling to compete: Quick & Reilly isn't easy for first-timers. For example, upon first visiting the site, you may reasonably decide to try the Visitor's Site link. Imagine how surprised you'll be when the site asks for your user name and password, as if you were already a member. Just hit the Cancel button, and a page appears with everything you need to register — but in my opinion, you should be able to demo the site without going through the tedious registration process. Then there's the question of commissions. Click the About Trading & Accounts link to find the commission schedule; then call me up and explain it to me. Be sure you have a calculator handy. To be fair, though, the site is fast and offers a good breadth of services. Best bet: Go to the Frequently Asked Questions page first.

Scottsdale Securities

www.discountbroker.com

Very low commissions and free research: All right, first things first: When you go to this site, check out the ultra-cool *Welcome to Scottsdale Securities Inc.* banner that develops along the bottom of your web browser (if you're using Navigator or Explorer). How can you not open a multi-thousand dollar account with a Web site that demonstrates such pizazz? Actually, a better reason may be the $9 commission on stock trades, which is as low as it goes. (You must have a minimum balance of $10,000 to enjoy that rate; otherwise, you pay $19 per trade.) Low prices make up for the lack of research tools, although the site does link to other service locations on the Web, where you can find newsletters and company reports. Bonds and options are available for trading. Scottsdale is a truly deep-discount broker with a reputation for good Web service without a lot of bells and whistles.

Waterhouse Securities, Inc.

www.waterhouse.com

Deep discounts and many extra services: If page attractiveness counts for anything on a financial service site, then Waterhouse Securities gets some points for nice design. A flat-rate commission of $12 for up to 5,000 shares is definitely worth investigating, and when you consider the many extra services offered, Waterhouse goes to the top of some discount brokerage lists. Tons of free publications; charts and quotes; IRAs without service charges; mutual funds; money transfers; and even a hearing-impaired telephone service set a high standard for extra services from a discount broker, especially one with such a drastically deep discount. Waterhouse points proudly to its number one ranking in a study of online brokers conducted by *Smart Money* magazine. The kudos are well earned.

Other Stuff to Check Out

www.abwatley.com
www.americanexpress.com/direct
www.ndb.com
www.optionslink.com
www.suretrade.com
www.wallstreete.com
www.wsaccess.com

Stock Quote and Portfolio Services

Some financial service sites concentrate on providing marketplace information in real time (or close to it) and help with portfolio management, but they stop short of the specialized field of brokering stock trades. Furnishing accurate and timely stock quotes is an Internet art in itself, and it's amazing how many different ways have been contrived to perform such a simple task. The wealth of services in this field gives online financiers tremendous choice in selecting where their information comes from, and in what format. The following sites are the current high points in a quickly evolving field.

Note: If you're just looking for financial news, check out the "Financial News" section in Part II. You'll find that many of those sites also enable you to search for specific stock prices.

Alphachart

www.alphachart.com

Stock-charting service: If you like your enlightenment tempered by a bit of

confusion, Alphachart is a destination that you should visit — but only with a Java-enabled browser (Navigator version 3.0 or later; Explorer version 3.0 or later) because Alphachart uses a Java applet to provide stock-charting services. It's pretty nice charting, too, although not the best on the Net — E-Trade customers get much clearer and more complete Java-based stock charting. However, it's free, which by itself is useful. The Java applet loads within a few seconds when using a 28.8 Kbps modem, and the charts can illustrate a variety of technical indicators — candlesticks, Bollinger Bands, and so on — on demand. Another nice feature is AlphaScan, which enables you to scan "the universe" for investment opportunities. Using AlphaScan, for example, you can ask for a printout of which NYSE, AMEX, or NASDAQ stocks finished the day 10 percent better than the day before. Unfortunately, the results aren't cross-referenced, and looking up the ticker indicators given can sometimes be mystifying. I was told something called GRN was up 10 percent, but Alphachart wouldn't tell me what GRN was. Still, if you're new to interactive charting or are just discovering technical indicators, Alphachart is a good place to get your feet wet.

ChicagoBoard Options Exchange

www.cboe.com

Online information site of the options exchange: If you're interested in options, and even if you have experience trading them, going directly to the source is the best way to get information. The ChicagoBoard Options Exchange is where most security options are traded, and the CBOE Web site is a treasure trove of facts about how options work. The site tells you which stocks comprise index options; how option prices reflect movement of underlying stocks; and, of course, the option prices themselves. You can order free printed publications from the CBOE by following the instructions on the Web site. Perhaps best of all, you can place yourself on the CBOE e-mail recipient list. Although I normally don't encourage opening your e-mail box to very many Web site updates, in this case, it's worth it. You can specify which alerts you receive, and I recommend at least getting the daily statistics of option trading. The CBOE is perhaps the best educational site about options available to the nonprofessional.

Cyberstocks.com

www.cyberstocks.com

Charts and quotes for technical stocks: For investors interested in technical stock issues such as Internet and computer companies, Cyberstocks.com is a good bookmark. A quick front-page summary tells you what the site is all about; click Cyberstocks Companies near the bottom to get to the meat, which is an alphabetical list that represents a virtual Who's Who of technology companies. The site also includes links to Hoover's Online, where you can dig up a wealth of information on individual companies or screen your stocks, snootily search for only the stocks of companies that meet your technical criteria in 20 categories, like a certain debt/equity ratio. The site also includes information about Initial Public Offerings, which are often in the technical market segment. Hoover's provides the quotes as well.

DailyStocks

www.dailystocks.com

Lots of stock information on demand: DailyStocks is the smorgasbord of quoting services. The links on the home page are profound enough, but when you type in a stock ticker, you get an impressive page bristling with links to quote sites that carry that stock, SEC online filings for the company, option information for the company, and news sources about the company. The Blitz version of the search does the same thing but without the tables, and uses subheadings links to help you get around faster. DailyStocks reverses the typical method of researching a company: Instead of going first to a quote site, then a headline site, and so on, you enter the company's ticker symbol in one location and are immediately linked to relevant quote and news sites. The idea is good, even if it's not executed as comprehensively as it could be.

DBC Online

www.dbc.com

Lots of quote and charting services: DBC (Data Broadcasting Corporation) Online is so bursting with information and services, there's no quick way to describe it. A glance at the home page tells you that you're in for some serious browsing, because each link spins off a whole different block of pages. DBC Online's main product is Signal, a software interface for real-time stock data. It's not free, and you can get information about it from the Software Downloads or Financial Store links. Returning to the front page, click any of the headline or charting links to get an idea of the depth with which DBC covers the financial scene. I can tell you from personal experience that the site's delayed quotes are the fastest and closest to real-time that I've encountered on the Internet, and the Personal Portfolio feature is excellent. DBC is a staple addition to your financial bookmark list, with good reason.

INVESTools

www.investools.com

High-quality research, some of it free:
Avowedly for "the independent investor,"
INVESTools provides stock charting from
Datek (see the previous section for a
review of this company). From the home
page, entering a company ticker symbol
delivers a stock quote plus links to
special reports from various financial
newsletters. However, this is where things
get pricey. Most of the reports cost
money to download; some as much as
$25. (And some as little as 25 cents.)
INVESTools has plenty of free stuff,
though, and it's definitely worth a visit.

Microsoft Investor

investor.msn.com/home.asp

★★ ★★

*Portfolio management and investment
research:* After seeing the Trading button
on the front page of Microsoft Investor,
you may think that Microsoft is in the
online brokerage business. In fact, the
Trading page just links to Ameritrade,
Schwab, Waterhouse, and other brokerages described in this section. The real
purpose and strength of Microsoft
Investor lies in research, magazine-style
articles, and portfolio-management tools.
The site is gathering a good reputation
for its design and high-quality services.
However, not everything is free, alas. A
subscription fee of $9.95 per month gets
you access to everything in the site,
which is part of The Microsoft Network
online service. (A free trial is available for
30 days, six months if you have Microsoft
Money 98 Financial Suite). Keep in mind,
though, that this rate structure may
change as Microsoft continues to redefine
and restructure its online network. In the
meantime, the excellent portfolio management page is open to anybody free of
charge (though you'll have to download
special software), and that feature alone
makes the site worth a visit.

NASDAQ

www.nasdaq.com

★★ ★★

Online site of the major stock exchange:
Your reaction upon first entering the
NASDAQ Web site may be the same as
mine: "Coool!" Colorful charts show you
how the NASDAQ Composite and Dow
Jones Industrial Average are performing
that day. One of the slickest quote
engines on the Net retrieves prices for up
to ten publicly traded companies,
whether they're on the NASDAQ board or
the New York or American exchanges, *and*
mutual funds. You can choose just basic
quote information (FlashQuote) or more
detailed information (InfoQuotes).
Relevant news stories are, of course,
linked to the reports; if CNBC/Dow Jones
video or audio reports are available on a
company, the NASDAQ site links to them
as well. Stock charting is accomplished
with intelligence and style. The portfolio
page is juiced with Java enhancements,
although NASDAQ asks you to fill out a
small survey before you get there. In a
word: Coool.

Quote.com

fast.quote.com/fq/quotecom/quote

Nothing but investment quotes: Quote.com
gets right down to business. You get a
ticker-symbol entry form, and that's *it.* No
links to news articles, no fancy graphics.
It's not by accident that Quote.com is one
of the most used services by *other* Web
sites that provide stock information — it
does a terrific job of delivering stock

quotes and charts. Right on the front page, as you type in your ticker symbol, you can also specify whether you want a simple quote or a particular price chart (minute, daily, weekly, or monthly). The simple quote isn't that simple, either; it provides high and low prices, direction of change, volume, earnings per share, price/earnings ratio, and more data tidbits. The Chart page brings up the price information in graphical form. Clicking the News link enables you to bring up recent relevant headlines, but to read full stories, you need a Quote.com subscription. Oh — there's also a rudimentary portfolio page, but you probably want to get portfolio services elsewhere. Go to Quote.com for what it's good for: quotes.

StockMaster

www.stockmaster.com

★ ★
★ ★   🗒

Excellent quoting service: StockMaster's front page used to display a tag line that was music to most Net surfers' ears: "All of our services are free to individual investors." Not everything is free anymore (the company's Baseline Reports provide in-depth info on more than 7,000 companies, but access costs you $5 per month), but the rest of the site is, in a word: excellent. StockMaster has one of the clearest presentations of price information around. Using larger typefaces for more important data categories makes a huge difference in readability, and even the spacious layout is soothing. The individual stock pages come with a volume and price chart for the previous 12 months. Furthermore, you can vote on a stock's future, according to your bullish or bearish sentiments, and then compare your prognosis with that of other visitors. StockMaster doesn't offer a broad range of data services, but what it does, it does very well.

Stockpoint

www.stockpoint.com

Market information, quotes, and charts: Stockpoint (formerly Investors Edge) is distinguished by an unusual and distinctly useful brand of information. The front page provides a list of the most active gainers and losers for the day; clicking the Most Actives link above them displays the biggest gainers and losers on each of the major stock exchanges, which is crucial information for momentum traders and option traders. The stock quote section enables you to search for a company or fund or enter the symbol directly, and then delivers clear price information with buttons for calling up a Java chart with various technical indicators traced on it. The integration of quoting and charting is impressive, even if the Java applet isn't as flexible as some others. (For example, you can't resize the Java window.) The portfolio page is for registered site members only, but registration is free. You also can sign up for a free e-mail newsletter to keep you abreast of the midday or end-of-day market news.

StockTools

www.stocktools.com

★ ★
★ ★

Unique research features for free: Previously a mediocre stock quote page, StockTools has come a long way — a very long way. The Database Query feature is one of the more sophisticated stock search engines, enabling users to retrieve information about companies that match characteristics they specify, such as stock price, degree of increase or decrease, and volume. Prefer a graphical representation? The Graph Wizard enables you to chart not only the price (in the color of your choice) but also the volume and other statistics. You also can include the industry's performance *and* up to four other individual stocks. The site has a beautiful design and innovative features.

Other Stuff to Check Out

www.bigcharts.com
www.dailystocks.com
www.isld.com
www.pcquote.com

Shelter is one of the basic human needs — along with Internet access, of course. Anyway, Web marketers are keen to servicing those basic needs, so you'll find lots of housing resources on the Web. Here are a few good sites, and if you'd like more, check out *Buying Online For Dummies,* by Joseph Lowery (IDG Books Worldwide, Inc.).

Homebuyer's Fair

www.homefair.com

★ ★
★ ★

More than just links: The Homebuyer's Fair site has an animated Ferris wheel on it's home page, which is appropriate: Ferris wheels make me dizzy, and Homebuyer's Fair has enough site links to do the same. If you want to buy a new house or find an apartment or simply find a moving van, Homebuyer's Fair can provide some direction. But more than just a links directory, Homebuyer's Fair

also has some truly unique programs that make a visit worthwhile. The Lifestyle Optimizer, for example, helps match you to a community by asking your opinions on things like town size, crime rate, and so on, comparing those answers to town demographics, and then producing a list of "ideal" communities for you to consider. The Salary Calculator compares the cost of living in over 800 U.S. cities and 200 international ones. Yes, this information is available on other Web sites, but Homebuyer's Fair pulls it all together in one convenient, unique package.

HomeScout

homescout.com

★ ★
★ ★

Lets the Web do your searching: HomeScout is one of those perfectly descriptive business names, because that's exactly what this site does for you — scouts out homes in the United States and Canada. The name sort of brings up images of an old American western film with a rider out ahead of the cavalry perching on the side of a hill, looking through binoculars for "For Sale" signs in a town up ahead. Anyway, you enter the city that you want to focus the search on, click Search, and HomeScout puts its electronic search engine to work. No fuss, no muss. The site claims to have a database of over 800,000 listings, and you can refine your search to existing homes, new homes, townhomes, condominiums, and so on. HomeScout also enables you to search for a good deal on mortgages and then apply online, and it has a few features that help you determine how much house you can afford, among other things.

International Real Estate Digest

www.ired.com

Properties for sale around the globe: An excellent first stop when looking to buy property outside the United States, International Real Estate Digest (or IRED.com) lists properties in 110 countries around the globe. Actually, it doesn't do the listing — instead, IRED.com links to the Web sites of real estate professionals and developers in the region that you're interested in. Judging from some of the letters to IRED.com, the quality of those linked sites ranges from good to needs improvement ("Your rating system leaves much to be desired," one letter began). Yes, *caveat emptor* — buyer beware. Still, for selection and breadth of coverage, International Real Estate Digest is hard to beat. And the site offers translation services into a number of languages, making it a must for the international home buyer.

Owners.com

www.owners.com

Homes for sale by owner: Some Americans think that they can sell their homes without a real estate agent. Must these independents put up their own Web pages to get their homes online? Hardly. Owners.com is one of a handful of Web sites that specialize in listing for-sale-by-

owner homes. Browsing the listings is as simple as entering the state you're interested in on the front-page search box, clicking Go, and then adding a few more details. Owners.com has a standard information form, and how much the owner wants to disclose online is indicated on the search results page via a diamond system (three diamonds, you can see it in your dreams; one diamond, you can drive right by it and not have the faintest clue). Some listings also have photographs and maps. Just to fill out the offerings, Owners.com adds things like mortgage links and basic buying information. You can also advertise your own home, at one of three levels. The most expensive listing costs $115, includes multiple photographs, and is put at top priority for search requests, but you can get a bare-bones listing for free.

REALTOR.COM

www.realtor.com

Professional agents' organization: One of the simplest ways to buy a home is to get a realtor and tell him or her what you want, and then wait for him or her to search for homes that match your wish list. Guess what? This site, from the National Association of Realtors, does the very same thing. But you knew that. You simply click Find a Home and click the maps to identify where you want to search, and then narrow your search by giving additional information. Ah, but you figured that out too, didn't you? Well, I bet you didn't know that the site has more than 1 million listings. Or that the search criteria page has a goofy required question at the top, before you even tell

REALTOR.COM how many bedrooms you're interested in. (During my visit, the site wanted to know if I owned a pager. Why? Can't the realtor just call my office?) One other warning: I found the mortgage rate section to be something of a black hole. I could get in, but I couldn't back out normally. It sort of left me reliving my childhood, when the parents moved without leaving a forwarding address.

Other Stuff to Check Out

www.fsbo.com
www.realtylocator.com
www.rentnet.com

Shopping

Polls indicate that many people still feel unsafe about shopping on the Internet. Granted, there are risks. Using a credit card in any medium carries risks, and until the Internet geniuses develop a more secure payment device (electronic cash, perhaps, or smart cards), each individual must tread through the rocky shoals of contemporary digital life as he or she sees fit. I routinely buy certain things — especially services — over the Web and feel comfortable with the security while enjoying the convenience. Obviously, nobody should do anything that makes them nervous, but at the same time, why buy blindly into Internet alarmism? One thing is for sure: Internet commerce is a fast-growing phenomenon.

Online retail outlets try to make you feel at home — relaxed enough to buy stuff, in other words — by providing a *shopping cart* that keeps track of your selections. When viewing a product, you can see a button that invites you to add the merchandise to your cart without actually buying it. Then, when you're ready to fork over the cash, you can weed items from your cart as you discover the horrendous bill that would ensue if you bought them all. Of course, you don't use actual cash. For the time being, credit cards are the prominent form of currency online. Shopping sites ask you for credit card information and your address, and some of them store that information so that you don't have to retype it every time you shop.

Clothes

Clothes shopping on the Web is a slower-growing phenomenon than buying books, music, and gifts, but I expect it to grow over the next year or two. The following sites are worth keeping an eye on.

Apparel.net

www.apparel.net

Link to online clothing stores: Perhaps the best first stop when clothes shopping on the Internet, Apparel.net is a directory of online shops specializing in wearables and accessories. Not every site linked from Apparel.net is a virtual store — some are clothing-related sites that don't sell anything. Nevertheless, this site is a great spot to find, say, a long list of online necktie stores. Clothing-oriented malls and catalogs are represented. Each link to an outside site is helpfully accompanied by a short description of the store that you're about to visit. The site also offers a nice directory of fashion sites.

Fashionmall.com

www.fashionmall.com

Collection of online clothing stores: With a beautifully designed site that can only be described as fashionable, Fashionmall.com makes for a stylish bookmark. A menu stretches down the left-hand frame of the home page, inviting you to choose categories like Women, Men, Kids, Shoes, and Jewelry. Each category leads to a page with links for selecting virtual stores. Linking to a store keeps you within the Fashionmall.com frames, and when you select an item for purchase, you're using a common shopping basket provided by Fashionmall.com. This shopping basket encourages spending, for better or worse, by making it easy to accumulate choices from many stores. The problem is, some stores don't offer online shopping at all! Only the ones with the faint *shop* indicator offer purchases online, but at least you can find contact information about the other designers represented in Fashionmall.com.

The Gap

www.gap.com

Mix and match clothes: The Gap — purveyor of hip casual khaki, cloth, and denim clothes that imply a relaxed but neat lifestyle, up to and including dress shirts and neckties for men and summer dresses and casual suits for women, not to mention a full line of kids' products, and don't forget the accessories — has opened shop on the World Wide Web. The site is so interactively cool that you can't pass it up. Several Virtual Style pages enable you to try various combinations of clothes using a drag-and-drop interface through the Shockwave plug-in. Pull a top onto a torso, add pants, change the

colors around, and get information about any garment that strikes your fancy. Ordering the darn thing is the next logical step, and The Gap has finally taken that step. If you're uneasy about ordering over the Internet, don't worry — like many retail Web sites, the Gap also has a store locator.

jcrew.com

www.jcrew.com

Order casual clothes from Web pages of the catalog: The J. Crew catalog has become almost a bible for the casual beachcombing set. The casual shorts, sport shirts, and easygoing footwear are *de rigueur* for trips to Nantucket and Cape Cod. Primarily a mail-order business, J. Crew has set up virtual shop on the Web. The site takes orders directly for merchandise illustrated on its pages; just click the picture of what you want, and J. Crew walks you through the rest. The online offerings are pretty extensive — perhaps not as deep as the printed catalog, but certainly deep enough to warrant a browse. And the moving page titles are a nice attempt to liven up the catalog. Visiting the site is a good way to familiarize yourself with the J. Crew "look" if you live inland.

L.L. Bean

www.llbean.com

Outdoor merchandise catalog: The most famous outfitter for outdoor hobbyists, L.L. Bean has been known for many years as a mail-order operation. The L.L. Bean catalogs are famous for providing high-quality boots, rugged shirts, jackets with seemingly hundreds of pockets, camping equipment, and all sorts of other indestructible plaid garments. L.L. Bean spreads out on the Internet with a site that enables you to order online from an online store or the printed catalog. Most intriguing is the search engine, which points you not only to products that are available at the site but also to helpful little articles about selecting the right merchandise for your needs. Enter **boots** in the search form, for example, and in addition to links for Rugged Walkers and Puddle Stompers, you'll find a piece called "How to Choose Great Hiking Boots" and a "Guide to Bean Boots." You can browse the site's offerings without using the search engine, but it may be the best way to maximize your experience.

Other Stuff to Check Out

www.eddiebauer.com/eb
www.grandstyle.com
www.islander-direct.com
www.mtco.com/~headwe/design/
   design.html
www.shopinvogue.com
www.yes.net/Marieka

Department Stores

Many department stores have online outlets. In most cases, they sell only a fraction of their inventory over personal computers — not because people are afraid of shopping that way, but because the department stores haven't geared up their sites to cover everything in their stores. The department store sites are partly promotions, and partly retail opportunities. Some of them enable you to make catalog purchases, but this feature is hardly more convenient than calling a toll-free number.

Bloomingdale's

www.bloomingdales.com

Stylish online shopping: The World Wide Web isn't very old, so pardon me while I pine for the "good ol' days" and

Bloomingdale's old Web site, which used to have a top row of blinking navigation buttons resembling the floor indicator lights of an elevator. First floor, menswear; second floor, home accessories; and so on. Sigh. Nowadays, Bloomingdale's online presence is a little less sentimental, though more functional. The Shopping page is the one area you'll want to enter, offering a number of traditional categories — areas for him, her, and it (the house), among others. Not to mention a fragrance shop. (Good luck smelling the perfect scent over the Net — they haven't invented a plug-in for *that* yet.) If you're the type who can't figure out what color shirt to wear with khaki pants, try the site's personal section, where you can communicate with actual Bloomingdale's employees who can assist you. You can also get news about store locations, openings, and sales.

CyberShop

cybershop.com

Upscale merchandise: A huge selection of upscale products and free shipping are the claims to fame for the CyberShop online department store. Don't look for bargains here. But if you're in the market for a $500 treadmill, modernistic and pricey Bose audio speakers, or some Waterford Crystal, CyberShop is the virtual spot for you. I strongly recommend the Gourmet Food department. Food-stuffed gift baskets are perfect gifts for computer book authors.

JCPenney

www.jcpenney.com

Online shopping, complete with music: What's shopping without the soothing tones of canned music drifting through the virtual aisles? That's just what the JCPenney site delivers. Ahhh, how soothing. Fortunately, the musical serenade is brief. Quasi-musical interludes notwithstanding, JCPenney does a good job of integrating its online and offline services. For example, if you have a printed catalog of JCPenney merchandise, you can use a special online form at the Web site to place a catalog order. Or you can browse from scratch. The home page delivers almost too much information — it's like an electronic magazine stuffed with articles and features. Of course, all the information relates to how great JCPenney is and what great brands you can find there. The none-too-subtle right-edge graphic, with "JCPenney, I Love Your Style" repeated over and over, sets the tone. Nevertheless, JCPenney is an expertly created shopping site.

Macy's

www.macys.com

Small collection of Macy's merchandise: In sharp contrast to the crowds sometimes found in big department stores (especially around an important shopping season, like National Author Day), the Macy's online site has one of the most spacious, uncluttered, relaxed page designs around. Part of the reason is that the company doesn't offer much merchandise online, compared to what you find in the offline store. The merchandise is divided up into two main categories: shop e-ssentials ("life's little necessities," like underwear, hosiery, men's dress shirts, socks, underwear, cosmetics, and gift certificates — gift certificates?) and gift e-ssentials (general things you'd buy for other people, which pretty much rules out the underwear). Another area is something called Personal Shopping, which enlists the help of a Macy's employee to track down what you want, and this service is also available via phone or e-mail.

Wal-Mart Online

www.wal-mart.com

Well-organized Web shopping: Extraordinary organization distinguishes Wal-Mart's Web store. Good thing, too, because when you have as many varied products as Wal-Mart does, you better present them coherently. The galaxy of merchandise offered through this site is organized in a style reminiscent of World Wide Web directories, with a top level of broad categories linking to a secondary level of more specific categories. In this system, you can start with Lawn Care & Pets, for example, and then click Pest Deterrents, and then on to the Ultimate Flea Trap. Products are pictured, though not always in their entirety. As an alternative to the directory browsing, Wal-Mart provides a keyword search engine.

Other Stuff to Check Out

www.fayettevillenc.com/belk

Flowers and Gifts

Gift shopping was the original Internet commercial application, and it's still going strong. Flowers and gifts seem inextricably intertwined — flower shops have gifts, and gift shops have flowers. Both types of virtual stores often carry gourmet food baskets.

American Greetings

www.americangreetings.com

Personalized greeting cards, both printed and electronic: A wonderful site with intelligently helpful features, American Greetings is an alternative to browsing forever through racks of greeting cards, only to finally select something that is never quite as personal as you'd like. Instead, try the Custom Greeting Cards section of this site, which enables you to personalize the front and the message of a card, which is then specially printed and sent to you. (The personalized cards cost up to $4.) The American Greetings site offers far more categories of greeting cards than you'll ever find in a store, so you're more likely to find something appropriate. If you're sending a card to someone who has an Internet e-mail account, you may consider an animated, electronic greeting or an e-mail postcard. The bad news: You can't send a single postcard; you have to buy them in groups of five ($5.95) or ten ($9.95). In addition to an innovative range of greeting cards, American Greetings offers gift baskets and Gorant Chocolates. (The latter is especially appropriate for sending to authors.) The free registration entitles you to create an address book of recipients — nice feature.

Flowernet

www.flowernet.com

Buy flowers directly from the growers: Flowernet provides an intermediary service between growers and end customers. The site takes your order, and your flowers come directly from the company that grew them. This setup affects the price quite nicely because a couple of distribution links are cut out of the middle, and also, presumably, results in fresher flowers reaching your

destination. Recently, a dozen long-stemmed roses cost only $39.95, which as any good wife, husband, daughter, or son knows, is a bargain price.

FTD

www.ftd.com

Online network of florists: The largest delivery system for flowers, FTD presents a Web site that makes your choices clear and coherent. FTD is more than just an agent for flowers — it's a network of florists. As such, it offers you two choices: shopping from the FTD catalog or shopping from an FTD florist's store selection. The Web site offers both alternatives. An easy-to-use search engine assists you in finding a local florist, using drop-down menus and keywords. The resulting list links you to Web sites where they exist, or otherwise provides the address. When you're ready to shop online, you're linked to the FTD catalog, where you can select types of flowers or browse by gift occasion. Some gourmet gifts also are offered.

Gifts on the Web

www.giftsontheweb.com

Well-illustrated gift selections: This extremely attractive gift site features a wide range of gifts, including chocolate, fragrances, books, jewelry, executive gifts, children's gifts, scarves and wraps, and gift certificates. The product descriptions are adequate, and the photographic illustrations are excellent. Each category offers about a dozen selections, accompanied by small, almost-unviewable photos. But not to worry — click any one to see a large photo and description. The home page is helpful, spinning you off into sections that enable you to choose a gift by category, price, or occasion. Here's a good feature: Reminder Service, which takes your gift dates and then sends you an e-mail poke in the ribs when it's time to send flowers.

Hallmark

www.hallmark.com

Electronic greetings for e-mail friends: Hallmark, the greeting card and small-gift chain that has reinvented itself at least once in past years, stretches into the Internet age with a pretty site that contains surprisingly hip features. Hallmark provides electronic greeting services for the thoughtful netizen. In a more traditional vein, you may expect the same wide selection of card types that you see in a Hallmark store, and you get it here. The Shoebox series and other Hallmark staples are well represented, and upcoming greeting card concepts are previewed. The e-mail reminder service is a helpful feature, and a community atmosphere is attempted — unusual in an online gift store — with a storytelling bulletin board.

Harry and David

www.harryanddavid.com

Gourmet delicacies: Stumped about what to get for Computer Book Author Day? I've heard that chocolate-covered pears are the perfect gift, especially for Internet

specialists. That's exactly the sort of delectable delicacy you find at the online gourmet food and gift purveyor, Harry and David. Specialty gifts aside, Harry and David offers an astonishing assortment of fruit packages to U.S. and Canadian residents, including a Fruit-of-the-Month subscription for 3, 5, 8, or 12 months. Other gourmet foods include bakery items, truffles, smoked salmon, ethnic specialties, and much more. The site index gives you some idea of the fantastic, mouth-watering range of goodies here, but you need to explore each section (always keeping Computer Book Author Day in mind, not to mention National Internet Directory Author Week, which I believe falls in this very week) to see the incredible number of products. And flowering plants. And gift certificates. Authors love those, too.

1-800-FLOWERS

www.800flowers.com

Fast, efficient gift shopping: From a simple bouquet to the Birthday Flower Cake (bleah), 1-800-FLOWERS offers more than 200 gift items at any given time through its Web site. If you're in a hurry, the Quick Shop page enables you to pick something nice, order it, and get out with a minimum of browsing around. But if you're in the mood to smell the cyber-roses, click through the entire selection, which varies somewhat depending on whether you're shipping within the United States or abroad. Flowers, of course, are the centerpiece offerings, but you also can find plants, balloons, gift baskets, and some gourmet food items. A very helpful selection page displays three drop-down menus for narrowing down your search by type of gift, celebratory occasion, and price. The drop-down menus stay with you as you browse, saving you the hassle of having to back your way out.

1-800-USA-4-FLOWERS

usa4flowers.com

Great U.S. flower delivery service: This site has a patriotic fervor that may please U.S. citizens but probably annoy everyone else. Hardly anyone can be immune to the annoyance of hearing a cheesy rendition of *America the Beautiful* that plays relentlessly on every page. (The solution is to scroll down to the page bottom and hit the Stop button. Whew.) 1-800-USA-4-FLOWERS offers same-day delivery within the continental United States for orders placed by 2 p.m. (recipient's local time). One interesting feature is the Celebrity List, which assists you in sending flowers to any one of a short list of actors and athletes. If you can stand the awful music, this site is a good place to send flowers and gourmet food gifts within the United States. The site provides links to international affiliates.

PC Flowers & Gifts

www.pcflowers.com

Pioneer virtual gift shop is still one of the best: A true pioneer, one of the first World Wide Web businesses, a landmark in the transformation of the Internet into a commercial domain, PC Flowers & Gifts continues its tradition of delivering roses, flower baskets, gourmet treats, and other gifty items to the friends and relatives of

netizens everywhere. From the home page, you can begin shopping by occasion, gift category, price range, and U.S. or international delivery; alternatively, you can zoom directly to special items on sale. The selection is fine, prices are good, overnight delivery is available, and the company has more experience satisfying Internet customers than just about anyone else in cyberspace.

Peet's Coffee and Tea

www.peets.com

Buy coffee and tea online: A diamond in the rough, the Peet's site is perhaps the least well-known of all the shopping sites in this section, but its beautiful design, warm attitude, and great selection definitely make the grade. The brown icons and the picture of the owners sampling the offerings make you want to head for the grinder right away, and the site offers a lucid education in types of beans, geographical characteristics, and shades of roast. Dozens of varieties are offered, each available in one of several grinds. The site also offers "Peet's Journals" — tales from experts in the field that offer insights into international coffee and tea culture. Next-day service is available if you're in a hurry.

Perfect Present Picker

presentpicker.com

Find an offline gift store: Perfect Present Picker is a fun and potentially useful site. It isn't a store — you can't actually buy anything here. Instead, it guides you toward merchants (mostly offline, but also a few Web-based stores) that carry the perfect gift for someone you have trouble shopping for. On the home page, you use a series of selectable scrolling menus to define who the recipient is.

Choose the recipient's interest, the gift occasion, and the recipient's personality (from organized to outgoing, from loner to lazy). You can select more than one choice in each category. Your quest then goes to another search page, where you can indicate the sex/age, occupation, and lifestyle of the recipient. Using this information, the site returns a list of possible gifts, along with store names and contact information. If this process sounds too confusing, click step wizard on the home page and let Perfect Present Picker lead you by the hand through the process. The site provides the perfect solution for the nostalgic and pensive history-buff lawyer who lives a workaholic life in a small town and is about to turn 45 — or anyone else on your hard-to-shop-for list.

Other Stuff to Check Out

flowers.xg.com
www.chilin.com/index.html
www.flowersworldwide.com

Miscellaneous Internet Shopping

The following are worthy shopping sites that don't fall into any other categories. They represent a few types of virtual buying that may increase in the near future: groceries, auctions, and event tickets.

First Auction

www.firstauction.com

Bid on discount merchandise: As Internet commerce continues to evolve with new, innovative ways to part you from your money, First Auction has come up with a humdinger. (*Humdinger* is a technical term much too complicated to explain here.) After joining through a registration process that includes entering credit card billing information, you can bid on merchandise placed on the block day and night. You can view ongoing auctions without joining, but you'll need to join to participate. First Auction is a subsidiary of the Internet Shopping Network, which, in turn, is owned by the Home Shopping Network. Therefore, it leverages the buying power of its parent companies to scare up good — sometimes great — deals on computer equipment, consumer electronics, and general items. Each item has a bidding deadline and an incremental minimum for bids (usually $10 or $20). You can review all the bids and then enter your offer on the Bid Page, and it's a good idea to sign up for the e-mail bulletins that alert you when your bid is no longer the highest. Remember to read all the fine print in the Help portion of the site before joining.

NetGrocer

www.netgrocer.com

Packaged groceries delivered to your door: Online grocery shopping has been tried with some success on local levels, but NetGrocer is the first attempt to provide Web-based grocery ordering and delivery on a nationwide (the U.S., that is) scale. By using FedEx for next-day delivery, it's a feasible idea. As you may expect, only packaged goods are available — no produce, refrigerated food, frozen food, fresh deli items, or fresh meat products. But for shelf staples like bottled drinks, condiments, pasta and dried grains, pet supplies, boxes of snacks, beauty and health products, and household items, NetGrocer is a good alternative, especially during crummy weather seasons. Admittedly, the selection is not nearly as extensive as in a major supermarket, but the selection keeps growing. One nifty feature: A tally of your shopping cart choices is displayed at all times in your browser.

Ticketmaster Online

www.ticketmaster.com

Buy tickets to events: It's a good match, and an obvious one: concert and event tickets over the Internet. Merge a big ticket database with the computer's ability to search by keyword, and happy concertgoers should be the result. You can angle into the database in a few different ways — by events (the most popular, or by state), categories (art, sports, music, and so on), theater (why this is a separate category is beyond me), or by linking to Ticketmaster affiliates in Canada, Mexico, Australia, and Great Britain. You also can search alphabetically or type in a keyword. Many of the listings include directions to the venue, an always-helpful feature.

Other Stuff to Check Out

www.avon.com
www.clinique.com/main.html
www.eddiebauer.com

Music and Books

I group book shopping and music shopping together, because books and music tend to be sold together in large offline stores like Barnes & Noble. Book and music shopping on the Internet get a lot of publicity, mostly surrounding just a few huge retailers that have set up shop on the Web. The beauty of buying books and compact discs over the Web is that you get substantial price discounts (partly made up by shipping costs, unfortunately), and in the case of music, you can sometimes listen to a selection before buying it. ***Remember:*** Be sure to get the RealAudio plug-in before shopping for music.

Amazon.com

www.amazon.com

Vast online bookstore with new music section: Don't ask me why it's called Amazon. Okay, you can ask, but I don't know the answer. Maybe because the online bookstore is a jungle of books? I doubt it. Anyway, Amazon.com is a legendary Web shopping location, having caught the Internet wave early and creating one of the very few successful virtual retail businesses. Arguably the world's largest bookstore with millions of titles available and with a new music store online, Amazon.com makes it easy to track down just about any book or CD you can think of, order it with a credit card, and receive it within days. Substantial price discounts are applied to every title, and the magazine-style interface is a pleasure to browse. Even if you don't have a book or CD in mind, you're likely to be tempted by a new release or a highlighted series of titles. Amazon.com is a wonderful place to browse for gift ideas — assuming, of course, the recipient likes to read or listen to music. You'd expect to find a topic directory and a search engine, and indeed you do, plus author information, occasional interviews (go ahead and look me up — I bare all kinds of secrets), photos of book jackets, and short descriptions of selected titles. Prices are good, delivery is quick, and there's just nothing bad to say about this incredible site.

BarnesandNoble.com

www.barnesandnoble.com

Online store of the giant book retailer: While Amazon.com (reviewed just before this site) may be the largest bookstore on the World Wide Web, Barnes & Noble is the largest offline, physical bookstore. Perhaps in raging envy over Amazon's cyberspace claim, Barnes & Noble squished its name together and set up virtual shop on the Net, setting up a price war that benefits all netizens. The Barnes & Noble site looks like an online magazine, with a few featured items on the front page and some category links on the left. Just click All Subjects to see the full list of book categories. Each subject area is another magazinelike affair, with an attached search engine and several highlighted titles with descriptions. The layout of this site is truly beautiful. BarnesandNoble.com (how ridiculous is that mashed name?) emulates its offline stores in the live events department by presenting author appearances in a chatting format, and encourages a community feeling by supplying bulletin boards, which nobody seems very interested in. And although Barnes — and — Noble (whew, that's better) doesn't have music, like Amazon, it does offer magazines and software.

Blockbuster Online

www.blockbuster.com

Atmospheric music and video shopping: Blockbuster, known primarily for its video rental stores, dabbles in online retailing with a darkly designed, multimedia-challenged Web site. It's a cool-looking place, though a bit hard to read at times. The album preview areas are sadly lacking in RealAudio capability, which has become the standard for online music stores. Instead, Blockbuster uses the AU format of music files, which can be played by version 3.0 or later of both Navigator and Explorer, but the wait time is much longer. Typically, you can either browse by musical genre or search with separate search engines for general or classical music. As for the online video store (which includes video games), well, it seems more like an online promotion to get you in the mood to rent a movie, rather than a place to actually rent the movie. The video games area provides general reviews, and the video area — although it does offer a few actual movies for sale and some QuickTime clips — works better as a filmography.

Borders.com

www.borders.com

New heavyweight in the book/music/video field: Just about any city in America that has a Barnes & Noble bookstore also has a Borders, so when Barnes & Noble went online, it was only a matter of time before Borders emerged with a cybershop. And while Borders folks weren't the first kids on the cyberblock, they obviously worked hard to produce a quality site. The magazine-style front page includes links and features that invite you to sit down and browse a while. The site's six main sections are Music, Books, Netcafe (for chat rooms and such), Children's, Video, and Computer Books — obviously the section for buyers with impeccable taste. The Music section includes RealAudio samples (yo, Blockbuster, are you listening?), and while the video store is lacking in clips, unlike Blockbuster, all the videos are actually for sale.

CDnow

www.cdnow.com

Popular online music CD store: One of the most popular shopping sites on the Web, CDnow has separated countless dollars from its Net-surfing owners during its tenure on the Web, justifying, in the process, the notion of buying music over the Internet. RealAudio has locked the value into this concept, and CDnow makes the most of audio streaming by enabling you to listen to selected excerpts of many albums before buying them. One of the beauties of this site is the terrific searching service that you can use to track down a recording by song title, artist, album name, record label, or soundtrack. Like Blockbuster, an entirely separate search engine is dedicated to classical music and the special complexities that go with that genre. CDnow has good prices and ships quickly.

Music Previews Network

www.mpmusic.com

  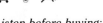

Listen before buying: The Music Previews Network sorts through the tangled jungle of music albums and product divisions by

emphasizing the customer's desire to hear before buying. Using RealAudio, the site selects a few albums in each of several genres and then presents three-minute audio previews of the CDs. The trade-off is comprehensiveness for a good, long listen. In three minutes, you can usually get the gist of an album's "sound," though it's not as luxurious as the listening stations in actual CD stores. The site uses a variety of audio formats — RealAudio, WAV, and MPEG, so most everybody should be able to hear the previews one way or another. RealAudio, of course, is the fastest and easiest.

Other Stuff to Check Out

www.englishbooks.com
www.internationalcd.com
www.leck.com

Online Malls

Online malls act like agents, gathering together various virtual merchants into one cyberspace and providing a common interface for browsing a wide range of products. The best malls enable you to shop among various stores with a single purchasing interface, commonly known as a *shopping cart.* This way, you can drift from store to store, dropping things in your shopping cart, and then pay for the whole mess with one credit card transaction billed to the mall. Other malls, not as efficient, provide the browsing interface but force you to buy separately from each store — just like a neighborhood mall.

220 Shopping

Cybertown Shopping Mall

www.cybertown.com/shopping.html

Neon stylings and unusual shopping choices: This site's home page, picturing android-like humans wandering through a futuristic mall, is science fiction. The stark neon design is maintained through-out the site's pages. Cybertown offers an eclectic range of products. A complicated "ATM" system is in place whereby you can collect points that you can later use to get discounts, but not more than once from the same merchant on the same day, except for Australian aboriginal holi-days — or something like that. It seems to be a registration lure, but why not? Go for all the savings that you can get while browsing an unusual and intriguing virtual mall.

Internet Mall

www.shopnow.com

One of the original online malls: The Internet Mall has been around cyberspace longer than most such sites, and it has figured out how to do this shopping thing *right.* The excellent ShopNow home page forgoes glitz in favor of clarity — good choice. You immediately feel that this is a site you can cope with. The site is nicely divided up into categories and subcate-gories, so, for example, you can browse Menswear under the Clothing & Accesso-ries department. Internet Mall functions

just like a regular mall in that each store has its own systems and accounting. When you click a link in a department, your browser goes to the merchant's site, with a link back to the mall remaining at the bottom of the page. You purchase items from the merchant's site and then link back to the mall and start over with another shop. This fragmented system, modeled as it is on the physical mall, seems less convenient in cyberspace.

Worldshop

www.worldshop.com

International shopping from your desktop: Worldshop is a cooperative online shopping mall with an international flair. Right up front, the site asks you to register — it's not necessary to browse, but a sign-up entitles you to receive e-mail circulars and a couple of other perks. When it comes down to buying, of course, you must be registered with credit card information — you can assign a PIN number to your account for added account security. Worldshop lists 24 categories of products — clothing, electronics, books, home office supplies, jewelry, toys, you name it. In each category, several participating inter-national merchants are linked. In the Music category, African goat skin drums compete for your attention with Swiss music boxes and Compact Disc Express. In the Food & Wine area, you can choose delicacies ranging from New York cheese-cake to imported caviar. A common Worldshop shopping system links all the merchants together.

Other Stuff to Check Out

www.cyquest.com
www.indiashop.com
www.rls.net/mall
www.window-shopping.com

Travel Services

A revolution of sorts is happening in the travel industry. In the past, if you wanted to buy airline tickets, you had to contact either an airline or a travel agent. Now you can check schedules, look up fares, and buy tickets online. This may not be an advantage for everyone; many people understandably prefer to leave itinerary planning to experts. But for those who like the idea of doing their own booking from a personal computer, the best online travel agents provide a great service.

In addition to virtual travel agents, other travel services are offered through the Web, from currency calculators to mapping services, rail travel packaging to foreign language assistance.

Miscellaneous Travel Services

This section is a miscellany of travel services besides booking air travel. Some of these sites are unexpectedly fun to use even if you're not planning a trip. In the following sites, you can schedule and book rail travel, find a bed-and-breakfast, get directions for a car trip, pick up foreign-language phrases, and calculate currencies.

Air Traveler's Handbook

www.cs.cmu.edu/afs/cs/user/mkant/ Public/Travel/airfare.html

Broad range of travel information: Because Air Traveler's Handbook isn't publicized on other Web sites and the text-based interface is unassuming and modest, you may easily overlook it, despite its mammoth address. However, the scope of information that it delivers is far from humble, and the site deserves a bookmark spot as a directory for just about any kind of travel information that you may need. Whether you're looking for an airline, a frequent flyer program, a travel agent, cruise information, a bed-and-breakfast, money and currency exchange data, a weather forecast, language sites, travel software, rail and bus information, or any of dozens of categories, this directory is bound to turn up something useful. The utter lack of graphics makes the site as swift as quicksilver. Air Traveler's Handbook is a no-nonsense, seemingly bottomless well of informative links.

American Bed & Breakfast Association

www.abba.com

Regional directory of bed-and-breakfasts: The rustic, informal quality of a bed-and-breakfast doesn't make you think of high-tech or computer databases. That may explain the relative lack of good B&B Web directories compared to other types of lodging and travel. The American Bed & Breakfast Association marshals its resources in providing an adequate repository of information about inns around the United States. Start by clicking a state in a U.S. map (which you can access via the Find a B&B page). The resulting page displays a list of member inns, alphabetized by city. Some of the listings contain a link for further information and a photo. More pictures would be welcome, because the visual atmosphere of an inn plays a big part in its charm. Contact information is, of course, provided (most B&Bs don't have Web sites of their own).

Amtrak

www.amtrak.com

Train schedules and reservations: The official Amtrak site is both promotional and useful, providing not only schedules and vacation packages but also an online reservation and booking system for buying train tickets. Modeled after Web-based airline reservation systems, Amtrak's Schedules page has one important difference: Rather than let you enter where you're departing from and where you're headed to, the site instead wants to know where you're departing from and how many connections you're willing to put up with. Not the way that I would have done it, but it's Amtrak's site. Anyway, Amtrak then spits out a list of destinations that you can reach in the given number of connections; you pick the one that you want from that list, and then train options appear. If you're traveling during the night, one great advantage of going by train is the possibility of sleeping accommodations. The site includes pictures and descriptions of the sleeping alternatives (you also can just buy a coach seat and doze as best you can). Coach seats tend to be less expensive than airfares to the same destination, and sleeping compartments are usually cheaper than first-class plane seats. The Amtrak site automatically searches for the lowest available fare.

AutoPilot

www.freetrip.com

Maps and driving directions: AutoPilot is a trip-routing service for auto travel that takes two locations in the United States or Canada and spits out directions from one to the other. Quicker and simpler than Maps On Us (also reviewed in this section), AutoPilot should be used for

getting quick directions without a lot of options. The value of such a service, naturally, lies in the quality and coherence of the directions, so I put it to the test. Take me from Princeton, NJ, to Nashville, TN, I requested. (If the directions are good, I thought, maybe I'll drive down and become a country music star.) Within 15 seconds, AutoPilot displayed a set of highly detailed directions that included the mileage and estimated driving time for each road segment. (The Remaining Miles and Remaining Time columns give the mileage and driving time in reverse.) More than a bare-bones list of instructions, the directions offer milestones along the way and inform you when you're approaching a city or major road. Small icons indicate whether the suggested road is a local, county, state, or federal highway. When selecting your itinerary, you can determine a preference for direct or scenic routes, or a mix, and whether to avoid tolls. Not bad! Certainly better directions than I'm likely to get from a friend. Now where are my slide guitar and boots?

Foreign Languages for Travelers

www.travlang.com/languages

Online multilanguage phrase book: Foreign Languages for Travelers takes a great idea and knocks its socks off. It's an online, interactive, audio-enhanced phrase book that teaches you common expressions in more than 60 languages. Choose a language that you speak from the drop-down menu; then select a language link below the menu that you'd like assistance with. The phrases are the same in all languages and are divided into Basic Words, Numbers, Shopping/Dining, Travel, Directions, Places, and Time and Dates. Selecting a category takes you to a couple dozen phrases, each of them hyperlinked in both languages. Click any phrase to hear it spoken by a native to that language. (The default audio format is AU files, which are automatically played when using Navigator 3.0 or Explorer 3.0 or later; RealAudio files are also available.) The site's strength is its breadth of languages rather than breadth of phrases, but it's a wonderful starting point for picking up some basic expressions before visiting another country. Helpful language and cultural links also are provided.

Maps On Us

www.mapsonus.com

Interactive maps: One of the niftiest and most fun interactive travel pages on the Web, Maps On Us provides U.S. maps (duh) and much more. On the home page, get started quickly by typing a street address. In less than a minute, another page displays a street map of the neighborhood. You can manipulate the image by panning in different directions, changing the scale by zooming in and out, and removing the street labels. (Click anywhere on the map to automatically zoom in.) You can set more detailed control over map displays by clicking the Map Settings button. Trip planning is part of Maps On Us, and it's a more sophisticated deal than the quick-'n'-basic AutoPilot (also reviewed in this section). You can set a street-level departure and destination address and include specific stops along the way. The result is a map (duh again) and also written, turn-by-turn directions that link to detailed maps of every turn. Maps On Us is really quite fantastic, and it's no surprise that Lucent Technologies created the site.

Stayfree Holiday Club

www.stayfree.org

Clearinghouse for home-exchange agreements: Although it's not your typical vacation, home exchange is a fairly popular type of traveling, used by people who open their home to strangers in exchange for spending some time living like a resident in another part of the country or world. The Stayfree Holiday Club provides a marvelous listing service and meeting place for those who want to

put a house or apartment on the home-exchange market. You can specify any restrictions that you care to, such as whether you allow smoking, kids, and pets in your home, what destination you're searching for, and what time of year you want to travel. Each listing offers a description (without pictures) of the home, its neighborhood environment, regional attractions, and anything else you can think of that may make somebody want to visit. All listings are divided geographically, and cover the globe. The directory is kind of fun to browse through, even if you don't intend to post a notice.

The Universal Currency Converter

www.xe.net/currency

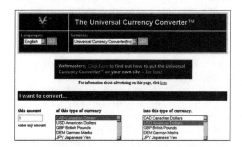

Count your cash in foreign denominations: Need a way to perform those pesky money conversions before traveling? Wondering how far your money will stretch (or be shrunk) in a foreign country? The Universal Currency Converter provides a quick and very easy way — actually two ways — to find out. First, you get the main converter, which uses two selectable menus. Choose your home currency in the first menu and the target currency in the second. Then click the Perform Currency Conversion button. A new screen displays with the values of the two currencies in relation to each other. For more information at a glance, use the Interactive Currency Table, which you can choose from the top selectable menu on the home page. A single menu appears in which you choose your home currency. When you click the Generate Currency Table button, a chart appears that translates a single unit of your home money into equivalent amounts of every major currency in the world. The database that fuels this site is updated often, so it's ideal for anyone traveling with a laptop that has an Internet connection. If you desire, you can even subscribe to a free e-mail service that sends you currency updates.

Worldwide Brochures

www.wwb.com

Get scads of travel brochures: You've never seen so many brochures. Actually, you can't see them, exactly, but you can get information about them, and then you can have them sent to you free of charge. I'll back up. Say you want to visit Disneyland, or go on a ski vacation, or take your kids on a Major League Baseball tour. The first step may be to visit a travel agent and pick up some relevant brochures. Alternatively, you can visit Worldwide Brochures on the Web and receive a flood of brochures. The site presents travel topics on the main Destination page, and the next page shows you a list of subtopics related to your main travel idea. Click one to see a list of available brochures, and click one of *those* to get information about the brochure (and about the company publishing the brochure). If the brochure seems to cover what you want to know, place it in your brochure cart by clicking an icon, and when you're done, type in your address to get them all sent to you. Worldwide Brochures is one of the easiest ways to get information about a trip.

Worldwide Guide to Hostelling

www.hostels.com

Read all about traveling on the cheap: Hostelling is a type of travel defined by

choosing hostel accommodations — very inexpensive, shared rooms and bathrooms located all over the world, usually available without reservation. More than a logistical feature of travel, hostelling is an attitude about traveling, centering around values of adventure, spontaneity, and community. The Worldwide Guide to Hostelling is a total resource for hostellers. Start with The Worldwide Hostel Guide link, probably the largest database of international hostels anywhere. You zero in on likely hostels by continent and country, and then the site provides you with addresses and phone numbers. (Most hostels don't have Web pages or e-mail addresses.) If you're new to hostelling, try the Frequently Asked Questions link — it's terrifically informative and gives you a good background in what to expect from the hostelling experience. The Virtual Bulletin Board is worthy of special note: Unlike many unused Web boards, this one is bursting with notices posted by people planning trips, looking for travel partners, and searching for great hostels by word of mouth.

Other Stuff to Check Out

babelfish.altavista.digital.com
www3.sympatico.ca/donna.mcsherry/
    airports.htm
www.bestfares.com
www.budgettravel.com
www.greyhound.com
www.stratpub.com

Online Reservations and Tickets

Most online reservation systems include an interface for checking airline schedules and fares. In all cases, the sites lease computer services from a few big systems that professional travel agents also use.

This setup results in a certain similarity from one site to another, though some crucial differences affect how easy the site is for nonprofessionals to use. Generally, you enter a departure date, time, and city; a destination city; and a return date and time. Some sites also enable you to specify how you want the results of your search to be sorted — by price, for example, or airline. Additional car rental and hotel booking services are sometimes provided. All of this is accomplished with varying panache by the major online travel agents listed here. If you want to comparison shop (or find a favorite), proceed through each system as if you were buying tickets but stop short of an actual purchase.

Air Travel Manager

www.airtm.com

Sophisticated airline reservation system: Air Travel Manager is unique among Internet reservations services and is most suitable for frequent travelers who are really serious about booking their transportation through a computer. The Web site is essentially a download station for special software that provides the interface for viewing fares and making reservations. After you download and install the ATM software, you connect to Air Travel Manager through your normal Internet connection and then take advantage of a standard point-and-click program with multiple windows for air, hotel, and rental car reservations. The site offers a rebate system which, for the very ambitious, can be the ticket to a modest at-home travel agency business. Air Travel Manager began on the CompuServe online service and recently migrated to the Web. The system is sophisticated and advanced. Those who only book flights occasionally should probably stick to simpler online systems that don't require a program download.

Note: The system is designed mainly for U.S. residents. International users can take advantage of it, but they have to set up their reservation system account themselves.

Flifo Cyberagent

www.flifo.com

Easy-to-use travel reservation system: Where did they get that name? I can't answer that question, but I do know that Flifo Cyberagent is an unusually user-friendly online reservation system that appeals to airfare bargain hunters. As with most virtual travel agents, you begin by creating a personal profile with your preferences. You then move on to planning your itinerary by entering cities and dates, using a page design that completely eliminates any possible confusion. Unfortunately, you can't sort results by price, and in fact, the results don't include the price of any flight that comes up. Instead, you get a *Show me the price* button after you've made your selections. Presumably, this setup is to allow the Flifo system to search its Fare Beater database for bargains. (Of course, you have to make sure the Fare Beater box is checked.) When the price information is finally displayed, Fare Beater alternatives are given that do, indeed, often beat the selected itinerary by mixing and matching different airlines for different legs of the trip. Flifo may have a strange name, but its service saves money and hassle.

Internet Travel Network

www.itn.net

Airline (and other) reservations with a sense of humor: I like a virtual travel agent with a sense of humor. At the Internet Travel Network (ITN), if you accidentally ask for a return date earlier than the departure date, you get this message:

"Hey! Airplanes are for transportation, not time travel!" Aside from the giggles, ITN provides a basic online reservation system encased in a user-friendly interface. It claims to be the first and only system of its kind — the latter claim certainly isn't true, and in fact, the itinerary screens (where you check available flights and prices for your destination) look identical to TheTrip.com, also reviewed in this section. All information is displayed in real time, and the site has millions of presumably happy — and chuckling — registered users.

Intransco

teleportal.com

Reserve tickets online and then buy them through the mail: Intransco is an online reservation and fare searching system with a couple of twists. For one, you can't actually buy tickets online, though you can make reservations. In what appears to be a reactionary resistance to online purchases, Intransco accepts only credit card orders sent through the mail or faxed. Intransco is unusual in another respect as well, in that the company is a travel consolidator, which means it buys plane tickets in volume at large discounts and then passes the savings to retail customers. The result is that you can get good prices, but you have less flexibility about when you travel. The packaged quality of the available tickets sometimes means that the same fare takes you 300 miles or 3,000. If you do end up buying a ticket through the mail, phone, or fax, your tickets are delivered by overnight courier.

Preview Travel

www.previewtravel.com

★★
★★

State-of-the-art airline reservation system: Anyone who thinks buying airline tickets

online is too complicated should try the Preview Travel system. Honed on America Online, the Web site leads you through the free registration process, setting up a personal profile, reviewing fares, and selecting an itinerary like a parent taking a child on a walk. Making a mistake or getting confused is just about impossible, which is a tribute to careful site design. More experienced users may be annoyed by the multiple screens, each asking for only two or three bits of information, but for beginners, the approach is reassuring and clear. When choosing dates for flights, calendars are thoughtfully placed on the screen — why don't all Web reservations sites do that? Flight data is presented more clearly than on some other systems and includes the number of available seats and an on-time record for the flights. Preview Travel was a pioneer in user-friendly computer interfaces for making reservations, and it continues that tradition on the Web.

TheTrip.com

www.thetrip.com

★★
★★

One of the best online travel-booking sites: TheTrip.com made a splash when it first appeared on the Web, partly because of what was, at the time, an astonishing new feature: the ability to track information on flights in progress. Although the site is avowedly for business travelers, it's just as useful and simple to use for anyone, even infrequent flyers. In a gallant attempt to apply itself usefully to all aspects of a trip, TheTrip.com is divided into five sections: The Flight, The Airport, The Ride, The Hotel, and The City. The Flight, of course, is where you compare fares, determine an itinerary, make reservations, and buy the tickets using a credit card. The Ride, The Hotel, and The City sections help you through your destination. Car rentals are handled as part of the flight reservation portion, so The Ride deals with limousines, shuttles, taxis, and trains within a country or city of your choice. The Hotel uses the same drop-down menus for selecting a country or city and then provides reviews and crucial data about lodging. In The City, descriptions of sightseeing, shopping, business resources, restaurants, entertainment, events, and recreation give you a good base of information before you travel.

TheTrip.com earns its hypes and awards. The page layout is clear; the site displays quickly; customer service assistance is quick, friendly, and capable when needed; and the information is solidly complete. Try signing up for the e-mail bulletins of travel bargains; they arrive about once a week.

Travelocity

www.travelocity.com

Full-service online travel agent: Travelocity, get it? Travel . . . city . . . velocity? Well, anyway, the Travelocity Web site is a combination destination guide and travel agent with a nifty feature or two. After you register (it's free), if you don't want to take advantage of the Flight Express airline reservation feature on the front page, the Travel Reservations section enables you to book a plane flight, reserve a rental car, or sign up for a cruise. You can check the arrival or departure time of a current flight, and even (here comes nifty feature number

one) arrange to have flight information changes sent to your e-mail address. I also like having the fare lists as separate data from the flight reservation page. In other words, you don't have to go through the process of booking your itinerary to get a general idea of what it'll cost. And here's niftiness number two: a B&B (bed-and-breakfast) directory. Travelocity is a bit on the slow side: Forget about using the Destinations Guide button; you could walk to your destination before you'd get any information about it.

Wholesale Travel Centre

206.235.50.10/wtc/index.htm

Discount travel tickets: Wholesale Travel Centre (WTC) is a discount online reservation and ticket purchase system. As a travel consolidator, Wholesale Travel buys blocks of airline seats at discount and sells them at rates usually below published fares. Using a somewhat complex but clear system of fill-in forms, WTC walks you through the itinerary-planning process of choosing departure and destination cities, and times and dates. Many more screens and button-clicks are required than in regular online reservations systems due to the necessity of checking multiple databases for discounts. The resulting fares are worth waiting for. Using a credit card, you can buy the tickets the moment that you make your reservation.

Other Stuff to Check Out

expedia.msn.com/daily/home/default.hts
www.easysabre.com
www.4airlines.com
www.webflyer.com

228 Travel Services

Part VI
Cultural Arts

"Awww jeez- I was afraid of this. Some poor kid, bored with the usual chat lines, starts looking for bigger kicks, pretty soon they're surfin' the seedy back alleys of cyberspace, and before you know it they're into a file they can't 'undo'. I guess that's why they call it the Web. Somebody open a window!"

In this part . . .

*E*ntertainment sites are among the most popular on the Internet. The World Wide Web is a perfect medium for presenting entertainment information because of its blend of graphics and information storage. Entertainment sites are among the fanciest, prettiest, glitziest sites on the Web. Often full of design graphics and photographs, entertainment sites can be a strain on the ol' modem. They also can be lots of fun to surf for that very reason — each site tries to be more eye-popping than the next.

Entertainment is a broad category, and I've divided it into the most popular sections. Of course, movies, television, and music get their due in this part, and I've also included sections on broadcast sites, literature, culture, personalities, and theater. Have a blast exploring the colorful Web world of entertainment!

Culture

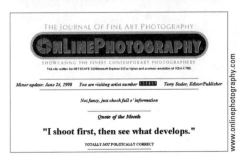

This section is devoted to the refined side of entertainment, including classical music, ballet, and photography. High culture, in other words. In a sense, just about everything that happens in the world is a cultural event when you think of culture as a sociological phenomenon. But that approach would make the topic too big for effective cataloging, so this section gathers just some of the best artistic sites and online publications.

Art and Culture Publications

The best Web magazines devoted to art present digitized prints of artwork, a range of news and feature articles, and current events coverage. Art e-zines aren't nearly as plentiful as finance magazines or general news sites, but the following is a directory to bookmark-worthy examples of the genre.

Critical Review

www.creview.com

★ ★
★ ★

Art criticism: Critical Review is an art review journal that carries its artsy

sensibilities straight to the design of its Web pages. Plain white backgrounds host sparse text links, and not a single upper-case letter is to be found. Modern and spacious, the site invites slow perusal and deep contemplation of the wise evaluations contained therein. Emphasizing New York galleries, but not restricting itself to them, Critical Review whispers sober analyses of current exhibits. Readers are invited to submit reviews of the shows. The Web site hosts discussion groups, but they work only erratically. (You wouldn't want to talk too loud in such a sacred gallery space, anyway.) In its tone, seriousness, and appearance, Critical Review evokes a refreshingly cool and unadorned (except by paintings, of course) downtown gallery in Manhattan on a summer day.

OnLine Photography

www.onlinephotography.com

Articles on photography: Calling itself "The Journal of Fine Art Photography," the home page of this online periodical gets off to a good start by animating the *O* in *OnLine* as a camera shutter opening and closing. The design reveals itself to be less clever as you scroll down the page. *Hint:* Widen your browser window as much as possible to accommodate the outdated table that houses the section links, and then back away from the computer screen as far as you can. Subtlety is not this site's strong point. Content, however, is. If you don't care so much about the articles and product reviews geared to active photographers and just want to view some great images, let your mouse gravitate toward two links in particular: Visual Resumes and The Masters Gallery. The first link contains amateur, but nonetheless stunning, portfolios, and the second is a professional gallery. The site's selection doesn't shy away from modern techniques of image manipulation, such as computer processing, and the results can be beautiful and weird. Other photographic Web sites are linked here, including a site of the month.

232 Culture

World Art Treasures

Sgwww.epfl.ch/berger

Art for contemplation and reflection: World Art Treasures had its genesis in the Jacques-Edouard Berger Foundation and the more than 100,000 art slides in its collection. Although the site is still evolving, World Art Treasures tries to build a specific approach for each art "itinerary," as the online displays are called. And those itineraries include many different types of media in many different areas. A recent visit found itineraries on topics as diverse as painting, Renaissance gardens, and the stone art on the temples of Angkor Wat in Southeast Asia. The site uses frames effectively for those whose browsers are so equipped. In the recent Johannes Vermeer itinerary, for example, viewers were treated to an enlightening biography of the Dutch painter right next to slides of his masterpieces.

Other Stuff to Check Out

users.bart.nl:88/~francey/byrne.html
www.kn.pacbell.com/wired/art/art.html
www.pbs.org/wnet/americanvisions
www.pictograph.com/TW3.html
www.theatlantic.com

Mixed Media

This section assembles miscellaneous classy culture sites that focus on a variety of specific artistic topics, as well as Web sites for specific institutions. Photography, classical music, theater, opera and light opera, Kabuki, ballet, and government agencies all find a home here. It's a grab bag of high-quality cultural sites.

American Ballet Theatre

www.abt.org
Web site of New York City ballet company:

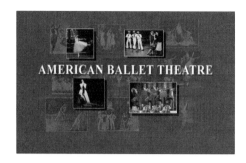

No self-respecting performing arts organization would forego a chance to promote itself and solicit contributions on its Web site, but the American Ballet Theatre rises above the purgatory of self-promotion with a site that goes way beyond its congratulatory review quotes and membership links. Although the American Ballet Theatre's headquarters are in New York City, the site has more than enough general information here to warrant virtual visits from out-of-towners. A recent highlight at the site was a fascinating article called *A Dancer's Life* by one of the company members. Of course, season schedules are listed here, as well as dancer biographies and a photo gallery. The Repertory Archives present an interesting historical database that you can access by ballet name, composer, or choreographer, all in a great Web interface that enables you to hide or reveal menu frames as you go.

ArtNet

www.artnet.com/home.html

Samples of art exhibitions around the world: ArtNet promises to be the most comprehensive art site on the Web. That claim may be true — it's certainly one of the most professional. Incorporating an online magazine and a list of online exhibitions, the site ends up displaying a lot of art on your screen. The exhibitions list is notable not only for its interesting selection but for its international scope. A recent visit pointed to museum shows from New York to Mexico City, from Chicago to Vienna. Each exhibition page gives thorough background text on the artist and contact information (and a Web link if there is one) for the gallery. In most cases, the site presents an online portfolio of the artist's work on separate pages. ArtNet also links the eager art-appreciator to auctions, art fairs, and art organizations.

Classical Insites

www.classicalinsites.com/live/splash/ fs_index.html

Classical music information: A virtual city for classical music lovers, Classical Insites is a multimedia fantasy land. The home page should get the honor of a bookmark. The city motif is carried forth with a splashy graphic of a town square whose buildings and other features divide the site into sections. The Hall of Fame is a good place to start — it's a gallery of performers with a featured artist who changes monthly (recently the conductor Serge Koussevitzky). The Conservatory is the site's learning center, offering an educational environment on the history and fundamentals of classical music. The Performance Center is like an online concert hall, featuring audio clips in RealAudio format and QuickTime movie clips from films with great scores (*Shine* was recently spotlighted). The Performance Center always carries a link to the Web site of WQXR, a classical radio station in New York City. Another major link from the city home page is the Bernstein Studio, an outside Web site devoted to the famous 20th-century conductor Leonard Bernstein. Classical Insites is worth spending some time with, whether you're an experienced classicophile or a newcomer.

Classical Net

www.classical.net

Classical music history: Classical Net is a sort of primer, or music appreciation site,

for classical music. Without being overly wordy or academic, the brief passages illuminate historical periods and composer's lives, painting a complete picture of the background of refined music. The Basic Repertoire page provides an excellent overview of the site's capabilities. The concise Musical Period paragraphs defining periods like Classicism and Romanticism may even be too brief, but they're enhanced considerably by the data available on individual composers, which you can access a number of ways. My recommendation: Use the Quick Reference link on the Basic Repertoire List page, and you'll find a page where all the composers are grouped by historical period in alphabetical order. You can also find composer information on the Composer Data and Works page, which includes chronological lists of composers sorted by birthday, date of death, and nationality. If you still can't find Beethoven, go back to the keyword search section of the home page. A CD buying guide helps new collectors, and the Reviews & Articles section includes contributions by several journalists and other music writers. Rounding out the site is a links area for finding other classical music Web sites and mailing lists.

CultureFinder

www.culturefinder.com

Find cultural events in different cities: CultureFinder has a few nice features, but here's what you should do first: Run for

234 Culture

the Calendar link on the home page, which leads to a truly great feature, the highlight of the site. The CultureFinder Calendar locates performances and other art events by date, city, or performing arts organization. At the time of this writing, over 1,200 such organizations participate in the Calendar. A series of entry forms invites you to specify a date range (month, day, and year), a type of event (dance performance, for example, or classical music concert), and a city. Within a few seconds CultureFinder lists the results, each with descriptive information about the event and box office phone numbers. (You can't buy tickets through the CultureFinder site.) An alternative browsing method for those who live in a large city involves selecting a city from a brief list of 22 metropolitan U.S. areas and viewing a list of performances beginning with the current evening. This method is a great way to quickly survey what's happening in town (as long as you live in a *big* town). The International Listings and Tickets link takes you to sites outside the United States. Taking a vacation to a big city? CultureFinder comes in handy when you're planning ahead.

Culturekiosque

www.culturekiosque.com

Broad cultural topics: Culturekiosque (a kiosk of culture, don'tcha know) takes a broad view of culture, extending beyond refined arts to archaeology, contemporary pop culture, and even technology. Demonstrating its global view, the site offers articles in a few different languages. Profiles of dancers, chefs, and opera singers rub elbows. The Operanet spin-off is a complete culture site in its own right, containing diva interviews, CD reviews, and opera news. Klassiknet takes the same approach to classical music, and jazznet — yep, you guessed it. What this superlative array amounts to is a connected circle of eight culture sites under the Culturekiosque umbrella. It's a full meal of cultural topics, to say the least.

Fiat Lux

bookweb.cwis.uci.edu/ AdamsHome.html

Photographic work of Ansel Adams: Created by the University of California, Fiat Lux is the closest thing to an official Web site for the legendary photographer Ansel Adams, one of America's seminal artists in black-and-white imagery. Fiat Lux includes a great deal of information, and the Web site presents it rather academically (no surprise for a university production) with an emphasis on text and a lack of icons, buttons, frames, or other standard navigational aids. Scroll down to the Exhibition Organization section and link your way to the history of the exhibit and then to the photographs. The link that you want is Tour the Fiat Lux Exhibition. The University of California commissioned Adams to document some of its campuses, and this exhibition is the result; the photographer's other work is not represented here. Nevertheless, the biographical and historical information is interesting, and the pictures display Adams's trademark clarity and contrast very well. And you can actually hear audio clips of Adams discussing his work.

The John F. Kennedy Center for the Performing Arts

www.kennedy-center.org

★ ★
★ ★

Retrospective of the performing arts center: The Kennedy Center site is primarily a placard for the Washington, D.C., performing arts center and its past and present achievements, but the information is presented with such vivacity that it's an irresistible cultural site. The Our History link leads to an especially interesting section of history and descriptions of some of the legendary performances since the Kennedy Center was built in 1971. You'll be amazed at how many luminaries in the classic performing arts have had memorials and on-stage birthday celebrations there. Education Programs is another good link, describing performances for children and adults. The National Symphony Orchestra, whose home is at the Kennedy Center, also has an informative section. Finally, the site describes Kennedy Center Internships along with guidelines for applying.

Kabuki for Everyone

www.fix.co.jp/kabuki/kabuki.html

Introduction to Japanese traditional opera: Kabuki is a traditional, slow-paced form of Japanese theater in which all roles, male and female, are played by men. Although this description sounds like a comic formula for television, in the context of Japanese stage art, Kabuki is revered and distinguished. The Kabuki for Everyone site excels at conveying Kabuki through text explanations, audio clips, video clips, and morphing animations that show a man changing smoothly into the image of a woman. The site presents schedules for the National Theater of Kabuki in Japan, which are useful if you're planning a trip there. Scroll down the home page to the Online Theater link for illustrated stories of Kabuki plays. The Kabuki Sounds link (again from the home page) leads to a fascinating section where you can hear audio clips of traditional Japanese musical instruments used in Kabuki, as well as examples of the encouraging shouts issued by enthusiastic audience members for their favorite actors. Kabuki for Everyone is an intriguing and educational glimpse into a formal cultural tradition that many people have little experience with.

National Endowment for the Arts

arts.endow.gov

Information on U.S. government arts grants: The National Endowment for the Arts (NEA) is a U.S. government agency that grants money for individual, collective, and institutional artistic endeavors. The NEA Web site empowers anyone to know who's getting the government's arts money. Three main sections present themselves. First is Arts.Community, an online publication spotlighting a featured artist, endowment news, and a writer's corner. Next is the Guide to the National Endowment for the Arts, an overview of the endowment programs and guidelines for applicants. Lastly, you find the Arts Resource Center, which includes both printed publications and online links. The NEA site is well done, compacting its voluminous information into summaries when needed and streamlining navigation by providing a text-only interface.

World Wide Arts Resources

wwar.com

Comprehensive directory of arts on the Net: Asking the question, "What comprises the arts?" always generates some debate. The World Wide Arts Resources strives to be the most complete guide to arts resources on the Internet and includes listings of theater and dance resources but not classical music. Not to quibble, though, what World Wide Arts Resources does, it does very well indeed. The left-hand menu column enables you to select among categories of artistic endeavors, including a few unexpected classifications such as Art History, Commercial Arts, Antiques, and Crafts. Each link leads to a second-level page of subdivisions within that category, and another click of the mouse reveals links to Web sites. This way, you can narrow down your interest from Arts Publications to Photography Magazines to a listing of about 180 online magazines on photography. You can switch categories from anywhere in the database, and a search engine helps those netizens who prefer cutting to the chase by entering keywords. World Wide Arts Resources should be on your bookmark list as a Web guide to *some* aspects of culture, with a strong emphasis on art.

Other Stuff to Check Out

architecture.simplenet.com
www.artpool.hu
www.dia.org
www.totemweb.com

Online Museums

The World Wide Web brings multimedia to network computing, and nowhere is that fact more appreciated than in the field of art online. Online museums shrink the globe and help justify the entire Internet phenomenon by bringing great cultural traditions onto your home desktop. As Internet technology develops, you can look forward to better, larger, and more fluid artistic presentations on the Net. For now, enjoy the following online galleries — they're among the best art collections on the Web.

Asian Arts

www.asianart.com

History and images of Asian art: Asian Arts is a kind of megagallery cum directory, in which you can browse among galleries exhibiting Asian art and then link to the online versions of those galleries. Asian Arts provides informative explanatory text around the images within the site, giving perspective and history. (A

separate Articles section is the most informative portion and also contains some images.) The site represents photography and paintings from such diverse Asian regions as Nepal, China (at various time periods), India, and Tibet. Because Asian Arts gathers so much artistic material to one central virtual location, it's amazingly educational and beautiful to look at.

Chateau of Versailles

www.Chateauversailles.fr

People who live in glass houses can have Web sites: Chateau of Versailles is one of France's most revered sites, a famous palace built by French King Louis XIV that doubles as the Museum of French History. This elegant Web site offers 360-degree images of the Court of the Chateau, the Hall of Mirrors, and the King's Chamber. The site offers information in both English and French, and images (accessed via the Masterpiece link) that speak to people of all languages — paintings, sculptures, furniture, decor, and other collections. Simply *magnifique*.

Digital Wave Imaging Gallery

www.digitalari.com/foyer.html

Unusual photographs: High-tech and cutting-edge photographs are the focus of Digital Wave Imaging Gallery. Generally hosting a few simultaneous online exhibits, the site is darkly effective. Sometimes the black backgrounds and mysterious typefaces make reading an eye-squinting chore, but you're not here primarily to read. Turn up your monitor's brightness setting and enjoy some remarkable photos. During a recent visit, I discovered a portfolio exploring the visual similarities of religious holy grounds and a starkly effective black-and-white collection of Puerto Rican landscapes. The site often highlights unusual exposure, development, and printing processes, but the exhibits aren't avant-garde in effect. The result is unusual but accessible.

Fine Arts Museums of San Francisco

www.thinker.org/index.shtml

Ambitious online museum: This museum site has an exciting ambition: to make the entire collection of the Fine Arts Museums of San Francisco available online. (The site has accomplished about half that goal.) The online exhibits offer slide previews or — if you have a Java-enabled browser or the Live Picture Viewer plug-in — virtual galleries. The Live Picture Viewer plug-in turns the Web site from a static collection of images to a multimedia playground with zooming, click-and-dragging capabilities. But if you'd rather bypass the download, just head for the Art Imagebase link, click I understand and agree!, and then click Highlights to begin touring the museum. Along the way, you'll get some ideas for using the search feature, and soon you'll be cruising around the virtual gallery like a veteran.

The Getty Institute

www.gii.getty.edu

Still under construction, but the possibilities. . . . : J. Paul Getty was a businessman who collected oil tankers, and when he

collected enough of them to become one of the world's richest men, he decided to collect art. J. Paul is gone now, but the Southern California–based trust that he left behind — called, naturally, The J. Paul Getty Trust — has become a multifaceted cultural force. The preceding URL leads to the Getty Information Institute, which promises to enhance "worldwide access to cultural heritage information for research and education by means of computer technology." The site is still evolving but is already impressive. You can take a quick visual tour of the new Getty Museum, quite arguably the most celebrated building in decades in the Los Angeles area. Given the stature of the Getty name in the art world, you can bet that the Getty site will be on the forefront of the cultural movement on the Web.

Leonardo da Vinci Museum

museum.brandx.net

Pictures of Leonardo da Vinci's work: This site serves a simple function and does so without any wasted time or design features. If the subject weren't so glorious, I would have to consider the site bleak, with its plain gray backgrounds and simple text interface. But stylish interfacing isn't the point, of course, the display of western civilization's greatest Renaissance figure is. Images take the front seat here, supplanting much in the way of biographical information. In fact, the following quote is the extent to which the Leonardo da Vinci Museum strives to enlighten us about the master's life: "Leonardo da Vinci was a great painter, designer, scientist, futurist, and thinker. His works are even more popular now than they were in his day." Okay, that quote does it for me, now on to the paintings. The site is divided into four *wings,* as in a real museum. The East Wing contains digital scans of oil paintings; the West Wing has Leonardo's engineering

238 Culture

and inventive designs; in the North Wing are drawings and sketches; and the South Wing has an historical exhibit of the Renaissance period. Typical of online galleries, each exhibit starts with small thumbnail reproductions, which turn into large versions when you click them.

The Louvre

mistral.culture.fr/louvre/louvrea.htm

Web site of the famous Paris museum: This URL takes you directly to the English version of The Louvre Web site, although you also can click for the French, Spanish, and Japanese versions. Many images from the famous Paris museum's collection are available here, although the site's organization is a bit on the haphazard side. Your best bet is to click Collections on the home page, and then scroll down the next page until you see the colored boxes representing Oriental antiquities, paintings, prints and drawings, sculptures, and other artistic categories. Each department dishes up small thumbnail images, which you can click to view larger versions. The collections represent "major works" but without explaining any reasoning behind the selection nor offering any search engine. This method makes The Louvre fascinating to browse through, as long as you're not looking for anything in particular. By the way: Clicking that morphing image on the home page takes you to a directory of the Louvre's newest building and its collection.

Museum of American Art

www.nmaa.si.edu

Exhibitions of historical American art: The Museum of American Art makes computer viewing easy with a series of online exhibition tours. Recent tours include *Singular Impressions: The Monotype in America, Renwick at Twenty-Five,*

American Kaleidoscope — Themes and Perspectives in Recent Art, and *The White House Collection of American Crafts.* The online tours start off with a screen that displays thumbnail pictures; click a pic to get a larger version. Underneath each full-size painting (or photograph), you find directional buttons for moving backward or forward through the tour — this feature is handy because it enables you to avoid revisiting the thumbnail page over and over. The images are high-resolution scans, which take a bit of time to display on the screen but are definitely worth the wait. And some tours include video clips that use the Vivo plug-in; the monotype tour, for example, includes video on the monotype process itself.

National Gallery of Art

www.nga.gov/collection/collect.htm

Extraordinarily fine online museum: The National Gallery of Art Web site sponsors a fun, attractive, and easy-to-use site. You can enjoy one of the finest art collections in the world with the help of a completely searchable and attractive interface, at no charge whatsoever, from the comfort of home. Short informative text (and sometimes RealAudio commentary) accompanies each image (just like in an offline museum). Browsing may be more enjoyable than searching, except if you're an art historian who really knows what to search for. Scroll down to the Tour the

Collection area and pick a category. The following page offers a handful of Selected Tours that offer three levels of viewing. Starting with small thumbnails, the next gradation is a larger reproduction with some history of the painting, followed (if you continue clicking the image) by a full-screen reproduction. The site places the images — which are high-resolution scans, resulting in beautifully detailed pictures — on white backgrounds without any framing or highlighting. The National Gallery of Art does an almost impossibly good job with this site. If you try only one online museum, this is the one.

WebMuseum

www.oir.ucf.edu/wm

Galleries of many artists: The WebMuseum is an online equivalent of a spartan art gallery that foregoes all comforts in favor of the brisk efficiency of simple displays — no chairs, water fountains, or rest rooms. The What's New in the WebMuseum? link is the key to the content, leading to an almost shockingly terse page consisting of nothing more than a list of a few hundred artist names. Click any one of the names, and a new page appears with a brief biography, some historical perspective, and thumbnails of featured paintings. If art history isn't your strong point (welcome to the club), then you're browsing in the dark. Not to say that you won't have fun clicking around and learning some miscellaneous art facts. WebMuseum has two big plusses. First, the lean design, bereft of all eye candy, makes the pages display lickety-split (that's a technical art term). Second, the full-size reproduction of the paintings (which you view by clicking the small thumbnails under each painter) are really big, enabling perusal of detail that is uncommon in virtual museums. WebMuseum may not provide a padded chair for viewing its wall hangings, but it delivers a good collection.

Other Stuff to Check Out

www.art.uiuc.edu/kam
www.mam.org
www.nhm.ac.uk

Entertainment News and Gossip

This section covers the entertainment supersites that provide news and gossip about movies, TV, and music. It also serves as a directory to entertainment publications on the Web. Because entertainment is such a huge Web topic, this section skims over the top, collecting the cream of the crop. You can find many great sites by linking away from these starting points, but you can't do better than the sites reviewed here. You'll see pics of your favorites stars, catch up on the latest gossip, meet people (if you want), and get up to speed on showbiz news.

I've divided the broad entertainment category into two subsections: Entertainment News and Entertainment Publications. As you surf around both categories, you may notice that they contain many of the same features: news, gossip, articles, and pictures. The Entertainment News sites tend to put a stronger emphasis on community features, such as message boards and chat rooms, and the Entertainment Publications sites tend to share magazine-style formatting features like headline links and sidebar navigation menus.

Entertainment News

General entertainment megasites — big Web domains covering movies, TV, music, videos, and other popular entertainment — are reviewed in this section. You've probably heard of some of them, even if you haven't visited them yet, because they're among the most popular locations on the Web and are sometimes mentioned in other media. In reading the following reviews, notice the differing emphasis of the sites. Some sites focus on style and glittery page design over substance. Others are serious about delivering news and don't distract you with bright colors. Some sites offer multimedia content by means of audio and video clips, which are great if you have a fast Internet connection. They're all among the best at what they do — delivering news about the entertainment industry and enabling fans to communicate with each other.

CNN Interactive – Entertainment

www.cnn.com/SHOWBIZ/index.html

Entertainment journalism: The famous news network's methodical and comprehensive style of information gathering is put to the service of the CNN Interactive–Entertainment site, which leads off with headline stories of the day, followed by a cartload of links to other background stories on entertainment topics. Links enable you to go to specific pages on books, movies, music, and TV. Each page has chat rooms and message boards,

showing that CNN has learned something about making online visitors feel at home. And many of the site's stories offer video or audio clips. Don't have the right plug-in? Don't worry — downloads are available. Highly respectable journalism matched with a clear, not-too-busy page design makes CNN Interactive–Entertainment a good mix of attractiveness and efficiency.

E! Online

www.eonline.com

Cool entertainment megasite: One of the major, ever-so-cool, must-see watering holes for entertainment news on the Web, E! Online dazzles visitors with flying text, plenty of photos, late-breaking gossip, enough TV and movie reviews to glut a cocktail party, online games, and lots of in-your-face, let's-have-fun attitude. Despite the multimedia glitter, you don't need any special plug-ins to see everything on this site. A chat area enables you to ponder the intangibles of the latest action blockbuster in the company of other netizens, and the find it! feature helps you locate (and even rent or buy) video titles. The E! cable channel creates E! Online, which includes a highlight guide of TV fare.

eDrive

www.edrive.com

Entertainment news and reviews: You have to look carefully to see what's left of the trademark smiling yellow star ("Ed") that used to greet visitors to eDrive, because all that's left is a blue silhouette. No need to fret, though: The eDrive site has plenty of things to keep you occupied. You can choose from daily updated feature stories, television schedules, David Letterman's Top Ten lists, chat and message boards, shopping, occasional contests, and the online home of Sexy Celebs. Ed, buddy, you won't be missed. Archives of photos and video clips keep things interactively interesting, and the Java-enhanced menu bars atop each page help you easily find your way around. Not that you wouldn't have fun losing yourself in the deep entertainment content of this varied site. The Today's Headlines section informs you of news and scuttlebutt from movie sets; the Cranky Critic curmudgeonly delivers reviews of current movies to an eager band of Cranky loyalists; and if you're an intermittent soap opera addict, check out the Chat & Messaging section to get straightened out on plot twists. Beginning as a family of phenomenally popular forums on theCompuServe online service, eDrive migrated to the Web in the fall of 1996.

Entertainment Network News

www.enn2.com

Directory of entertainment Web sites: This is what Entertainment Network News says about itself: "ENN has been created to be a total ENTERTAINMENT world megasite on the World Wide Web." It falls far short of that goal, but ENN deserves a bookmark spot thanks to what will eventually be a side benefit but for now is the impressive main feature: a very good directory of Web sites in various fields of entertainment. You won't find anything innovative about the categories of this directory; typical divisions of Movies, Television, Music, Video, and Magazines prevail. (A few unusual classifications are

present: Sixties and Radio among them.) The long list of quality links within each category is what commands your attention. And the site offers chat rooms and "Romance" — a chance for you to find someone online who shares your entertainment tastes.

Jam!

canoe1.canoe.ca/Jam

Offbeat entertainment and cultural news: An entertainment Web site can easily fall into the trap of rehashing the same industry news and gossip as everyone else — that exclusive terrain is occupied by the blockbusters of online showbiz: E! Online, CNN Interactive Entertainment eDrive, and Hollywood Online. Any other site without comparable news and production resources is doomed to also-ran status on the hypercompetitive World Wide Web. Jam! sidesteps the issue by creating fresh angles on all aspects of entertainment, from movies, to theater, to TV, to music (including a separate category for you country fans). Games, surveys, and quizzes add spice to the mix of news and reviews. Stories are informative without being too long, and they dig deeper into niches of showbiz that other sites don't always cover. The site's tone isn't academic or bookish in the slightest, but Jam! always strives to be interesting, and usually succeeds.

Mr. Showbiz

www.mrshowbiz.com

News and plenty of photos: If you're in the mood for an entertainment news and gossip site that's well organized and isn't trying to frazzle your brain with screaming colors and icons streaking across the screen, try Mr. Showbiz for a comprehensive, fairly sober offering of stories, reviews, and photos. Lots of photos. Tons of photos. A vault of photos. Besides the photos (did I mention how many there are?), Mr. Showbiz is distinguished by an array of sponsors that contribute interesting content, such as Wall of Sound (reviewed in the section "Music," later in this part), which furnishes music stories. Imaginative games — like the Plastic Surgery Lab in which you can alter the visage of your favorite star, for better or worse — spice things up.

MTV News Online

www.mtv.com/news/headlines

Music and entertainment news: A shocking, deep-blue, mysterious background greets you and draws you into the alternate culture of MTV News Online. The site's design is striking, but not painful, to the old retinas, and the news is definitely geared to the MTV generation. The site prominently features tour information for hot bands, and for some reason, the site tends to provide a lot of lawsuit stories involving rock stars. Anyway, clicking a headline link takes you to the full story, where the belligerently blue background persists. The fine white text against the deep-ocean azure may require some squinting, depending on your monitor. The site is a simple, no-frills (except for the colors — did I mention the blue background?) presentation of about two dozen daily updated news stories from the universe of rock 'n' roll.

Yahoo! Entertainment Summary

www.yahoo.com/headlines/ entertainment

Entertainment industry headlines: Yahoo!'s tradition of providing fast headlines leading to fast stories for fast updates of news, continues in the entertainment section. Lest I forget to mention it, the Yahoo! Entertainment Summary is fast. Don't even think about viewing a picture here because Yahoo! doesn't consider furnishing any. Instead, you find a gray background and down-and-dirty headlines and stories. Organized into entertainment topics (People, Music, Arts, and so on), the site updates its news frequently. Yahoo! Entertainment Summary is one of the best ways to get up to speed in a hurry.

Other Stuff to Check Out

theguide.gim.de/ETRANS/Index.HTM
www.mrmedia.com/mrmedia
www.wsin.com/entertainment.html
www.xplore.com/xplore500/medium/ entertainment.html

Entertainment Publications

Reading about entertainment is almost as good as the entertainment itself. Most of us love going to movies, for example, and when we're not in the theater, we pore over movie reviews to determine what to see next or find if the movie scribe agrees with our verdict on the latest flick. The World Wide Web hosts electronic editions of printed entertainment magazines and newspapers, and the following collection of sites shows you how to see the best of them.

Details

www.swoon.com/mag_rack/details.html

Entertainment and lifestyle magazine:
Entertainment as lifestyle, and lifestyle as
entertainment — that's the editorial
viewpoint of *Details* magazine, a fat glossy
book in the real world and a slick cutting-
edge Web site in the virtual world. What
does it say about the Details reader when
the Horoscopes section has its own major
link on the home page? Well, never mind,
it's a nicely designed section, updated
daily. The chat area requires a software
download, and the popular forum
message area is more devoted to relationships than entertainment. *Tip:* Go for the
Q&A Archive, a vault of interviews with
entertainment icons from Mira Sorvino to
Elton John.

Entertainment Weekly Online

www.pathfinder.com/ew

*Online version of the entertainment
magazine:* Entertainment Weekly Online is
another of those friendly URLs from
Pathfinder, the Time Warner megasite
that publishes several virtual magazines.
A jumbled home page menu of feature
articles expands into awesome, profound
content (profound in both quantity and
quality). Every article page seems to
explode into a dozen more items, and you
can easily get happily lost worming
deeper into the glut of multimedia

entertainment news. Reviews abound,
and the site archives them for past-tense
browsing. A movie-centric approach
prevails, but that doesn't prevent Entertainment Weekly Online from running
specials on TV shows, such as the "Top
30 TV Shows." Additional content is
available for registered users (a 30-day
trial is available). The site is alive with
multimedia enhancements that don't bog
down your browser, and strikes a good
balance between information and graphic
style. It's a keeper.

The iZine

www.thei.aust.com

Entertainment news from down under:
Australians may think they're a long way
from the other continents — I mean, you
can't just pack up the family in the ol'
minivan or sedan and drive to Australia
from North America or Europe — yet
Australian entertainers have had a major
impact on the rest of the world. As I write
this, Natalie Imbruglia's *Torn* is tearing up
the U.S. music charts, and ads for Mel
Gibson's latest *Lethal Weapon* flick (are
they up to *Lethal Weapon 41* yet?) are
unavoidable. This online magazine's
cover links include Music, Film, Art, and
Books. If some of the names mentioned
aren't familiar, don't worry — in a few
years, they probably will be.

Los Angeles Times Entertainment Section

www.calendarlive.com

Entertainment journalism: The *L.A. Times*
takes an exceptionally thorough approach
to entertainment, including more elevated
cultural subjects like art, books, and
theater. As you may expect, the *L.A.
Times* presents the whole package with a
journalistic flair, which is a polite way of
saying that it's a bit on the dry side
compared to other online publications.
I'm not complaining, though — the
benefit of Web sobriety is usually a fast-
moving site, and the display times of the

L.A. Times pages won't keep you sipping your chilling coffee. A long front page contains small pictures that don't drag down your modem's performance, and a side navigation bar offers more links to internal features than you'd be able to cover on a leisurely Sunday of entertainment surfing.

Metaverse

www.metaverse.com/vibe

Neon-styled entertainment magazine: Metaverse is one of the most richly designed, graphically indulgent entertainment sites around. Pages don't exactly fly onto your screen — you may have time to teach yourself Portuguese while browsing through this site. However, the intense background and near-psychedelic headlines are worth locking your eyes onto if you have the patience. One of the great visual features appears right beneath the main artwork, where a scrolling Java ticker clues you in on the themes in the CyberSleaze gossip column. Besides cornea-wrinkling visuals, Metaverse slyly slips enough film 'n' tune content into your cranial cavity to keep you dreaming of smoky stages and silver screens for many nights. *Tip:* Link over to the HorribleScopes page for a cynical, tongue-in-cheek message from the heavens.

The Nando Times: Entertainment

www.nando.net/nt/enter

Online entertainment newspaper: The entertainment section of The Nando Times, a prominent Internet news publication, forks over a standard headline-to-full-story link scheme, without a lot of miscellany — miscellany like pictures, quizzes, games, message boards, or chat rooms. Come to think of it, that's a lot of missing miscellany. But no complaints here. The Nando Times: Entertainment is a fast, grounded, online entertainment newspaper for people who don't have time to download graphics. If you're really in a hurry, simply scroll the headlines on the main page — a selection of one-paragraph stories gathered on the same page. Adding to the quick-read ethic of the site, the headlines contain one-sentence summaries that give you the gist of the story and help you decide whether or not to pursue the link. The Nando Times: Entertainment page isn't comprehensive or gossipy, but it's fast as lightning.

National Enquirer

www.nationalenquirer.com

Fine, respected journalism — NOT: One day recently while I was at the supermarket, a *National Enquirer* headline grabbed my attention, and I was soon astonished to learn that Elvis had been reincarnated as an alien from Alpha Centauri and had impregnated Elizabeth Taylor. I was amazed that such a startling, newsworthy story wasn't picked up by any other publication I could find, and I was determined to find the *National Enquirer* on the Web. I did. Guess what else I learned? Bill Gates was allegedly arrested! Yes, *the* Bill Gates, the head of Microsoft. Of course, he was 22 at the time and had simply forgotten to take his driver's license along when he was pulled over. These things happen when you're thinking about how your company is going to dominate the computer software field and not watching the road. Anyway, if you find this kind of fine journalism titillating, simply zip to this site and click one of the links to find the current edition's headlines.

People Online

www.pathfinder.com/people

News and gossip with a serious tone: The People Online site delivers the insight into celebrity personalities that you'd expect from its parent publication *People* magazine, with the addition of a serious tone more suited to a newsmagazine. The newsier approach still centers around personalities, but it adds a dry seriousness to the proceedings that isn't entirely welcome. Nevertheless, the site is professionally produced, dishes out plenty of eavesdropping character, and is cheaper (that is, free) than its printed counterpart. The Daily Peephole isn't as scandalous as you may think (or hope) — it's just breaking news. You'd expect photo galleries from a picture-oriented magazine, and you get 'em on the Web site. Bowing to Internet expectations, a keyword form enables you to search the news database. People Online, like the magazine, represents the conservative end of celebrity gossip.

USA Today Life

www.usatoday.com/life/lfront.htm

Online version of the newspaper's entertainment section: As a transposition of the national newspaper's daily Life section, the USA Today Life Web site enhances the print version's gossipy information value with an impressive variety of computer resources. An index and site-specific search engine start you off efficiently, and the Web site's contents are much more extensive than that of the newspaper section. The site offers reviews of current movies, TV shows, and music albums and then archives them in a vast library that's easy to navigate. No matter which direction you proceed in this Web site, you're likely to be surprised by the depth of information, the clarity with which it's organized, and the speediness of the page displays. Classified ads are thrown in as an unexpected extra. If you appreciate the sensibilities of the *USA Today* newspaper, you'll love how it translates to the Internet. And it doesn't even cost 50 cents a day.

Other Stuff to Check Out

members.aol.com/beatgeninc/beatgen/beatgen.html

www.99lives.com
www.dispatches.org
www.gigaplex.com
www.nashscene.com
www.webgenesis.com

www.gogaga.com

Looking for cyberspots to exercise your new browser plug-ins? You've come to the right place. Receiving media broadcasts over the Internet is a unique kind of entertainment — but only entertaining if you have a fast enough Net connection. The following sites are appropriate only for 28.8 Kbps or faster connections.

GoGaGa

www.gogaga.com

Unusual music programming: GoGaGa, the Internet radio station that says, "We take weird seriously," is for the musically restless — those who thirst for diverse and free-form programming. The site divides the Netcast day into blocks, just like a broadcast radio station, and includes Music for Cubicles during workdays — "From our cubicle to yours, music to ward off management." (The show descriptions are almost as good as the shows.) GoGaGa calls its evening program Velvet Grotto, with Tabitha Angst as one of the hosts ("Be afraid, be very afraid"). The Web site also provides a playlist, although you may have trouble making sense of it because the musical selections aren't scheduled (you can imagine the difficulty in listing times when the listenership is global). The DJs announce the musical selections, and as for the selections themselves, eclectic is definitely the word, with an emphasis on world music.

NetRadio Network

www.netradio.net

All kinds of music programming: The NetRadio Network is an Internet-only station that's a little on the odd side. Live programming isn't the point at NetRadio, which features many channels of genre music and entertainment news. The site is more like a jukebox, but with a lot of ever-shifting content surrounding it. Clicking the What's New button on the home page makes you think the site is strictly a heavy-metal affair, but a glance at the left-hand menu reveals a range of musical choices from Christian to classical, new age to vintage rock. The site delivers celebrity and entertainment news in text format enhanced by audio clips — for example, a recent story portrayed one musician as a whiner, with the incriminating word hyperlinked to an audio clip of a baby whining. I'm not sure what NetRadio is — part radio station, part multimedia entertainment newspaper, part online album collection. But it's definitely fun.

ON-AIR.com

www.on-air.com

Three genres of music: You'll be seeing more of this type of Web site in the future, I'm sure: a totally automated, Internet-only radio station. No chattering DJs, and by the same token, no personality or sense of

topicality. ON-AIR.com provides wallpaper music programming over the Net in three musical genres: Popular, Oldies, and Dance. The Netcast quality is very good. All the music is delivered in stereo, and you should have RealAudio 5.0. (ISDN users get a special link for better-quality audio over the higher bandwidth.) I like the fact that ON-AIR.com keeps it simple in all departments: the home page, which doesn't make you click around forever searching for the music, and the programming, which is easy to understand and always available. "The most music on the Net. Period," they say. It's probably true.

theDJ.com

www.thedj.com

Music programming: An Internet-only radio station of sorts, theDJ.com doesn't use announcers. The site is a preprogrammed playlist of musical selections in various genres. When you click the icon to start the station (after waiting an eternity for the graphic-loaded home page to display), a window opens that resembles a car radio with ten buttons; Ska, Mega BPMs, Modernmix, New Wave, Progressive, Psychadelic, Goodtunes, Trance, Smooth, and Awesome80's are the defaults. Clicking one of these buttons starts that playlist in RealAudio, with the delectable feature of displaying the artist and album name in the RealAudio window. (How I wish all Netcast stations had this feature.) The site presents the music in stereo, which works best in very high-speed connections, preferably over 28.8 Kbps. But wait — there's more! If you don't like the ten default categories, scroll beneath the buttons to find more than 60 other categories that you can use to replace one of the defaults. Interestingly, theDJ.com offers a special software program for listening without a browser or RealAudio, but downloading this program offers no apparent advantage.

Timecast

www.timecast.com

Comprehensive directory of RealAudio and RealVideo broadcast sites: RealAudio isn't the only media-streaming game in town, but it's far and away the most prevalent format for live audio (and video, in version 4.0) on the Web. Timecast is RealAudio's guide to streaming events — both live and archived — on the Net. The image-intensive directory includes three main sections: Live, Audio/Video Sites, and Radio/TV Stations. Browsing the site gives you an idea how the Web is struggling to become the successor to radio and television. Receiving video through regular modems is still a problem, but audio is definitely acceptable if you have a 28.8 Kbps or faster modem and version 3.0 or later of RealAudio. Many radio stations now simulcast on the Web, and television is following suit gradually. Timecast keeps its finger on the pulse and is the place to go when you want to know "what's on."

World Radio Network

www.wrn.org

Live international newscasts: World Radio Network is like having a short wave radio set in your computer. Talk about a global perspective! During any given day, you can hear live newscasts from countries all over the world, 24 hours a day. (Whaddya mean, you don't *want* to listen to Radio Netherlands at 3:00 in the morning?) General news, arts, culture, sports, and science are all areas the site covers at one time or another. The site also provides complete schedules of which programs, from which countries, are carried at the site. For people living abroad, World Radio Network is a great way to stay in touch, and for everyone else, it's an invaluable way of gaining a broad perspective on the news.

Other Stuff to Check Out

www.broadcast.com
www.king.org
www.tbn.org
www.virginradio.co.uk/radio.html

Compared to the high-tech image of cyberspace, books seem almost like antique anachronisms, dusty remnants of a previous era. But the truth is, the book industry in general is thriving, big bookstores are doing big business, more titles than ever are being published, and books are a fairly big topic of interest on the Net. These trends don't seem to reflect any danger that a computer monitor is on the verge of replacing the comforting, familiar bound book. How cozy is it to curl up in your favorite chair with your computer, scrolling through a book? About as cozy as sleeping on a large circuit board.

This section surveys Web sites that give general information about books and the book industry and book reviews, plus a few of the best author sites and a few literary e-zines.

248 Literature

Authors

Book authors are somewhat more amenable to participating in official Web pages about their work than other celebrities, especially movie stars. Even so, about half of the following sites are unofficial fan sites. Fans create these unauthorized tributes with the best of intentions and usually don't include reproductions of the authors' works. I certainly haven't included any copyright infringements here. Official sites generally afford e-mail contact with the author — though you may actually be writing to the author's publisher or agent. Unofficial sites don't have that feature, but they do provide background about the writer's life and work.

Unfortunately, I can't include *all* author sites without creating a book heavy enough for weight lifters. So I've included some of the most popular writers.

The Anne Rice Page

www.annerice.com

Anne Rice's official home page: It's official! The page, that is — it's not a fan site. How Anne Rice, who writes with astounding fertility of imagination and in such quantity, has time to answer letters on a Web page is beyond me. But respond she does. You also can get information about her upcoming projects and take an Anne's-eye-view tour of New Orleans (the setting of at least one of her most famous books). You aren't required to sign in unless you want to get on the mailing list.

Arthur C. Clarke Unauthorized Home Page

www.lsi.usp.br/~rbianchi/clarke

Respectful fan site devoted to the science-fiction author: The eloquent and respectful description of Arthur C. Clarke's work — "He is an author who takes an idea and drops it into a quiet pool of thought." — is an evocative justification of this almost reverent fan site. Arthur C. Clarke is one of the great science-fiction writers of the century, author of the classics *Childhood's End* and *2001: A Space Odyssey.* The site presents a biography, bibliography, and filmography, illustrated with photographs (probably as unauthorized as the text, but certainly used with the best of intentions). The creator of this page takes most of the material from the *authorized* biography, which he credits liberally. The site is a good overview of the man and his work. And the site isn't limited to English-speaking (or reading?) fans.

Danielle Steel

www.daniellesteel.com

Information on the author plus interview audio clips: The official Web presence of the best-selling author, Danielle Steel, this site takes a stab at being a well-rounded Internet attraction. Of course, the site promotes her books. The Meet Danielle Steel section is a mystifying one-paragraph rumination, presumably by the author, on a timely topic: I left wonderfully illuminated after learning she likes mariachi music on Father's Day. Having thereby gained an intimate acquaintance with Ms. Steel, you can move on to The Screening Room, an impressive list of the TV movies based on Danielle Steel novels. The site doesn't provide any TV clips. RealAudio interview clips are here, but they don't include any insightful biographical information.

James A. Michener

www.jamesmichener.com

Home page for the author: If you like the travel and destination writings of the late author James A. Michener, this is the site. Comprehensive but not exactly elegant, this site offers a complete chronological biography of the author's life, including release dates of his writings. You can browse photos and video clips filmed around the author's home in Texas. A See the World feature uses an interactive map to describe books that he has written on certain geographic areas. Perhaps the most interesting portion of the site is the collection of autobiographical stories written by the man himself.

Stephen King Web Site

members.aol.com/skingsite/index.html

Unofficial site of the bestselling author, with lots of pictures: This unauthorized tribute to the very prolific writer, Stephen King, is well intentioned and rich with material. The site makes at least one thing clear: Mr. King is not shy in front of a camera. The Media Gallery features a tremendous list of photographs of the writer at various ages, with his dog, on a motorcycle, at work in his office, and on and on. The same section offers audio clips of interviews, including a long *60 Minutes* dialogue. The site delivers the expected fan attributes: a biography, links to other sites, lists of King's work, reviews, and even an online crossword puzzle.

Book Reviews and News

This section lists the most prominent sites covering books in general, with news, reviews, and sometimes author interviews. General book sites usually aren't as elaborate as other types of Web publishing, such as sports sites or general news. Credit this trend, perhaps, to the book industry being somewhat threatened by the Internet, with its potential for copyright-smashing, bootlegging of published titles. But the fact is, you almost never see current fiction displayed on the Net, although technology makes it pretty easy to do so. The World Wide Web remains a place to read *about* books but not the books themselves.

Book Stacks Unlimited

www.books.com

Information, author interviews, and bookselling: Look at this site's URL. You'd think the *books.com* domain name belonged to Barnes & Noble or some other giant bookseller. In fact, it belongs to a local bookstore in Cleveland that had the foresight and pioneering spirit to establish an online site as early as 1992. With the catchphrase, "Your local bookstore — no matter where you live!" Book Stacks Unlimited obviously understands the essence of the Internet. Modeling the online site after all the services and niceties you find in big chain bookstores these days, Book Stacks Unlimited comes across as a folksy, friendly site that's surprisingly equipped with the latest multimedia gadgets. Audio programs feature author interviews and store updates. Yes, you can buy online, and the site has an ever-changing array of suggestions and new-release information on the right side of the page. The site even has a cafe with message board discussion groups. And Books Stacks Unlimited supports its online ordering by delivering to anywhere in the country.

BookPage Online

www.bookpage.com

Readers may contribute book reviews: BookPage is a book-review publication (printed and virtual) that wants to help you select books and learn more about their authors. Much of the Web site content is either original or an enhanced version of the printed reviews. In each monthly edition, the site usually offers over 50 reviews, plus an archived backlog of previous reviews. The write-ups are divided into categories and the reviews themselves are of moderate depth, sometimes including author interviews. BookPage Online invites readers to upload their own reviews for consideration.

Booktalk

www.booktalk.com

Publishing industry buzz: Many literature sites on the Web are governed by a conservative sensibility that seems to treat books as sacred objects, deserving the utmost gravity and serious consideration. Booktalk throws that attitude in the circular file cabinet with a gossipy, stylish raft of industry buzz. Divided into five main sections — Authors, Publishers,

Agents, Bookstores, and Slush Pile — the writing in this site's pages is a blend of advice to would-be writers, industry listings, and news. In the Agents area, for example, the page includes articles about how to obtain representation, and then it follows with a long list of agencies and contact information. The Slush Pile, in case you're wondering, is the catch-all section containing miscellaneous articles of interest. All aspiring writers should put Booktalk on their bookmark lists.

BookWire

www.bookwire.com

Publishing information plus a Web directory: BookWire recently upgraded its visual appeal without losing track of what makes the site important — content. BookWire is a one-stop resource to other literary sites on the Web as well as general information about the publishing industry. The best way to start digesting the sprawling content: Hit the BookWire Navigator link to see a site index. From the index, you can link to the *Publishers Weekly* bestseller lists, lists of booksellers and libraries, magazine and book-review sites, Soapbox message boards, and quite a bit more. Even updated, this site is no multimedia playground, but it's full of useful book info.

Independent Reader

www.independentreader.com/
  irhome.htm

Reviews supplied by bookstores: Book buying is both easier and harder than it used to be. Easier because the proliferation of large bookselling chains brings huge inventories of titles within reach of most towns in the United States. Harder because of the impersonal nature of those stores. Fast disappearing are the days when a trip to the bookstore meant exploring a relatively small collection handpicked by the proprietor of a local shop. The Independent Reader takes a stand for the old days, ironically using the most modern form of media: the World Wide Web. This site offers advice, short reviews, and recommendations from independent bookstores around the country. The result is a review site unaffected by the purely market-driven considerations of a large chain bookstore. Dozens of topic categories lead to short book reviews, some of well-known titles, but more of gems that may get lost in the mass marketplace shuffle. The reviews give ISBN numbers, so after consulting with your Web advisor, you can stroll into the local behemoth bookstore, grab a cappuccino, and special-order the book.

Internet Road Map to Books

199.165.129.36/index.html

Web directory to book sites: A fine literature directory, the Internet Road Map to Books is straightforward and text-oriented, dishing up a guide to book links around the Web. Although the organization of the site is informal rather than rigorous, you shouldn't have trouble finding valuable sites from this starting point. You can track down book-review sites, publishers, bookstores, and online editions of books. Some pages include keyword searching, and what the site lacks in elegance it makes up for in usefulness.

Publishers Weekly

www.publishersweekly.com

Online version of an industry bible: Publishers Weekly, the printed magazine, is a sort of bible for writers and publishers alike. (I keep my copies on an altar.) It reports on trends, statistics, and industry news in the publishing business. The Web site carries much of the printed content, sometimes enhanced, and in the case of the famous bestseller lists, the site posts them three days before they appear in the magazine. Those lists, in fact, are a core portion of Publishers Weekly; they're divided into genres and niches of publishing that enable you to see exactly what's selling best in which fields. The Publishers Weekly site is primarily of interest to people in the business, but for interested onlookers, it provides an insider's glimpse.

Other Stuff to Check Out

www.geocities.com/Athens/Delphi/7915
www.cs.cmu.edu/books.html
www.indolink.com/Book/index.html

Literary Magazines

The field of online literary publications is still very young. Something about reading literature from a computer screen goes against the grain of the editors and writers. Salon Magazine and Slate, both reviewed in this section, are pioneers in virtual territory, and The Missouri Review is an electronic edition of a printed literary journal.

Cortland Review

www.cortlandreview.com

Reading — and hearing — the author's voice: Ever read a great book and then gone to see the movie version, only to be disappointed? Not surprising, really.

252 Literature

Sometimes no one can convey the feelings and drama of poetry and fiction quite like the author. This delightfully sublime site publishes poetry and fiction (a rarity in itself) *and* enables you to read along with the authors by using RealAudio. To keep fans entertained between issues (three issues had been published in a little over half a year at the time of this writing), the editors of Cortland Review add monthly features and columns, including advice for would-be writers. Free registration is encouraged but not necessary, unless you want to join the chat rooms in the TCR Speakeasy section.

IndiaStar

www.indiastar.com

Book reviews from an Indian perspective: IndiaStar tells you right at the top of the page that it's a literary art magazine. And *that* IndiaStar is, with poems, fiction and nonfiction stories, fiction and nonfiction book reviews, and film and multimedia reviews. The topics, naturally, tend to be Indian in nature but not exclusively (one recently reviewed book was *The Inscrutable Americans*). The design is uneven — page displays aren't consistent from one article to the next, and occasionally you find an article with a couple of paragraphs that drift well beyond the margins of the rest of the piece — but the content is important. And given the recent

tension between India and Pakistan, this site can help people of all nations better understand the troubled region.

The Missouri Review

www.missouri.edu/~moreview/
main.html

Newly published fiction: The Missouri Review Web site is one of the best cyberplaces to read new fiction. Placing the contents of this marvelous journal on the World Wide Web is a service to netizens everywhere and should be rewarded with a bookmark and frequent visits. *The Missouri Review* holds an annual Editor's Prize contest, and the Web site archives current and previous winners in fiction, poetry, and essays. The result is an award-winning collection of some of the best unknown writers anywhere. The site also carries book reviews and interviews (recently featuring sound clips of a poet reading his own work), but they're only icing on the cake. The heart of *The Missouri Review* is the writing. Pour yourself a glass of sherry, settle into a cozy chair with a laptop (or better yet, print out the stories from your computer), and get reading.

Salon Magazine

www.salon1999.com

Literary articles: Salon Magazine, a Webzine for wry sophisticates, has gained fame for taking the idea of presenting literary values on the Net (who in the world thought of *that?*) to the logical next step of doing it well. Putting out at least two editions every week, Salon Magazine archives its past articles in a sensible, easy-to-find way; provides a search engine for finding stuff; and generally is up to speed with Web perks that most netizens expect from a major site. The literary content here ranges from political commentary to media hazing, movie reviews to book surveys — all dished up with style and breeding. Culture effectively becomes digital culture in Salon Magazine.

Science Fiction Weekly

www.scifi.com/sfw/

Sci-fi e-zine: Science Fiction Weekly is an e-zine produced by the Sci-Fi Channel, and it covers literary science fiction on an equal level with televised and cinematic expressions of the genre. Hit the Off the Shelf link first for book reviews; a recent visit uncovered a review of an installment in the Second Foundation Trilogy and *Antarctica* by Kim Stanley Robinson. The Classic Sci-Fi link often focuses on past-generation books and sometimes movies (from a literary viewpoint). News of the Week deals equally with literature and screenplays, as well as any other arenas where genre news occurs. No fiction, unfortunately, but the site recently reviewed and rated upcoming science-fiction games.

Slate

www.slate.com

Literary articles and columns: Slate is probably the most famous electronic-magazine experiment yet on the World Wide Web. Started by the Microsoft

Corporation with the famed Michael Kinsley as the editor, Slate enjoyed a publicity splash when it mounted its first issue on the Web and was immediately beset by technical problems and bad reviews. But time, perseverance, and backing off from pretension have worked their magic, and Slate is now generally considered one of the most literate, sophisticated offerings on the Internet — satirical jabs are usually somewhat respectful. The table of contents is stuffed with interesting articles, reviews, and ongoing dialogues that stretch from issue to issue. Learned commentary on current events, in the tradition of *The New Yorker,* is high on the agenda. One of my favorite features is the In Other Magazines link, a weekly rundown of the content in *TIME, Newsweek, The Economist, The New Yorker,* and others. The only problem: Now that Slate has established itself, the site is no longer totally free. To get at some of the more stimulating features, you'll have to subscribe, for a fee (about $20 annually). Too bad.

Other Stuff to Check Out

www.echonyc.com
www.execpc.com/~catrina/pen/
www.mala.bc.ca/~mcneil
www.randomhouse.com
www.writepage.com

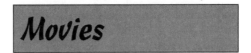

254 Movies

If you cast your eyes back over the entire history of the movie industry in the United States, you'll be overwhelmed by how many films have been made. I would guess at least a hundred — and that's just counting the number of movies Sean Connery has been in. The Internet is perfect for keeping track of Hollywood's prodigious productivity (try repeating that a few times). Movie databases have gotten so good and are so easy to use that I don't bother watching the credits at a theater. I just go home and look up the actors who played in the movie I just saw. But then I don't have much of a life. You'd probably prefer going out to a Starbucks after the show, sipping decaf cappuccino, nibbling a cranberry scone, and discussing the subtle derivations of Bruce Willis's newest performance. Fine, I'm not envious.

In addition to the databases, this section surveys movie studio Web sites, which tend to be elaborate exercises in self-congratulation, with graphics so heavy your computer is likely to fall through your desk. As a group, studio sites have a way to go before reaching a high level of entertainment value, but they're good places to get advance information about upcoming features as well as a sense of the stars as people.

Movie Databases, Directories, and Reviews

Making a movie is a complex venture: a collaboration of dozens of people plus the participation of an entire industry that promotes and reviews films. Movie databases track all the small cogs in the gigantic filmmaking industry, delivering the results to you in a highly searchable, easy-to-use format. (At least, the best of them do.) The following list includes some of the best databases, and getting in the habit of using them can really enhance your movie-going experience by making you more aware of all the forces that combine to create a film. In addition, you can learn a lot about the industry movers and shakers.

Academy of Motion Picture Arts and Sciences

www.oscars.org

Online home of the Academy Awards: I used to have a friend who could recite obscure facts about the Academy Awards, like who won the Oscar for Best Cinematography in 1953. The rest of us, who aren't blessed with such recall, can find every winner and lots of other wonderful facts about Hollywood's most important awards show at this online home of the AMPAS, the organization that presents the golden statuettes. The Academy Awards page includes a special page for the last Oscar ceremony, links to pages for the four prior ceremonies, and a searchable database of winners and nominees, wonderfully cross-indexed. The site even includes a list of where the ceremony has been held over the years. Information on the other AMPAS programs is also provided. And who did win the Oscar for Best Cinematography in 1953? Trick question. Two were given — one for a black-and-white film to Burnett Guffey for *From Here To Eternity,* and one for a color film to Loyal Griggs for *Shane.* Now if I can just find my friend's phone number. . . .

Boxoffice Online

www.boxoff.com

★ ★
★ ★

Reviews and articles: As King George XIV once said when his third wife bungee-jumped off the cliffs of France, "Wow."

That's exactly what I said when I saw the gorgeous home page of Boxoffice Online, and I'm not even a student of exclamatory European royalty. This site is the online edition of a print magazine of the same name, and although the splendid graphic that starts off the site isn't replicated on every page (thank goodness, or you'd have time to take up dangerous hobbies), the design is effective throughout, and the content is very worthwhile. Reviews and feature articles dominate the pages, and the virtual edition contains a three-year archive of reviews.

Cannes Film Festival

www.festival-cannes.com

Online site for French film event: Arguably the second-most coveted prize a film can win, after the Oscar for Best Picture, is the Golden Palm award at the annual Cannes Film Festival. I'm sure the French organizers would say that the Golden Palm is *the* top award, but I'll avoid that discussion. The French festival does have a top-notch Web site in French and English, which includes historical information on the festival and the winning films (justifying the site's inclusion in this category). But the site also includes a calendar of the festival's 12-day May run; travel information; information on the nominated films and others being featured; daily news updates during the festival; and video clips of some of the key festival moments, including press conferences, the red carpet ceremony, and the closing ceremony. (You'll need RealVideo and another server plug-in to watch, but download links are provided.) Best of all, you can enjoy the memories year-round, as the clips are left up well after the festival's close. Not a Golden Palm effort, but one well worth applause.

Cinemania

cinemania.msn.com

★★
★★

Great movie information: You have to like a site that headlines its gossip page with "pssst!" Cinemania is full of great design features, no-holds-barred reviews, articles about current and upcoming movies, and exclusive celebrity interviews. A site of The Microsoft Network (MSN), Cinemania is open to everyone, and you don't need an MSN membership. The stories are liberally embedded with hyperlinks to other pages that comprise an enormous database of anyone in the movie business that you can possibly think of (except maybe the assistant gaffer of *The Mole People*). Movie Times is an interesting feature for U.S. visitors that asks you to enter your zip code and tells you what's playing within a selectable number of miles from your residence. A great all-around movie site.

CineMedia

**ptd15.afionline.org/CineMedia/
    welcomes/hello.html**

Web directory to movie sites: A megadirectory to movie sites around the Web, CineMedia wastes no time connecting you to sites and takes the broadest possible approach to the subject of movies. You can enter a search keyword right from the home page or select the Browse link to see the directory categories. The subject divisions really cover the bases — ranging from Actors and

Video to Studios and Theaters, from Festivals to Production, and even finding a place for TV and Radio sites. The link lists themselves are extensive, to say the least. One hint: If you search for sites related to specific movies, under the Films directory category, often you end up with broken pages because many film-specific sites are taken down after the movie has enjoyed its theater run.

Film.com

www.film.com

Reviews and movie multimedia: This high-profile watering hole for movie buffs drags your modem through quicksand when delivering its pages, but the wealth of features makes the slow process worthwhile. (Maybe you can watch a video while surfing Film.com.) Reviews are the big attraction here, and a keyword search engine helps you find reviews of almost any flick you can think of. You can access current movies by using a drop-down menu, but beware of the site's strange logic. On my first visit, I called up the movie *Men in Black* and got a review of an entirely different movie. My second try worked fine, proving that movies exist in an alternate dimension. (Either they do, or I do.) The site recommends plug-ins, especially RealPlayer (RealAudio 5.0 that includes RealVideo) for viewing video clips.

Hollywood Online

www.hollywood.com

Movie information, especially soundtracks: I'm glad to see a movie site that gives soundtracks heavy play. Hollywood Online's MovieTunes section is a data-base of soundtrack selections, accessed by browsing or searching, and you can play some of the tracks through

RealAudio. The black-background, nuts-and-bolts site design makes you feel like you're in a movie vault, and in fact, that's pretty much what the Multimedia Library is — an archive of photos, sounds, videos, trailers, and production notes. Hollywood Online presents a variety of formats, and you may be able to get away without downloading any fresh plug-ins, although the site recommends Shockwave and Vxtreme. Hollywood Online mixes database services into a slick design with special skill and panache — one of the best movie database sites.

The Internet Movie Database

www.imdb.com

Everything you want to know about every movie: The Internet Movie Database (IMDb, as it's affectionately called by devotees) occupies a place of honor on most movie fans' bookmark lists. Having first gained attention for its revelations of film bloopers, the site now grabs atten-tion for its flexible search engine and its wonderful cross-referencing of all kinds of movie information. You can locate a movie by title or keyword, and you can find actors the same way. After you find your way to a movie, a large array of icons link to plot summaries, reviews, production notes, release schedules, financial information, and much more. The main page for each movie lists every person involved with the production from the director and leading actors to the assistant caterer in charge of keeping the ice cubes square — most names include links to dedicated pages giving that person's entire career history. You can angle into information by person, film title, or career niche. Always current and even forward-looking, IMDb covers movies from the first day of release (and sooner in some cases). You no longer have to be frustrated with peering through a milling theater to catch the credits. Just do what I do — look up the movie in IMDb when you get home.

Movie Guide

www.tvguide.com/movies/index.htm

Film information, reviews, and database searching: Movie Guide, part of the TV Guide Entertainment Network, is one of the best of these general movie sites at putting dazzling page design in a format that doesn't take all weekend to display. Some of the other movie sites give you time to run out and see a flick while their competitively resplendent pages struggle through your modem like sand through an hourglass. The Motion Picture site is pretty and reasonably fast. The site focuses on current movies — you can scroll down the home page, find the movie you're interested in, and click a RealVideo clip or the review. The movie listings include ratings and a somewhat snappy summary. Consider this intro to the review for Sandra Bullock's *Hope Floats:* "No, it sinks slowly." Ouch. If you want an older film, simply use the keyword search form at the top, which connects to a solid database.

Moviefinder.com

www.moviefinder.com

Find movies that correspond to your tastes: How would you like a Web site telling you which movies you do and don't like?

I didn't think so. Fortunately, Moviefinder. com isn't quite that presumptuous, but it does attempt to make intelligent (or at least lucky) recommendations of films based on what you teach the site about your tastes. Here's how the site's "We recommend" feature works. First, you must complete an utterly obnoxious registration process that should, in my cranky opinion, be banned from the Net. Don't try skipping any of the approximately one zillion questions; the site won't accept your membership until you answer 'em all. Sheesh. At least the site is free — nobody should have to pay for such registration torture. Anyway, after the sign-up is out of the way, you get to rate a selection of movies, and the site presumably gets the gist of your preferences, using that information for its recommendations. Alternatively, you can dump the recommendations entirely and use the built-in directory to search for a movie by genre, title, or rating. When you find a movie in the database, you get a serving of production data and a small review.

MovieLink

www.movielink.com/?UID:13001

Local movie schedules: MovieLink is the premier Web site for finding what's playing down the street, no matter where you live in the United States. It works by asking for your zip code and then remembering it every time you visit. Displaying a list of theaters in your region, MovieLink lists all the showings, and links to information about the movies. You can even buy tickets through the site for participating theaters. MovieLink doesn't work as elegantly as Cinemania (also reviewed in this section), a site that enables you to determine the distance to the theaters. But MovieLink shines in its flexibility, letting you search for a movie by theater, show time, title, or type of movie. The site fills in the gaps with a chat area, previews, trailers, and a merchandise store.

Other Stuff to Check Out

www.99lives.com/filmogs/index.htm
www.cinema-sites.com
www.moviesounds.com
www.movieweb.com
www.mybonbon.com/midi-go-round/
movie.htm

Screen Classics and Cults

One of the delights of film is its long legacy. Whether you believe that the golden age of moviemaking is upon us or is long gone, the past offers a rich repository of movies that were produced with different sensibilities than you see in modern theaters and that reflect the different eras of American life. The following sites celebrate past-era filmmaking in general or some single aspect of it.

American Movie Classics

www.amctv.com

Web site of the cable channel: If you have cable TV and you love classic movies, you probably know about the American Movie Classics channel, featuring nothing but one stroll after another down memory lane, occasionally throwing an odd documentary. The Web site promotes the

cable channel with information about the current star of the month, schedules, and so on, but the site offers enough original Internet content to warrant a bookmark. The Dressing Rooms area is especially diverting, featuring stories about legendary actors and actresses, presented almost as a detective story with embedded hyperlinks leading you from one page to the next. One problem: The site is attractive to look at but difficult to read, with white and sometimes olive text that's difficult to see against the black background.

The James Bond Movie Page

**www.dur.ac.uk/~dcs3pjb/jb/
jbhome.html**

All you need to know about 007: Prime info nugget: Half of the world's population has seen a James Bond movie — now that's what I call a cult following! This startling fact greets you right off as you enter The James Bond Movie Page, perhaps in self-justification, perhaps in mere glorification of Ian Flemming's suave detective who catches the imagination of so many. The site does a fine job of presenting the entire repository of Bond arcana in Web format: the movies, the women, the gadgets, the villains, the actors, and more. If you read no other page, read the Gadgets page.

Mining Co. Guide to Classic Movies

Classicfilm.miningco.com

Debate over and learn about the classics: As with the several dozen sites offered by the Mining Co., this page focuses on one topic and serves as a destination and a gateway to other sites. The site offers "In the Spotlight" features, which recently included "Classic Doomsday Movies," "A Tribute to Frank Sinatra" (who had just died), and "A Tribute to Bob Hope" (who was still alive enough to joke about the rumors of his demise). The stories aren't deep and certainly won't pass for any in-depth film-school research paper, but they're friendly and informative, and full of links to the movies mentioned. You also can search for Internet links in more than two dozen categories and participate in bulletin-board and chat-session discussions.

The Palace

www.moderntimes.com/palace

Hollywood's golden era plus B Movies: A site dedicated to Hollywood's so-called Golden Era, The Palace is a sober, multimedia-rich collection of material that's fun to browse even for casual admirers of past-generation moviemaking. Particularly welcome is the B-Films section because *bad* (pathetically low-budget but often surprisingly resourceful) movies don't receive much representation on the Net. The Midnight Ramble section (about Black Hollywood) is likewise enlightening, and the Great Women gallery is another way the site displays its scholarly and studious inclination. The Palace sorts photo images by decade. The handful of audio clips don't amount to much because they're formatted with such good fidelity that the files are huge, and the site doesn't use RealAudio, so listening takes too long. But the rest of the site is a fine project indeed.

Vintage Hollywood

www.geocities.com/Hollywood/Studio/ 5217/

Nostalgic view of Hollywood: Ooh, nice home page — at least, after you scroll down below the very large ads. (The same bad design afflicts several pages.) The Hollywood Home of the Stars Tour is a good link to start with — it's a postcard-style picture tour of the people and neighborhoods of one of the world's most glamorous neighborhoods in the 1940s. The Salute to Katharine Hepburn is also worthwhile, as is the Vintage Hollywood Site Directory. Vintage Hollywood isn't going to win any design awards, but the pages are fun to browse even when they're clunky.

Other Stuff to Check Out

www.call-us.demon.co.uk/cary.html
www.filmsite.org/genres.html

Studios

Movie-studio sites tend to be absolutely gorgeous and include content that doesn't live up to their designs. In other words, gear yourself for some disappointment. Naturally, the studio sites don't promote movies from other studios. And because most people don't keep track of which studio makes which movie, browsing studio sites can be a frustrating way to look up your favorite flick. Use the movie databases to find specific films, and check out the studio sites for beautiful graphics and advance information about upcoming movies, sometimes including video clips. In this section, I've gathered the sites representing the largest Hollywood studios, plus a few not-so-large studios that have interesting pages.

MGM

www.mgmua.com

Spectacular studio site: Metro Goldwyn Mayer (MGM) has a great studio Web site. Of course, the pages may take all night to display because most of the studio Web palaces try to outdo each other with graphic intensity. The site makes a play for community by providing message boards, with chat rooms under construction at the time of this writing.

You find both forums in the Club section, which is the best place to escape (partially) the relentless studio promotions. MGM doesn't require you to register, but the lure of winning contest prizes encourages you to fork over your demographic info.

Miramax Cafe

www.miramax.com

Great graphics and celebrity information: Miramax is the movie studio that's well known for high-quality mainstream films (like *Good Will Hunting* and *Bullets Over Broadway*) produced with relatively inexpensive budgets that are only slightly larger than the gross national product of small nations. Miramax does a good job making self-promotion jazzy and fun. The More News Not Fit to Print section sounds like a gossipy news area for the movie industry, but — surprise! — all the news relates to Miramax movies and stars. The Concession portion looks interesting — that is, if you crave Miramax-related merchandise. Okay, the site is a shameless advertisement, but what studio site isn't? At least Miramax has great graphics and posts a more personal brand of celebrity information, such as interviews, than many other sites. Now, if the Miramax folks would only learn that dark backgrounds and dark text are hard to read. . . .

Sony Pictures Online

www.spe.sony.com

Major studio's online site: Sony Pictures realizes that in order to attract people to a studio Web site, you need to provide something more fun than the usual "Look how great we are" rundown of Oscar nominations and movie posters. Although Sony Pictures Online has its share of self-congratulation, the site squeals *fun* right from the start and makes finding your way around easier by providing several different paths through the maze of pages. A good multimedia setup helps, as well as having time to spare watching pages display their terrific graphics — talk about fun! Sony Pictures Online manages to avoid much of the pomposity that afflicts some other studio sites.

Twentieth Century Fox

www.foxhome.com

Information and clips: The Twentieth Century Fox movie studio and Fox TV network merge their resources and properties in this sprawling, egotistical, hidden-gem type of site. The site has a self-congratulatory tone to it and certainly rests on its laurels — actually, it does have substantial laurels upon which to rest. The site highlights the past year's movies too prominently, but the decade-by-decade History of Fox is interesting and even too brief. Given the "keeping up with the Joneses" attitude that pervades Hollywood, it's not surprising that the site recently added an online store. You can also download a screen saver, search the site, view upcoming movie hype, and read press releases.

Universal Pictures

www.universalstudios.com/
universal_pictures/

Production notes, photos, and clips: Don't attempt to view this site if you have an imminent plane to catch. You can build your own aircraft in the time it takes to display these pages. Nevertheless, coolness reigns at the Universal Pictures site, which serves mostly to promote current movies. Pick a movie, and the site treats you to several pages of production notes, still photos, video clips, star biographies, and sometimes a game or contest based on the movie. The graphics are good, but the waiting is wearying — what else is new at a studio site?

Warner Brothers

www.movies.warnerbros.com/
main.html

Information and movie previews: Primarily promotional, the Warner Brothers movie site redeems itself with its heavy and innovative use of streaming multimedia. You really need a battery of plug-ins for this site to come alive, but of course, they're all free downloads, with the site supplying links to them. During a recent visit, a live video Webcast from the set of *Lethal Weapon 4,* just released during this writing, was featured on the site. Furthermore, the previews of current releases enliven your browser to full effect with the Macromedia Flash plug-in. The black page design creates the feeling of being in a darkened movie theater, and all the video clips help sustain the illusion.

Other Stuff to Check Out

www.disney.com/DisneyPictures/index.html
www.flf.com
www.trimarkpictures.com

Music

Music lovers take note: The Web is now a very musical cyberspace. Music was a popular topic on the Net even before audio files were so easy to listen to, and now that RealAudio and other *streaming* formats are so simple to use, music is playing through logged-on computers everywhere.

If music is one of your big Net interests, I recommend getting RealAudio for your browser before diving into these sites. The basic version of the RealAudio plug-in is a free download, and you can upgrade later to a fancier version that costs a bit of money. Go to this URL to download either version: www.real.com.

RealAudio enables you to hear music clips (if they're RealAudio files) without downloading them first. Just click the sound file on a Web page, and the music streams through your computer's sound card.

This section directs you to many kinds of music sites but not to classical music, which I cover in the "Culture" section, earlier in this part.

Directories of Music on the Web

Because music is such an enormous topic on the Internet, you may need help finding your way around the thousands of musical sites. In this section, I gather the best music-specific Web directories. Using these sites is a great way to discover the Net locations that will eventually become your favorite bookmarks.

Charts All Over the World

www.lanet.lv/misc/charts

International music charts: For the truly adventurous music-loving, statistic-minded netizen, Charts All Over the World is an irresistible, if arcane, bookmark. The site is a single l-o-n-g page, listing music chart sources for music all over the world. Putting a new spin on the meaning of *world music,* this site is awesome in its relentless thoroughness. Have you ever lain awake at night, wondering what song is number one in Estonia? Distracted at work because you can't put your hands on the dance chart for a local Slovakian radio station? Hankering for a quick glance at the Hungarian radio playlists? Now you know where to go — Charts All Over the World provides links for all those and hundreds more. A quick warning: Most of the links from this page go to international servers, so expect delays.

Internet Music Resources

www.siba.fi/Kulttuuripalvelut/
   music.html

Musical Web links: The Sibelius Academy of Finland established itself a few years ago as a powerful music presence on the Internet. Specializing in cataloging and delivering musical information, one of its main Web sites is Internet Music Resources, a terrific guide to what's on the Web, musically speaking. You may think that classical music is the order of the day, but that's far from the whole truth. Categories of links in this directory include Music Magazines; Computer Music, MIDI, and so on; Rock and Pop; Jazz and Blues; and Instruments. Each category link leads to a reliable international list of interesting sites. Music libraries and music education receive special attention in the directory. The site is simple and quick to use.

Musical Web Connections

www.columbia.edu/~hauben/music/
   web-music.html

Massive lists of music links: Musical Web Connections is a little old but still one of the greatest music link sites you'll ever encounter, as long as you don't mind the complete lack of graphics or presentation pizzazz. This site is nothing more than a list — an enormous, classified list of music sites on the Web. The list previously resided on a single Web page that took several minutes to load into a browser; now, due to viewer demand, the site breaks down its list on various pages according to categories. Each category is an unorganized list, without even the benefit of alphabetization. Musical Web Connections is a browser's paradise, but if you want to find something in particular, hit the search link to explore the entire megalist by using keyword searching.

Sites & Sound Links

www.servtech.com/public/koberlan

Musical Web directory for musicians: "Music Resources For Musicians" — that's what you see when you enter Sites & Sounds Links. Although the graphically intense Web site doesn't contain much of interest to the recreational music lover looking for entertainment value, Sites & Sounds Links is a treasure trove for musicians, both amateur and professional. Basically a directory of music resources on the Web, categories include MIDI Files, Music Electronics, Music Marketplace, Music Software, Recording Studios, Record Labels, and Samples/ Patches. You can choose between a framed and no-frames version, but even the frames path moves quickly. Sites & Sound Links has been up and running for almost two years, and musicians hope the site continues for a long time to come.

Ultimate Band List

www.ubl.com

Find Web sites of bands: The folks at Ultimate Band List (UBL) don't call it *ultimate* for nothing. The UBL database is so massive that the search for any one band is broken down into a few steps. At this site, your ultimate goal is to find all the resources on the Web about a band or artist. Start by clicking a letter of the home page alphabet, or if you know the name you're looking for, just type it in the search keyword entry form. When you arrive at the page for that artist, the site provides links to relevant Web sites, along with brief descriptions of them. I can't exaggerate the importance of those descriptions and how they distinguish the Ultimate Band List from more generic directories that provide only raw lists of links. Knowing a bit about a site *before* linking (or not linking) to it saves time

and makes surfing more fun. Whether the UBL database of artist links is complete is impossible to know. But I can't believe anyone wouldn't be satisfied by all the choices, which include bands and radio station links from a number of countries. Ultimate Band List is the place to start when you're looking for a band on the Internet.

Unfurled

www.unfurled.com

★ ★
★ ★

New, hyped music directory: Unfurled is a hip new major music site on the Web. A collaboration of MTV and the Yahoo! World Wide Web directory, Unfurled grabs the universe of musical Internet locations by the neck and attempts to tame it into an Internet music directory. Successfully? Partially. The site is sort of a cross between a directory and a Web magazine. Whether this new venture attains its goals in every respect, so soon after its birth, is not necessarily the point. All music-loving netizens should instantly add this site to their bookmark list for the many things it *does* do better than ever before. Then they can watch it mature and improve over time.

The top directory level comprises five broad topic areas — Smarty Rants, Encyclomedia, Gossip Gossip Gossip, Totally Wack, and Riffs Online — and the next level down contains only five or six links in each category. You can hardly consider such an anemic level of content to be a directory at all, but the chosen sites (presumably chosen with extraordinary care) are excellent, and the reviews are entertaining. To be fair, snuggled down in the lower left of the pages (and near the bottom of the home page) are some clickable unreviewed topic headers, including Labels, Mags, Tours, Charts, Genres, and others. These categories lead to long lists of unreviewed links. On every second-level page, the site presents a clickable alphabet — what could it be for? A little experimentation reveals that the letters comprise a gateway to a separate artist directory. Having stumbled on to the artist directory, and perhaps realizing, as I did, that it's the finest feature of the whole site, you may wonder why Unfurled doesn't highlight it a bit more.

One problem is that some of the news needs updating. On a recent visit, I found the Release Calendar to be two *months* out of date. Talk about yesterday's news! Still, Unfurled's flag has only recently been set snapping in the virtual breeze. Considering the scope of the project and the corporate partners involved, it's bound to keep improving.

Other Stuff to Check Out

www.musicmap.com
www.music-on-line.com
www.stl-music.com/hub.html
www.theinfoguide.com

General Music and News Sites

General music sites present news of the recording industry, concert information, album reviews, and thick layers of style and attitude. Some sites emphasize multimedia (streaming audio, mainly) more than other sites that concentrate on news. The Web represents rock music better, by a long shot, than any other genre, but I include a couple of great jazz and country sites. Live Internet simulcasts of concert events is one of the more exciting recent developments that you sometimes find on these sites.

The Blue Highway

thebluehighway.com

History of, and tribute to, the blues: A romantic attitude about the rich history of the blues pervades The Blue Highway with good writing, plenty of listings and links, and even a shopping opportunity. In fact, why not cut right to the chase and go shopping first? Hit the Blues Mall button for a list of online shopping venues more or less related to blues music or culture. From lithographs to home-brewed beer, from collectibles to a map of blues musicians, the Blues Mall offers the most quirky excuses to exercise your credit card that you're likely to find on the Net. Having purged your spending impulses, go back to the home page and try the Blue Highway button for essays and tributes to the masters of the blues. RealAudio Blues Links features radio listings and links, and The Gutbucket is a virtual dumping ground for miscellany that doesn't fit elsewhere in the site. Humor and reverence make an odd mix, but if you have a taste for down-home music, perhaps the melancholy-yet-exalted character of this site will appeal to you.

Festivals.com

www.festivals.com

Information on music festivals: Festivals.com's mission is simple: Deliver information about gatherings around the world. A combination online magazine and directory, the home page is dominated by headlined stories about festivals — recently, for example, the 95th anniversary celebration planned by Harley-Davidson enthusiasts in the birthplace and home of that classic American motorcycle line, Milwaukee, Wisconsin. Click one of the links across the top of the page to see similar stories on Arts, Music, Children, Sports, and Motor festivals. Seem U.S.-centric? Well, many of the stories are, but don't give up. Clicking the world map brings up a search page with three basic ways to search: by clicking on another world map until you arrive at your area of choice; by searching for a festival by name; or by seeking all the registered festivals in a given country at a given time. Want to know about festivals in South Africa in September? Festivals.com can help you. Too bad English is the only language available. Still, as more festivals register, this site will become even more valuable. By the way, if you're a music lover in the United States, check out Festival.com's sister site, Festival Finder (Festivalfinder.com).

Great American Country

www.countrystars.com

Tribute to country music and its stars: Like the music it represents, Great American Country is lean, down-to-earth, and straight to the point. The site is attractive, yet unburdened by extra graphics or multimedia gadgets that would only slow it down. The main features include a country stars section with biographies and background career information; a concert info area, streamlined to give you dates and locations on a per-artist basis for all the current country music tours; a top-40 list; some photo pages; and a feedback section. Great American Country also includes links to other country sites. The photo albums could be better organized, and they're mainly publicity shots, not candid or live photos.

But you find lots of them, and the pics are reproduced very well on the site. Great American Country is the real deal for fast information about country music.

iMusic News Agent

imusic.interserv.com/newsagent

Music headlines and news: iMusic News Agent doesn't write a word of original reporting. The site functions as a gather-and-sort Internet agent, continually collecting and categorizing news headlines from other Net sources and presenting them in a centralized, coherent fashion. This site is sort of a *Reader's Digest* of hard news affecting the music industry. Dividing music news into five areas — Music, Industry, Label, Celebrity, and Movies — iMusic manages to be comprehensive yet concise, and include a smattering of non-music entertainment news. The Reviews link to the side offers CD reviews from Addicted to Noise (also reviewed in this section) and other sources. The front page is a marvel of clarity, despite the tremendous number of news options it wields. Expanding out a bit from pure music, entertainment and movie headlines also provide links. The site maintains an alphabetical scheme by source, except for the very useful Top Stories portion of each category. Whenever you click a headline link, the site takes your browser on a side trip to the Web source carrying the story, which is perhaps grounds for a small complaint — the site would be better if iMusic licensed the stories and carried them on their own very efficient server. But who am I to tell the folks at iMusic how to run their business? iMusic News Agent is incredibly useful exactly as it is.

Internet Underground Music Archive

www.iuma.com

Unknown bands: Internet Underground Music Archive (nicknamed IUMA) is the Internet watering hole for people whose thirst for new, independently produced music can't be slaked. Independent music, known as *indie music,* constitutes an underground movement of bands and solo artists creating original (or derivative), brilliant (or boring), and progressive (or regressive) music that's hard to market in today's corporate pop hit machine. IUMA is the online hangout for indie music and its fans, and the site's presence is growing stronger as its features expand. Currently, you can browse among IUMA's member bands, most of which include audio clips in their listings. RealAudio and Liquid Audio plug-in links are offered. You can sample and then buy albums online, but that's passé. IUMA's Liquid Lounge now enables you to buy and download songs straight to your computer. You need Liquid Audio to take advantage of this feature. The site also highlights indie record labels. If you love new music, you need to know about this site, and if you're new to the indie scene but have a taste for sonic adventure, try IUMA as an experimental bookmark.

Note: Liquid Audio files aren't easily transferable to other media, so you're limited to playing them on your computer unless you can somehow hook your computer up to your stereo to record them. On the other hand, you sometimes can get music on the Web first, because some bands release music over the Internet before their CDs hit the stores.

Jazz Online

www.jazzonline.com

Jazz for the beginner: Jazz Online is smooth, streamlined, simple, and probably fits other adjectives that don't begin with the letter *S.* Especially suitable for the less experienced jazz listener, Jazz Online guides you through newly released music without assuming you know a thing about jazz, refusing to categorize the music according to academic divisions like mainstream, fusion, or be-bop. Instead, the site uses evocative expressions like "In the mood" or "Groovin'," which may turn off veterans but give novices a reassuring understanding of what they're getting into. Feature stories are educational as well. Jazz Online emphasizes recorded jazz; it announces and reviews new releases and classic reissues, with a kind of *joie-de-studio* that makes you want to rush to your local jazz record shop. Because most towns don't have a jazz record shop, Jazz Online conveniently links to CDnow, the online CD store, so you can vent your credit card. Jazz Online is a breath of fresh air in the smoky world of online jazz.

MTV Online

www.mtv.com

The music channel online: MTV doesn't compete with itself by trying to play music videos effectively over the Net, which wouldn't be successful over most Internet connections. Instead, it uses just the right amount of multimedia technology to deliver a blend of news, program guides, enhancements to the television content, and live events. Headlines, feature stories, and music chart updates comprise the News portion — to browse through the backdated archives, click Gallery (although the link is misnamed). The Unplugged area (on the Tubescan page), representing one of MTV's most popular features, is a warehouse full of information, including sound files and video clips, some of which the channel never aired. Videos are in QuickTime format, which plays automatically through most modern browsers after a download period.

Those of you in Europe will probably be glad to know that MTV Europe has a page (`www.mtveurope.com`). Just don't tell your parents you heard it from me.

Music Previews Network

www.mpmusic.com

Listen before you buy: Compact disc (CD) collectors benefit from the listening stations at large CD outlets, which enable buyers to preview new releases before buying them. Music Previews Network furnishes an online version of the same idea, catering not only to its customers' desire to make informed purchases but also to a variety of computer configurations. This site fully supports RealAudio as well as other listening formats — using RealAudio is probably your best bet if your browser contains the RealAudio plug-in. (The plug-in is a free download.) In fact, Music Previews Network supports versions 2.0 *and* 3.0 of RealAudio, as well as WAV and MPEG file formats. This audio stuff is all very technical, but it basically means that you should be able to hear some music clips no matter what software you're using. Every album previewed on this site enjoys a three-minute treatment of excerpts, accompanied by a bit of spoken introduction and a one-paragraph on-screen text summary of the CD's style and personnel. The trade-off

for such lavish audio treatment is that the site doesn't preview very many albums by record-store standards. Still, a good cross-section of music is here, broken down by musical genre, plus specialty lists such as *Billboard* charts. Needless to say, you can purchase any CD with a credit card, right through the Web site.

N2K

www.n2k.com/index.html

Commercial, yes, but cool: N2K represents a growing trend on the Internet — a comprehensive site that offers three genre-based music channels and what N2K claims is the world's largest online music store. In short, N2K wants to win you over with the music and then sell it to you. But what sets this site apart from other online shopping services (touched on in Part V) are the three music channels — Jazz Central Station, Rocktropolis, and Classical Insites. You can access all three from the N2K site, and all three are worth the trip. For example, take a quick visit to Jazz Central Station. Right at the top are four track links — Jazz Journey (covering interesting items about the history of jazz), Jazz Talk, Recommended Listening, and Voice Your Opinion. Jazz Journey is particularly cool; the feature during my visit was a multipage rundown of jazz's "Third Stream," a post–World War II movement that sought to integrate some classical music elements with jazz. At the end of the journey was a test. Just kidding. Actually, the site ended with relative sound samples. You can buy stuff, link to related Web sites, look up individual musicians, search the site, track down record companies on the Net, and much more. Sure, N2K is a commercially based venture, but window shopping here is a lot of fun.

Pollstar

www.pollstar.com/

★★
★★

Who's playing when and where: Many entertainment sites cover concert tours as part of the news fare they dish up. Pollstar's agenda is to provide the most comprehensive music tour information on the Web, and nothing else. Pollstar is a bookmarkable site for anyone who likes attending live music events. A few thousand performing artists and several thousand live events are catalogued in what's described as "The Internet's most accurate, comprehensive, and up-to-date concert tour database." Does Pollstar live up to its own hype? It certainly throws a lot of information in your face from the moment you enter the site. The site's a bit confusing, in fact, but here's the deal: Start up top with the upper frame of the site, which doesn't change as you roam around. It contains a searching interface that encourages you to type in an artist, city, or venue. (Too bad you can't specify two out of three — that would save some hassle.) A search results page enables you to narrow down the search by entering desired dates. One way or another, you end up with a list of performers and the venues where they're appearing. Both the artist and the venue (concert hall or nightclub, in most cases) are hyperlinked to further information — artist information specifies other upcoming venues, and venue information includes upcoming artists.

The Recording Academy

www.grammy.com

Online home of the GRAMMY Awards: Perhaps better known by its full name — the National Academy of Recording Arts and Sciences, Inc. (NARAS) — The Recording Academy site is a subtle salute to the music industry. Subtle, because on the visual design scale, the NARAS site is

more like Bach than Van Halen. Anyway, the site has everything of interest to NARAS members, from organization activities and joining information, to news updates about things that affect the industry. One of the best sections is InForum, a collection of articles by those who have "made it" to help inspire those who haven't. And, of course, the site has everything you'd like to know about the GRAMMY Awards, including Webcasts during the show (near the end of February). Oddly, I wasn't able to find any sound files available during my visit.

Rock Online

www.rockonline.com

Relatively mellow rock 'n' roll site: Having garnered its share of awards, Rock Online remains satisfied with a fairly staid presentation, compared to digital palaces like N2K's Rocktropolis and Jazz Central Station. Dark backgrounds, modest logos, and clear page layouts give your crossed eyes a break from the graphical shenanigans of the more ambitious page layouts currently in vogue. Hey, who says a site isn't worthwhile if it doesn't initiate dyslexia in the viewer? Rock Online is content with message boards (you must register to use them), a couple of feature stories, and a handful of channels devoted to indie labels, college radio, and chat rooms. The site's attitude attempts grunginess occasionally, but a sweet and helpful core shines through. The site isn't *baaaad,* but it's not bad, either. Give it a try when you're in a mellow mood.

rockhall.com

www.rockhall.com

★★
★★

The music museum, online: The Rock and Roll Hall of Fame puts virtual reality to great use at its Web site, rockhall.com. The home page shows the Hall, located in Cleveland, Ohio, and displays head shots of honorees (Ray Charles, Janis Joplin, Jimi Hendrix) flashing against the building along with the year of their induction. You also can get visitor's information, making the site a good resource if you're planning to make the trip. Armchair travelers can tour exhibits, peruse a list of 500 songs that defined rock, and — best of all — read extensive information sheets about all the inductees and hear their music clips through RealAudio and other formats. For anyone who grew up on rock and roll, this site is a blast to prowl through.

SonicNet

www.sonicnet.com

★★ ★★ 🎤 ✍

Live concert simulcasts on the Web: You can easily say that SonicNet sacrifices coherence for classy design, but I'm not sure it's a complaint. A Web site has a certain appeal when it forces you to browse and explore the site to learn what's in it. Even this newly redesigned SonicNet site forces you to poke around a bit; the animations and ads, while entertaining, don't help much. The site focuses on three main areas, all linked to the front page (way over there on the left — yeah, those colorful little buttons). The News site offers daily music reporting and

features. The Guide site serves as a guide to music sites around the Web. But if you have a 28.8 Kbps connection, the RealPlayer plug-in, and a taste for Internet adventure, go to the Station link. SonicNet offers Radio SonicNet, In Concert, and The Streamland Preview Channel. SonicNet aims at a young audience and ravenous Net browsers.

VH1

www.vh1.com

Modest online version of the cable channel: One of the growing complaints about the VH1 cable channel is that it doesn't play much music anymore. Well, you have to hunt to find the music on the VH1 Web site, too. The best site for fans is the inside VH1 page, which features the channel's artist of the month, events, and interviews, with video clips for most. The Score is VH1's online magazine, with good features and coverage. The disc-o-tech (the online store venture with CDnow) was still being developed during my visit, and the site even sent me to Music Boulevard once, not CDnow. Then there's the Links page. No matter what you find on the page or how it's put, the page is about links. During my recent visit, the Retro flat out asked the question, "What ever happened to the 1980s all-girl band The Bangles?" So I clicked, expecting the cable network that brings me "Pop-Up Videos" to tell me, duh, what happened to the 1980s all-girl band The Bangles, or at least send me to one specially chosen site that answers the question. Instead, I got page 2 of the VH1/Lycos search engine results on "bangles." (Not even the first page of results.) The first entry on the page I got was "Beads, Baubles, and Bangles by Mrs. B." Interesting baubles but nothing about girl guitarists.

WILMA: The Internet Guide to Live Music

www.wilma.com

Concert and touring information: WILMA is an Internet legend among musicians. A Jetsons-type persona, she enables you to find touring information — concert and venue listings — through the Search-O-Matic live music database. The Search-O-Matic is brilliantly designed; it invites you to enter an artist, city, or venue and de-livers cross-referenced results so you can zip back and forth between a band playing in a certain club to that club's entire schedule for the next month. My only com-plaint: WILMA is a bit slow. The searches take too long, but they're worth the wait.

Other Stuff to Check Out

bspaa.com/newscenter/newscenter.html
www.imusic.com
www.jamtv.com
www.musicnewswire.com
www.sonicstate.com

Music Publications

From online editions of music trade magazines to Web-only electronic publica-tions, this section covers the best of music periodicals. These e-zines sometimes carry the same sort of news as the sites in the previous section, Music Directories, but generally their informational focus is on articles and columns. The Web sites usually enhance the online editions of print magazines, such as *Rolling Stone,* by offering search engines for browsing archived articles and back issues.

Addicted to Noise

www.addict.com

Rock and alternative music: Thankfully, Addicted to Noise gives you a choice of Hi-Fi (lots of pictures, slower to display) and Low-Fi (more text, faster). The site bails you out if you mistakenly choose Hi-Fi with a regular modem by splashing a big Low-Fi link on the Hi-Fi home page to lead you to the right track. Did you follow that discussion? Here's the deal: Unless you have a 28.8 Kbps connection, an ISDN line, or cable Internet access, choose Low-Fi. It saves you the trouble of watching your nails grow while the Hi-Fi page is loading. Addicted to Noise covers the cutting-edge rock and alternative scenes with a comprehensive irreverence that makes this the site to keep for cutting-edge music stylishness. As you would expect, feature stories, columns, and reviews are present, but the core attraction of Addicted to Noise is Radio ATN — an Internet rock-and-roll radio station. Oddly, this virtual station includes no *real-time* programming, but it does produce shows and then archives them for random access on the Net. Just hit the Radio ATN link for a guide and make sure you have RealAudio 3.0 or Shockwave plugged into your browser. (The RealAudio performance from this site is exceptionally smooth and trouble-free.) The mission of Addicted to Noise is apparently to get you addicted to its site, and it works.

Billboard Online

www.billboard.com

Music industry newspaper: Billboard is a trade newspaper for the music industry, and Billboard Online replicates most of the press releases and trade reports that you find in the printed edition. The renowned *Billboard* charts — setting the standard of success for albums, singles, country, and R&B recordings — appear on the site in their entirety and offer a good reason to bookmark the site. Conforming to the lean style of *Billboard,* the Web site doesn't waste time with superfluous graphics or multimedia fluff. Although much of the site's content is free for everyone, Billboard Online offers two subscription plans for deeper access.

New Music Express

www.nme.com

Music news and gossip: New Music Express takes a floodwater approach to delivering music news and gossip, pouring out text like a raging river. The site has recently been redesigned, simplifying the look without losing its Web-grunge style visual edge. The top news stories of the day take up most of the home page, with links down the side. One interesting feature: Some of the links reveal definitions when you point your mouse at them. I think I could have figured out that Reviews carries "Reviews and CD Sales," but I applaud the site for trying to improve workability for the readers. The site still carries record reviews, tour dates, charts, and gossip. RealAudio clips are available with many reviews. New Music Express is a good mix of music information — let it wash over you like a cool stream.

Rolling Stone Network

www.rollingstone.com

Music articles and reviews: Rolling Stone Network, the online edition of the landmark music magazine, is a dizzying Rube Goldberg array of spinning logos, shifting pictures, and darting icons. The front page is dizzying, anyway, and then things settle down after you get inside. My advice is to start with the News page, a self-contained Web publication with its own editorial staff. Features and columns are representative of the solid and only slightly daring music journalism found in the printed version, and the site's best feature is Random Notes Daily, which is, of course, updated every day. If you want samples from the actual magazine, click The Magazine, but the site has plenty of other things to keep you occupied. The Video page offers RealPlayer videos that you can play when you want, while the Radio page offers streaming Pop Hits, Modern Rock, or New Wave to your desktop. The Gallery is a good use of computer space, featuring concert pics and *Rolling Stone* covers, and you can keep up with the latest Performance news (where you can learn about Webcasts) and Recordings news. Not to be outdone, Rolling Stone Network also offers you numerous opportunities to purchase music through links to CDnow.

Vibe

www.vibe.com

Online edition of the magazine: Vibe is concerned with more than just music — it's a magazine of image, lifestyle, and attitude. The Web site incorporates *Vibe* magazine and surrounds it with added features. The home page leers out at you with garish impact, and the links are way too small (see those itty-bitty words on the left side of the graphic?). But don't be turned away; after you get past the home page, the site's sensibilities settle down to a level of stylish interest, without ever treading across the line of bad taste. Vibewire is the site's news department, but the daily news updates extend beyond the music field, making the pages take nine years to load. (Well, maybe only eight years, but that's still too long.)

Wall of Sound

www.wallofsound.com

News and reviews: Wall of Sound is one of the most balanced music sites on the Web. The balance is between information and design, substance and style, clarity and élan. News headlines, album reviews, release notes of upcoming recordings, feature articles, interviews, and charts share space without cluttering the site. Wall of Sound presents stories with just enough pictures and a sprinkling of listening opportunities by way of RealAudio. Interviews are off the beaten path, well conducted, and archived for future browsing. Wall of Sound is a model of what an intelligent-yet-hip music site can be. The intelligent, hip thing for you to do is bookmark it.

Other Stuff to Check Out

www.mayo-ireland.ie/irishmusic.htm
www.rockrgrl.com
www.singout.org

Personalities

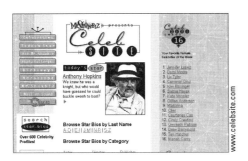

The Internet isn't only about information — real, breathing people are behind the data. Well, at least you find information *about* people. The personalities that inhabit the entertainment world — celebrities of movies, television, music, even politics — don't often make themselves available through the World Wide Web. If they do surf the Net, they do so incognito, probably appreciative of the built-in anonymity. E-mail addresses for the stars of film, stage, and concert are very hard to come by. But that doesn't stop people from trying. This section is devoted to Web-based attempts to crack the privacy of celebrities by way of e-mail, Web site, or postal address. The following directories are often created by fans who take celebrity contact as a kind of manic hobby and like to share the results of their research.

You need to remember a couple of things about sites that offer celebrity addresses. First, they tend to be personal sites, created by fans rather than industry organizations like studios, agencies, or — perish the thought — actual famous people. Although the lists in these sites are produced with the best of intentions, they don't carry any authority. The second point, which is related to the first point (but unrelated to the third point, which I haven't thought of yet), is that many of the addresses represent agencies, studios, and post office boxes; in other words, you won't get a hot line into the bedroom of your favorite star. And the third point (aha!) is that more often than not, you won't find an e-mail address at all. Most celebrities (and their agents and studios) haven't exactly embraced cyberspace. Yet.

Alan's Celebrity Addresses

www.geocities.com/Hollywood/Hills/ 9842

A fan's address list: Alan, autograph hound supreme, does an incredible job of collecting postal addresses for celebrities. He is liberal in sharing the autographed photos he has received, although I suspect that even if he placed twice as many photos on these pages, they would amount to only a tiny fraction of what he really has. When tracking down a celebrity address, start by clicking the Address Page link on the home page. Click an alphabet letter at the top of the home page and then squint your way through the extremely small type of his lists. (At the time of this writing, Alan was updating the list; if the letter you need doesn't respond, simply click the Older Address List link to the left and proceed.) Alan is in the process of compiling over 12,000 famous names on this list — certainly one of the most extraordinary private celebrity research jobs anywhere.

Celebrity Addresses

www3.islandnet.com/~luree/ fanmail.html

Find celebrity Web sites: The Celebrity Addresses site is a little misleading because it doesn't really focus on providing celebrity postal or e-mail addresses (although it does offer recommendations for tracking down a famous person's e-mail address). However, it's a good resource for finding Web sites about actors, comedians, athletes, musicians, and authors — some sites are officially authorized sites and some are created by fans. After choosing a category of performer, select from an alphabetized list of links. The variety is impressive, and the link quality is generally good, although you never know what you're in for with fan sites.

Celebrity Connection

members.tripod.com/~jonnykat/ index.html

All kinds of celebrities: The Celebrity Connection list is unusually valuable because it includes musicians, politicians, athletes, and even musical bands and sport teams. In this respect, the site veers from the movie-centric adulation of most celebrity lists. The list itself, which you must link to (not once, not twice, but three times) from the home page, can hardly be more basic or less graphically interesting. It's just a list — plain font and very long. Very sensibly, the site reminds you over and over to be polite and not to use any address for harassing intent.

Celebrity Site of the Day

www.net-v.com/csotd

Links to the best celebrity sites: A variant on the Cool Site of the Day concept, you can think of Celebrity Site of the Day as an homage to copyright infringement because most celebrity sites are fan sites and most use unauthorized pictures and plagiarism. But copyright infringement isn't really your problem, and if you're collecting celebrity sites for your bookmark list, Celebrity Site of the Day is a good place to start. You're likely to find all sorts of features here — from reverent tributes to Elvis to one that compares Mariah Carey to a goddess. Celebrity Site of the Day encourages viewers to nominate a site and to browse through previous daily selections back through 1996. The site claims high standards of selection and ineffable good taste, but it has to keep cranking out the picks every day, so as you can imagine, the quality is bound to be uneven.

Celebrity Snack Palace

www.catch.com/snack

Funny, informal celebrity site: This irreverent, quirky site is a treat for jaded eyes. After you've surfed up and down the Web, and the sites all begin to look the same, go to the Celebrity Snack Palace. Let me warn you right now: This site is no place for surfers with tender language sensibilities. You won't find a bit of erotica or porn in the Celebrity Snack Palace, but the writers don't exactly take a Victorian approach to language. The turns of phrase are informal, to say the least. Kick off your shoes and enjoy the Primal Scream Button or Mounds of Sounds (take your audio plug-ins). Unexpected sound bites turn up here, including a background loop of a Tom Jones song that you can sing along to, and the site's offbeat style never stops.

CelebSite

www.celebsite.com

★ ★
★ ★

Celebrity profiles: CelebSite is a brilliantly designed Mr. Showbiz site that accomplishes its modest goals perfectly. It doesn't try to be a complete entertainment magazine, but it does give you a complete current picture of any celebrity in its database. Refreshingly, the database isn't limited to movie stars, but includes musicians, comedians, models, directors, publishers, TV actors, and writers. You can search by typing in a celebrity name, but you may have more fun browsing by category. When you land on a celebrity page, you see a photo and can select what kind of information you want to view. Biographies, credits, and related Web sites are available for each person. CelebSite maintains a clear page format throughout the site, which makes browsing a delight.

Country Bytes

www.premrad.com

Audio interview clips: Part of the Premiere Radio site, Country Bytes is available by clicking — all together now — the Country Bytes link on the home page. Country Bytes has a narrow focus: to provide sound bites of country music stars discussing their projects in digitized audio formats. In most cases, the audio files represent celebrities' responses to a single question, not an entire interview. A short introductory paragraph describes the singer and the question asked. By clicking the singer's name you can listen to the answer. The audio quality is good, too; these clips don't sound like telephone interviews. The selection is sometimes limited, but Premiere Radio has enough other goodies to make a visit worthwhile. Grab your RealAudio-enabled browser (or click on the download link) and head over to this site because it's a blast to explore.

Driveways of the Rich & Famous

www.driveways.com

Self-mocking celebrity interviews: As a public access cable TV show, *Driveways of the Rich & Famous* makes waves, even so far as getting a flattering nod from *The Wall Street Journal.* The idea is not to interview the celebrities themselves but the ancillary people that surround them like nonchalant gnats — gardeners, mailmen, neighbors, and doormen. The interviews shed some light on the lives and personalities of the hidden celebs, but the interviews aren't even the point of the show. The show — and to a certain extent the Web site — attains brilliance by using a self-mocking tone that reaches out to infect the entire celeb-fawning culture with irony, thereby partially redeeming it. Often, the interviews reveal nothing whatsoever, bringing their mock-reverential tone to full effect; sometimes, the least revealing interviews are the funniest and most worthwhile. Even if some of the tone is lost in the translation to the Web, the subtext remains strong — although it requires a bit more imagination on your part. Give the Web site a try and see what Whoopi Goldberg's pool man has to say. (Here's a teaser: "She really doesn't use the pool that much.")

Other Stuff to Check Out

pages.prodigy.com/BAPT37B/cesa.htm
www.geocities.com/Hollywood/8506
www.kcweb.com/super/awards.htm
www.starbuzz.com

Television

You here lot of talk about TV on the Internet, the Internet on TV, and the general convergence of computers and televisions. (And telephones. And maybe some day, if you're good boys and girls, toasters.) That total convergence is still a long way away, so in the meantime, you can turn to the Web to help you more fully enjoy TV. What I'm getting at with this tedious introduction is that this section doesn't review television broadcasts on the Internet. This section deals with Web sites about popular shows, TV network sites, and online schedule guides.

Networks

The following section includes some major network television sites. Almost every cable and free TV network has a presence on the World Wide Web, and many of the networks make a dreary job of it, believe me. Apparently thinking that self-promotion excites netsurfers, the networks do nothing more than plug their shows (as if you didn't get enough of that by watching their channels), list their schedules (as if you needed to go on the Web to see what's on), and — did I mention this? — plug their shows and plug their shows and plug their shows. However, a few sites actually provide some interest beyond network self-adulation.

ABC.com

www.abc.com

The network's Web site: Watching television may be a passive activity, but ABC.com begs visitors to get involved. The Message Boards section offers you the chance to post comments, complaints, praise, verbal tomatoes, and whatever else is on your mind about virtually any show on the ABC schedule. If you'd prefer just to know more about the shows, you can use the drop-down menu on the home page or work your way through the front page links. Online features and activities are also offered, while pages on Books and Music (and the shopping that goes with them) are provided in conjunction with Barnes and Noble and Music Boulevard, respectively. The final touch is the ABCNews ticker and link on the front page. ABC may not be the network behind "Must-See TV," but the Web site is highly recommended viewing.

A&E

www.aetv.com/index2.html

Program listings and previews: The Arts & Entertainment cable channel receives lots of attention for its fine original programming, particularly the Biography series. The Web site invites you to "Escape the Ordinary," and although the saying refers to the cable channel's programming, the site has a few features intended to do the same thing. The Web site accommodates your research by e-mailing you program listings (if you want them), previewing upcoming series, providing a weekly quiz (good luck!), and setting up an online store. A&E even provides study guides for the classroom. The Now On A&E box tells you at a glance what's happening in the next couple of hours (on the tube, of course, not in your life specifically).

Comedy Central

www.comcentral.com/jshome.html

Funny in its own right: The Comedy Central site apparently strives to both frazzle your optic nerves and tickle your cerebrum while getting you as interactively involved with the site as possible. Games, quizzes, and activities lure you at every step. On a recent visit, you could try to *Win Ben Stein's Money* (so to speak) with an online version of the game show; play an *Ab Fab* online shopping game (the goal: to spend $5,000 in such a way that you bring out your chosen character's "inner self"); and visit a playground from the animated hit *South Park*. (Parents, a warning: Just because it's animated doesn't mean you shouldn't check it out first.) One of the best features is the Download This! link, which leads you to archived libraries of video clips from popular Comedy Central shows. The site is graphically rich, with little Java applets that keep things moving around. The Web site is fun, which befits the virtual home of the Comedy Central cable network.

Eye on the Net — CBS

www.cbs.com

Bland but comprehensive: Major network sites tend to be fairly bland, and CBS does nothing to violate that grand tradition, although the site has improved. Don't be surprised to be asked information that helps the site track down your local CBS affiliate and don't be surprised to find that information integrated into what the site presents you. Spin-off sites cover Primetime, Daytime, and Late Night programming; Specials, and the CBS Kidzone. If you try to find any program directly by using the drop-down box near the top of the page, you still have to pretty much go through those categories.

What's a little confusing is that additional links at the top of the page cover topics like News and Sports, and the resulting pages have a hearty blend of local affiliate content. Still, the site does a nice job of picking some of the network's best features, and the extensive video offerings make a visit worthwhile.

FOXWORLD

www.foxnetwork.com

 ★ ★
★ ★

Good content from the network's online site: FOXWORLD conveys the impression that the Fox television network has created a fantasy domain that provides endless fascination and delight. Although that characterization may be stretching the truth, the Web site certainly goes beyond the call of duty in providing service to netizens. More than just a promotion for the network and its shows, the home page (which is gorgeous, by the way) enables you to search for specific shows, daily schedules, and network affiliates from drop-down boxes at the top. Links at the bottom connect to sites dealing with children's programming and activities, general Fox shows, Fox news, Fox sports, the FX Network, News Corp (Fox's parent company), the Fox movie studio, and Gamestorm, a News Corp–owned online game.

HBO

www.hbo.com

Generous displays of HBO content: You can tell immediately, upon entering the HBO site, that it's fat and fun. But you have no idea how generous the premium cable network is with sharing its content for free on the Net. Click to Dennis Miller's page, for example, and read highlights of his opening monologue. You find similar translations of TV content to the Web throughout the sprawling online real estate of HBO. Furthermore, HBO produces Web-only *shows* as well; these shows are innovative virtual programs written and designed to be viewed through your web browser. You can find these virtual programs under the Web Originals section of the site — the links connect you to dedicated Web locations for those shows. (Parents, be careful of III: am, one of the Web shows that contains adult content. If you say it's okay for your kids, you'll need either the Vivo or QuickTime plug-ins to watch; you can find Vivo on the CD that comes with this book.)

NBC

www.nbc.com

Lots of information, nice style: NBC has enjoyed good fortune in the network ratings wars, and many people turn to the official sites of such hit shows as *Frasier, ER,* and *Friends* to get updates, cast biographies, and previews. The site is nice but not flashy — but then, the site is supposed to make you want to turn on the TV, not be an end destination in itself. The site almost could be. You can look up show information, check out behind-the-scenes scenes, play games, enter chat rooms or view program forums, check out original Web content, and link to CNBC,

MSNBC Sports, and MSNBC News. The NBC Web presentation is more useful than most network sites. Catering to the still-learning netizen, the site advises you about browser plug-ins and links to source sites, connects you to search engines, and basically tries to be your friend in cyberspace.

Nick at Nite & TV Land

nick-at-nite.com

Games, prizes, fun, and trips down memory lane: Nickelodeon — the cable network for a mixed audience of kids and adults who enjoy trips down the memory lane of television entertainment — produces a Web site full of interactive fun. Sure, it promotes the television schedule of Nick's stations, which is useful by itself. But the real fun is in the games and special content that you find only on the Web. Check out the Arcade section for interactive activities with some pretty impressive prizes attached. My favorite area is Retromercials, which presents images and audio reminiscences of TV commercials from the 1960s and 1970s — with sound and video. The splashy design of this site's home page isn't helpful, and you have to explore a bit to find what you like.

Sci-Fi Channel: Dominion

www.scifi.com

Like another world: The home page is beautiful, in a retro-scientific way that seems to meld the technology hopes of the past with the awesome possibilities of the future. The site also shows some of the imagination of the cable channel. Yes, it has show information, chat rooms, games, neat downloads — the basics. But the site also has something very unusual: Seeing Ear Theatre. Yes, you read it right. Touted as "The Premiere Site for Science Fiction Audio Drama," the offerings include both archived material from the golden days of radio and more recent offerings. Some of the material is specially produced for the channel, including the recent *Alien Voices* project with Leonard Nimoy (he was Spock in the original *Star Trek*), which has re-created some classic H.G. Wells and Sir Arthur Conan Doyle works for broadcast. You'll need RealPlayer 5.0 to listen, but the download link is provided. All told, the Sci-Fi Channel site has enough cool content to merit a following worthy of the cable channel itself.

Other Stuff to Check Out

tnt.turner.com
www.bbc.co.uk/television
www.cnbc.com/wsjrpt
www.pbs.org
www.the700club.org
www.upn.com/home.html
www.zdf.de/homepage.asp

Television Schedules and Guides

Some people think that logging on to the Web to find out what's on TV is strange. The fact is, online schedule guides are useful beasts, and I use them quite a bit. (Of course, my life has less intrinsic interest than a mollusk's.) In addition to

seeing a grid of what's playing now, you can search for individual shows or movies, and the database aspect of online TV guides is what makes them valuable — you can instantly find exactly what you're looking for. Here are some of the best sites.

GIST

www.thegist.com

Listings and articles: GIST is an enhanced TV listing service with aspirations to be an electronic magazine. It's an interesting read, with feature articles and Web links. For general listings, you first select the region of the United States in which you live and then examine a time-channel grid to see what's on. Of course, you can define the time and day and limit the channels shown. For a more topical approach, the home page enables you to select a type of viewing — movies, sports, soap operas, sci-fi, news, drama, kids, or comedy — and each choice throws you into a separate section with its own articles and listings. A free, optional registration process makes the listings more accurate for your specific location.

Special TV Resources

www.specialweb.com/tv

Directory of television Web sites: Formerly known as Internet TV, Special TV Resources is a directory to television sites on the Web. Extremely user-friendly, especially for Internet beginners who appreciate the New to the Net tutorial, the site divides its links into nine basic categories — General Sites, Shows, Actors, Commercials, Magazines, Usenet, Bookstore, Trivia Blitz, and Networks. The directory isn't meant to be exhaustive (or exhausting, for that matter), and this site's claim to fame is the excellence of the sites it chooses for its listings. The frame-based design makes it easy to keep your bearings while roaming through the directory.

Television Schedules of the World

www.buttle.com/tv/schedule.htm

Global TV listings: No matter where you live on this planet, Television Schedules of the World connects you to an Internet guide to local programming. Local, that is, to different countries. Basically a specialized Web directory on a grand scope, the site breaks down its listings by country, providing links to sites that cover TV programming schedules for that country. Some countries, such as Canada, have several sites, whereas Brazil and many other countries have only one Web television guide to represent them. You'll be amazed at how many countries are in this list.

Total TV Online

www.tottv.com

Network television listings: Total TV Online goes for simplicity, and the strategy works. The home page presents a few special features — articles, Web directories to hit shows, and the occasional contest. When you click the Listings link, the site really gets down to the basics. A very clear procedure enables you to zero in on your cable provider; then you can determine any

three-hour block of time within the following week or search for program scheduling by keyword. I prefer the Grid view option — which brings up a nice, clear chart with all the major cable channels and the major free networks. Total TV Online color-codes the shows so that you can easily distinguish between sports and movies. All movies and some shows provide links to brief plot and cast summaries. The service that Total TV Online provides is basic, but it shows you what's on at any given time — and it always works.

TV Guide Entertainment Network

www.tvgen.com

The online home of TV Guide*:* Note the fancy site name. Although *TV Guide* has always been one of the most compact published products, both in name and format, the Web site has pretensions of grandeur, in both title and content. Stretching beyond mere television coverage, movie reviews and music articles push the envelope. What about the TV listings? They're pretty good if you can find them. (The site embeds a small link near the top of the home page.) TV Guide Entertainment Network works by swallowing up your zip code and then spitting out local programming timetables. A standard scheduling grid appears — using standard color-coding for program types — in a standard three-hour time increment, covering all the standard cable and free channels. (Yawn.) *TV Guide* is treading on thin ice here by competing simultaneously with the big electronic entertainment magazines and the dedicated TV programming guides. The site is good, but it doesn't excel in either direction.

Ultimate TV

www.ultimatetv.com

Schedules and articles: Ultimate TV is an online magazine covering television from all angles — personalities, schedules, previews and reviews, columnists, sports, feature articles, job listings in the television industry, Nielsen ratings, and Web-based television broadcasts. The site promotes community through message boards, chat rooms, and polls that invite you to vote on the quality of TV shows. Wire service reports provide TV-related news, so you can keep up with your favorite stars' latest salary demands. Although you can search the site for schedule listings, providing them isn't Ultimate TV's strong point. The site is sort of like *TV Guide* in reverse: more emphasis on feature articles and news, and less emphasis on scheduling.

Other Stuff to Check Out

www.a-perfect.com/sat/guide
www.erols.com/mwyatt/tvnow.html
www.microserve.net/tvhost

Various and Sundry TV Sites

In this portion of the TV section, I gather a few sites that don't fit into any particular category but are righteously good nonetheless. Because the sites are unrelated to one another, I don't have much to say about them as a group, except that they're righteously good, which I already said. Some deal with the history of television, which traces the personal history of its viewers. Others offer commentary on shows. One of the following selections updates soap opera plots. The goal of this section is to provide interesting, well-designed sites covering any aspect of television.

Academy of Television Arts & Sciences

www.emmys.org

Information on the Emmy awards: The Academy of Television Arts & Sciences has a beautiful site that opens with a rotating photograph of an Emmy — it's one classy home page. Ten areas define the site structure, including membership information section, historical information, news, a Hall of Fame, and an index of everything in the site. One good place to start is the Awards portion, which delivers information about the upcoming awards and details the winners, facts, and trivia for the past year. The site doesn't bog you down with unnecessary graphic do-dads (or don't-dads, either), yet it manages to look great every step of the way, like an Emmy-award recipient.

Audiences Unlimited

www.audiencesunlimited.com

Free tickets to television show tapings: Audiences Unlimited is a specialty firm that has been brokering free tickets to TV studio tapings since long before the World Wide Web was created. With the Internet creeping steadfastly into people's homes, Audiences Unlimited decided to provide its service on the Web. You can request tickets for about four dozen shows, mostly situation comedies. (The shows last a half hour, but the tapings run four or five hours.) This service is great if you're planning a visit to the Hollywood area or if you live near there. You can search by show title or date, and the site works for two months in advance. A side benefit of Audiences Unlimited is all the information it gives about the shows and their stars. Even if you don't go to a taping, you can learn a heck of a lot about a show's cast by browsing this site.

History of TV Advertising

adage.com/news_and_features/ special_reports/tv

Television history from the advertising angle: Created by *Advertising Age,* a trade journal of the advertising industry, History of TV Advertising goes beyond its own mission. The site really provides a blow-by-blow history of television from the 1940s to today, with an emphasis on advertising. You pick a decade from the home page and then read capsulated descriptions of important industry events that transpired during that decade. Many of the tidbits make no reference to ad programming but spark reminiscences for anyone who lived through that period. The emergence of color TV in the 1960s, for example, affected advertising because companies became self-conscious about airing their black-and-white ads. This site allows you to learn even more about that period if you want. History of TV Advertising is a fascinating trip, presented mostly with text and illustrated by some photographs. You won't find any video clips of advertisements, unfortunately.

Hole City

www.holecity.com

Cynical commentary on the media: "The Net used to be brief and biting, now it's often vague and corporate. How convenient: Here we are to fill the void." Such is the mission of a brilliant but biting band of writers who actually aimed their first cyberbarbs at TV but have since expanded to also include ads, movies, sports, and videos. If you want to find articles that convey your own nightly frustrations with the media, surf over to TV Hole as soon as you hit your desk in the morning. (Corporate managers around the world, please pretend you didn't see the previous sentence.) You'll

be pumping your fist with a relished "Yeah!" as you absorb the caustic criticisms of this literary and sarcastic daily update. No multimedia clips here — just good writing and good taste.

Soap Dish

www.tvgen.com/soaps

Concise soap opera plot updates: You can find a number of soap opera update sites on the Web, but Soap Dish is probably the best, blending an easy, time-saving interface with just the right amount of feature content in the form of articles and interviews. Cutting right to the chase, you get summaries for all the daytime soaps for the past week, updated every afternoon after the last one airs. Drop-down menus enable you to select a show and day, and the synopses are concise without being mysteriously brief. Soap Dish avoids the trap of telling the story in too much detail, a style that so often plagues other update sites.

The X-Files Episode Guide

www.thex-files.com/epiindx.htm

Show-by-show plot updates: I don't know about you, but the X-Files Episode Guide is just what I need to stay up to speed with the dramatically intriguing, metaphysically challenging, storyline-convoluting quasi-sci-fi series. If you've ever enjoyed the creepy scares of Scully and Mulder but wondered what the heck was going on, welcome to the club, and welcome to the site that straightens out your tangled confusions. An episode-by-episode rundown of stories from *The X-Files* is especially useful for the past year or two because the show has veered into a more continuous story that requires you to be aware of what has come before. Each plot summary is concise but complete, with embedded links leading to background character information. The video and audio clips are fun but not necessary.

Other Stuff to Check Out

hip-huggers.com/entertainment/television/
   index.html
www.clicktv.com
www.cs.cmu.edu/afs/cs.cmu.edu/user/
   clamen/misc/tv
www.mca.com/tv/xena
www.mtr.org
www.sofcom.com.au/TV/
www.timelapse.com//tvlink.html
www.ugcs.caltech.edu/st-tng

Theater

www1.playbill.com/playbill

The sites in this section cover all aspects of theater, including musicals and plays. You also can find reviews, historical information, listings, and much more.

Aisle Say

www.escape.com/~theanet/
   AisleSay.html

Online theater magazine: Aisle Say is an online theater magazine that stakes its claim to fame on good writing and a solid database of reviews. The site isn't enhanced (or burdened) by grand graphics, fancy frames, or scintillating sidebars. The home page is a long textual affair that links to feature articles and reviews. The enduring value of the site lies at the bottom of the home page,

where you find a list of review databases divided into cities. You can browse through review indexes for Phoenix, Cleveland, Toronto, New York, and other cities, and Australia. Click a city to see a list of reviews, and then select a review to revel in intelligent, savvy, sometimes caustic writing. The editorial standards of Aisle Say are high, and the spartan site design never keeps you waiting. Aisle Say is a Web stop for true theater lovers who enjoy great and sometimes controversial commentary.

American Association of Community Theater

www.aact.org

Community theater: Before visiting this site, I didn't know that community theater houses play to more audience members than any other performing art in the United States. The American Association of Community Theater (AACT) supports local theater by establishing standards of excellence and providing resources to help meet those standards. In a broader sense, AACT is an advocacy group that establishes such public awareness events as National Community Theater Week. The Web site primarily helps its members and offers sources for obtaining plays. In addition, it provides AACT event info, Web links, job listings, and various tips and helpful facts.

Gilbert and Sullivan Archive

math.idbsu.edu/gas/GaS.html

Tribute to the light opera composers: Since September 1993, the Gilbert and Sullivan Archive has been the premier site covering the light operas of the masterful 19th-century duo. You would expect an index of all the operas, but the Archive goes even further with complete librettos in many cases, accompanied by MIDI music files of the songs. The site also abundantly provides plot summaries and clip art. Furthermore, the site is now adding some MPEG audio files, presenting classic recordings of portions of the operas. (You need different browser plug-ins for the MIDI and MPEG files. MIDI is computer-generated instrumental music; the MPEG files are digitized live recordings.) A directory to festivals and other sites around the Web finish off the main menu.

London Theatre Guide

www.londontheatre.co.uk

Guide to the West End and beyond: Many of the world's most renowned musicals in recent decades have originated in England, and this site keeps abreast of happenings around the London theater scene. Visitors find news, listings, reviews, and seat plans, most cross-referenced to one another. The site also includes information on purchasing tickets, backstage tours and theatrical museum tours, and a place to post messages. The London Theatre Guide isn't fancy, but it doesn't have to be — after all, the play's the thing.

Playbill On-Line

www1.playbill.com/playbill

International theater news: If you've ever been to a show and received the slim Playbill program, containing scant information and multitudes of advertisements, you may wonder how such a slight publication can pass itself off as a magazine. The Internet version makes up for its printed cousin's deficiencies by providing a full range of international theater news, Tony award updates and recaps, listings of shows from New York to London to Brazil, audio clips and other multimedia goodies, Broadway quizzes, financial information on current shows, a keyword entry feature for searching the database, a way to buy tickets and

souvenirs online, and feature articles about the stars and future productions on and off Broadway. Whew, quite a difference! Playbill comes alive on the Web, and it's a great bookmark if you love theater. It's also a valuable resource for aspiring actors, singers, and technicians, thanks to the industry job postings.

Theatre Central

www.theatre-central.com

Theater information for audiences and professionals: Created by Playbill Online, Theatre Central is a locus of theater news, links, listings, industry jobs, and features. Theatre Central is unique in providing interactive industry listings into which aspiring and established theater pros can enter their own classified information. Truly international, Theatre Central covers Broadway, Off Broadway, regional productions, national tours, summer stock, and theater in London, Brazil, and Canada. The site offers a good deal of technical information, such as theater box office gross revenues, as well as a question-and-answer section and quizzes — a section I assiduously avoid. Theatre Central is the best all-purpose theater site on the Web for both pros and audience members.

Theatre Development Fund

www.tdf.org

Nonprofit theater organization: If you've ever been to Times Square in New York City, you've probably noticed the big red and white TKTS banners, beneath which you can buy half-priced theater tickets for the current day's performances. TKTS is a seminal part of the New York City experience, and it's but one of the community outreach services innovated by the Theatre Development Fund (TDF). The TDF Web site describes its educational programs, travel programs, awards, events, and various U.S. and international services. Visiting this site and joining the mailing list entitles you to receive offers on discount tickets that TDF periodically makes to its entire membership roster. ***Note:*** Not just anyone can join, but if you're a student, retiree, or performing arts professional, you can get on the list.

Tony Awards Online

www.tonys.org/index.html

Information about the Tony awards: Although this site is dedicated to Broadway's biggest night, it's a year-round affair. Vacillating between anticipation of coming awards and reflection on past awards, Tony Awards Online is updated daily and presents a lot of theater information along the way. The What's Playing section is a multimedia showcase of current shows, including photos, music, and ticket information. The News page brings you theater headlines, and it links to full stories about comings and goings of star players, openings and closings of shows, and other items of news and gossip. Message boards and chat rooms enable you to share your passion for theater with other fans.

Other Stuff to Check Out

members.aol.com/bpsprtfan/bpbdwy.htm
members.aol.com/mgmfanatic/index.html
www.broadwaytheater.com
www.geocities.com/Broadway/1336
www.geocities.com/Broadway/9395/
    index.htm
www.nycopera.com
www.stage-directions.com
www.theater-express.com
www.theatrenet.co.uk
www.thesofa.com

Part VII
Fun and Free Stuff

The 5th Wave   By Rich Tennant

ORICHTENNANT

IT WAS ACTUALLY ON THE WEB ONE NIGHT THAT CAPT. AHAB CAUGHT UP WITH HIS OBSESSION.

WHALE CHAT

White? Really? Where can we meet?

In this part . . .

The beauty of the Internet is its interactivity. Unlike TV,
it doesn't play programs at a sometimes numb,
passively receptive audience. The Internet may turn into
glorified television eventually, but for now, most of the
Net won't do a blessed thing until you do something first.
You must hit a link to start seeing things, and this
interactivity — which enables you to determine the
course of the "programming" — is what gives the World
Wide Web its unique character. Interactivity is always fun,
and many sites on the Web are geared to maximize the
Net's entertainment value with games, puzzles, contests,
humor, and multimedia streaming features. Perhaps the
most interactive aspect of the Internet is the potential for
community, as manifested in message boards, chat
rooms, and virtual Net cities. All these fun manners of
interactivity are featured in this part.

Audio and Video Multimedia Sites

Multimedia is making a valiant attempt to arrive on the Net. The software tools for playing sound and video through a connected computer have gotten better and better, and now audio sounds pretty good — as long as you have a fast-enough modem (28.8 Kbps or faster) and the correct application (RealPlayer 5.0 or later with its RealAudio browser plug-in, is the current champ). Video is a tougher nut to crack: Although it works (after a fashion) through 28.8 Kbps modems, you really need 56K or ISDN (or cable access at home, or institutional access at work) to make video come alive.

As problematic as multimedia still is on the Web, it's so much fun to play with — and even harder to avoid, actually, as more sites consider it to be an indispensable design feature. This section gathers some of the most interesting, fun, impressive, and cutting-edge Web locations featuring audio and video.

So what are you likely to find on a multimedia site, anyway? The World Wide Web would like to be just like TV, but the truth is that it's too far from that lofty goal to be compared with that medium. For now, radio stations successfully transmit their programming on the Web, and other audio features, like those presented in 60 Second Theater, work very well. Another

great implementation of audio through the Web is the Net-casting of live concerts. On the video side, some television stations simulcast on the Web; some of these stations are listed in other sections of this book. For this section, I selected a couple of sites that feature archived video presentations for viewing on demand.

Alternative Entertainment Network

www.cummingsvideo.com

Entertainment and documentary programming: AEN is a legitimate Internet network and one of the most dynamic multimedia sites on the Web. The focus is decidedly not on live programming, but all kinds of entertainment features are available on demand. From previously censored clips of "The Smothers Brothers Comedy Hour" to Abbott and Costello performing "Who's on First?" on television, from a library of stand-up performances at the Improv to "Leonardo DiCaprio: In My Own Words," from documentaries to "The World Business Review," the Alternative Entertainment Network tosses up a smorgasbord of Internet shows. To see everything, you need RealPlayer 5.0, a link for which is conveniently included on most pages.

Ann On-Line

www.annonline.com

Online talk show: Ann Devlin has been a radio talk-show host for many years and now hosts an Internet-only program. Shows are uploaded daily but aren't broadcast (or Netcast) on a certain schedule — the show is on-demand only. Devlin goes for literary guests in a big way, often accommodating authors who have written books about social topics or medical discoveries. The site really does the Net-show concept right: You can post messages to the host with guest ideas for future shows, chat or exchange messages with other listeners, and browse months' worth of back shows. You need RealPlayer — and yes, Ann On-Line provides a link to download it.

InterneTV

www.internetv.com

Internet television in its infancy: The Internet's first dedicated television station, InterneTV resembles television only by a stretch of imagination. The site's first central item of programming in 1997 was "Austin," a video-based soap opera set in the Texas city. Promised soon are series based on the rave culture and "Bartenders," which will be about — well, you don't need me to tell you. InterneTV offers video collections of some movie trailers, music videos, and performance clips of a dance company. In other words, InterneTV is struggling for programming content. But at least the "station" is in operation, and you can watch it grow and develop. Links are provided for all the plug-ins that you need.

LiveConcerts.com

www.liveconcerts.com

Live Netcasts of rock concerts: This gorgeous site has a noble cause: to bring live music to the Internet through RealAudio. LiveConcerts.com hooks up with KCRW in Santa Monica, California, to provide some radio simulcasts on the Net, but the main focus is concert Netcasts of popular rock acts — no household names (depending on the household, I guess), but three or four concerts per week are simulcast through this site. Upcoming events are searchable, and every concert is archived. The archives may be the site's most valuable feature, providing hours of good live music for the taking. Free membership is offered but not required; the site tries to lure you with prizes. LiveConcerts.com is so well done in every respect, it's almost ridiculous. Great site!

Prairie Home Companion

phc.mpr.org

Online site of the public-radio program: It's ironic, but Garrison Keillor is on the Web. Why ironic? Because the star and host of "A Prairie Home Companion," the long-running public-radio variety show that emphasizes Midwestern United States down-home values and old-time music, can hardly be considered at the forefront of the digital revolution. Keillor is best known for his evocative storytelling feature, "Lake Wobegon," where the Internet is probably considered to be an impenetrable big-city quirk. Anyway, this site is a treasure for PHC fans, but don't expect to find archived audio programs of the radio show. You can listen to the Internet simulcast Saturdays at 6 p.m. Eastern Standard Time; the program is not available after that hour. But you can look at photos, post questions to Keillor, and try the Comedy Seminar.

60 Second Theater

www.letusout.com

Short radio-style plays: You've got to love this site's URL. You'll also have a hard time resisting the brief radio-style audio plays streamed out from 60 Second Theater, where the one-minute dramatic presentations are refined to an art. At last visit, 56 "works" had been completed, featuring acting that ranges from pretty good to downright boffo, as well as sound effects. The Hitchhiker is a recurring play motif and character who has been picked up by suicidal hot-rodders; are they trying to save him or kill him? In another play, a man finds himself in a strange city, but he's really the one who is bizarre, speaking an unrecognizable language and fighting off people-eating dragons. The plays are all almost 60 seconds long and never more than a minute and a half. The RealAudio transmission is uniformly and gratifyingly excellent. These productions are addictive — try to listen to just one!

Superman Radio

www.dccomics.com/radio/index.html

Original 1940s Superman *radio broadcasts:* This is fantastic: Now you can listen to original Superman radio episodes that were first broadcast during the 1940s. The 15-minute episodes bring back the old radio-serial days perfectly, from the heroic quaver in the announcer's voice to the resourceful special sound effects. The programs are optimally presented in RealAudio 3.0, with a reduced-bandwidth path available for users with Version 2.0 and 14.4 Kbps modems. Unfortunately, the site doesn't have a library of past episodes, and the episodes run in sequence, so to start at the beginning of a serial, you have to wait until it comes around again. Look! Up on the screen! It's a site, it's a plug-in, it's Superman on the Net!

Tribute to Laurel & Hardy

www.exit109.com/~smazoki/index.html

Homage to the comedy duo: This labor of love lists all the famous comedy duo's films and throws a rich mix of multimedia at your browser. Make sure that you're equipped with RealAudio (Version 3.0 or later), or you'll miss out on the fun of hearing this site's pages as they go by. Best enjoyed as a sequential series of photos and old musical soundtracks, the site tailors itself to your preferences by expanding to the size of your screen resolution or staying within the bounds of your browser. You can also turn off the music or the graphics, but why? This tribute is a multimedia feast and a great deal of fun.

Other Stuff to Check Out

alf-nt.city.at
cartalk.com
www.amw.com
www.cryptnet.com
www.hardradio.com
www.jerrylewiscomedy.com
www.man-with-no-name.com
www.msbet.com
www.there1.com/radio.html
www.webactive.com

This section contains reviews for sites whose content deals with either comic books or comic strips. Fear of reprisal from my editors kept me from putting these reviews in the "Culture" section.

Calvin & Hobbes Gallery

www.okidoki.com/calvin_and_hobbes

Everything you want to know about the strip and its creator: This site is somewhat misnamed because it adheres to copyright laws by not displaying *Calvin & Hobbes* strips. It's not so much a gallery as an information site, and a far superior one to the official Calvin & Hobbes site, which likewise doesn't display any strips more recent than 1987. The official site is so lame that it's not getting into this book. This unofficial site is lovingly dedicated to the famously rambunctious and imaginative boy, Calvin; his not-so-real tiger, Hobbes; and his mystified parents and teachers. The site does stretch copyright laws by reproducing Bill Watterson's (the artist's) own text characterizations of his cast, taken from one of the books. Book lists, other Web sites, and some miscellaneous pictures round out the site.

Comic Book Continuum

**www.detnews.com/metro/hobbies/
comix**

Comics news: Comic Book Continuum covers news from the world of comics in the broadest possible fashion. The site's daily updates report on television shows or movies if they bear some relation to comic characters or strips that served as inspiration for the show. A recent example was an update on a Superman movie that may — or may not — star Nicholas Cage. Message boards enable comic fans to connect with each other.

ComicZone

www.unitedmedia.com/comics

Strips from United Media: ComicZone presents information about the serious and funny funnies brought to by United Media. The site is wonderfully simple: You select the comic you want from the drop-down list at the top of the page (or click another link, if there is one), and you're off. Not only do you get that day's version of the comic, you can browse through a four-week archive. All your Sunday favorites are here, including *Peanuts, Dilbert, Robotman, Eek & Meek, Herman,* and *Nancy.* The site also enables you to meet the mind and pen behind the funnies by featuring many of the artists. One oddity: United Media's wonderful editorial cartoonists aren't included in the drop-down list. To get to their work, simply click Editoons on any secondary page.

Marvel Online

www.marvelonline.com

Online site for comic book company:
Marvel Comics is the home to some of the world's most famous comic characters (Spider-man, Captain America, and the X-Men, to name a few) and arguably the world's best-known comic character creator (a man named Stan Lee). They're all well represented on Marvel Online, which doesn't display the comic books online — unless you want to sign up for The Marvel Zone, which broadcasts original "cybercomics" in streaming audio and video for an annual fee of about $30. Still, there's plenty here that's free, from the threaded chat rooms that enable readers to offer their suggestions on how stories should twist, to Excelsior Theatre, which featured an animated Captain America cartoon during my visit. Parents, one warning: Marvel Online includes plenty of opportunities to shop for comics, software, and other items online, so don't naively let your kids have your credit card when they're at Marvel Online. Other than that, turn 'em loose.

Universal Press Syndicate Comics

www.uexpress.com/ups/comics

Archives of UPS strips: United Press Syndicate (UPS), a distributor of many favorite comic strips, is generous in its online offerings. This site archives about a month of UPS strips, starting about two weeks after they appear in newspapers. *Doonesbury* is here. *Pavlov, Foxtrot, Stone Soup, Cathy, Crankshaft, Garfield, Tank McNamara, Ziggy* — all here. A drop-down menu enables you to select strips from a particular date, and Sundays are conveniently marked next to the date. UPS doesn't stop with just the strips — the site also delivers artist information and message boards for meeting other fans, and an opportunity to buy a frame-worthy copy of the comics.

Other Stuff to Check Out

comics.ch
www.dccomics.com
www.execpc.com/~icicle/main.html
www.geocities.com/SoHo/5537
www.uta.fi/yhteydet/sarjikset.html

Contests, Puzzles, and Tests

Puzzles, which are a trend on the Net, are a fun way to participate in online prize giveaways without getting involved in the questionably legal area of online gambling. (Gambling is not covered in this book.) Not all puzzle pages offer prizes, and I include some favorites whose rewards range from money to pure gratification.

Online puzzles take various forms: sweepstakes that depend on pure luck, contests that rely on specific knowledge, and traditional puzzlers such as crosswords and word scramblers. There's also the question of commitment: You can play some puzzle pages briefly, in passing, but some require dedicated work. As usual, I try to include a variety in the following sites, which represent different skill and time demands.

Best Contests and Sweepstakes on the Web

www.webmagnet.com/
   bestcontests.html

Reviews of gaming sites: Finding the best of anything on the Internet, including contests and sweepstakes, isn't easy. Contests are especially hard to track down because they're sometimes short-lived or seasonal. A contest timed to promote a new product or movie, for example, may last only a few weeks or a couple of months. The value of this site is that it does a great job of collecting, reviewing, and linking to virtual contests of skill and luck. By this site's definition, a *contest* is a game of skill and a *sweepstake* is a game of chance. Those definitions work for me. Each recommended site is reviewed briefly and then graded according to ease of entering, value of prizes, and other criteria.

The Bulwer-Lytton Fiction Contest Home Page

www.bulwer-lytton.com

Worst-opening-sentence competition: The Bulwer-Lytton Fiction Contest has drawn the attention of *TIME* magazine, *Smithsonian Magazine, People* magazine, *The Wall Street Journal,* and many other mainstream publications. Too literary, you say? Hardly. The BLFC (you try typing the unabbreviated name a few times) is a *bad-fiction* contest with the goal of finding the worst opening sentence of an fake novel. The contest is an annual affair with a deadline of April 15 —

"a date Americans associate with painful submissions and making up bad stories" — although this year, attempting to be "no less magnanimous than the IRS," the deadline was extended to June 15. Reading the rules and history of the contest is half the fun of this site. Should you be inspired to enter an awful first sentence for consideration, you may do so either electronically or by postal mail. Browse the archive of winners to get the hang of it.

IMDb's Guess the Name

us.imdb.com/M/quiz

Movie trivia: The Internet Movie Database (IMDb) presents a movie-trivia puzzle for those who feel ready to test their wits against one of the finest movie databases on the Net. (See the review of the Internet Movie Database in the "Movies" section of Part VI.) Using multiple choice in some cases and a spell-the-answer system in others, Guess the Name asks for the voice of Marge Simpson, Susan Sarandon's husband, the sister-in-law of Shirley MacLaine, and other composure-rattlers. Unfortunately, the spell-it-out quizzes force you to use an on-screen keyboard instead of providing a simple form for typing the answer at your own keyboard. That arrangement makes things more cumbersome than necessary. Still, you don't have to actually enter the answer; just make a guess, click the Reveal the Answer button, and move on to the next puzzle.

Mensa Workout

www.mensa.org/workout.html

Nonqualifying test for would-be geniuses: Ever wonder whether you have the supercharged brain synapses that you need to join Mensa, the society of high intelligence? Now, before those insecurities kick in, you should remember that intelligence has yet to be defined with any certainty, and the value of intelligence tests of all sorts is highly questioned in the fields of education and psychology. (While you're at it, please disregard the *Dummies* part of this book's silly title.) The Mensa Workout is an official creation of Mensa, but it isn't a qualifying test. As the fine print in the ads says about those psychic hotlines, this site is for recreational purposes only. So if you want to torture yourself with questions like "If it were two hours later, it would be half as long until midnight as it would be if it were an hour later — what time is it now?" sharpen your mouse and surf on over to the Mensa Workout. The test takes a half hour to complete, but even if you spend three weeks on it, who's going to know? I've been working on the darn thing for a year and a half, and I'll have it finished any day now.

Puzzle Depot

www.puzzledepot.com

Online puzzles and games: The Puzzle Depot is dedicated to online puzzles and games of all kinds, from crosswords to trivia to puzzles (*pun*nish word scramblers). The main site, at the preceding URL, spins off into a several different areas, including a software library and a puzzle center that offers modest prizes. Lots of links also send visitors to fun sites around the Web. Mainly, though, Puzzle Depot isn't so much interested in luring visitors with cash or prizes as much as it is in turning them on to the fun of online games.

Rock Mall Trivia Challenge

www.rockmall.com/arcade.shtml

Music, entertainment, and culture trivia: If you're stumped by trivia games because the categories aren't right (yeah, I've used that excuse a million times myself), surf right over to the Rock Mall Trivia Challenge — assuming that you're at home with music and pop culture in general, that is. More than 150 categories are available for the choosing, each with dozens or hundreds of questions. All kinds of musical genres are represented, plus TV shows, sports, and personalities. Recent additions during my last visit included Frank Sinatra, Elvis, Godzilla, Boxing, Sex Symbols, and the Spice Girls. (Hmmm. Spice Girls in a separate category from Sex Symbols. Is Rock Mall trying to say something?) Clearly, this trivia challenge isn't about music only, despite Rock Mall's being the sponsoring site. The challenge is a solitary one, in that you're not competing against other gamers in real time, but a database of high scores is kept, and you basically compete against other people's results.

Strawberry Macaw's Puzzle Page

www.serve.com/games/puzzles.htm

Virtual puzzles: Strawberry Macaw (a big red bird, don't you know) is the host of a puzzle site with eight games. Although they avowedly aren't designed for kids, the bird and the games attract a younger audience. Even so, I found myself intrigued by the Twenty-Three Matches Game, in which you battle the site to avoid removing the last match. The site offers tic-tac-toe, which is clearly a kid's game, but it also offers a poker puzzle. A couple of sliding-picture puzzles are fun for kids of all ages. All of Strawberry Macaw's games require many mouse clicks, but the pages display quickly, so the worst that can happen is that your Back-button log gets glutted with game pages.

Other Stuff to Check Out

roguemarket.com
weber.u.washington.edu/~jlks/
    mindgame.html
www.contestclub.com

Internet games are some of the best family sites on the Web. But not every site in this section is perfect for young kids because some sites require mature skills of the sites. None, however, have inappropriate content.

Electronic gaming is a bigger industry than ever. Electronic games began in arcades, then migrated to CD-ROMs, and are now flourishing on the Internet. Action games have a deservedly violent and bloody reputation, and they aren't the focus of this section, for two reasons:

- They're too gruesome to be highlighted in a G-rated book.

- High-graphics action games don't work well over the Internet unless you have a high-speed digital connection.

The following gaming sites provide nonviolent fun. Most of these sites are for solo players, but a couple enable you to hook up with real-time opponents.

By the way, if you really want to get into Internet gaming, *Internet Games For Dummies* by John Kaufeld (IDG Books Worldwide, Inc.) is a great resource.

Big Network

www.bignetwork.com

Channel your extra energy: With a name like Big Network, you half expect this site to be the end-all of online gaming, with hundreds and thousands and gazillions of games. Actually, Big Network isn't that intimidating, with a few dozen well-chosen games organized into "channels" aimed at different demographic groups. Main Street is the family offering, which had just two games during my visit — the Chinese solitaire game mah-jongg and an intriguing game called What on Earth?, where you pick from among five live international Web camera sites and try to guess the location. If you need help, fairly easy trivia questions provide clues. If that sounds a lot like the computer game *Where in the World Is Carmen Sandiego?*, that's because one of the co-creators of that game reportedly helped design What on Earth? Big Network has other games, of course, including a chess game where the opponent's pieces are invisible. Isn't regular chess hard enough? Multiplayer games require that you register (it's free) and download the site's Big Player plug-in (which is also free, but needs Internet Explorer or Netscape 3.0 or later and Windows 95).

chess.net

www.chess.net

Virtual chess: Chess.net is the premier interactive chess-partnering site on the Web. Providing its own software, the total package enables you to log into the chess.net server, find a playing partner, and view the game in progress on your monitor. (Some people also like to keep a chess board next to their computer.) Registering and downloading the software are both free, although the software program isn't really necessary if you can cope with a text-based move indicator, such as BxN for Bishop Takes Knight. But if you prefer seeing a representation of a board and pieces, and using your mouse to move the pieces around, go for the free download. Game instruction is featured at the chess.net site. You can also chat — but remember, don't distract the players.

'80s Games & Trivia

www.80s.com/Trivia

Electronic games celebrating the "me" decade: Citing the best obsession-inducing electronic games of the 1980s — PacMan, Tetris, Asteroids, and others — '80s Games & Trivia makes a case for that decade's being the best gaming period (sort of the golden years of wasting time, I suppose). Anyway, '80s Games & Trivia brings it all back to life with Java applets and regular Web interfaces that not only resuscitate the electronic classics but also present nonbeeping challenges such as Rubik's Cube and Trivial Pursuit. You don't need plug-ins to join the retro-gaming fun, but you do need a Java-capable browser, such as a recent version of Navigator or Explorer (Version 3.0 or later works fine in both cases). The Daily 100 offers a Hollywood sound clip (using AU files) to challenge your movie memories. Registration is required, but only for score-keeping purposes, and it's free.

Gamesville

www.gamesville.com

Online bingo: The prizes aren't much for winning a Gamesville game, but prizes are indeed promised. That's the rationale for asking you to complete a long and thoroughly repellent free registration process before playing, when in fact Gamesville just wants your demographic information for its advertisers. The site turns disingenuous once again when it tells you to wait for all the graphics to load on a certain page before clicking the Play button, explaining that the game won't work without them. The truth is that the graphics are banner ads that have nothing to do with the game. Such sleaziness is unwelcome in my book, but I must admit that playing bingo online is kind of a blast. Each game has a board design that you must replicate in order to win, and you get three bingo cards (boards). New numbers appear at the top of the game window, and a new game begins every 20 minutes, 18 hours per day. (Can you spell a-d-d-i-c-t-i-o-n?) You can also play Acey Deucey and something called Picturama.

Hollywood Stock Exchange

www.hsx.com

Virtual trading in the movie industry: How many times have you wished that you could invest money in the careers of stars and the fortunes of movies? Neither have I. Nevertheless, the Hollywood Stock Exchange (HSX) is a good idea, it's well implemented, and it's dangerously addictive to play. Yes, you can find pots of prizes at the ends of the rainbows, in case the sheer joy of succeeding in a game of insight isn't enough motivation. Registration is required to open your HSX account, but the game is free. All money in this game is imaginary. Upon registration, you're given $2 million in HSX dollars and access to some information pages about movie productions and personalities. The game is run much like a real stock exchange, with share prices and daily gains and losses — except that the trading day never ends in this 24-hour game.

Internet Gaming Zone

www.zone.com

Microsoft's entry into gaming: Give Microsoft its due — although the company was late to embrace the Internet, Bill Gates's crew is making up for lost time quickly. This rapidly growing online game community is a perfect example. Once you sign in (for free), you can enter a game's room and begin playing and chatting. Price-wise, the games fall into three categories: free ones that you can play at the site; games where you need the CD version of the game in your machine, and then the Internet Gaming Zone plays "matchmaker," pitting you against others; and premium games that require a small fee (around $10 per month for *Fighter Ace*). The offerings are diverse but generally family friendly, ranging from Microsoft's own *Age of Empires* to Bridge to *Jedi Knight: Dark Forces II* to Spades. Internet Gaming Zone also stages tournaments and ranks players. Strangely, you won't find a game about dominating the computer industry at Internet Gaming Zone. Guess Microsoft saved that one for real life.

Mr. Showbiz Plastic Surgery Lab

www.mrshowbiz.com/features/games/
   surgery

Virtual plastic surgery for the stars: The Plastic Surgery Lab is part of the broad Mr. Showbiz entertainment site (reviewed in the "Entertainment News and Gossip" section of Part VI), and invites you to rearrange the facial features of the stars, like John Travolta and Nicolas Cage in the movie *Face/Off* or recent Oscar

nominees. You can make wholesale substitutions of one actor's face for another while keeping the hair or take the more subtle approach of mixing the features of several celebs. Whichever method you choose, you're in for high-quality dilution of your valuable time at this site — no question about it. The simple interface of radio buttons for selecting features makes this site a no-learning-curve bit of foolishness, and several "labs" are available for your wicked experiments.

Prizes.com

www.prizes.com

Contests, lotteries, and big prizes: Prizes.com represents a new trend in online contests — one that involves money. The prizes in the site's name refer to cash winnings, as in a lottery. Some of the games, in fact, are distinctly lottery like, involving number selection and pure chance. As you do in a government lottery, you also must pay for the privilege of playing, in some cases. Prizes.com has free games that pay their winnings in either cash or tokens, which are the site's virtual currency. You can use accumulated tokens to play the cash games, most of which cost 50 cents (one token) to play. Furthermore, you can buy tokens outright by using a credit card, maintaining a balance of tokens in your Prizes.com account. Tokens never expire. Prizes range up to $100,000, with better odds for smaller prizes. When playing this sort of Internet lottery, you must feel comfortable that the site is honest and doesn't avoid posting numbers that you have selected. Although I have no reason to mistrust this site, I would engage in such pleasures in strict moderation.

Riddle du Jour

www.dujour.com/riddle

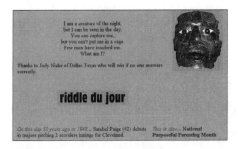

Riddles posted daily: I am a "sea" of knowledge. But if you remove the "sea," I become something that functions erroneously. What am I? That riddle is an example of the brain-puzzlers dished up daily at Riddle du Jour. This site is fun in a couple of ways. First, the game is highly participatory, with members typing possible answers to each of the daily riddles, competing for fairly substantial prizes. Also, everyone is invited to submit original riddles, and if you stump the members, you get the prize. Past riddles are archived for a week (you can't browse farther back, unfortunately). Oh, the answer to the preceding riddle? The word *faculty* — remove the *c,* and it becomes *faulty.*

Riddler

www.riddler.com

 $

Games, puzzles, and surprisingly few riddles: Oddly, riddles are de-emphasized at the Riddler site. Browsing this site is like visiting a baseball page that covers basketball, hockey, tennis, lacrosse — and down at the bottom of the home page, you find an inconspicuous link to baseball. So it is with riddles on the Riddler site, but that's not a complaint. This site is a fun and varied Web gaming location that offers crosswords, trivia, and multiple-player games, in addition to riddles. Oh, and prizes — let's not forget

about the prizes. You must register to play some of the games or win any of the prizes; registration is free but complicated and extremely bothersome. After you waste an hour filling in multiple forms, a surprise awaits you: Some of the games have entry fees if you want to qualify for prizes. You can play for fun for free, however.

The Station

www.station.sony.com

No Vanna, no Alex, but lots of fun: Sony, in addition to owning a pretty good chunk of the home electronics market, owns a pretty good chunk of Hollywood, including the production company behind the television game shows *Jeopardy!* and *Wheel of Fortune.* This Sony Web site includes — not surprisingly — online versions of both. Online *Jeopardy!* and online *Wheel of Fortune* are played pretty much the same way as the famous, enduring television contests, except that you play alone and not with two other live contestants and a somewhat stiff, if erudite, host, or beautiful letter-turner. (You know, if you really watch Vanna, she doesn't turn letters anymore, she just touches the letters. What a gig.) Other games are also offered. Be sure to have your browser cache turned on (it usually is on by default, so if you've never messed with your cache setting, don't start now); otherwise, the games proceed too slowly to be fun. If playing the games doesn't hold your interest, you can use the message boards or chat rooms. If you work your browser windows with skill, in fact, you can chat *while* playing.

Trivial Pursuit

www.trivialpursuit.com/htdocs

Online edition of the board game: Thank goodness — now I can be humiliated in private by playing the solo online version of Trivial Pursuit. The object of this virtual game is to fill in all the slices of a pie by correctly answering questions in six categories. You get six tries in each category — six opportunities to demonstrate exactly how little you know about stuff. My general knowledge is barely up to the task, and I learned an important lesson about careful typing. In response to the question "What monument took 1,700 years to build?" I meant to answer "Great Wall of China" but accidentally entered "Great Mall of China," which, as everyone knows, took only 1,000 years to build. (The Great Mall was a deterrent to invaders, largely because of its inadequate food court and lack of parking.) As both caustic consolation and sardonic reward for your wrong and right answers, the site spits out comments such as, "Is now a good time to tell you that your boss is behind you?" No registration or prizes are available — just good old-fashioned degradation of your self-esteem.

Virtual Chess Coach

home.rmci.net/tvchess/coach

Chess instruction: Virtual Chess Coach is not a playing site but a nicely done instructional site for improving your game. From the starting-line basic of learning how the pieces move to intermediate maneuvers such as forks, pins, and skewers to advanced techniques including types of openings and closings, Virtual Chess Coach presents a wealth of illustrated help that should make any aspiring chess maven drool. Anybody can understand the simple, clear explanations and illustrations. Short articles geared to coaches and parents are included, as well as a book list and links to other Web sites.

Other Stuff to Check Out

info.gte.com/cgi-bin/battle.cgi
www.casinocenter.com
www.gamehut.com
www.netlink.co.uk/users/pagat
www.shockrave.com
www.smalltime.com/nowhere/findthespam
www.snacking.com
www.uschess.org

Humor and Comedy

www.comcentral.com/jshome.html

Humor is alive and well on the Internet. Like all other topics, but perhaps more glaringly, some Web humor is decidedly mediocre. But that mediocrity just makes the good sites seem all the better.

The following sites cover the gamut from literary humor to outright silliness. I emphasize written humor but include a couple of multimedia sites.

BRETTnews

www.brettnews.com

Hilarious, literate commentary on modern culture: Brett Leveridge is his name; he's a humor columnist in the tradition of Andy Rooney (but far funnier, I assure you), and this Web site contains his collected ruminations. You may have come across

Brett Leveridge before, either in print or over National Public Radio; a page on this site enables you to hear some of those vocal essays in either RealAudio or Shockwave format. *BRETTnews* is a virtual periodical consisting solely of Leveridge's funny, observational, tasteful essays. He lambastes advertising, corporate downsizing, and similar topical issues with a resigned, "can-you-believe-it" sort of style, with great turns of phrase and hilarious examples. Bob Costas gave his thumbs-up to the site, which is a favorite of mine, too. (Generally, I follow Bob Costas around as much as possible.)

Comedy Central

www.comcentral.com/jshome.html

Online comedy, sponsored by the cable-TV channel: Much more than just a promotion for the comedy cable network, the Comedy Central site is like a channel unto itself, feeding laughs and plenty of interactivity to chuckle-starved netizens everywhere (well, everywhere in the English-speaking world, anyway). Many of the stalwart Comedy Central TV shows have online surrogates at this site, including *Win Ben Stein's Money* and *The Daily Show.* You can play the game in the first case and access *Daily Show* features (such as "5 Questions") in the second. My favorite portion of the site — it keeps me going back often — is the Today's Headlines section, which puts a comic spin on current events, especially entertainment stories. Irreverence is the rule, of course, and the writing is witty and scalding.

The Corporation

www.thecorporation.com

Corporate-culture satire: This humor site is everyone's over-the-top nightmare of corporate arrogance. Playing it deadpan all the way, The Corporation has page upon page of tongue-in-cheek memos, statements, and press releases concerning its affairs, labor relations, and policies. The Corporation opened a school in Arkane, Indiana, for example, so that its child laborers can get a quality education without having to leave the plant. The Corporation appropriates the entire Internet as its own network. Some pages don't carry the corporate-memo motif but are separate comedy products — the Cybermuseum of Modern Art (COMA), for example. A tremendous amount of work has gone into this site, which is one of the underpublicized humor gems on the Net. Even though The Corporation hasn't issued any new memos in a while, check it out, but remember to keep telling yourself, "It's not true!"

Ditherati

www.ditherati.com

Ridiculous quotes: Ditherati must be a medical site; it documents foot-in-mouth disease wherever it occurs in our digital world. Concentrating primarily on the ditherati of the digerati — that is, the endearingly foolish things said by news-media moguls and media-challenged politicians — the site is clean and spare. Just one hilarious quote per day graces these pages, each prefaced by a one-sentence commentary. Fortunately, past dithers are archived for your enduring pleasure. Revel retrospectively in the day when a software company president remarked, "Next to food and water, the human race needs things, and that's what we design." In many cases, the quotes require a veteran netizen's experience with computers and Silicon Valley companies, without which getting the humor may be hard. But in many cases, the dumb hilarity shines clearly for everyone. And you can sign up for the e-mail service, which sends the stupidity to you for free.

L.A. Times Laugh Lines

**www.latimes.com/HOME/NEWS/LIFE/
LAUGHS**

Hollywood chuckles: One of the stereo-types of Southern California is that of the starving actor struggling to be discov-ered. Well, a lot of starving comics in and around Los Angeles hope to get some attention, too, and the *Los Angeles Times* helps out by publishing a daily column called Punch Lines that includes comic observations from the discovered (Jay Leno) to the not-so-well known. The site also has a daily Pint-Sized Punch Lines column with jokes for and by kids; a somewhat daily column called Off-Kilter that offers news and observations about events that are, well, a little out of the ordinary; and a weekly self-explanatory piece called Wide World of Weird. Other sites may be funnier, and the jokes sometimes tend to have a Southern California bent, but for consistent chuckles about the world at large, this page at the *Los Angeles Times* site is a great way to start your day.

NeoScience Institute

www.necrobones.com/neosci

Science satire: It's a good thing this page has *Neo* in NeoScience; otherwise, you may be tempted to take it seriously. The credo of the page authorizes anyone bearing the NeoScience membership card to "perform any experiment in the name of science, regardless of any hazards, moral issues, or legalities, while free of liability for the results." The NeoScience Institute explores potentially ground-breaking experiments, such as animal training through high-energy explosives and artificially intelligent tooth implants. A photo gallery shows off the Institute's equipment and staff members, including Igor, the general-purpose assistant. My only complaint is about the wimpy yellow type, which is tricky to read against the blazing blue backgrounds. But just

consider that design to be another misguided experiment on your eyes, and enjoy this fine satirical page.

The Onion

**www.theonion.com/
contentframemain.html**

Tongue-in-virtual-cheek satire: "Congress Passes Americans With No Abilities Act." "Aspirin Taken With Bottle of Bourbon Reduces Awareness of Heart Attacks." Such are the blazing headlines of The Onion, the Web's finest satirical newspa-per, which specializes in deadpan literary prose that often verges on bad taste. (One story on "Educators Alarmed by Poorly Written Teen Suicide Notes" devolved into a hilarious article about split infini-tives and dangling participles among desperate, suicidal teens.) The idea behind the site's name is that it makes you cry — with laughter. To be fair, The Onion isn't *only* a satirical publication; it features serious interviews with enter-tainment personalities in the A.V. Club section. But most people that I know visit the site for the weekly updates of fake news, and that feature is certainly what brings me back again and again. **Note:** Parents, The Onion's humor can some-times run to more adult themes, so you may not want to let your children browse here alone.

Rodney Dangerfield

www.rodney.com

The comedian's Web site: "I tell ya, I don't get no respect — no respect at all." It would seem strange if Rodney's perennial complaint *didn't* come piping through from the home page of the official Rodney Dangerfield site, and indeed it does. The legendary comedian has been delivering morose one-liners to an eager audience for — how many years? Nobody knows for sure; historians are stumped. But the man keeps up with the times, with appearances on *Mad TV* and the creation of his own, quite slick Web site. Rodney Dangerfield (the site, not the man) relies on video and audio clips for good effect, presenting a Joke of the Day and other odds and ends, including video highlights from his career; you need RealPlayer to view them. A few contests, selected merchandise, and the chance to e-mail the legendary comedian himself fill in the gaps around the jokes. Rodney may not get much respect in the real world, but this site is a virtual shrine.

TeeVee

search.intertext.com/teevee

Poking fun at TV programming: Television is so frustrating for the critical, sated, jaded viewer that some sort of release is necessary. You could throw your TV set out a tall window, David Letterman-style, but you'd feel remorseful if it squashed a cat. You could compare caustic notes with your friends, but that would just motivate you to watch the same awful programs again so that you could hold up your end of the conversation. The best solution is to spend wasted TV-watching time visiting TeeVee, soaking up the funny cynicism of this cybercritique. Go for the Must Read TeeVee section on the left (with the convenient slide bar) to find the archived back issues. Who knows? You may end up spending more time staring at your computer monitor than at your TV — and only you can decide whether that's a lifestyle improvement.

Other Stuff to Check Out

www.bobsfridge.com
www.netlink.co.uk/users/humornet/
   biblio.html
www.scottibros.com
www.sfcomedy.org

Kids' Sites

www.girltech.com/index.html

Kids take to the Net like fish to water. Like birds to air. Like bees to flowers. Like — well, enough metaphors. Kids love the Internet, a lot of kids are around, and a lot of kid-oriented sites are around, too. This section is one of the largest in the book because I couldn't stop showing off these sites to kids and parents both. In finding your own Web locations for children, remember the Yahooligans! directory, reviewed in the "Directories" section of Part I. This directory is a kid-safe universe of Web links, divided by topic, and is one of the best resources on the Net for young folks. Here's the URL: www.yahooligans.com.

Information for the Young Mind

The sites in this section aren't necessarily educational, strictly speaking; they don't all attempt to replicate and supplement school subjects. The following sites do, however, provide some kind of information geared to the young mind that's more substantial than just an activity or game. Some of these sites are in game format, make no mistake about it, but fun is a vehicle for conveying information.

Alaska Space Science Adventures

dac3.pfrr.alaska.edu/~ddr/ASGP/
   INDEX.HTM

Alaskan science: A production of the Poker Flat Research Range in cooperation with other Alaskan science foundations, the Alaska Space Science Adventures site brings space down to earth for young viewers. Splashing a picture of the aurora borealis on the home page gets things off to a good start and gives kids a multitude of further choices. (The Aurora Gallery on the What Makes Alaska Different page has more images.) Some of the information is about Alaska, and some material is about physics, unrelated to space exploration. The Straight Scoop button leads to pages written for older students.

Biography.com

www.biography.com

Online companion to the A&E series: This extraordinary site is produced by Arts & Entertainment, the cable-TV channel famous for its *Biography* programs. Although the TV programming is promoted somewhat, this site is genuinely educational for people of all ages. The site maintains a list of current biography books on the Read page, providing links to reviews and, in some cases, the entire first chapters of the books. A biography quiz awaits on the Play page to humiliate you as it did me. If you want something simpler (hah!), try the anagram game; get it right the first time and you can use the

site's online anagram engine to scramble the letters in your own name. A search engine enables you to track down information on historical figures (or choose among an alphabetical list of 15,000 people), and a message-board section features literally hundreds of ongoing discussions about famous people, past and present. Biography.com is an awesome, beautifully designed site.

Discover Learning

www.bc.sympatico.ca/learning

A broad learning site for kids, parents, and teachers: Discover Learning is a sprawling Web site for kids, mainly, but this Canadian site provides sections for parents and teachers as well. The Student Skull Cramp section is designed with an eye to satisfying kids of all ages, from language puzzles to games to jokes. Discover Learning is nicely balanced among online activities, learning resources, and Web tools for making the most of the Internet. A Beyond Learning section (in the Parent Braindump) stretches young minds beyond school. Free registration is required to participate in the Forum message boards, but the rest of the site is unrestricted. Huge Web link lists are categorized by topic, with an especially impressive collection of environmental-awareness sites.

Dole 5 a Day

www.dole5aday.com

Nutrition information: On the World Wide Web, as on television, many companies produce children's programming sites that inform while selling products. I generally avoid listing such sites in this book, but in this case, the information is so valuable, and the site is so colorfully presented, that it's a worthwhile stop even if the Dole company wants to equate its name with health in the mind of every child in the world. Bobby Banana is the site's host, promoting the idea of five daily servings of fruits and vegetables, and purportedly is the voice of the "5 a Day" theme song that comes blasting out when you reach the home page. You can view much of the site without plug-ins, but Shockwave is used well on some pages. The Nutrition Center teaches kids facts about fruits and vegetables, and breaks down foods according to what nutrients they contain. Sometimes the fruits and vegetables use WAV files to tell you about their goodness. Christopher Canteloupe, for example, is high in Vitamin A. Don't believe me? Just ask him.

Educational Web Adventures

www.eduweb.com/adventure.html

Great learning games: The folks behind Educational Web Adventures have teaching experience that ranges from kindergartners to adults, so it should be little surprise that they've produced a great Web site that should appeal to both. For example, A Pintura: Art Detective is a classy piece of work that delivers a lesson in art history disguised as a detective game. Using mostly text, supplemented with photographs of art reproductions, the story is written in an amusing, exaggerated detective-novel style. The case involves identifying paintings in an attic and, in the process, picking up some basics on art history. Is art the only subject? Nope. Science and social studies topics are also covered, with suggested age ranges conveniently included. Parents, ignore this site at your own risk. If your children discover "The Tiger Talks Back" game before you do, they'll tease you with questions like, "Why do tigers have stripes?" (Hint: camouflage. Now you're on your own.)

Encyclopedia of Women's History

www.teleport.com/~megaines/ women.html

Profiles of famous women, written by children: This remarkable encyclopedia is written entirely by, and for, kids, and young visitors are encouraged to submit their own entries about historical women. The result of multiple submissions is that some famous women have more than one descriptive article. Topic duplication doesn't pose a problem, especially considering the extremely abbreviated length of some submissions. The entries aren't edited — at least, not for spelling and grammar, and presumably not for content — so the educational value of the Encyclopedia of Women's History may not be on a par with the *Encyclopedia Brittanica*. No matter. I've never found any egregious errors, and half the value of this site is the invitation to young visitors to do some research and publish a report on the Web.

Family PC for Kids

www.yahooligans.com/content/fpc

An easy-to-navigate site for kids: Simplicity is appealing to young netizens, and a kids' site can get away with substantially simpler content than an adult site can. That fact is demonstrated at Family PC for Kids, a three-part site whose large type and memorable categories make it easy for kids — especially those on the young side — to call the site their own. A recent Celebrity Profile described a producer of animated TV programming. MegaNews posts news about software for children, and GigaBrain's Page Picks is a link list to other kids' sites.

FreeZone

freezone.com/home

Online magazine for kids: FreeZone is an interactive kids' e-zine covering culture, science, sports, puzzles and games, and communication with other kids. Loaded to the hilt with graphics, FreeZone trades quick display times for an engaging, busy, animated, lively, colorful page design that's sure to attract attention and catch the eye of any surfing child. Encouraging curiosity (the site is produced by Curiocity) and communication, FreeZone provides plenty of chat and message-board space, as well as lessons on Internet safety. (The chat area is monitored full-time.) The chat rooms are usually fairly crowded, even during times when no official meetings are scheduled. Free registration is required for using the message boards.

Girl Tech

www.girltech.com/index.html

Resources for girls: The clean, simple home page of Girl Tech is deceptive — it doesn't give any indication of the deep range of resources that are available to young female surfers at this site. More than a virtual club, Girl Tech is a haven and a point of empowerment for girls around the world who feel underrepresented on the Internet. Hailed by CNN, *Ms.* magazine, and the national

director of the YWCA, Girl Tech provides lots of features and lots of interactivity (like threaded message boards) to encourage girls to get involved. Tips for parents are sprinkled throughout the site, and articles on girls and technology appeal to parents as well as kids. Resources (including lesson plans for teachers), bibliographies, links, reviews, and a resource list round out this all-star site.

John Ward Elementary School

hammer.ne.mediaone.net

School's Web site: Of all the school Web projects posted to the Internet, John Ward Elementary School is one of the best. Educational as well as fun, the site spins off pages about civil rights, the environment, geography, Hawaii, handicaps, and science. On the fun side, interactive games downplay competition while emphasizing logic and strategy. The site features a special tribute to the Boston Marathon, which runs through Newton, Massachusetts, where the school is located. The links page is broken down in the style of a Web directory. John Ward Elementary School has put together a well-rounded site and updates it fairly often.

KidSat

kidsat.jpl.nasa.gov

NASA-sponsored space site: Although KidSat is a NASA-sponsored Web site about astronomy and space, it's designed and run by kids. The site's goal is to provide kids with tools for participating in the exploration of space by following the progress of shuttle missions, meeting the crew, helping plan observations, and using images generated from the exploratory missions. The site is still under development, and some of these goals remain just goals for the time being. For now, the photo gallery is one of the best parts of the site. From ground systems to NASA logos to space views, every image in the database is available to kids free of charge for use on their Web pages and in school reports.

KidsCom

www.kidscom.com

Global site for kids: For an active, entertaining, fun, and educational site, kids get a good deal with KidsCom. The site maintains a global perspective, especially in the Around the World section, where children can learn about life in other countries, view other cities, and connect electronically with KidsCom members all over the place. The site even provides e-mail links to presidents and prime ministers. A well-designed Graffiti Wall Chat area (on the Make New Friends page) is a kind of chat environment where kids can connect in real time. (The chat areas are monitored at all times.) Quizzes, news, contents, games, and a chance to submit a story based on supplied characters and places enliven the proceedings. KidsCom is a great starting place for any child's Web session.

kidsworld-Online

www.kidsworld-online.com

Virtual creative center for kids: The online home of *kidsworld* magazine, kidsworld-Online has one of the best e-zine designs for children that I've seen. A cartoon map of the site starts you off, but if you have trouble figuring out what the locations mean, the text-based Guided Tour below the map saves the day. Movie reviews focus on kid-appropriate flicks; Around the House features recipes and games; the School section has science experiments and other activities; a Poetry Wall enables kids to put up their own verses; kidsworld News features headlines from a young perspective; and Cool Links sends viewers off to other kids' destinations on the Web. The site is consistently entertaining in its design without resorting to cuteness or condescension.

Knowledge Adventure

www.adventure.com/kids

Learning and fun for kids of various ages: Knowledge Adventure built its reputation on excellent, fun, and educational CD-ROM products for children. The tradition continues on the Internet with the Knowledge Adventure Web site, and kids should head immediately to the Jump Start Activities link on the home page. The following page is divided into grade levels, each one offering a variety of interactive learning activities. Online sticker books, slider puzzles, and coloring books entertain young viewers, while the fourth-grade crowd (the oldest age group) can connect the dots and do more advanced coloring. Knowledge Adventure imported many of the multimedia goodies that its CD-ROMs are famous for, but they work less smoothly over the Internet, using a standard 33.6 Kbps modem. Kids should get a big kick out of the frog-numbers game, a Java applet in which you solve an equation by flicking a frog's tongue at the correct answer. Plug-ins aren't required, but a Java-capable browser is needed.

The Locker Room

members.aol.com/msdaizy/sports/
   locker.html

Sports information for young fans: The Locker Room exhibits all kinds of information about various sports in a format that kids appreciate and find easy to navigate. The site describes the rules of the games and provides information such as history, fun facts, important dates in each sport's season, glossaries, necessary equipment, variations on the main sport (such as softball in the baseball section), and children's leagues. The writing is brief and clear without being condescending — even adults can learn a thing or three from these pages. Baseball, soccer, tennis, ice hockey, basketball, football (American), gymnastics, swimming, running, field hockey, volleyball, and bowling are covered. Additionally, a page gives kids instruction on stretching and warm-up exercises.

Penpal Box

www.ks-connection.com/penpal/
   penpal.html

International pen-pal exchange: Penpal Box is a service for kids up to 16 years old who seek e-mail pen pals. Straightforward in design, the site invites you to click a box labeled with the appropriate age and then read a selection of letters (like classified ads) by kids describing their interests. A truly international

meeting place, the letters come from everywhere from Malaysia to Sweden. The Penpal Box Help link describes how kids can post their own names and letters to the site. Safety and problem-solving are covered in detail.

SchoolHouse Rock

genxtvland.simplenet.com/
   SchoolHouseRock/index-hi.shtml

Online companion to the TV series: Fans of the innovative, clever, and effective education series probably would agree that the *SchoolHouse Rock* songs are among the best educational songs ever produced. Sometimes difficult to find in CD stores, the good news is that *SchoolHouse Rock* is now available on the World Wide Web. The entire *SchoolHouse Rock* oeuvre is filed in five categories: Grammar Rock, Science Rock, Multiplication Rock, America Rock, and Scooter Computer and Mr. Chips. Songs such as "Conjunction Junction," "Busy Prepositions," and "Naughty Number Nine" swing, jazz, and rock through principles of math, language, science, computer basics, and history. Words are included for singing along with the RealAudio and WAV audio clips, and some numbers have the original QuickTime videos.

Starchild

starchild.gsfc.nasa.gov

Astronomy information: Starchild is a learning center for young astronomers. One of the site's best features is its division of information into two levels. Level one is for young kids; it keeps explanations simple and brief. Level two goes a little deeper, assuming more knowledge of science and language. The Solar System, the Universe, and Space Stuff are the three main sections of the site; a fourth section is devoted to a glossary. Occasional quizzes pop up, and the site encourages kids to study hard in school.

Tech Wizards

www.hompro.com/techkids

Information on robots and space explora-tion: Tech Wizards is produced by an engineer, a mother of three kids who owns a technology-consulting business. Featuring an emphasis on robots and space (and robots *in* space), the site is essentially a lengthy link list, with some commentary. In less-capable hands, this site wouldn't be too extraordinary, but the site's range and quality of links are excellent, even though some of the news links are getting a little long in the, uh, tooth? Sections include Robots in Space, Robotics for Beginners, Featured Labora-tories, Field Trips, Robots in the News, Robot Folks, Wired Women, Electronics in the Classroom, Cool Clubs, Zines, and a book list. Definitely for older kids, Tech Wizards is a terrific Web resource.

UNICEF: Voices of Youth

www.unicef.org/voy

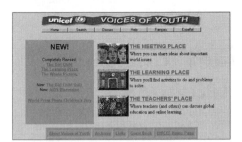

Social issues around the world — for teens: For older children, Voices of Youth is an opportunity to learn about global issues of health, peace, sufficiency, and different ways of life, and also to connect with other kids. Games and interactive features inform kids about issues in parts

of the world where life, especially for children, is sometimes desperate. This site is designed for teenagers; younger kids may be frightened by some of the pictures or at least may not comprehend much of the site's content. The bulletin-board area invites kids to post opinions and ideas about world hunger, child neglect, and other adult issues, and the message community is truly international.

The Why Files

whyfiles.news.wisc.edu

Science for kids: This site is a clever, edutaining way of hooking kids into learning about science, especially if they're familiar with the similarly named *The X-Files* TV show. The Why Files seeks to explain the background behind headline science-news stories. A recent visit featured a story, called "Running on Empty," about the depletion of natural resources here on Earth. The related articles broadened the topic by explain-ing how overfishing, overpopulation, and land-use practices are causing, or will soon cause, scarcities in fish, fresh water, and, yes, even chocolate. The site sometimes tackles difficult or controver-sial subjects, such as the selling of elephant-tusk ivory in African countries. The site is a model of clarity, both graphically and editorially.

World's Greatest Speeches

www.audionet.com/speeches

Collection of 20 speeches: From Franklin Delano Roosevelt's first inaugural address in 1933 to a speech by George Bush in 1991, World's Greatest Speeches dishes up 20 RealAudio presentations of famous (and infamous) public addresses. The site, which is part of the Broadcast.com system of Web audio programming, is actually a promotion for a CD-ROM of 400 speeches. Whether the CD-ROM appeals to you or not, the Web page is a nifty way for kids to hear speeches that they may not have been around to hear the first time, as well as to familiarize themselves with RealAudio.

Yak's Corner

www.yakscorner.com

Fun and attractive magazine for kids: Calling itself "America's coolest news magazine for kids," Yak's Corner lives up to its own hype in both page design and content. Created by the *Detroit Free Press* (see the review of the Freep Web site in the "Newspapers" section of Part II), the stated mission of the site is to get kids to read more. In an era in which children get their information from TV, enticing them to read through a computer monitor may not be a bad idea. (A printed version of Yak's Corner is distributed with the *Detroit Free Press*.) Certainly, Yak's Corner lures kids in with stunning graphics and news stories that appeal to a child's world — reviews of new movies for kids, for example, and reports that quote kids more often than adults. The interactivity of the site comes to life in many ways. The Your Art section invites kids to send in art (by postal mail) and then displays it on a gallery page. The Yaktivities section has an online story for which readers are invited to submit the next chapter, or an invitation to e-mail the site, called, of course, Yak Back to the Yak. As if that's not enough, the site also has a

Fun & Games section which includes — I swear I am not making this up — a Yak Yuks page.

ZuZu

www.zuzu.org

Online magazine partly written by Web visitors: Often visited and frequently updated, ZuZu is an online magazine for kids, featuring artwork, stories, poetry, creative writing, jokes, interviews, Broadway reviews, and profiles of kids. Original contributions are encouragingly solicited on a page (Get Published!) that explains exactly what's needed in upcoming issues and how to send stuff. Stories and artwork are welcome submissions. The past several issues are available for browsing.

Other Stuff to Check Out

co-nect.bbn.com/WorldBand/
   CoNECTMusic.html
kidshealth.org
litcal.yasuda-u.ac.jp/LitCalendar.shtml
www.childrensmusic.org
www.realkids.com
www.usinteractive.com/stomp/home.html

Kids' Games and Activities

Activity sites are usually produced by not-for-profit organizations, Web-savvy parents, or commercial companies seeking to promote their offline products. Some schools have created activity pages to share with the world at large. The educational factor in sites that provide on-screen activities for kids is usually prominent, but some of the following sites are games, pure and simple, that don't attempt to teach a thing.

Brain Teasers

www.eduplace.com/math/brain

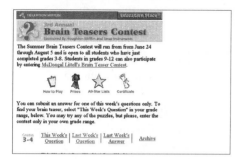

Math puzzles: The Brain Teasers site reminds me of my grammar-school days, when arithmetic puzzles were the bane of my young life. I still can't do those puzzles, as I recently discovered with certainty after roaming the challenges of this site. The puzzles are of the real-world-challenge type, such as decorating a room of certain dimensions or calculating how many miles are traveled by a man walking backward through a train (or something like that; my brain is too weary to remember properly). All the puzzles are divided by school grade, but settling into the youngest group didn't help me any. The Web page holds occasional contests, but just working on the archive of past puzzles is fun for kids who have a flair for problem-solving. If you know any of these kids, have them e-mail the answers to me.

Carlos' Coloring Book

coloring.com

Online coloring book: An online coloring book? Carlos' Coloring Book has been online since 1994 and is going strong with a fun, simple site for young kids. Offering a selection of bold, clear line drawings with color palettes on the pages, the site invites kids to select a color, click a portion of the picture, and see a fresh display with that portion colored in.

Continuing that way eventually colors the entire picture, which typically has fewer than 20 portions. The pictures are happy, kid-friendly renderings of fruit, leprechauns, Santa Claus and Rudolph, and others.

CBC4Kids

www.cbc4kids.ca/

Canadian site for children: Hosted by the Canadian Broadcasting Corporation, CBC4Kids is a wonderfully designed, inviting site that entertains while it manages to educate. Visitors are offered the choice between an Intense page or a Regular page. Either way, you find that the site is divided into sections, four of which (Shhhh! Our secret!) relate to school subjects: The Lab (science), Words (language), Music, and Time (history). CBC4kids also has a Kids Club that's more like a show-and-tell, with jokes, practical money advice, a "name that sound" contest, a pet arena, and more. The Kids Club has a Clubhouse where registered guests (registration is free) can post messages, play games, and let others know what they think of movies, books, and the like. But a child can have lots of fun at the other pages without ever making it to the Kids Club section. Take Music, for example. Kids can listen to the Sound Bar Jukebox (they need the Shockwave plug-in, which is on this book's CD), listen to a feature about a band and take the Sound Bar Quiz, or use the Hum Link 4Kids for help when they can remember the words to a song but can't remember the title. And those just three of the offerings on the Music page.

FUNBRAIN.COM

www.funbrain.com

Math and spelling made fun: Nothing ever pleases both parents and their children, but FUNBRAIN.COM is a site that comes close — very close. FUNBRAIN.COM offers games that reinforce basic educational skills, but in a fun way, making games out of math, spelling, money, and so on. For example, Math Baseball frames arithmetic problems in a baseball format. Kids can select one of four levels of difficulty and specify whether they want addition, subtraction, multiplication, or division problems, or a combination. A math problem is posed on each page. The player must type an answer and then click the Swing! button to see whether the answer is correct. If so, the answer is a hit; if not, it's an out. Games last for three outs (if only real baseball games were so brief). The game is fine for very young kids because the easiest problems are on the 2 + 1 level. (I'm pleased to report that I got that answer right.)

The Headbone Derby

www.headbone.com/derby

Game requiring research performed on the Internet: The Headbone Zone seeks to provide an Internet learning experience while giving kids a good time. The site succeeds through opulent graphics and intriguing, well-designed games, not to mention weekly prizes. Using text in a cartoon format, the games are multiple-episode research adventures in which kids must learn to proceed, and the research can be performed on the Internet. As kids learn and proceed through the adventures, they accumulate points. Anyone can play as soon as he or she arrives at the site, but winners must have registered at the beginning.

Java Solitaire

hammer.ne.mediaone.net/solitaire.html

Virtual Chinese checkers (surprise!): Java Solitaire isn't the solo card game that most people are familiar with. Instead, the on-screen game is a one-person version of Chinese checkers, in which you try to remove as many marbles from the board as possible by jumping one over another; the jumped marble is removed. With a Java-equipped browser, you can play the game effortlessly by clicking and dragging; the computer does the book-keeping, moving the marbles off as they're jumped. The game is fun for all ages and surprisingly challenging.

Kids Domain

www.kidsdomain.com

Gentle site for kids and parents: The dancing teddy bear on this home page serves notice that this is a bright, cheery, nonthreatening site. Kids Domain has four main areas (Kids, Grownups, Downloads, and KD Review) that offer online games, activities, downloads, links, software reviews, Web site reviews, advice — you name it. The Holiday section in the Kids section is especially nice, offering themed activities and crafts for beleaguered parents. Another very helpful section is the Questions link, which, in addition to offering the standard "Who we are" information, includes tips on where parents with older computers can find software. All told, the bear could give Kids Domain a big thumbs-up — if the bear had opposable thumbs.

Kids' Space

www.ks-connection.org

Well-planned international site: The home page of Kids' Space has something rare: The option to customize the framed version of the page for left-handers and right-handers. Clicking one simply puts the site index frame on one side of the page or the other, but that's typical of some of the small, thoughtful touches put into this site. Whichever hand you go with, you'll find the site built around two main sections — an International Kids' Space section for creative activities, and a Kids' Space Connection section for communication activities. The site is rich with visitor-submitted material from around the globe, from the story submitted by an English language class in Russia to an audio clip of a 9-year-old French girl playing a Schubert waltz on the piano (obviously a child who listened when her mother told her to practice). Anyway, lots of interesting interactivity makes this a very worthy bookmark for younger netizens.

Mastermind

hammer.ne.mediaone.net/ mastermind.html

Engaging game against a computer: Mastermind is a one-page Web game for kids that looks simple. Playing the game isn't hard, but beating the computer isn't easy, either. Win or lose, though, the game is addictive enough that I almost missed my deadline for this portion of the book by playing it too much. For Java-enhanced browsers only (Version 3.0 or

later of Netscape Navigator or Internet Explorer works), the game requires you to guess the computer's sequence of colors by placing colored pegs in a board with holes. You have eight tries; the computer supplies hints about the correctness of your preceding attempt. Younger kids can approach the challenge as a fun guessing game; older children may appreciate it as a game of logic.

Mister Rogers' Neighborhood

www.pbs.org/rogers

Online companion to the TV series: Mister Rogers has a home in cyberspace, and it's located at this Web site. Designed to correlate with the themes of the television program, the site offers kids a range of activities and fun. One of the most valuable sections contains an extensive reading list on topics covered by the show. The Children's Corner area displays line drawings that can be printed and colored. The site has a distinct psychological bent, instructing kids in activities that, for example, help them deal with frustration and anger (drawing angry feelings, dancing fast, running, pounding on modeling dough). Parents' Pages give hints for the difficult moments of child rearing, such as bedtime.

National Wildlife Federation Games

www.nwf.org/nwf/games

Games, puzzles, and information on wildlife: This site, which is a subset of the National Wildlife Federation (NWF) Web domain, offers links to sections of the main site where kids can get information about the NWF or send for a catalog. But fun is the specific mission of the Games portion, although a child's brain cells certainly won't atrophy after he or she spends some time at this site. Mix-'em and match-'em games enable mouse-enabled kids to shuffle around parts of a picture — a simple jigsaw puzzle, really — to make a complete animal drawing. Riddles are clever, and the answers are placed on separate pages from the questions. (What kind of water should you drink when you are sick? <Fig click> Well water.) The I didn't know that! link definitely falls into the "teach them without their knowing it" category, featuring Gee Whiz Facts, such as how wolves can communicate by howling over a distance of two miles, or how cockroaches can go three months without eating, as long as they have water.

Seussville Games

www.randomhouse.com/seussville/
 games

Online companion to the Dr. Seuss books: Random House, publisher of the Dr. Seuss books, created a Web site filled with three types of games for kids, most of which involve the Dr. Seuss characters. Printable games include a connect-the-dots puzzle and The Cat's Hat Maze. Another section of games can be played online without any browser plug-ins. A third section contains Shockwave and may be accessed by browsers equipped with the large Shockwave plug-in (an accompanying link sends you to the download location). If you have a child who really likes this site, signing up for e-mail site updates on the Seussville home page is a good idea; the updates are delivered by the Cat in the Hat.

Wacky Web Tales

www.eduplace.com/tales

Create hilarious, nonsensical stories: Parents who remember the side-splitting *Mad Libs* books from their young years have the gist of Wacky Web Tales, except that the Web version can be played by a single person. Stories that contain crucial blank spots are provided. The idea is to fill in the blanks before ever seeing the story and then read it back with outrageously irrelevant nouns, verbs, and adjectives sprinkled through it. Withholding the story until the end is a good idea, allowing a child to play alone if no friend is around, as long as he or she knows how to make up a past-tense verb, a singular noun, an adjective, an adverb, and other basic word types. Players choose among a list of site-supplied stories or a much longer list of reader-supplied stories, and you can upload your own tale via e-mail.

www.thekids.com

www.thekids.com

Storytelling site: Storytelling is a much-beloved activity for most kids, perhaps because their imaginations are so free and active. This site is devoted to literature of high imagination, from legends to fantasy to folktales to sacred stories from different traditions. Placing a value on interactivity, this site invites kids to upload their own original stories, which then appear, signed, on the Web. Kids must know how to type or be with an older person who does. Monitored chat rooms are an upcoming feature.

Young Eloquent Authors' Haven

home1.pacific.net.sg/~lambert/
 yeah1.htm

Meeting place for young writers: Budding novelists and poets find a home at the extremely welcoming Young Eloquent Authors' Haven (YEAH) site, where eloquence is more of a goal than a requirement. Kids need to join to submit stories or poems, but anyone can browse the literature stored at the site. A friendly community, YEAH enables kids to sign up on the Keypals list; it also offers a collection of graphics for kids to use on their Web sites. YEAH is for all ages, and any piece of writing can be submitted for inclusion on the site; nothing is rejected.

Other Stuff to Check Out

204.96.11.210/jchuang/Music/Mozart/
   mozart.cgi
alabanza.com/kabacoff/Inter-Links/fun/
   b_games.html
craftsforkids.miningco.com/mbody.htm
imagiware.com/mancala.cgi
imagiware.com/masterweb.cgi
personal.nbnet.nb.ca/renhold/crafty.htm
www.bu.edu/htbin/pegs
www.cyberkids.com
www.cyberteens.com
www.kidnaround.com
www.kidscook.com
www.ozemail.com.au/~wprimary/acts.htm
www.tjw.stanford.edu/adventure

Kids' Personal Sites

The following sites are some of the best sites produced by children. In some cases, adult help clearly was involved, but the idea, writing, and basic design of the site belong to a child. Some of these kids are ambitious; some are brilliant; some are enthralled by global networking. All these children are the young pioneers of a new virtual community.

I must mention something about the stability of kid-produced sites, obvious though it may be: Kids grow. Quickly. Their enthusiasms burgeon, shift, and fade. These sites are not the most stable on the Web. I chose these listings with an eye to endurance, so one or two may be out of date or even discontinued when

you link to them. Sorry about that, but even out-of-date sites can provide ideas that are worth sharing with your kids (or borrowing for your own site, if you *are* a kid).

Adam Jones for President

www.mich.com/~jones

Web site for 16-year-old's 2024 presidential campaign: Have you decided who you're going to vote for in the U.S. presidential election of 2024? Well, start thinking ahead at Adam Jones's ambitious campaign headquarters. Adam is a 16-year-old Republican from Michigan, shown posing with the governor of that state. Adam, who began his campaign when he was 14, claims that the United States can't afford not to elect somebody who has devoted his life to improving the nation. He may have a point. At any rate, the site has won numerous awards (including one from Bob Dole) and is one of the most professional kid sites around. Check out Adam's platform, follow his links, and play his favorite game (Dark Horse).

Astronomy Net

**members.aol.com/stevehben/
   sastro.html**

Astronomy news and photos: Astronomy Net would be an impressive accomplishment of Web design and comprehensiveness for a person of any age, and it's an astounding feat for young Steven Benjamin. The phenomenal link directory of astronomy sites is a professional-level reference source. A recent visit turned up a 3-D photo of Saturn (you needed glasses from *Astronomy* magazine to get the full effect), as well as trivia questions that I couldn't answer. Steven also provides keyword entry forms for several major Web search engines — a major technical accomplishment. Finally, a chatroom interface invites astronomy buffs to connect for real-time conversation. Astronomy Net, at the very least, is educational for other kids. The site also is an inspiring example of the potential of the Internet when it's approached by an imaginative child.

The Bowen Family Page

www.comlab.ox.ac.uk/oucl/users/ jonathan.bowen/children.html

Web greetings from the banks of the Thames: Okay, maybe calling this a children's site is unfair — after all, Daddy (Jonathan Bowen) is a British college computer professor, and "Mummy" (Jane S.M. Bowen) is a museum curator, so the Bowen children (12-year-old Alice and 10-year-old Emma) probably had a little help with the page. Regardless, youngsters will still find this a delightful yet personal destination, and a great online resource. Yes, all the Bowen family members have personal pages (although Emma is a bit distressed that her sister's comes first alphabetically) that give a little bit of biographical information, complete with photos and AU sound files greeting visitors. Yes, there are games and poems and jokes and activities that the girls have collected or written. But what makes the site remarkable are the links. Sure, lots of personal sites have links, but the Bowen family has nearly 200, on everything from game sites to other family sites to museums to family resource sites, from all around the globe. And the links are not only in list form on the front page but also integrated into the girls' biographies. For example, Alice sang in a performance of Handel's *Messiah* in 1997. Click the word "Messiah" on her page, and you're transported to a biography of Handel on a Texas university site. Yes, all the members of the Bowen family probably had something to do with the construction of this site — but it's a site that probably every family can find something worthwhile on.

Christopher Johnson's Home Page

www.chris.com

ASCII art collection: Christopher Johnson is a teenager who discovered one day that the chris.com domain name was still unregistered on the Internet. To hear him tell the story, that fact was his entire motivation in creating a Web site. He registered the name for himself, posted his favorite Web links, and included the centerpiece of the site, which is an awesome collection of ASCII art. ASCII art, if you don't know, is a drawing made out of common typewriter characters, mostly punctuation. The idea is silly, but when taken deep into the realm of human ingenuity, the results can be amazing. Christopher collected hundreds of state-of-the-art examples, ranging from an astounding Betty Boop to trains and cars. This site has far and away the finest collection of ASCII art that I've ever seen.

Heather's Happy Holidaze Page

www.shadeslanding.com/hms

Music and holiday material: The 7-year-old Heather received coding help from her mom and dad in constructing the Happy Holidaze site, but the impressive design is hers. When you enter the site, a MIDI rendition of classical music streams out of your computer's speakers (assuming that you have a MIDI plug-in). Heather seems to be taken with Web technology in general and even promotes Internet telephony at the site. The holiday links form the site's core; each link gets its own little rhapsody, complete with advice, photos, a short spoken audio clip by Heather, and/or activities.

Ivan!

www.asiaonline.net.hk/lilywong/kids/ ivan.htm

Original artwork: Ivan Feign is a 6-year-old artist and world traveler (no kidding) whose site won a CorelDRAW Web site contest. Ivan's page features his artwork, all of which was created with traditional materials, not on a computer screen. Nonetheless, he is obviously talented, and it's a pleasure to see his renderings of a dolphin, an airplane, a boat, an octopus, and portraits of his family. As a surprise treat, Ivan sings a couple of songs in RealAudio — a serenade of sorts to accompany your visit to his virtual art gallery.

Katie's Basset Hounds

nashlinks.com/ginger.htm

Dog stories and information: This popular and touching site tells the tale of 12-year-old Katie's two basset hounds, in her own words, and invites other hound owners and dog lovers to leave their own greetings, notes, and dog stories. A MIDI music soundtrack follows you around the various pages of the site, playing an entertaining array of jazzy tunes. Katie gives her viewers hints on bringing up basset hounds, particularly along the lines of not allowing them to eat spools of thread, but the site's main purpose is sharing a love for dogs with friends of all ages.

Lindsay's Page

www.athenet.net/~suec/lindsay.html

Jokes and original artwork: Lindsay, who is 7 years old, likes jokes and mazes, and young kids will love her page. The jokes, all of which are riddles, are presented in a page format that displays a new chuckle with every click of the Reload button. The mazes are shaped like animals and, as Lindsay sensibly points out, are meant to be printed — no writing on the monitor. A short sound file enables you to hear Lindsay's voice, and a gallery link (wchat.on.ca/merlene/kid.htm) displays a slide show of the talented youngster's drawings.

Other Stuff to Check Out

home.sprynet.com/sprynet/balgassi/ adria.htm
worldkids.net/kids/adam
www.geocities.com/Heartland/3333
www.geocities.com/Paris/6699
www.iconsult.co.at/seta/private/pippa

Speaking as broadly as possible (kind of with a Midwestern accent), the Internet can be divided into three characteristics: information, commerce, and community. The community angle is what this section is all about. People actually meet other people in cyberspace, as the news programs sometimes remind us with occasional horror stories of seduction and invaded privacy. But considering the millions of meetings that occur every day, the Net is a relatively safe place, especially if you take these basic and easy precautions:

- **Don't give personal information to someone you meet online**. Guard your postal address and phone number, and even your e-mail address.

- **Don't fall into the temptation of believing that you know somebody well through online chatting.** The Internet is a one-dimensional environment.

- **Don't get addicted to virtual contact.** Keep the online world in its place.

With those precautions in mind, you can now trip gaily into the world of online chatting and message boards. I began my online citizenship through message boards, and I still consider them to be a wondrous way to get to know people all over the world who have similar interests. Chat rooms are fun, although far less sophisticated than message boards, generally speaking, with less substantial content.

Chatting and Message Boards

Remember those naysayers who said that the growing popularity of the Internet would only exacerbate one of society's secret ills, namely that we weren't spending enough time with other people? Check out any Web chat room today and

you'll find thousands of people spending some quality time with each other, albeit in electronic form. And chat rooms are becoming more popular every day, thanks to software improvements and more powerful — and affordable — personal computers. Where are those naysayers now? Probably logged into some chat room on the Web, that's where.

The following sites are chat and message-board communities. In all cases, intense adult supervision is required when kids are attracted to online chatting. In most cases, chat sites should be off-limits to children.

Astro-Chat

**astrochat.realitycom.com/astrochat/
   index.cfm**

Astrology topics: As astrological sites go, Astro-Chat is a semiserious community of people who enjoy talking about the ancient art (science?) of planet prognostication. The message boards use a bold, large, garish, and somewhat annoying blue type that takes up too much window space, but the site compensates for that drawback by placing all responses to an original message on the same page, saving you the trouble of endless mouse clicks. The Open Forum is for general chat, and other broad topics include Lover's Lane, Astrological Chat, World Visions ("How to make the world a better place, if you can be bothered"), Questions & Answers, and Books. Live chat is promised in the future. A new feature enables you to listen to your sun-sign forecast (weekly) through RealAudio. The audio feature is available only by subscription, but the preceding week's forecasts for all signs are archived for listening by anyone. My astro-forecast indicated that *Internet Directory For Dummies* will be the biggest-selling book of the century. Who would have guessed?

Chathouse

www.chathouse.com

Wide selection of chat rooms: Spectacular graphics on the home page set a high tone for this universally accessible chat domain, which means that anyone can see discussions, no matter what computer system or software configuration is being used. That doesn't mean you can always get by without special software: One of the free chat rooms (The Screening Room) features cyberconversation about independent films, which you can view clips by using the VDO plug-in, which you can find on the CD that accompanies this book. Chathouse is a large communal meeting place where anyone can cope with the software requirements (none) and begin meeting people right away. A phenomenal number of chat rooms are available for a variety of topics, but be aware that the clientele of Chathouse tends to be young and that the conversations often ignore the stated purpose of the room. Four levels of paid subscriptions are available, each offering a different selection of extra features, but you can (and probably should) ignore them all and just try the free rooms.

ChatPlanet

www.chatplanet.com

Directory of sites that use ChatPlanet software: ChatPlanet is a directory of Web chatting locations that use the ChatPlanet software. ChatPlanet created a Java chatting program that any Web site can use, turning that site into a ChatPlanet channel. What this means to you, if you visit ChatPlanet, is quite simply a big selection of chat alternatives on any number of subjects. ChatPlanet provides the directory. Just click your way into Arts & Entertainment, for example, find an interesting subtopic, and then link to the host Web site. The Java chat window looks the same in every case, so you should feel right at home; that's the advantage. The disadvantage is that the Java applet must load from scratch into your computer with every channel you visit, even if your visit occurs during the same Web surfing session. *La grande bummere,* as the French almost never say. Nevertheless, ChatPlanet is a good way to find the best chat sites for your interests — the ones that you'll return to again and again.

CoolChat

www.coolchat.com

Chatting and free Web sites for members: CoolChat is a more recent Web incarnation than GeoCities (reviewed in the following portion of this section), but it has the same ideology: a complete, planned Internet community. Whereas GeoCities centers on free Web pages and e-mail, CoolChat centers on chatting. But you get a free Web site, too, as well as an internal e-mail system. Membership is free, and the registration process is fairly harmless; several demographic questions are optional.

Cybercise

www.cybercise.com/forintro.html

Health and fitness topics: A high-quality message-board system with serious, friendly discussions that don't veer off-topic often, Cybercise is a well-designed, well-maintained virtual community. The topics of the site are exercise, fitness, diet, preventive medicine, and related health-empowerment subjects. The boards operate smoothly and quickly, using a text interface uncluttered by burdensome graphics or frames. Personal profiles are created during the required sign-in process, and you can access anybody's profile when you read that person's message. Each message is on a separate page, making the site a good exercise routine for your mouse but keeping things nicely organized. The tone of discussions is down-to-earth, sympathetic to health problems, full of advice, and sharing. The unmoderated boards receive the most traffic and are predominantly safe and polite, but for added security, you can use the moderated boards, in which every message is read by the site's staff before being posted publicly.

HomeArts Network

homearts.com/cgi-bin/WebX

Domestic topics: HomeArts is a family-oriented online community emphasizing home, food, garden, marriage, health, puzzles, family, and style. The preceding URL leads to the HomeArts chat rooms, though you can find the message board section with just a few clicks of your mouse. Registration (it's free) is needed before joining the chat rooms, but the other members are typically friendly. The message boards use the all-responses-on-one-page style, which has its plusses and minuses. Active topics grow into *very* long pages that take longer to load, but you can conveniently read everyone's

responses without reaching for the mouse every couple of seconds. Conversations on the HomeArts boards are mature and often last for months on a highly detailed topic, such as how to wire a newly built home for future technologies.

Talk City

www.talkcity.com

Chatting for adults and teens: Talk City is one of the big chat emporiums on the Web. You need special software to communicate in Talk City, but the software downloads automatically, and you have a choice of three program levels; the Lite version is the fastest to acquire. (Plug-ins aren't needed, but your browser must be Java-capable.) On the home page, use the drop-down list to choose which of the approximately two dozen chat rooms you want to enter. The topics are mostly innocuous sports or entertainment topics, and a teen room is available. This area isn't a secure, safe area for kids, however, and as is true of other chat domains, only adults should be present.

This Old House

boards.pathfinder.com/cgi-bin/ webx?14@@/This%20Old%20House/ This%20Old%20House

Home-renovation topics: A Pathfinder message community, This Old House is a meeting place for those who are interested in home renovation. Just browsing the board yields an education in removing caulk, venting a stove, patching walls, recoating clawfoot tubs, painting steel doors, coaxing attic bats outside, using paint sprayers, repainting masonry, and other handy skills. No registration is required; the Pathfinder approach to message boards is one of immediate gratification, and the linked message threads are presented up front on the home page.

Other Stuff to Check Out

boards.pathfinder.com/cgi-bin/
 webx?14@^470604@
paris-anglo.com/cafe
www.aidem.com.sg/madonna
www.bluemarble.net/~amyloo/phinished/
 index.html
www.esociety.net
www.yellowroom.com

General Communities and Directories

General communities usually provide a range of community services, including chat rooms, message boards, internal e-mail, and sometimes free Web pages. These sites are typically more family-oriented and generally somewhat safer for kids than message-board-only sites are — and certainly safer than chat-only environments.

Bla-Bla

www.bla-bla.com/chat

Great message boards for informal discussions: With the encouragement to "just keep talking" appearing all through the site, it's no wonder that the Bla-Bla message boards contain more than their share of fluff. In an apparent realization of this propaganda mistake, Bla-Bla recently sported imploring admonitions to its community, asking users to respond to messages more substantively. Time will tell whether the new instructions work. In the meantime, the Bla-Bla message board system is a loose, informal, fun place to meet people without having to think too much. One of the eight "rooms" (message boards) is called The Thinker; it contains conversations that are slightly more elevated toward the cerebrum. Other rooms emphasize gossip, humor, and bedroom topics. The boards work flawlessly, with quick displays and easy response forms with automatic quoting of the preceding message. The new chat rooms require the iChat software, which you can download from the site. And you can also get a free home page at Bla-Bla.

Excite Talk

www.excite.com/channel/chat

Generic virtual community: More than a message board and more than a chat room, Excite Talk has the grand ambition to become a complete Internet planned community. Chatting and messaging are included in the mix. Chatting is accomplished in Java format or by means of a downloaded program that significantly enhances the meeting experience by representing each participant with a small graphic image; all these images float in an undefined window space on-screen. Balloons appear above the heads of each person's image with the words that they type. Considering that the Java applet doesn't work well, you should spend the ten-minute download time to acquire the chat software. Messaging doesn't require any special programs, but you must register before posting a message. The boards work moderately well, displaying every message in a discussion thread on a single page. Community sections are defined by topic: Music, Film, Shopping, Sports, Books, and the like. Regional chat rooms (United Kingdom, South America, Japan, and so on) are also offered.

320 Meeting Places

Forum One

www.forumone.com

Search engine for online messaging communities: Forum One is a complete multilingual information resource about online communities that are based on message boards. Although the site serves the community leader who owns a discussion forum, with a newsletter, a bookstore, and a library of software tools, many people who just like meeting others in cyberspace use its search engine and forget the rest. The site is a worthy search engine, to say the least. Entering a keyword compares that word to a large and comprehensive list of Web bulletin boards, and the results are divided into two convenient parts. Suppose that you enter the keyword **spirituality**, looking for message-board discussions of religion or New Age topics. First, the results point you to forums in which spirituality is a primary topic. Second, links to specific message discussions containing the keyword in the title are listed — usually at great length. The search engine cross-references the Web message boards brilliantly, enabling you to discover friends and discussions in areas where you wouldn't think to look.

GeoCities

www.geocities.com

Virtual community complete with neighborhoods: GeoCities is a unique and growing phenomenon on the Net that began a couple of years ago as a quirky idea. World Wide Web observers have watched it grow into a significant virtual community — arguably the most significant and visible community on the Web. If you've surfed the Web for at least a couple of days and kept your eyes on the URLs streaming by, you've no doubt seen the geocities.com domain name more than once. GeoCities offers its members free Web-site space, and they take advantage of it with a vengeance. Free e-mail, too. All for free, notwithstanding a subscription service that provides much more server space (for creating much larger Web sites) at a nominal cost of about $5 per month. (GeoCities is not an Internet service provider, which means that you have to get on the Net by some other means to use its services.) GeoCities provides a directory of its members' Web sites and permits commercial pages; in fact, it offers a library of programming modules that make virtual commerce easier when the modules are installed on a site. Playing the community theme to the hilt, GeoCities calls its topics *neighborhoods.* The site offers a chat area, which is used mostly by members. The site has too much to describe fully, but this is the bottom line: If you're interested in online community and in having your own Web page, check out GeoCities first.

PowWow

tribal.com/powwow

Travel the Web in groups: An innovative software invention for small virtual communities, PowWow is catching on quickly throughout the Web. Completing a free registration and downloading the PowWow program gives you the sudden freedom to page other PowWow users in real time (or send them a voice message), forming a group of up to nine people for chatting and exchanging certain types of files, even from remote computers. Staying linked while surfing around effectively creates a gang of friends roaming around cyberspace together, chatting all the while and tossing URLs and files back and forth. Because picture files may be shared among the group members in real time, you can imagine the uses to which PowWow is put among presumably unmarried people. You're free to leave any unsavory group that you enter. A kids' version of PowWow is now available; it blocks inappropriate content.

Yack!

www.yack.com

Directory of live chatting events: A chatter's guide to cyberspace, Yack! has a fine reputation for comprehensiveness, which it earned by displaying chat schedules not only for the World Wide Web but also for online services such as The Microsoft Network and America Online. Because of its wide range, linking to one of its events could be problematic if you aren't a member of the hosting service; check the given location of a chat before trying to attend. The schedule is helpfully broken down into broad subject categories; you can also browse the master list of the day's events. Yack! provides all the basic information about a scheduled chat event, such as starting time, duration, required software (if any), and cost (usually, nothing), and it even invites you to sign up for an e-mail reminder of weekly events.

Other Stuff to Check Out

www.itl.net/vc

Web-Based Entertainment

Web site designers are ingenious at providing online entertainment. In this section, I gather some unusual pleasures — but nothing too controversial, I assure you. From streaming multimedia to online mysteries, from role-playing games to interactive novels, this section highlights ongoing entertainment and unique graphical features.

Affairs of the Net

www.jaynscott.com/affairs

Romantic soap opera for e-mail peeping toms: Follow the developing e-mail romance of adults Elizabeth and Richard or teenagers Samantha and Markos through this fictional collection of their correspondences. A soap opera for netizens, the ups and downs of an online relationship are tracked through what might seem like voyeurism for the wired generation: reading someone else's e-mail. With stories of Internet love occasionally making the headlines, maybe Affairs of the Net represents the new wave of entertainment drama. Well, maybe not. But it's entertaining.

AncientSites

www.ancientsites.com/index.rage

Role-playing games and more:
AncientSites could have been included in
a number of sections in this book. The
site offers 3-D games, quizzes, and tours,
all related to the ancient world. Chat and
shopping are also offered. If you register
(it's free), you can select the ancient
world that piques your interest —
Babylon, Rome, New York, and so on.
One hint: Don't get carried away when
registering your password, because
you really don't want to type in
Nebuchadnezzar every single time you
visit. Trust me. Anyway, AncientSites
qualifies in the online entertainment
category for four online games — *S.P.Q.R.,
BombsAway!, Acropolis!,* and *Nieuw
Amsterdam* — that will please any hard-
core computer gamer. For example,
S.P.Q.R., which stands for Senatus
Populusque Romanus (a Latin phrase,
literally translated as "Bill Gates for
President"), is a graphical role-playing
game set in ancient Rome. The year is
205 A.D., and the capital of the ancient
world is threatened by a mysterious
saboteur, Calamitus. Your job is to save
Rome — before dinner, if possible. The
game plays like one of those cryptic CD-
ROM adventures (MYST is a good
example). The site presents beautiful
graphics, and you spend too many hours
floundering around, trying to figure out
what to do next. It's not all that bad,
actually, and certainly not as befuddling
as MYST. For one thing, you're given some
information to start with, and even the
first picture gives you something to pick
up. You move by clicking an item in the
graphic and watching what appears. No
other clues are forthcoming, either from
the site or from me. Good luck!

As the Web Turns

www.metzger.com/soap

Episodic, text-based soap opera: As the
Web Turns calls itself an Internet soap

opera, and it takes the form of a serialized
novel. As of this writing, the soap opera
contains 52 episodes, each only a few
paragraphs long. Missing a few episodes
is no problem, either, because they're all
archived on the home page. More drawn-
out than a novel, more compact than a TV
soap, As the Web Turns is unique and
humorous and is gaining a reputation as a
"must-see" site.

Blender

www.blender.com

Streaming content for fast Net connections:
Blender is a unique interactive Web
experience that requires special software.
Fortunately, the needed program is a free
download from the Blender site. After you
install the software, you can access more
than six hours' worth of special streaming
content at the Blender site. Like all sites
that feature streaming multimedia,
Blender works best over very fast
Internet connections. If your computer
can match Blender's speed, you get
games, video interviews, interactive
cartoons — basically, a multimedia
magazine on a high level. Blender calls
itself "interactive television," and it's
definitely on the forefront of the cutting
edge. One warning, parents: Some of the
games may cross the border of what you
deem acceptable for your children, so
don't go wandering off while the little
ones are on the Blender.

Nick Click

www.coolcentral.com/nick

Online mystery: Starting with the tense
soundtrack music emanating from the
home page, Nick Click sets an atmosphere
of dark, campy, suspenseful fun. An
ongoing interactive detective case, Nick
Click appeals to mystery lovers who

aren't in it for prizes or awards, but just for the sheer joy of a cheesy story and bad dialogue. Each part of the story opens with an update on what occurred before, forestalling total confusion. As you follow along page by page, you see occasional invitations to interact, starting with an invitation to choose a name for yourself — you're part of the story, you see. Nick orders you around and enlists your help with the case. I won't tell you any revealing secrets, mainly because I'm clueless about these things. But I know this: Nick Click is one of the better mystery sites.

Stereograms

www.teleport.com/~jrolsen/
   stereograms/stereo00.html

3-D pictures on your monitor: You may have seen stereograms in books. Stereograms look at first like random dots on a page, but if gazed at for a long time, they transform into depictions of objects and abstract designs that seem to leap out of, and recede into, the page. (You should give up if the effect doesn't work after, oh, maybe three hours.) Now you can thrill to these deep depictions on your computer screen. I was doubtful that a stereogram would work over a computer, but I found it to be no more difficult than printed stereograms, for whatever that's worth. The coolest feature of this site is the animated stereogram of a whirlpool, which justifies technology's interference in this art form. Downloadable audio stereograms are also available. No plug-ins are required for the animation, but your browser has to be recent enough to understand Java script. Version 3.0 or later of either Navigator or Explorer works, and WebTV works, too.

TheCase.com

www.thecase.com

Online mysteries: If you haven't guessed that TheCase.com is about mysteries, you probably shouldn't try solving any of the puzzlers put before you weekly at this site. Even if you don't care to try your deductive skills, however, you can read mysteries that are presented at sched-uled intervals during the week (along with, considerately, the approximate time it takes to read them). A message board enables people to share impressions of the stories and help one another solve them, making this site a fun community spot for mystery lovers. Just don't ask me for help. No matter how many clues you give me, I'm clueless.

WebRPG

www.webrpg.com

Information about role-playing games: Role-playing games are popular among a loyal, almost cult following. RPGs are fantasy adventures, usually written in historical or science-fiction settings, that are completely interactive — that is, nothing happens until you set things in motion. The games can be text-based (in the old days, that format was the only one) or graphical, and can be distributed on CD-ROMs or on the Web. Web-based RPGs are somewhat slower than their CD-ROM counterparts, depending on the speed of your connection. WebRPG is the primary networking site for role-playing enthusiasts. At this site, you get conven-tion news, links to the top RPG sites, an art gallery, chat rooms, a free e-mail newsletter, general game hints, and all kinds of indexes and "best-of" lists.

Other Stuff to Check Out

goan.com/soap.html
www.communitysites.com/index.rage
www.directnet.com/~gmorris/title.html
www.lightfiles.com

Part VIII
The Part of Tens

The 5th Wave   By Rich Tennant

MEN

PRINTER PAPER

In this part . . .

The World Wide Web is useful, it's informative, and it's commercial. But it's also fun! And lest you forget the fun aspect of cyberspace, I've roamed the back alleys, country roads, and the remote outposts lying along the Net's fringe, collecting fun and quirky sites for those who like to take the road less traveled.

Ten "Cool Pick" Sites

The phenomenon began soon after the World Wide Web began sprawling into cyberspace: sites that attempted to separate the wheat from the chaff, the cool from the uncool. It all started with a single site called "Cool Site of the Day," reviewed later in this part. The fad quickly spread, and coolness became a commodity. This section surveys the results of the "Cool Site" genre of Web sites — the locations that feed you daily, weekly, or even hourly sites that meet a standard of coolness.

Anyone can run a "Cool Pick" site, so it stands to reason that the quality among them differs. In choosing the following sites, I considered the quality of their picks, as well as the ease with which you can use them. Because the "Cool Pick" site itself isn't of inherent interest — you're after the picks, not the picker — I don't like sites that contain too many graphics or don't archive the picks conveniently. (The original Cool Site of the Day is exempt from all such considerations, because it has attained legendary status.)

Cool Banana

www.coolbanana.com

★ ★
★ ★

No-nonsense cool sites: One problem with "cool" sites is that their coolness is often based on splashy graphics, which seem to take forever to display on your monitor. Especially when a recent "cool" award increases traffic at the site, the delays can be coma-inducing. Cool Banana's mission is to find great sites that meet its three criteria: fast, simple, and universal. As the folks at Cool Banana put it, "No T1 Required; No Plug-ins Required; No Best Viewed With." (A T1 is a high-bandwidth telephone cable, and "best viewed with" refers to sites that require a certain browser.) Obviously, the Cool Banana site itself is both quick and attractive, and its designers manage to find some great Web locations that meet the standards. Though the site hasn't been updated in a while, browsing through past picks is worthwhile and made easier by the site's dual methods of organization: chronological and by subject.

Cool Central

www.coolcentral.com

Frantic and cool: Cool Central has an icy-blue design motif and covers all the bases. Generating a site of the moment, site of the hour, site of the day, and site of the week, it's almost frantic (is that cool?) in its attempt to keep you surfing constantly. The sites of the moment and hour are probably culled from a database in a more or less random fashion. The Cool Central Site of the Day is an editorial selection, and the weekly choice is apparently the result of a vote among the site's editors. The selections range widely from corporate promotions (Disney's official *Mulan* page), to quirky personal sites, to new search engines. Of course, you can browse backward among the daily picks for several months.

Cool "Cool Site of the Day" Site of the Day

crayon.net/about/cool.html

This is getting ridiculous: The "Cool Site of the Day" phenomenon got so out of hand that this site was set up (as a joke) to pick the daily coolest "cool site" site. Sort of like this section of the book, come to think of it. CCSOTDSOTD (as it's conveniently abbreviated) began on April 1, 1996, and continued making daily picks until May 13, 1997. Whether it will resume is anybody's guess, but even as it stands now, with its archive of past picks, it serves as a great directory of the best "cool site" sites. The site doesn't provide any descriptions of the picks, unfortunately — just raw links and an amusing explanation of the site's creation. Now the next step, if enough sites like this one spring up, is there likely to be a Cool "Cool 'Cool Site of the Day' Site of the Day" Site of the Day, which would be easily abbreviated as CCCSOTDSOTDSOTD?

Cool Site of the Day

www.coolsiteoftheday.com

The first judge of hipness: The original site that began the entire "Cool Site" craze when the World Wide Web was almost a brand-new phenomenon, Cool Site of the Day is revered among netizens for its judgment of hip sites. Growing from its humble beginnings, Cool Site now sports dazzling graphics and the élan of a celebrity site. It's also probably the *only* site on the Web that doesn't display awards — after all, who can praise the king? Best of all, past cool picks are archived, so the site is full of excellent links. Cool Site of the Day extends its mission by giving an annual award, the recipient of which is subject to great speculation and debate, and the site's creators encourage the conjectural atmosphere by posting nominees. If you visit no other "cool site" site, make sure you hit the original one.

Cybersmith Site of the Day

magneto.cybersmith.com/hotsites

Great cool-site descriptions: Cybersmith is your basic daily cool pick, housed in a well-constructed site with attractive, minimal graphics, and great organization. The organization of the archives, in fact, is what sets Cybersmith apart. Set up like a Web directory (Yahoo!, for example, or Infoseek), the archive is divided into 15 categories, each of which links to past daily selections. You can go back chronologically, too, but looking for certain kinds of sites — like Cool Technology,

Reference, or Just Plain Fun — is more satisfying. While browsing through site selections, the concise descriptions really help you make sense of the sometimes cryptic titles.

Dr. Webster's Web Site of the Day

www.drwebster.com

Advice to cure your Web ills: If you're sick of less-than-enthralling Web pages, then the good doctor has a prescription for you, right up top, under the Today's Prescription header. Click it and you'll get the doctor's sage advice, with past recommendations conveniently included. What, that's not where you're aching? Well, try the doctor's search engine page, which includes not only links to major search engines but also more specialized directories that might improve your mood. Or you can click to get the weather, get advice on Windows 95 (useless, of course, because we all KNOW that Windows always works perfectly), check the wires for news, or get your daily horoscope. All told, the good doctor has lots of good features — and this doctor makes house calls.

Family Site of the Day

www.worldvillage.com/famsite.htm

Sites for the family: As wholesome as can be, the Family Site of the Day picks sites safe for all ages, with some appeal for the whole family. You can find many learning sites — dinosaurs, foreign countries, history — in the archive list, as well as sites *about* kids *for* parents. On some days, you'd think this site is really Parents' Site of the Day, but then 100 Winnie-the-Pooh links show up as the day's link, or The Hole in the Wall Gang Camp, and you realize that this site is truly family fare. Family Site of the Day is part of the even-more-wholesome WorldVillage site, and you can link to WorldVillage KIDZ, the Gamer's Zone, and other WorldVillage locations from the site.

Incredibly Useful Site of the Day

www.zdnet.com/yil/content/depts/ useful/useful.html

Useful sites . . . really: Compiled by Yahoo! Internet Life, the online-offline magazine of Web browsing and searching, the Incredibly Useful Site of the Day targets fact-finders, appliance-fixers, fact-locators, browser-updaters, travel bargain-hunters, Web searchers, newsgroup-perusers, audio players, and question-answerers, proving in the process that the World Wide Web need not be a mindless, time-sucking black hole of wasted energy and futility. Not that anybody really thinks it is, but just in case the thought crossed your mind, this site remains the best argument against such heresy. Underneath a daily general listing, 12 Library Categories help guide you to the Web site of your dreams — for at least the moment. One complaint: Two of the five links on the Recent Useful Sites list didn't work during my visit. But I'm sure that's just an oversight for a page that is — how should I put it — a very *useful* directory.

Political Site of the Day

www.penncen.com/psotd

Great political sites: The title says it all: daily picks among politically oriented sites. The home page shows the selections for the past week, and deeper archives are housed in the Library area. This excellent resource manages to dish up a fresh political site every day, and darned if they aren't all good. The selection is particularly strong internationally, because a substantial number of picks deal with either sites *about* political procedures in non-U.S. countries or are sites *from* non-U.S. countries. Recent picks include the U.S. Conservative Caucus, the party of European Socialists, and a site seeking human rights equality for Indonesian Chinese. No sluggish graphics or cute come-ons here — just a sober review of politics on the Web.

Shockzone — Shocked Site of the Day

www.macromedia.com/shockzone/ssod

The place to find sites with Shockwave: Shockwave is one of the major web browser plug-ins, and perhaps one of the least understood. What beginners mostly seem to know about it is that it takes longer to download than most other plug-ins, and therefore remains unacquired on many computers. Also, because Shockwave delivers more than one multimedia function, some confusion exists about what it really does. So here's the deal: Shockwave plays multimedia productions created with the Director animation-video-sound software, and some of the hippest multimedia sites on the Web use it. Also some of the slowest — Shockwave sites are, in my experience, generally the slowest sites around to load. The results are worthwhile, though, especially if you have a fast modem or digital Internet connection. If you have Shockwave, the Shocked Site of the Day is where you want to go to find sites for flexing your new browser muscles. If you don't have Shockwave, the site gives you a good reason to get it. Unfortunately, you have to squint mightily to read the green and white text on the black background at the Shocked Site of the Day, but it's still the best "Where's the Shockwave?" directory around.

Ten Sites for Seniors

www.elderhostel.org

The singing duo of Jan and Dean made the charts in the 1960s with their song about "The Little Ol' Lady From Pasadena," a lead-footed grandma who taught anyone who dared challenge her to a drag race that "there was nobody meaner." Well, that image needs some updating. First, get rid of the "little" part; that depicts frailty, and senior citizens have never been more active than they are today. And that "old" stuff — put it away, too. Seniors are "life experienced" today.

And as for the car — well, it's probably in the garage, not because grandma doesn't like driving it, but because that groovin' grandma is now racing around the Web with a Pentium II computer with 64 megs of RAM and a 4 gig hard drive. Seniors, you see, are one of the fastest-growing demographic groups on the Web, and more and more sites are catering to this senior audience. Here are ten that should appeal to cyberseniors.

Better Business Bureau

www.bbb.org

Words to the wise: Sad to say, but con artists seem to love picking on the elderly. The Better Business Bureau (BBB) can help seniors (and others) fight back by keeping them informed, using reports from numerous BBB agencies around the United States and Canada. The BBB's simple Web site offers numerous services, including scam alerts and bulletins, business and charity reports, ways to help mediate a dispute with a business, and good, solid information resources. An online database that enables you find out if anyone has filed a complaint against a business is already available in prototype form. The BBB site can't stop the cons, but it can help you spot them.

Elderhostel

www.elderhostel.org

"Adventures in lifelong learning": Elderhostel is a program for people age 55 and over based (roughly) on Europe's youth hostels, combining inexpensive places to stay with opportunities to learn.

Since its founding in 1975, this U.S. and Canadian program has seen tremendous growth, with nearly 300,000 participants annually enjoying programs in some 70 countries on everything from literature to art to science to music. Service programs, where seniors can "combine adventure with making a difference," are now included as well. Typical programs run five or six days, and although the "tuition" fee doesn't cover transportation to and from the location, it does cover just about everything at the location, including the room, meals, instruction, and field trips. The Elderhostel Web site includes an online catalog that enables you to search for upcoming programs that may interest you, learn more about the specific program and accommodations, and register online. The site is simple, complete, and enlightening — much like the programs it offers.

Eurolink Age

www.eurolinkage.org/euro

Network of European senior sites and programs: Eurolink seeks to be a resource directory of programs for the estimated 120 million senior citizens in the European Union. The site isn't fancy — in fact, it has very few graphic elements — but the information is invaluable. The Programmes page includes information on ActiVAge, a program designed to create opportunities for seniors in Europe, and Ageing Well Europe, a "programme" of health promotion among seniors. Equally important are the Networks, Links, and Members pages, which include information and connections to a number of other resources.

Fifty-Plus.Net

www.fifty-plus.net

Canadian Association of Retired People (CARP): Fifty-Plus.Net is produced by CARP, which is to Canada what the American Association of Retired Persons is to the United States — a large group dedicated to education of and advocacy for seniors. (The AARP site, by the way, is reviewed in Part III.) You find some standard elements here, including feature stories, news about the organization and its activities, and chat and message boards. All are nicely put together. What makes the Fifty-Plus.Net page stand out is that it also has a Just For Fun section with quizzes and jokes. Fifty-Plus.Net is a nice stop, regardless of where you are on the road of life.

GrandsPlace

www.grandsplace.com

Community for special parents: GrandsPlace is a work in progress that I mention because of its noble goal — to be an online resource for grandparents and others who have put off retirement to raise their children's children. The Every Day Living page promises links and articles on such topics as home schooling, genealogy, spiritual thoughts, and household hints. Already up and running are chat rooms, moderated message boards, and a page with re-source links. Even in prototype form, GrandsPlace is a valuable resource for those raising their second family.

Resource Directory for Older People

www.aoa.dhhs.gov/aoa/resource.html

Directory site for seniors: A joint venture between the U.S. National Institute on Aging and the Administration on Aging, this directory is nothing fancy to look at (except for the fluorescent blue AOA logo at the top corner). But looks can be deceiving: Check out the Table of Con-tents, and you'll find a vast listing of organizations and agencies from A to Z. Okay, it's really A (Administration on Aging) to Y (Young Men's Christian Association), but you get my point. What really makes this site special are two things: First, the list isn't limited to sites that automatically scream "senior citizen," meaning that it reflects the wide interests and needs of today's seniors; and second, that the site is now search-able. The directory is of particular use to people trying to find information on specific illnesses.

SeniorCom

www.senior.com

Award-winning senior site: The people behind SeniorCom started their site when a search engine search using the word *senior* brought only two matches. Now, of course, hundreds of sites cater to seniors, but SeniorCom remains one of the best. The main pages include SeniorCom Money Club, Senior Chat, Senior News Network, Town Square (links to other sites of interest to seniors), Health and Wellness, Professional Services, Travel, and Doctor Directory. Senior News Network includes material from various magazines around the United States, from *Maryland Maturity Lifestyles* to *Southern California Senior Life.* An SNN Global link is also included, although during my visit those pages linked mainly to the already listed sites. Registration is required to use the chat rooms, message center, and activities bulletin boards, but registration is free and not very intrusive (SeniorCom doesn't even ask for your street address).

SeniorNet

www.seniornet.com

Information on the information age: SeniorNet is a nonprofit organization of computer users 55 and older who seek to share their technological wisdom with others. The organization has more than 130 learning centers around the United States, holds national conferences, and participates in research on older adults and technology. And that impressive résumé doesn't include their Web site, which offers round tables (message boards) on more than 350 topics. Dream of designing your own Web page? The SeniorNet site has round tables that can help you. Or you can click the Education link, where you find online courses on HTML, the language of the Web. (I can think of a few nonseniors who would probably benefit, but I digress.) Registration is encouraged but not required. No matter what your level of technical expertise, SeniorNet has something that will appeal to you.

SeniorsSearch

www.seniorssearch.com

Directory for senior sites: SeniorsSearch (say that three times fast) purports to be "The Only Search Directory Exclusively For The Over 50 Age Group." The sites are grouped into some 64 categories that range from general topics (Pets, Community, Travel) to more specific subjects (Golf Related Sites, Travel Accommodations, Senior Discounts). If you need to be even more specific, click Fast Search on the right and you're directed to a page that divides those 64 categories into subgroups (Hotel Chains, Hotels Europe, Hotels USA, and so on). But that's not all — SeniorsSearch also includes links for Today's News, Business News, Stock Quotes, and On-Line Trading; contests; and bulletin boards. And links to SeniorsSearch sites in Australia, Britain, and Canada are included at the bottom of the page. This site is a must bookmark for cyberseniors.

Third Age

www.thirdage.com

Online community for seniors: If Third Age isn't the ultimate virtual community for seniors, then it comes very, very close. What's a Third Ager? According to the site, Third Agers are people who have pursued their careers, raised their families, and are now ready to "come into my own." (They're also people who are "self-reliant," "involved," "savvy," and "curious." Hey, wait a minute — I'd like to be a Third Ager!) The home page invites readers to Connect with chat or message rooms, or explore areas of interest like Health, Money, Romance, Work, Family, and so on. Each interest section typically has an Insider column ("Cellulite Happens" headlined the Health page during my visit), a Tool page (a Career Advisor quiz on the Work page, for example), and a feature. The pages are simple but attractive, and contain links to related chat rooms and forums — a handy feature, even if you are "self-reliant."

Ten Unusual Sites

This section is nothing if not strange. The only thing linking the following sites together is oddness. From a site that turns your whole Web experience backwards to a page that relives your past lives, these bizarre sites are all gape-worthy.

!sdrawkcaB

smeg.com/backwards

Read other Web pages backward: Amazingly fun, if a total waste of time and brain power, Backwards! (if you'll excuse me for writing it forwards) takes any URL that you enter into it, surfs you over to that Web page, and displays it on your screen with all the text written backwards. You should definitely try looking at The New York Times Web site in this fashion. In fact, whenever you're sick of the news, try reading it backward at your favorite headline site — it really takes the edge off. Many graphics also are reversed by the magic of Backwards!, though some others just don't display at all. After you reach a destination site, displayed in reverse, your computer reverts to normal thereafter, unless you return to Backwards! and enter another URL.

The Cyber Toaster Museum

**www.spiritone.com/~ericn/
 museum.html**

In case you haven't seen it all yet. . . . : Pause for just a minute and reflect with me on the crucial question of our time — where would we be without the toaster? Actually, this site doesn't answer that question either, but it does trace the history of the toaster, all the way back to General Electric's D-12 model in 1909. The text is nicely interspersed with pictures and broken up by crucial time periods. A product of the Toaster Museum Foundation (a legitimate nonprofit organization that you can join), this site will leave you in awe. And if it doesn't, click over to the TMF home page, where you can link to other Unusual Museums of the Internet, a group that includes everything from the Sugar Packet Museum to the British Lawnmower Museum. Come to think of it, where would we be without sugar packets. . . .

KissThisGuy

www.kissthisguy.com

Archive of misheard lyrics: Admit it — you've found yourself singing along with the radio, only to realize that the words you're singing don't actually match the song. I know the feeling. My revelation came when I was 12, riding in the car driven by a friend's older brother, and I realized the Beatles were singing "Hey, Jude," not "Hey, dude." Well, I'm not alone. This site gives cybersurfers the chance to come clean, to admit their vocal transgressions — and to check out the nearly 1,800 confessions of others. Judging from some of the entries, I'm not the only one who regretted singing in a friend's car. You can view the entries by song or by artist, or just view recent submissions. And when you submit your entry, make sure that you vote on whether your version is better than the original. The archive's stats show 61 percent think their lyrics are superior.

Learn2.com

www.learn2.com

Learn to do just about everything: This site is a major award winner, and it's not shy about hanging its medals in full view. You can't avoid the self-congratulatory quotations on the home page, but wade through them to the Browse link on the

left-hand menu sidebar and begin coming to grips with an intensely deep, useful, and fun site. (In other words, the awards are justified.) Learn2.com is essentially a series of tutorials (called *2torials,* get it?) on an incredibly wide range of topics, from carving a turkey to curing hiccups; making origami to leasing a car; flossing your teeth to buying used skis. I'm not talking about one-paragraph, glib instructionals here, either — the 2torials are detailed, multipage affairs written with great clarity and care, often supplemented by entirely new, related topics that don't appear on the main browse menu. This site is, in a word, incredibly deep and unexpectedly useful. (In my universe, that's one word with a few spaces in it.)

Mining Co. Guide to Urban Legends and Folklore

urbanlegends.miningco.com

Forum for disbelievers: Admit it — someone you know has warned you that if you download a screen saver featuring the Budweiser frogs, you'll get a terrible virus that wipes out your hard drive. Or you've heard that someone flushed a baby alligator down the toilet in New York City, and now the full-grown beast is roaming the city's sewers. If you have, you've heard what is now commonly known as an urban legend (or UL) — a false story that gains credibility simply by being retold and retold. This site debunks these myths with a number of ULs featured right on the home page (including, during my visit, the Budweiser frog story). And if the half-dozen or so featured ULs aren't enough for you, try any of the links on the right-hand side of the page for more far-fetched stories, from Animals (like the sewer gator) to the Classics to Show Biz (Bert the Muppet dead? Say it isn't so!). Most, obviously, are false, but occasionally you can find some truth to the rumor, and the site helps separate fact from fiction. And the story of the guy who tried to blow-dry his poodle in the microwave? Well, that *really* happened to a friend of a friend of mine. . . .

The hosted site is just one of some 500 offered by the Mining Co. (www.miningco.com). Each of the single-topic sites is hosted by someone who is charged with keeping up on the topic, meaning the pages all offer links to related sites around the Web and recommendations for books on the topic. The sites also offer chat rooms, message boards, and e-mail newsletters to keep you up on the topic (or, in the case of urban legends, forewarned).

roadsideamerica.com

www.roadsideamerica.com

A guide to "strange and wacky vacation wonders": Roadside America, a wonderfully designed site, is a spin-off of a book of the same name. The site requires some exploration, refusing to yield its contents — except in very cryptic

terms — on the home page. Follow its instructions, and you're likely to spend your next vacation visiting beer-drinking goats or Mother Goose Village. The suggestions at this amusingly written site all are geared around car trips, and it provides no advice concerning plane or rail travel.

Songs of Crickets and Katydids of Japan

www.asahi-net.or.jp/~UN6K-HSMT/ English/ENGindex.htm

Just when you think you've heard it all: This unusual personal page is something of a labor of love from Kazuyuki Hasimoto, a resident of Fujieda-shi, Shizuoka, Japan. This site contains dozens of photographs and recordings of crickets and katydids that Mr. Hasimoto has collected personally. You can hear them individually (on the Crickets and Katydids page) or in chorus (on the Nature Song page). He even has one page that helps you to understand the Variation of Songs between seasons. And clicking the individual cricket photos brings up information about the cricket, including Japanese and Latin names. You need RealAudio to hear the recordings, but Mr. Hasimoto includes a download link. And he offers free backgrounds for computers and Web pages to download, too, in case you want to take a souvenir from your visit but know that chirping will bother the person in the next cube. The preceding URL takes you to the English language site, although a Japanese site is offered as well. Hasimoto-san, Yoku dekimashita!

Underbelly

www.underbelly.com

Where not to go: Sort of an anti-destination guide to the real world, Underbelly defines its editorial charter as, "Where not to go, and what to do when you get there." Using a blend of hip, cynical writing and a shockingly deep blue color scheme that threatens to liquefy your consciousness, Underbelly hilariously strips famous itinerary spots of their glamour and then points you toward underpublicized gems within their seamy borders. New York, San Francisco, Paris, and Galveston (Galveston?) suffer through Underbelly's paces. The site is mostly text and thus moves quickly. A collaborative work of almost a dozen individuals, Underbelly is perfect for those who either hate to travel or have traveled too much.

The Useless Pages

www.go2net.com/internet/useless/

The worst (?) of the Web: I list this site because, after completing almost an entire book of really cool Web pages, U.S. government regulations require me to give equal time to the, uh, shall we say, not-so-cool Web pages. And few sites are up to the challenge of documenting the truly mediocre as the Totally Useless Page. If it's kitsch, it's here, with categories that range from Elvis (of course) to Wacko. Although the site at first appears dated, the links still work, and the Useless Updates link jumps to recently modified pages with links to all of the featured

sites. My personal favorite is the page that interspersed Dean Martin singing *That's Amore* with sound clips from *Star Trek: The Next Generation,* all the while paying mock tribute to Martha Stewart. Useless, yes; unimaginative, no.

WebCam Central

www.camcentral.com

Directory for video voyeurs: What's unusual about this site isn't the site itself — it's a pretty straightforward resource directory of live cameras available through the Web. No, what piques your interest is wondering why some guy named Bob would stick a Web camera on his deck in Washington, or why German authorities think you need a live shot of the Autobahn, or why anyone would put a Web camera in his or her home. Does anyone watch? Of course we do. And no matter what your interest, WebCam Central probably has a link for you. That's not to say that you'll find *every* Web camera site listed, because while other Web camera directories exist, WebCam's discretion makes it the family-friendly choice for this book.

338 **Ten Unusual Sites** _____

Appendix A

A Surfer's Guide to the Internet

· ·

*T*his appendix takes you on a whirlwind tour of Internet basics. If you don't already know, here's where you discover what the Internet and World Wide Web actually are; what else the Internet offers; what software you need; and what you need to get online in the first place. For a lot more information, grab a copy of the latest edition of *The Internet For Dummies* by John R. Levine, Carol Baroudi, and Margaret Levine Young (IDG Books Worldwide, Inc.).

Acquainting Yourself with the Internet and the World Wide Web

Equating the Internet and the World Wide Web is easy, and many people use the terms "the Net" and "the Web" interchangeably. I don't mean to be a stickler for details, but knowing that there is an important distinction between the Internet and the Web is useful; so, here it is: The World Wide Web is just a portion of the Internet, not even the largest portion, and some people feel that it's not the most important part of the Net. Nevertheless, the Web has certainly gotten more publicity, and it's the subject of more controversy than any other part of the Internet. Read on to discover how the current state of affairs has developed.

The Internet

The Internet has existed since the dawn of civilization, predating the rise of Mesopotamian culture. Well, that may be an exaggeration, but my point is that the Internet was around long before most people heard of it, and for a couple of decades before most people started using it. Developed by the U.S. government and used primarily by academicians, the early Internet enabled university professors to share research around the globe. The Internet of the 1970s and 1980s didn't look remotely like it does today; it was almost completely text, and it worked similarly to the DOS operating system. (If you're not familiar with DOS, count your blessings and move on.) As an institutional resource, the Internet was completely noncommercial, and nobody had any thought or interest in developing it beyond what it was.

The original purpose of the Internet was to provide *security for information.* During the Cold War in the United States, the powers that be figured out that storing important information in networked computers would be a good way to preserve it in case of physical attack. Because computers, when connected by telephone lines, can be located anywhere just as conveniently as if they were centralized in one city, the network system diluted the risk of information loss. So, a system was born that today, having emerged into social and political maturity, enables you to view an animated Captain Kirk leading a sing-along. Such is progress!

The World Wide Web

The World Wide Web changed everything just a few short years ago. A bright young fellow, who amazingly has been neither elected president nor ostracized from polite company, invented a software system for navigating the then-thorny landscape of the Internet. An earlier menu system called Gopher had attained quick popularity among the academic professionals who used the early Internet, helping them find stuff online, but Gopher didn't catch the imagination of regular folks. The World Wide Web's most important feature was (and still is) the *hyperlink,* which enables anyone to move from one location to another in cyberspace by just clicking one hyperlink. No more typing text instructions. This radical development coincided perfectly with the rise of the Windows operating system, which got most computer users familiar with using a mouse.

The World Wide Web is basically just a language — and a simple one, at that. The language is called HyperText Markup Language, which everyone calls HTML for short. World Wide Web locations on the Internet are created with HTML, which communicates with a specialized viewing program called a web browser. The result of the synergy between HTML and browsers is *Web sites* — screens that may contain text, pictures, and all kinds of multimedia files, such as music and video. You reach all these virtual goodies in the basic Web way: clicking the ol' mouse on hyperlinks. The process could hardly be easier, and when the Web was introduced, it really *did* catch the imagination of regular, nonacademic people. The result has been the spectacular emergence of the Internet as a public, commercial, controversial, exciting, end-of-the-millennium cultural force, with this book being the pinnacle of the cyberspace revolution. (Okay, maybe I overstated that last part.)

Getting Online

The Internet isn't much fun if you aren't on it. And if you're a newcomer to the scene, you may feel a bit bewildered. Allow me to help. Starting from scratch, here's what you need:

✔ **A computer.** Any computer purchased in the last few years will do. If you're planning on using an older model, you may need to upgrade your RAM or your hard-drive size to use the latest Web software.

✔ **A modem.** A modem connects your computer with a telephone line (see the next item). Most new computers come with built-in modems, but be sure to ask before you buy. Modems are rated by the speed (bits per second, or bps) at which they transfer data. Surfing the Web with a 14.4 Kbps (or 14,400 bps) modem is frustrating. 28.8 Kbps modems are a big improvement, and now that they're common, you should even consider getting a 56 Kpbs modem. (One word of warning: Be sure to check with your Internet service provider (ISP) or online service to make sure that your modem is compatible with your ISP.) You also can get specialized telephone lines called ISDN lines for even some faster data transfer, but they're beyond even some advanced Web users. ISDN lines are expensive, too.

✔ **A telephone line or cable connection.** Most people connect to the Internet over the phone. If you really like the Net, you can do what lots of other people do: get a dedicated line (a separate phone number) for your computer. Just plug the phone line into your modem, and you're almost ready to go. If you're really lucky, you live in an area served by a cable company that offers Internet access through a dedicated cable. Cable access costs — you typically have to pay a one-time setup fee and pay again for a network card, and *then* you can begin paying the monthly service fee — but if you don't mind the extra outflow of cash, you find yourself with extra inflow of data, as cable connections are faster. You also don't need an Internet service provider, so you cable folks can skip the following bullet.

✔ **An Internet service provider (ISP).** You need to get an account with a company that specializes in connecting people to the Internet. Your account comes with a local phone number that you call to log on, an e-mail address that's your home base online, and, in most cases, some storage space on your ISP's computer to put up your own Web page if you so desire.

Online services like America Online (AOL) and The Microsoft Network (MSN) act as Internet service providers, in addition to displaying their own sites for members. You also may choose a dedicated ISP, in which case you have two basic choices. First, you can sign up with a national or international provider that furnishes local dial-up phone numbers all over your country. Alternatively, with a little research, you can probably locate a small, local company.

✔ **Software.** The main piece of software that you need to access the Web is a web browser. In many cases, ISPs supply browsers free of charge, but local ISPs don't always furnish software. In that case, you need to either buy a software kit in a store or get a friend to download a copy for you (some browsers are legally free of charge). You can find more information about Internet software in the "Software" section, later in this appendix.

The Internet Community

If you get intrigued by the colorful pages of Web sites and the increasingly multimedia playground of cyberspace, you can easily forget that the Net is a populated community. Other people — a *lot* of other people — are logged into the scene. Surely there's a way to meet some of these people, to turn the Internet from a relatively static universe of virtual billboards into a living, breathing, realm of individuals. In fact, three main ways exist.

Newsgroups

It may seem strange at first, but electronic message boards are a great way to not only meet people but also engage in fascinating discussions on any number of topics and develop substantial online friendships. The primary message board system of the Internet is called Usenet, and the discussion groups hosted by Usenet are called *newsgroups.* The newsgroup name is a holdover from the early years of the Internet when the message boards served a more utilitarian, less social purpose than they do now. These days, much more than just sharing research news, Usenet newsgroups feature informal discussion forums on thousands of topics.

I must point out, though, that Usenet newsgroups are an *adult* feature of the Internet. For one thing, to put it bluntly, some newsgroups are pornographic. Even aside from the sexual newsgroups, a highly informal, sometime controversial atmosphere prevails in some groups. Long, sometimes scathing arguments and debates are commonplace. Language isn't edited or censored in any way. The Usenet isn't owned by any company or agency, and most newsgroups aren't moderated by a discussion leader. Having issued all these warnings, I encourage adults interested in meeting people online to check out the newsgroups. Many of them are delightful communities, and you're almost certain to find a newsgroup dedicated to a topic that you're interested in.

Mailing lists

Internet features sometimes have unfortunate names, and *mailing lists* are one such feature. In the day-to-day offline world, you think of mailing lists with apprehension, associating them with unwanted junk mail. But online, the term refers to e-mail discussion groups. Mailing lists are sometimes called *listservs,* which is a more nerdy and accurate term. I personally call them jellybeans, but I doubt if anyone else does. Whatever you call mailing lists, they are another way of networking with kindred spirits online. Mailing lists are automated systems that distribute any e-mail sent by a list member to everyone else on the list. On the receiving end, you get every e-mail sent by all list members delivered to your e-mail box. On the sending end, all your responses are sent to the whole group.

Mailing lists usually are centered around a particular topic, and membership is restricted to people with a genuine interest in that topic. You don't need to be an active participant — just reading is perfectly acceptable. Mailing lists aren't publicized widely, so you must dig a little to find one you like. A good source of mailing list information is this Web site:

```
www.liszt.com
```

You join a list by sending an e-mail to the *listserv* — that is, the automated program running the list. In most cases, you just put a "join list" command in the subject line or the body of the message. (The Web site located at the preceding URL gives complete joining and quitting instructions for each mailing list.)

A note of warning: Popular mailing lists with lots of members can swamp your mailbox with more e-mail than you may want. Of course, you don't have to read it all. Still, make a note of how to quit the group when you join. It's information you may want to use.

Chatting

Chatting is one of the most controversial aspects of the Internet. The reason for all the publicity mostly centers around the anonymity afforded by the Net, allowing people to misrepresent themselves to other people. Men can pretend they're women. Adults can pretend they're kids. Online deception in chat rooms can lead to risky situations if anyone gives personal information (like a phone number or street address) to a stranger or recent acquaintance. The solution: Don't give away your personal information in a chat room! Not even your last name. End of lecture.

Warnings aside, chatting is a fun part of the Internet experience. You can find chat rooms as an added feature of many Web sites, and in Web locations specifically dedicated to chatting. You may need to search a bit to find a chat room that consistently hosts the kind of people you want to talk with and the topics that interest you. Check out my suggestions in the "Meeting Places" section of Part VII of this book.

Software

Software is the heart of computing. Without it, you'd own an expensive but useless piece of metal with a screen. When it comes to Internet software, here are a few things that you should know about.

Web browsers

Web browsers are either free or inexpensive, thank goodness. If you sign up with an online service or a national U.S. Internet service provider, you get the browser free. Some local ISPs throw in a browser with your account, too. After you're on the Net, you can get upgrades by simply downloading them.

Two brands of web browsers dominate the Internet scene. The first is Netscape Navigator, which at one time almost everybody used, and it's still the most popular browser — barely. The second is Microsoft Internet Explorer, which has nearly caught up, in part because it was the first of the two to be given away totally free of charge. (You can get them both free now.) The version numbers of the two programs are in sync, conveniently, making it easy to compare features between them. Versions 3.0 of each program aren't the most recent, but they're still quite prevalent. Versions 3.0 contain many built-in features that make Web surfing pleasurable. In some cases, you may want to download extra features, especially plug-ins (I'll get to them in a minute), but you can have a good browsing experience with just the basic 3.0 browsers. Although the 3.0 browsers do well, upgrade to the 4.0 version as soon as you can. The newer versions have significant new features to add to your browsing experience.

Plug-ins

Plug-ins are a fascinating niche in the Internet software field. Small programs that enhance the function of your web browser, plug-ins are usually free, downloadable, and easy to install. Plug-ins enable you to view (or hear) the multimedia features of a Web page that aren't part of the basic browser language. Here are a few crucial plug-ins and their functions:

- **RealAudio.** In terms of music and sound on the Internet, RealAudio is the most important plug-in you can have. RealAudio enables your browser to *stream* audio programming through your computer in real time. Audio streaming is a big advantage over past methods, which required downloading sound files — often requiring long waiting periods — before beginning to listen to them. With RealAudio, you begin hearing the audio program almost immediately. You can get RealAudio (or RealPlayer, the newest version that includes a RealVideo video streaming viewer) at this URL:

  www.real.com

✔ **Shockwave.** Shockwave is one of the largest plug-ins (requiring a longer download time than most), but it also gives you a lot. The function of Shockwave is to display multimedia created in another program called Macromedia Director. Director enables Web producers to put animation, video, and audio in an integrated package on their sites. Because it's such an advanced tool and because the plug-in is more cumbersome than most others, Shockwave hasn't become as popular and prevalent as RealAudio. But Shockwave displays are usually very entertaining. If your browser does not already have Shockwave (Explorer 3.0 has Shockwave built in and Explorer 4.0 has an installation option that helps you get Shockwave, but Netscape users must download the plug-in), you can get Shockwave on the CD that accompanies this book or at:

```
www.macromedia.com/shockwave
```

✔ **Crescendo.** Crescendo is a little plug-in that enables you to hear MIDI music (music produced on computers using synthesized instrument sounds) on pages that provide MIDI files as background music. One nice feature of Crescendo is the small control panel that appears on Web pages providing MIDI background music. If you don't like the tune that's playing, you can just turn it off. Here's the site for downloading Crescendo:

```
www.liveupdate.com/midi.html
```

E-mail programs

The Netscape and Microsoft browsers provide software for reading, organizing, and sending e-mail. Some people prefer using a separate, more sophisticated e-mail program, though I find that both Navigator's and Explorer's features are sufficient for my needs. Here are the basic features that you want in an e-mail program:

✔ **The capability to create folders for storing categories of e-mail.**

✔ **A program that accepts *attachments*, files that are hitched to a written note.** E-mail attachments can contain pictures, programs, and other nontext files.

✔ **The capability to easily format a letter with color, different fonts, and other layout properties.** One caveat: When formatting your e-mail in different fonts, remember that your recipient must have those fonts installed on his or her computer in order to read them.

✔ **Automatic checking of e-mail.** Good programs can check your e-mail box for new deliveries at specified intervals.

> ✔ **An address book.** If you can't store the Internet addresses of your correspondents, you're in for hassles. Make sure that the e-mail program you choose can easily transfer an e-mail address from an e-mail message to the address book, preferably with just a click of an on-screen button.

One e-mail program, Eudora, is widely lauded for its excellent, sophisticated features. It comes in two versions: a free, reduced-feature program (Eudora Light) and a full-featured version that costs money.

You can find a copy of Eudora Light on the CD that comes with this book. Check out Appendix C for more details.

Appendix B

Tips for Trolling the Web

● ●

*N*obody says that surfing the Web is hard. Click a link, and you're somewhere — not exactly neurosurgery. But there's plain-vanilla surfing, and then there's expert, impress-your-friends, timesaving, corner-cutting surfing. Everybody knows that expert Web surfing is much harder than neurosurgery. The following tips share some of my surfing habits, especially ones that can cut through the waste when you're trolling the Net for good sites.

Look Before You Link

Those URLs, cryptic though they seem, actually tell a story. Not a very interesting story, mind you, or one that you'd want to tell your kids at bedtime, but a story of some usefulness to you. One thing is certain about the Internet: There are too many choices. Surfing, browsing, and especially searching for stuff is largely a matter of deciding what *not* to visit. If you could eliminate all the disappointing and broken sites from a Web session, imagine how much time you'd save. Why, it could add up to . . . to . . . *minutes!* Of course, you can't eliminate all the disappointing sites, but in some cases, the URL flashes a red alert worth paying attention to. Fortunately, Netscape Navigator (and some other browsers) shows the URL in its bottom-of-the-window taskbar as you run your cursor over a link before you click it. This feature works with both text and graphic links. (Version 3.0 of Microsoft Internet Explorer lacks this basic feature, showing you instead the title of the site at the end of the link; however, version 4.0 does incorporate this feature.)

Here are a few points to watch out for when reading URLs:

✔ **The tilde tells you something.** A *tilde* is the "~" symbol. It's often located in the upper left of a keyboard. You can commonly (though not always) find it in the URLs of personal home pages. Many Web site leasing services — such as Internet service providers whose customers receive a certain amount of online computer space to put up their own Web sites — identify a customer's leased computer space with folders beginning with the tilde. Now, I'm not saying that personal home pages are bad! But if you're looking for corporate sites only or Web locations that are likely to be stable over time, you can scan links (in a directory page, for example) for URLs without the telling tilde. Here's an example of a tilde-distinguished personal home page URL (fictional, of course):

```
www.isp.com/~brad/cappuccino.html
```

✔ **Brief is beautiful.** Short URLs, the ones that don't use any single slashes after the double slash, indicate two important things. First, that the site has its own domain name. Owning a domain name simply means that at the very least the site creator has paid for the privilege, and may mean the site is running on its own Internet computer (server). Such a brief URL is generally a sign of a corporate site, as opposed to a personal one, although individuals can buy "virtual domains" running on someone else's server. Second, short URLs mean that you're about to link to a main page of a site, because all the inner pages are distinguished by filenames after a forward slash. Here's an example of a short, domain-name-only URL:

```
www.publication.com
```

And here's an example of a URL for an inner page of that same site — a link that you can access from the main page:

```
www.publication.com/fakenews.html
```

✔ **Watch for international extensions.** Cruising for international sites is one of the great pleasures of the Web (it is the *World Wide* Web, after all), especially for those who have always been intrigued with short-wave radio and other globe-shrinking technologies. You can spot international (that is to say, non-U.S.) sites by their domain extensions. Domain extensions are the *com, net, org,* and *edu* endings that you see attached to domain names. Sites housed on international servers may use extensions that denote the host country, such as *ir* for Ireland, and *uk* for United Kingdom. This info is handy if you want to visit such sites or if you want to avoid them — international sites often operate much more slowly for American visitors, thanks to the long physical network distances being spanned.

Bookmark Now!

Bookmarking is one of the great, necessary features of Web browsing. Experienced netizens have bookmark lists that look like Sean Connery's film résumé — long and complicated. Most browsers (certainly Navigator and Explorer) enable you to set up folders to keep your favorite sites in categories, and take it from me, a netizen of long experience, having a list that's too long rather than too short is much better. You can more easily prune your bookmarks than locate a site that you forgot to add. A stitch in time saves nine — but that doesn't have anything to do with what I'm talking about. My point is that you should bookmark sites quickly when you first visit them if you think you may ever, in this life or your next life, visit them again. Keep a trigger finger on your bookmark button and sort things out later.

If One Browser Window Is Good, Then Five Must Be Better

Some people don't know that you can open more than one window of your browser. That's right, it's twins! You can have two, three, or ten browsers running at the same time, just by continuing to open new windows. Opening a browser window isn't like booting up a program from scratch; a program runs once and supports multiple windows. (Browser windows get crabby if they don't feel supported.) So why would anyone want to do such a thing, anyway, aside from inclinations toward schizophrenia? Because keeping multiple windows open can keep you from getting lost on the Web.

Even though the Back button enables you to retrace your steps, relying on it too much can cause problems. For one thing, new Web design technologies mess up the function of the Back button sometimes, and you may find that you *can't* retrace your steps exactly as you thought. Or you may want to take a major excursion somewhere without having to tediously retrace your steps, even if the Back button keeps track of them flawlessly. If you're at a page (perhaps a major directory page) and want to remain anchored there while you explore, just open up a second window and take off. Shut down the second window or leave it parked when you're ready to resume your original track.

This technique is addictive and very useful. The downside is that sometimes your computer complains that you don't have enough memory. Personally, I generally have four browser windows open — but nobody ever accused me (or any of my multiple personalities) of being normal.

Disregard Most Search Results

Searching the Web is a mixed bag. (Not as bad as a mixed metaphor, but not nearly as good as a mixed breed.) You can use some great Web services called search engines to help you search — see the "Search Engines" and "Directories" sections in Part I of this book and also run right out and buy multiple copies of *World Wide Web Searching For Dummies* (IDG Books Worldwide, Inc.). (Sorry about the plug; Jay Leno made me do it.)

The problem with search engines, in fact, is that they're *too* good. They display more results than you could possibly explore even if you were as demented about the Internet as I am, which I trust for your own sake you're not. The solution: Ignore most of the results. There are ways to find what you're looking for, but rummaging through page after page of results isn't one of those ways. If you don't see anything useful-looking on the first page of search results, you've probably used the wrong keywords. (Using bad keywords is something you should never admit to in polite company.) You can save time by entering new keywords five times over rather than traipsing down 20 virtual dead ends. Be as specific as you can. For example, rather than just searching for just **car**, search for **Stutz**.

Once you've got the basic techniques down, learn to take advantage of your favorite search engine's advanced search options. Most search engines enable you to use symbols (usually the plus sign) or words (usually *and*) to indicate that you want sites with more than one word, so you can enter **Stutz+Bearcat** or **Stutz and Bearcat**. You can also usually exclude words by using a minus sign, or sometimes the words *and not* (as in **tuna–dolphins** or **tuna and not dolphins**). Quotes around an entry tell most search engines that you want sites with exactly those words in exactly that order (such as **"Anthony and Cleopatra"**). Some sites also enable you to specify where on the Web page you want to find the given search words (such as **title:Anthony and Cleopatra** for sites with "Anthony" and "Cleopatra" in the title). And some sites also include a percentage match, giving you a clue what percentage of the words the site returned. The point is, just like the Web, the search possibilities are virtually endless.

Learn the Value of Cache

Whether you know it or not, your web browser is stashing stuff on your hard drive. Pretty nervy, I know, and the worst part is that it didn't even ask first. But the truth is, your browser is looking out for your interests. It wants to save you time when revisiting Web sites. So it stores elements of every page you visit in a special folder on your hard drive. Then, when visiting a page after the first time, the browser loads the big stuff — pictures, especially — directly from your hard drive, which is much faster than loading them all over again through your modem. So what's the problem? Hey, don't get defensive. There's no problem, all right? I just want you to know that you have control over your browser's cache (rhymes with stash): You can change its size or even eliminate it completely.

Make your cache smaller if you need to conserve hard drive space, or enlarge it if you have tons of storage space. You may want to try eliminating the cache if you enjoy a high-speed Internet connection (ISDN or faster, that is) because when your connection runs at a high speed, the cache doesn't save much — if any — time while taking up just as much hard drive space.

Use <Gasp!> Identical Passwords

This tip goes against common wisdom. (Oh, how I love being contrary.) Ever since site registrations began appearing on commercial (even free-of-charge) Web sites, it has been advisable to submit a different password for each site you join so that evil acquaintances can't get into all your favorite Web sites and gaze at your settings. Software utilities have been developed to help you keep track of all the passwords skittering around your brain like animated M&Ms. I myself, in earlier books, advised against using the same password over and over in different Web sites. My evil secret was that I did exactly that in most cases. Fortunately, all seven people who read my previous books have been arrested for illegal sheep-cloning (a genetic crime ring that stayed in touch over the Web, apparently) and don't have Internet access in prison, so I'm free to come out of the closet.

Of course, there *is* a good reason to be cautious about your passwords. Some commercial sites enable you to store credit card information on the site's server, so you can repeatedly order products or services without entering all your info each time. If someone were to break into your account at that site, that despicable hacker could order an air conditioner online with your money and send it to someone in Alaska, where it's really not needed.

To guard against such a misuse of unnatural resources, diversify the risk by choosing different passwords for valuable Web accounts. If your browser has a feature that saves password information for you, don't use it for things like shopping sites where you've registered and recorded your credit card number. As big a pain as it is, enter the password manually every time you enter such a site. In my case (and I'm being serious now), I use special clusters of letters and numbers to gain access to my online brokerage accounts and the sites where I often buy services, such as my favorite online travel agency. All the other hundreds of sites I've joined have the same password — even the same user name. If you can figure it out, you're welcome to gaze at my settings.

Conserve Bandwidth

This is a public service announcement. Bandwidth is basically the amount of driving space everyone has on the information highway. Using the space inefficiently is like taking your car on the interstate and parking it there. If enough people did that, the information highway would turn into the information parking lot. Bandwidth is scarce now, though technology companies are working hard to reverse that trend in the foreseeable future. Examples of hogging bandwidth are logging onto your unlimited Internet account and taking a vacation to Antibes while your computer is still connected, or tuning into a live Netcast just before leaving your house for a walk across the country. Okay, those examples are a bit extreme. And there's no reason to become a raging activist, but if you want to be smart and considerate to the whole Internet community, avoid wasting an Internet connection and the bandwidth it takes up.

Guard Personal Information

Even though I've become complacent about passwords, I do think that protecting your personal information when you're online is vitally important. Meeting people online is a pleasure and one of the greatest appeals of the Internet. At the same time, one of the biggest traps is to assume that you know somebody well, based solely on interaction in a chat room or message board. Trust seems to build quickly when chatting online despite the anonymity or perhaps *because* the lack of physical presence encourages people to drop their guard and open themselves to more revealing, honest communication. It's important to never forget that the person you're talking to could be totally unlike his or her online persona in the offline world. Be very cautious when giving offline information to an online acquaintance — a lesson that kids especially need to hear. Offline information includes postal addresses, phone numbers, and even your real name if you're using an online alias. I'm not saying that real friendships can't develop from online meetings, sometimes extending into the daylight world — I can testify from many experiences that they do. Caution is the keyword. Going into a chat room is like attending a masquerade party; enjoy the fun of meeting disguised people but don't mistake the mask for the real face.

Bookmark Directory Pages

I've already given one tip about bookmarking, but I'm hoping you've forgotten that already. Besides, this particular piece of stellar advice is worth its own tip. Web directories can be a great help finding your way around, but they're big and complicated, usually consisting of hundreds of Web pages —

or thousands, in the case of the Yahoo! Directory. When browsing, you're bound to come across a great directory page that suits your needs perfectly and that you don't want to risk losing. The solution, of course, is to bookmark it immediately. I have such pages scattered throughout my bookmark folders, placed in the appropriate topic, not gathered together into their own folder.

Remember Reload

The poor Reload button (called Refresh in Internet Explorer, the champion browser at renaming common terms that everyone just learned) is misunderstood and underused. It's enough to make you weep. But then, I sniffle over TV commercials. Reload is commonly used to update a page whose content changes quickly, like a sports scoreboard page. Indeed, reloading to get updated information is a fine, upstanding use of the button. But the situation in which I use it even more often is to break a page stall. A page stall is when a new page begins to display and then stops in its tracks like a somnambulist walking into a telephone pole. Nothing budges it, not even muttering and glaring, two foolproof methods of dealing with crises in life. Often, a page stall is just bad luck — you requested the page at the same moment as 937 other impatient people, and the Internet server is choking under the pressure. Break out of your personal logjam by smacking the Reload button, and you're likely to get into a different and much quicker queue. The Reload button isn't designed to work on in-laws who drop by your house unexpectedly, but it's worth a try.

If the Site Won't Appear, Tinker with the URL

The most frustrating number in cyberspace is 404 — the error message that you get when your browser discovers that your requested site has moved without leaving a forwarding address. What can you do? Well, you can slap the computer, but that'll just end up costing you money if you break something. Or you can try begging, but browsers are notoriously unresponsive to emotional pleas. No, a better solution is to alter the address just a bit.

For example, say you tried unsuccessfully to reach the following URL:

```
www.isp.com/~Brad/cappuccino.html
```

My experience is that many times the Brads of the Web world are still out there; they've just changed their addresses a bit. The site's new URL may be something like

```
www.isp.com/~Brad/latte.html
```

But because you've been so specific, the browser tells you — logically — that the cappuccino page is no longer out there. Simply shorten the address to:

```
www.isp.com/~Brad/
```

and if Brad still exists at the same server, you'll soon be sharing the cyberaroma of his site.

In short, don't let a few bad experiences browsing the Web overshadow the many joys you can find in cyberspace. As a recently coined saying goes, give a man a fish and you feed him for a day; teach him to use the Internet and he won't bother you for weeks.

Don't Let Your ISP Slow You Down

Ever buy a zippy new modem and go to the great pain of installing it, only to discover that you're still getting the same, slow performance when loading pages. Did the modem company cheat you? Probably not. A more likely answer is that your modem is faster than your Internet service provider's. Check with your ISP to see what speed their modems operate at. Remember, information travels along the Internet only as fast as the slowest modem in the chain. So if you've got a 56 Kbps modem but your connection speed is limited to your ISP's top end of 28.8 Kbps, you can patiently wait for pages to load and for your ISP to upgrade, or just get a new ISP.

Check That Line

So you've got that zippy new modem in place, your ISP has a modem that offers the same high-speed access, and yet pages are *still* loading slowly. Now what? Check the phone line. You may have some noise in your connection that's holding up data transfer. Most times you can solve the problem by simply disconnecting and then reconnecting. In other words, hang up to get rid of the problem — just like hanging up gets rid of those problem phone salespeople. If the problem persists, call the phone company and have them fix the problem — with the phone line, that is. If you've got a way to get rid of problem phone salespeople, we'd all like to hear it.

Appendix C

About the CD

● ●

*T*he CD that comes with this book contains a wide variety of software helpers for getting on the Internet and making your visits to cyberspace more pleasant. The CD amounts to a virtual tool kit of programs that enhances your web browser. The included programs enable you to use files downloaded from the Net, view multimedia files more easily, and add features to your browser. In addition, the CD provides hyperlinks for every site listed in this book (see the upcoming "Using the Directory Links" section for details), which should save you hours of manually typing URLs. Read on to find out everything you need to know about the CD.

System Requirements

Before you install the CD, make sure that your system meets the following system requirements. If your computer doesn't meet the minimum requirements, you may have trouble using the programs on the CD.

✔ A 486 or faster PC running Windows 3.1, 95, or 98, or any Macintosh with a 68030 processor or better running System 7.5 or higher.

✔ At least 8MB total RAM installed in your computer (16MB recommended).

✔ A CD-ROM drive — double-speed (2x) or faster.

✔ A sound card with speakers.

✔ A monitor capable of displaying at least 256 colors or grayscale.

✔ An Internet connection — a 14.4 Kbps or faster modem (some programs may need a faster modem to do things such as playing audio and video directly from the Internet) or network access.

What Do I Do First with the CD?

Knowing what to do first with the CD depends on what kind of operating system you're running. Read on. . . .

Windows

To start the CD using Windows 95 or 98, follow these steps:

1. **Insert the CD (label side up) into your computer's CD-ROM drive.**

2. **Select <u>R</u>un under the Start menu.**

3. **Type** D:\SETUP.EXE.

   I'm assuming that your CD-ROM drive is labeled as the D drive in your computer. If not, replace the "D" with whatever letter designates your CD-ROM drive.

   The first thing that you see is the IDG License Agreement.

4. **Accept the terms of the IDG License Agreement.**

To start the CD using Windows 3.1, follow these steps:

1. **Insert the CD in your CD-ROM drive.**

2. **In the Program Manager, choose <u>F</u>ile⇨<u>R</u>un.**

3. **In the Run dialog box, type** D:/SETUP.EXE.

   Substitute your actual CD-ROM drive letter if it's something other than D.

4. **Click OK.**

5. **Accept the terms of the IDG License Agreement.**

After following the instructions that relate to your computer, a window appears called Internet Directory For Dummies. That window is the *installation shell* for the CD. It's harder to crack than a peanut shell but not as pretty as a sea shell. The purpose of the installation shell is to install programs from the CD to your hard drive. Installing any single program could hardly be simpler:

1. **Click one of the four CD sections.**

2. **Click one of the programs.**

3. **Click the Install button for that program.**

Macintosh

To install the items from the CD to your hard drive, follow these steps:

1. **Insert the CD into your computer's CD-ROM drive.**

   In a moment, an icon representing the CD that you just inserted appears on your Mac desktop. Chances are, the icon looks like a CD-ROM.

2. **Double-click the CD icon to show the CD's contents.**

3. **Double-click the Read Me First icon.**

   This text file contains information about the CD's programs and any last-minute instructions you need to know about installing the programs on the CD that I don't cover in this appendix.

4. **To install most programs, just drag the program's folder from the CD window and drop it on your hard-drive icon.**

5. **Some programs come with installer programs — with those you simply open the program's folder on the CD, and double-click the icon with the words Install or Installer.**

   Once you have installed the programs that you want, you can eject the CD. Carefully place it back in the plastic jacket of the book for safekeeping.

Using the Directory Links

For your convenience, I've placed all the URLs that are listed in this book on a couple of Directory Links pages that you can open in your web browser. Any site reviewed in this book is just a mouse click away. To use these links pages, follow these steps:

1. **With the CD in your drive, launch your web browser.**

2. **If you have Microsoft Internet Explorer, choose File⇨Open. If you have Netscape Navigator, choose File⇨Open File.**

   An Open dialog box appears.

3. **Select the HOME.HTM file.**

   If you're using Windows, type **D:\HOME.HTM**. (If your CD-ROM drive isn't D:\, please be sure to use the correct letter for your drive.)

   If you're using Mac OS, use the Open dialog to display the contents of the CD. Select the HOME.HTM file and then press Return.

4. **When the home page opens, you can begin browsing the links pages.**

Select a part by clicking the part title on the left side of the page. You can then move through the selected part by using internal jumps that take you from section to section.

Clicking a link opens a second browser window. The second window enables you to browse the Web site without ever losing track of the Links pages from the CD. You can always bring the Directory Links pages back to the top of your desktop and select another link. Selecting additional links changes the Web site in the second browser window, so you don't have to worry about having more than two browser windows open at one time.

What Else Is on the CD?

After you get the CD up and running (see the "What Do I Do First with the CD?" section of this appendix), the following programs present themselves for your examination and installation. As the following sections indicate, the CD is divided into four sections.

Internet tools

The Internet Tools portion of the CD features a large selection of software programs that get you onto the Net and get you busy doing things more productively.

- ✔ **Anarchie 2.0.1 (Mac):** This shareware Macintosh File Transfer Protocol (FTP) program copies files between your Mac and a computer on the Internet. It's useful for such technical activities as uploading your own Web pages.

- ✔ **BBEdit Lite 4.1 and BBEdit 4.5.1 Demo (Mac):** BBEdit Lite, from Bare Bones Software, Inc., is a Macintosh freeware text editor with powerful features that make creating HTML scripts for your Web pages easy.

  The commercial version of this program, BBEdit 4.5.1, has stronger HTML editing features. I include a demo version of BBEdit 4.5.1 on the CD. This demo is fully featured but cannot save files. You can learn more or register your version of BBEdit 4.5.1 at www.barebones.com.

- ✔ **Dreamweaver (Windows 95/98 and Mac):** Dreamweaver from Macromedia is a visual HTML editor that enables you to have plenty of control over your HTML code. That means that if you don't want to learn HTML, you can still make Web pages, but if you're a bit of a control freak or want to do real Webmaster stuff like work with Dynamic HTML, this tool will still do the job for you.

✔ **Eudora Light (Windows 3.1/95/98 and Mac):** One of the leading e-mail programs, Eudora Light is absolutely free, and you can use it as long as you want without registering. You should realize that both popular web browsers — Netscape Navigator and Microsoft Internet Explorer — have e-mail programs attached to them. However, many netizens swear by Eudora, the big sibling of Eudora Light. (Eudora is a commercial program that you have to pay for; it's not free like the Light version.) So trying Eudora Light is a good way to determine if Eudora is an alternative you'd like to use.

✔ **Free Agent (Windows 3.1/95/98):** Free Agent is a popular Usenet newsgroup program that enables you to read and participate in the electronic bulletin boards of Usenet. Both Internet Explorer and Netscape Navigator provide Usenet functionality, so consider Free Agent an alternative if you use one of those web browsers.

✔ **HomeSite 3.01 (Windows 95/98)** HomeSite from Allaire is an excellent program that enables you to create and edit HTML, the markup language for making Web pages. If you're feeling brave about editing HTML yourself, this program makes it much easier to get started.

✔ **Internet Coach (Windows 3.1/95/98):** This software teaches you about the Internet without actually logging on to the Net. Graphic and informational files give you an idea of what the Internet looks like and how it works.

✔ **Internet Explorer 4.01 (Windows 3.1/95/98 and Mac):** This application is a powerful web browser. It's also free, which makes it a true bargain.

✔ **MindSpring Internet Access (Windows 3.1/95/98 and Mac):** MindSpring is a complete Internet service provider (ISP) package that you can use to get on the Internet for the first time, or as an alternative to whatever service you're currently using. This software installs Internet Explorer. If you prefer Navigator, don't worry, you're not burning your bridges behind you. (Though you may be burning your britches — that'll teach you to sit on the stove while reading this book.) You can install the Netscape software right from this CD, and it will work just grand with MindSpring.

After you're signed on, one of the first places you may want to check out is the MindSpring Web site at www.mindspring.com.

You need a credit card to sign up for MindSpring Internet Access.

Important note: If you already have an Internet service provider, please note that MindSpring Internet Access software makes changes to your computer's current Internet configuration and may replace your current settings. These changes may stop you from being able to access the Internet through your current provider.

- **Net Nanny (Windows 3.1/95/98):** Designed primarily for parents, Net Nanny monitors and blocks Internet content that may be objectionable or inappropriate for young viewers. Net Nanny also blocks certain functions within your computer, if you want it to, establishing a more private and secure computer environment.

- **Netscape Communicator (Windows 3.1/95/98 and Mac):** Communicator is actually a free suite of programs that includes e-mail, online conferencing, and an HTML editor, as well as the popular web browser, Netscape Navigator.

- **WebWhacker (Windows 3.1/95/98 and Mac):** WebWhacker enables you to save Web pages (the text, graphics, and HTML links) directly to your hard disk so that you can quickly open and view the pages with your web browser while offline. The program copy included on this CD is a demo copy that expires after you've used it for a little while. Follow the instructions in the program for purchasing a permanent copy.

- **WS_FTP LE (Windows 3.1/95/98):** How's that for an easy-to-remember program name? Quick, without looking, what's it called? You looked. Anyway, ol' what's-it-called is very useful for transferring Web pages that you create to your Internet server. If that's a meaningless sentence, you probably aren't creating Web pages or are doing so through America Online or CompuServe, each of which provides different FTP software. Portions of this software is copyright © 1991–1997 by Ipswitch, Inc.

Multimedia tools

The programs in this portion of the CD give you enhanced multimedia functionality, either online or offline. Here are the goodies:

- **Adobe Acrobat Reader (Windows 3.1/95/98 and Mac):** Web pages can look great, but some publishers are unhappy at having to change the original page layout of publications to conform to HTML design requirements. (HTML is the language that all Web pages are written in.) To get around HTML, some publishers use the Adobe Acrobat format instead, which preserves all the fancy layout characteristics of the original publication — formatting that would be lost in the translation to HTML. The Adobe Acrobat Reader enables you to view Acrobat documents in all their original glory.

- **GraphicConverter 3.3.1 (Mac):** By shareware author Thorsten Lemke, GraphicConverter is an ultra-cool program that you can use to view and save images in virtually any graphics format that you're likely to encounter on the Internet.

- **Paint Shop Pro (Windows 3.1/95/98):** With Paint Shop Pro, a graphic viewer and software art program, you can view downloaded picture files and then alter them beyond all recognition with several special effects. It's a very cool program for playing around or attempting serious computer artistry.

- **Shockwave (Windows 3.1/95/98 and Mac):** Shockwave enables you to view streaming multimedia over the Web — you can watch movies, listen to CD quality audio, and even play games. Shockwave is one of the most popular formats for multimedia on the Web. After you've installed Shockwave, check out the Shockwave Web site, at shockrave.macromedia.com, to see what all the fuss is about.

- **VDOLive Player (Windows 3.1/95/98 and Mac):** VDOLive Player is a web browser plug-in that streams video files so that you can watch them right away when logged in to a Web site — you don't have to wait until they're completely downloaded before they start playing.

- **VivoActive Player (Windows 3.1/95/98 and Mac):** Another video streaming plug-in (see the preceding description of VDOLive Player), VivoActive also saves download time by playing video files as soon as you click them. The two plug-ins (VDOLive and VivoActive) aren't interchangeable or compatible. Some Web pages use one; some use the other. It's a good idea to install both.

Utilities

The programs in the Utilities portion of the CD aren't Internet-related but are very useful for general computer tasks. Here's what the CD gives you:

- **CleanSweep (Windows 3.1/95/98):** Like Complete Program Deleter described later, CleanSweep gets rid of all the system files associated with any program that you're deleting from your hard drive.

- **ClipMate (Windows 3.1/95/98):** ClipMate replaces the standard Windows clipboard — the built-in utility that stores text or graphics that you cut or copy from a program. Whereas the regular clipboard is a simple utility that saves only one thing at a time, ClipMate saves several bits of text or graphics, enabling you to access a list of cuts (or copies) for future pasting.

- **Complete Program Deleter (Windows 3.1):** Veteran users of the Windows 3.1 operating system can tell you that deleting a program from your hard drive is no simple matter. Many programs place files all over your hard drive, in many different directories. Complete Program Deleter scours your system, rounds up all the scattered files associated with the program that you want to get rid of, and plucks them off.

✔ **DropStuff with Expander Enhancer (Mac):** This shareware product from Aladdin Systems enables you to compress files into StuffIt files by dragging and dropping the files on the DropStuff icon. Stuffing files into StuffIt archives squeezes the files into a smaller space on your hard disk, saving space. DropStuff also adds more abilities to the freeware program StuffIt Expander (included on this CD). With DropStuff installed, StuffIt Expander can decompress ZIP archives from PCs and also decompress files more quickly on Power Macintosh and compatible computers.

✔ **StuffIt Expander (Mac):** StuffIt Expander 4.5 from Aladdin Systems, Inc., is an invaluable file decompression freeware utility for Macintosh users. Many files on the Internet are *compressed* — that is, compressed in size via special programming tricks — to save storage space and cut down on the amount of time required to transmit files. After you download a compressed file, you should use StuffIt Expander to decompress the file and make it useable again.

✔ **StuffIt Lite (Mac):** This is Aladdin's freeware compression program. It doesn't do all the cool stuff DropStuff does, but it does enable you to make StuffIt archives, and, like I said, it's free.

✔ **ThunderBYTE (Windows 3.1/95/98):** ThunderBYTE detects and eliminates viruses. A computer *virus* is a tiny bit of software code created to wreak havoc in unsuspecting systems. The truth is, viruses are relatively rare, and you may never encounter one. (I never have, and I've practically lived on the Internet for years.) Nevertheless, ThunderBYTE makes your Web surfing safer.

✔ **WinZip 6.3 (Windows 3.1/95/98):** WinZip is a Windows decompressor for downloaded ZIP files. Almost all large files available on the Internet for downloading are compressed in the ZIP format, and WinZip is an indispensable part of any netizen's tool kit. Use WinZip to decompress downloaded files, after which they can be used.

Fun stuff

Fun Stuff is . . . what's the word . . . oh, fun! A couple of programs are included that you may get a kick out of:

✔ **ACT! (Windows 95/98):** Act! is what organized people call a personal information manager, or, if you don't have time for that — a PIM. It gives you a calendar, address book, and reminder service in an easy-to-understand single program.

✔ **Escape Velocity (Mac):** Pilot a space ship in this combination of classic trading game, arcade shoot-out, and strategy simulation. Escape Velocity is an exciting, open-ended shareware game that's different every time you play it.

✔ **Eclipse (Mac):** Want a screen saver on your Mac that doesn't eat up memory or crash your system? Eclipse from Ambrosia Software is a small shareware program with a powerful set of features to keep your Mac's screen safe and your machine running smoothly.

✔ **MVP Backgammon (Windows 3.1/95/98):** Backgammon with style! MVP Backgammon pits you against the computer, disguised as one of several opponents. If you register for the official version, you get more opponents and lots of fancy graphics.

✔ **MVP Euchre (Windows 3.1/95/98):** This version of the game enables you to pick from six characters at either beginning or intermediate skill levels to be your partner and opponents, or get on a network and play against your friends.

✔ **MVP Spades (Windows 3.1/95/98):** Like Euchre, with Spades you get to pick a partner and your opponents from six virtual players. In addition to the fun and challenging game play, the graphics and easy controls make the MVP games a great way to sharpen your skills for the next family get-together.

✔ **Snood (Mac):** Snood is an addictive, nonviolent puzzle game. Free the Snoods trapped on the ceiling by launching other Snoods at them. If you connect three or more Snoods, they escape, dropping any other Snoods that were connected only to the disappearing Snoods. This game has no time limits and endless variations. Register this shareware version to be able to design your own puzzles and register your high scores on the Web.

(If you think this game sounds interesting, but all you have is a PC, check out David Dobson's site on the Web at `www.personal.umich.edu/~dob/pcsnood.html`. He is working on a PC version that wasn't ready in time to be included on this CD.)

How Shareware Works

Installing shareware, such as GraphicConverter or WinZip or Escape Velocity on your computer carries a few responsibilities you should be aware of.

Shareware programs are not free. Shareware is commercial software that you try out at no charge and then pay for if you decide to keep it. You can use a shareware program for a certain time period without paying for it in order to decide whether you like it enough to use it in the future. This time period is called an *evaluation period,* and you don't have to pay for this evaluation period. The shareware distribution system is run on a code of honesty to everyone's advantage. Software authors can distribute their products inexpensively online, and customers can browse shareware products by the thousands right from home and try them at no cost.

After you've evaluated the software and the way it works, decide whether you want to keep it. If you decide you don't need it or don't like it, you should delete it from your computer. If you decide you do like it, you must register your copy of the software. You can find instructions for registering shareware software, including the registration fee, in the shareware software files. Payment for shareware programs is based on the honor system. Incidentally, besides making you an honorable person, registering the software entitles you to upgrades, information, and other goodies from the software company.

If You've Got Problems (Of the CD Kind)

I tried my best to compile programs that work on most computers with the minimum system requirements. Unfortunately, your computer may differ, and some programs may not work properly for some reason.

The two likeliest problems are that you don't have enough memory (RAM) for the programs you want to use, or you have other programs running that are affecting installation or running of a program. If you get error messages such as "Not Enough Memory" or "Setup Cannot Continue," try one or more of these methods and then try using the software again:

- **Turn off any antivirus software that you have on your computer.** Installers sometimes do some of the things that viruses do (but without hurting your computer), and your computer may get hysterical, assuming that it's under attack by a virus.

- **Close all running programs, including the CD interface.** The more programs you run, the less memory is available to other programs. Installers also typically update files and programs. So if you keep other programs running, installation may not work properly. You can install any program on the CD through the CD directory.

- **Have your local computer store add more RAM to your computer.** Of course, adding memory costs money. However, if you have a Windows 95 or 98 PC or a Mac OS computer with a PowerPC or G3 chip, adding more memory can really help the speed of your computer and enable you to run more programs at the same time.

If you still have trouble with installing the items from the CD, please call the IDG Books Worldwide Customer Service phone number: 800-762-2974 (outside the United States: 317-596-5430).

Index

• C •

(continued)

(continued)

• S •

(continued)

(continued)

IDG Books Worldwide, Inc., End-User License Agreement

READ THIS. You should carefully read these terms and conditions before opening the software packet(s) included with this book ("Book"). This is a license agreement ("Agreement") between you and IDG Books Worldwide, Inc. ("IDGB"). By opening the accompanying software packet(s), you acknowledge that you have read and accept the following terms and conditions. If you do not agree and do not want to be bound by such terms and conditions, promptly return the Book and the unopened software packet(s) to the place you obtained them for a full refund.

1. **License Grant.** IDGB grants to you (either an individual or entity) a nonexclusive license to use one copy of the enclosed software program(s) (collectively, the "Software") solely for your own personal or business purposes on a single computer (whether a standard computer or a workstation component of a multiuser network). The Software is in use on a computer when it is loaded into temporary memory (RAM) or installed into permanent memory (hard disk, CD-ROM, or other storage device). IDGB reserves all rights not expressly granted herein.

2. **Ownership.** IDGB is the owner of all right, title, and interest, including copyright, in and to the compilation of the Software recorded on the disk(s) or CD-ROM ("Software Media"). Copyright to the individual programs recorded on the Software Media is owned by the author or other authorized copyright owner of each program. Ownership of the Software and all proprietary rights relating thereto remain with IDGB and its licensers.

3. **Restrictions on Use and Transfer.**

   (a) You may only (i) make one copy of the Software for backup or archival purposes, or (ii) transfer the Software to a single hard disk, provided that you keep the original for backup or archival purposes. You may not (i) rent or lease the Software, (ii) copy or reproduce the Software through a LAN or other network system or through any computer subscriber system or bulletin-board system, or (iii) modify, adapt, or create derivative works based on the Software.

   (b) You may not reverse engineer, decompile, or disassemble the Software. You may transfer the Software and user documentation on a permanent basis, provided that the transferee agrees to accept the terms and conditions of this Agreement and you retain no copies. If the Software is an update or has been updated, any transfer must include the most recent update and all prior versions.

4. **Restrictions on Use of Individual Programs.** You must follow the individual requirements and restrictions detailed for each individual program in the "About the CD" section of this Book. These limitations are also contained in the individual license agreements recorded on the Software Media. These limitations may include a requirement that after using the program for a specified period of time, the user must pay a registration fee or discontinue use. By opening the Software packet(s), you will be agreeing to abide by the licenses and restrictions for these individual programs that are detailed in the "About the CD" section and on the Software Media. None of the material on this Software Media or listed in this Book may ever be redistributed, in original or modified form, for commercial purposes.

5. **Limited Warranty.**

   (a) IDGB warrants that the Software and Software Media are free from defects in materials and workmanship under normal use for a period of sixty (60) days from the date of purchase of this Book. If IDGB receives notification within the warranty period of defects in materials or workmanship, IDGB will replace the defective Software Media.

   (b) **IDGB AND THE AUTHOR OF THE BOOK DISCLAIM ALL OTHER WARRANTIES, EXPRESS OR IMPLIED, INCLUDING WITHOUT LIMITATION IMPLIED WARRANTIES OF MER-CHANTABILITY AND FITNESS FOR A PARTICULAR PURPOSE, WITH RESPECT TO THE SOFTWARE, THE PROGRAMS, THE SOURCE CODE CONTAINED THEREIN, AND/OR THE TECHNIQUES DESCRIBED IN THIS BOOK. IDGB DOES NOT WARRANT THAT THE FUNCTIONS CONTAINED IN THE SOFTWARE WILL MEET YOUR REQUIREMENTS OR THAT THE OPERATION OF THE SOFTWARE WILL BE ERROR FREE.**

   (c) This limited warranty gives you specific legal rights, and you may have other rights that vary from jurisdiction to jurisdiction.

6. **Remedies.**

   (a) IDGB's entire liability and your exclusive remedy for defects in materials and workmanship shall be limited to replacement of the Software Media, which may be returned to IDGB with a copy of your receipt at the following address: Software Media Fulfillment Department, Attn.: *Internet Directory For Dummies, 2nd Edition*, IDG Books Worldwide, Inc., 7260 Shadeland Station, Ste. 100, Indianapolis, IN 46256, or call 800-762-2974. Please allow three to four weeks for delivery. This Limited Warranty is void if failure of the Software Media has resulted from accident, abuse, or misapplication. Any replacement Software Media will be warranted for the remainder of the original warranty period or thirty (30) days, whichever is longer.

   (b) In no event shall IDGB or the author be liable for any damages whatsoever (including without limitation damages for loss of business profits, business interruption, loss of business information, or any other pecuniary loss) arising from the use of or inability to use the Book or the Software, even if IDGB has been advised of the possibility of such damages.

   (c) Because some jurisdictions do not allow the exclusion or limitation of liability for consequential or incidental damages, the above limitation or exclusion may not apply to you.

7. **U.S. Government Restricted Rights.** Use, duplication, or disclosure of the Software by the U.S. Government is subject to restrictions stated in paragraph (c)(1)(ii) of the Rights in Technical Data and Computer Software clause of DFARS 252.227-7013, and in subparagraphs (a) through (d) of the Commercial Computer–Restricted Rights clause at FAR 52.227-19, and in similar clauses in the NASA FAR supplement, when applicable.

8. **General.** This Agreement constitutes the entire understanding of the parties and revokes and supersedes all prior agreements, oral or written, between them and may not be modified or amended except in a writing signed by both parties hereto that specifically refers to this Agreement. This Agreement shall take precedence over any other documents that may be in conflict herewith. If any one or more provisions contained in this Agreement are held by any court or tribunal to be invalid, illegal, or otherwise unenforceable, each and every other provision shall remain in full force and effect.

Installation Instructions

• •

To start the CD using Windows 95/98, follow these steps:

1. **Insert the CD into your computer's CD-ROM drive.**
2. **Select Run under the Start menu.**
3. **Type** D:\SETUP.EXE.
4. **Accept the terms of the IDG license agreement.**

To start the CD using Windows 3.1, follow these steps:

1. **Insert the CD in your CD-ROM drive.**
2. **In the Program Manager, choose File⇨Run.**
3. **In the Run dialog box, type** D:/SETUP.EXE.
4. **Click OK.**
5. **Accept the terms of the IDG license agreement.**

To install programs from the CD to your Windows computer, follow these steps:

1. **Click one of the four CD sections.**
2. **Click one of the programs.**
3. **Click the Install button for that program.**

To use the CD with a Mac OS computer, follow these steps:

1. **Insert the CD into your computer's CD-ROM drive.**

    The CD icon appears on your Mac desktop.

2. **Double-click the License Agreement icon.**
3. **Double-click the Read Me First icon and read the document.**
4. **Double-click the CD icon to show the CD's contents.**

Some programs have an Install icon that you click to start the installation. Other programs have you drag and drop a copy of the program from the CD to your hard drive. If you see icons with the words "Setup," "Installer," or ".sea," you need to double-click the icon to install the program.

For more information, see the "About the CD" Appendix C.

Discover *Dummies*™ Online!

The *Dummies* Web Site is your fun and friendly online resource for the latest information about *...For Dummies*® books on all your favorite topics. From cars to computers, wine to Windows, and investing to the Internet, we've got a shelf full of *...For Dummies* books waiting for you!

Ten Fun and Useful Things You Can Do at www.dummies.com

1. Register this book and win!
2. Find and buy the *...For Dummies* books you want online.
3. Get ten great *Dummies Tips*™ every week.
4. Chat with your favorite *...For Dummies* authors.
5. Subscribe free to *The Dummies Dispatch*™ newsletter.
6. Enter our sweepstakes and win cool stuff.
7. Send a free cartoon postcard to a friend.
8. Download free software.
9. Sample a book before you buy.
10. Talk to us. Make comments, ask questions, and get answers!

Jump online to these ten
fun and useful things at
http://www.dummies.com/10useful

For other technology titles from IDG Books Worldwide, go to
www.idgbooks.com

Not online yet? It's easy to get started with *The Internet For Dummies*®, 5th Edition, or *Dummies 101*®: *The Internet For Windows*® 98, available at local retailers everywhere.

Find other *...For Dummies* books on these topics:
Business • Careers • Databases • Food & Beverages • Games • Gardening • Graphics • Hardware
Health & Fitness • Internet and the World Wide Web • Networking • Office Suites
Operating Systems • Personal Finance • Pets • Programming • Recreation • Sports
Spreadsheets • Teacher Resources • Test Prep • Word Processing

IDG BOOKS WORLDWIDE
BOOK REGISTRATION

Register This Book and Win!

We want to hear from you!

Visit **http://my2cents.dummies.com** to register this book and tell us how you liked it!

- ✔ Get entered in our monthly prize giveaway.

- ✔ Give us feedback about this book — tell us what you like best, what you like least, or maybe what you'd like to ask the author and us to change!

- ✔ Let us know any other ...*For Dummies*® topics that interest you.

Your feedback helps us determine what books to publish, tells us what coverage to add as we revise our books, and lets us know whether we're meeting your needs as a ...*For Dummies* reader. You're our most valuable resource, and what you have to say is important to us!

Not on the Web yet? It's easy to get started with *Dummies 101*®: *The Internet For Windows*® *98* or *The Internet For Dummies*,® 5th Edition, at local retailers everywhere.

Or let us know what you think by sending us a letter at the following address:

...*For Dummies* Book Registration
Dummies Press
7260 Shadeland Station, Suite 100
Indianapolis, IN 46256-3945
Fax 317-596-5498

™
...FOR DUMMIES

BESTSELLING BOOK SERIES